JUNG'S GLOBAL VISION
Western Psyche Eastern Mind

Science is the tool of the Western mind... The East teaches us another, broader, more profound, and higher understanding – understanding through life. ... But (we) wholly misunderstand the realism of the East...

Western imitation is a tragic misunderstanding of the psychology of the East... it is not for us to imitate what is foreign to our organization or to play the missionary; our task is to build up our Western civilization, which sickens with a thousand ills.[1]

— C.G. Jung

Our Western psychology has, in fact, got as far as yoga in that it is able to establish scientifically a deeper layer of unity in the unconscious.[2]

— C.G. Jung

---

1   C.G. Jung, as reported in Richard Wilhelm, 1962, p. 82
2   C.G. Jung, 1975c-2, p. 573.

The cover design includes images of two paintings by the author.

THE PLACE OF THE SACRIFICE
The main cover picture is called *The Place of the Sacrifice*. By way of amplification, the Vedic sacrifice takes place at the spot between the two opposites, fire and water, where fire is masculine and water is feminine. The Vedas of India are regarded as the original scriptures brought into being by early seers. In this image, there are four horizontal water drop shapes, referring to the still unconscious wholeness of the feminine. There are 15 or 16 more or less distinct phallic shapes, which symbolize the masculine principle. Qualitatively, the number 15 refers to relationship with the archetypal psyche and manifest world. The number 16 = 4x4 symbolizes the differentiation of the four central aspects of the Self – wisdom, power, relatedness and devoted service – by each of the four functions of consciousness. Their blue, green and yellow colors indicate qualities of introversion and reflection, the living spirit of nature and hope, and illuminating insight. In India, Shiva is a powerful male god associated with fire as both creative and destructive, while Shiva's lingam (phallus) is sometimes referred to as a pillar of fire. Thus, in this image, there are both masculine and feminine energies, which bring wholeness through sacrifice to the Self, where subjective encounters are a defeat for the ego and an opening to more consciousness.

GOLDEN FISH 4
The image of the golden fish on the top right hand side of the book cover, with both vertical and horizontal golden waves, suggests relatedness to cosmic energy (left and right waves) as well as relatedness to both spiritual (upward waves) and material (downward waves) energy. The four waves flowing in each of the four directions indicate potential differentiation of the central aspects of the fourfold Self, wisdom, power, harmonious relatedness and devoted service by each of the four functions of consciousness. Gold has high value; it is a metal that does not tarnish, and is a symbol of the sun and eternity. In alchemy it is related to the water of life and the philosopher's stone, the goal of the opus. The fish is intelligence that emerges from the depth of being, here symbolized by the background dark blue water. In many cultures, the fish is a symbol of the manifest God, for example, in Christianity, Christ is depicted as a fish, while in the Puranas of India, Vishnu, the god of creation, is symbolized as a fish. These reflections and amplifications suggest that this image is a symbol of the cosmic Self with potential for spiritual differentiation.

JUNG'S GLOBAL VISION
Western Psyche Eastern Mind

David T. Johnston, Ph.D.

With References to
SRI AUROBINDO • INTEGRAL YOGA • THE MOTHER

Agio
PUBLISHING HOUSE

PUBLISHING HOUSE

151 Howe Street, Victoria BC Canada V8V 4K5

Permission to reproduce images 54, 64, 121, 125, 154
and 155 from *The Red Book* by C.G. Jung was graciously
granted by W.W. Norton & Company. Permission was
granted by Inner City Books to reproduce the images and
diagrams on pages 88, 173, 194, 196, 217, 260, 269 and
287. Permission was graciously provided by Sri Aurobindo
Ashram Trust to quote from Sri Aurobindo's *Saviri*. The
Trust also provided the photographs of Sri Aurobindo and
the Mother. Illustrations of C.G. Jung and Marie-Louise
von Franz are copyrighted by Ken Faulks.

Jung's Global Vision:
Western Psyche Eastern Mind
ISBN 978-1-927755-21-1 (paperback)
ISBN 978-1-927755-22-8 (ebook)

Cataloguing information available from
Library and Archives Canada.
Printed on acid-free paper.
Agio Publishing House is a socially-responsible enterprise,
measuring success on a triple-bottom-line basis.
10 9 8 7 6 5 4 3 2 1c

CONTENTS

DEDICATION

To the Mother

ACKNOWLEDGEMENTS

After having completed the initial draft for this book, I met Thomas Davis at a symposium at the Pacifica Graduate Institute. We began to communicate by e-mail and I eventually sent him the draft, which he read and on which he briefly commented. He diplomatically cajoled me into what amounts to a re-organization of aspects of the first part of the book, which I did. I am very thankful for his intervention. Interestingly enough, just prior to the book's completion, I met Thomas at a later symposium at Pacifica and we acknowledged and rejoiced in the synchronicity involved in our meetings at both bookends of this publishing project.

I would also like to extend thanks to my friend, Ken Faulks, who masterfully crafted two images, one of C.G. Jung and another of Marie Louise von Franz, for the book. I would also like to thank my editor, Nowick Gray, who helped me considerably in presenting the material in an acceptable fashion. Finally, my thanks go to Bruce and Marsha Batchelor, for their continual guidance through the publishing process, without which I would have been entirely lost. Marsha also came up with a book cover design which pleases me enormously.

Marie-Louise von Franz

C.G. Jung

The Mother

Sri Aurobindo

PREFACE

This study is principally about Jung's individuation process as a full-bodied spiritual path and yoga. In order to present my argument, I first examine the case for essential intelligence behind life in the world at both a macrocosmic and microcosmic level. I begin with a personal touch, by examining Jung's relationship with the natural world and his own psychological evolution. I then summarize the story of the intelligent unfolding of the universe, followed with a look at what astrology has to teach us regarding archetypal intelligence informing life at both the cosmic and individual levels of being. Subsequently, I study evolutionary evidence from biology and the science of the brain. I then return to Jung's personal narrative and demonstrate how his life unfolded intelligently from below, fully engaging the instinctive, dynamic and creative psyche, as well as under the direct influence of a descent of the spirit from above. I emphasize how his consciousness of this double action is a measure of his greatness and importance as a guide for the contemporary seeker.

My original interest in comparing Jung's path to the Integral Yoga of Sri Aurobindo and the Mother was initiated by a dream I had of Jung back in 1973 in relationship to Sri Aurobindo's book, *The Synthesis of Yoga*. I recount this dream and amplify its meaning below. In referring to the works of Sri Aurobindo and the Mother, I demonstrate similarities to Jung's path as well as differences, using the former as my hermeneutic lens. As the etymology of the word hermeneutics suggests, Hermes, the Greek messenger of the gods, is an ever-present guide in bringing the disparate threads of this study together. My principle interest lies in shedding light on Jung's psychology of the individuation process, taking Jung himself as an example of the further reaches of the process. I also often refer to Marie-Louise von Franz, Jung's foremost disciple and creative thinker in her own right. By alluding frequently to Sri Aurobindo and the Mother, I also present their Integral Yoga to some extent as well as its intensive and extensive effect on the world and humanity. Throughout the study, there are inevitable unconscious biases with their inherent tensions, based on my close inner associations with all the above mentioned personalities and their teachings. The writing process itself, which involves a dialogue with different aspects of the projected unconscious, helps them become conscious. Otherwise, without going into specific implications for the organization of my document, my research style reflects my introverted intuitive, feeling, judging [INFJ] personality type. In my particular case, this means that intuition and the feeling function as well as thinking dominant the research, while the sensation function serves to relate the research to concrete reality. As an introvert, the subjective element is also dominant, which translates into the fact that there is an intense subjective interactive process with the research material, which has had a transformative effect on me personally, and this over many years dating back to 1967, when I first began studying and then becoming intimately involved with the teachings of both Jung, and Sri Aurobindo and the Mother. After the final draft of this study had been completed, I was put on to a book, *The Wounded Researcher,* by the author, Robert Romanyshyn, who had been my research instructor 19 years ago. On reading the book, I realized my approach to researching this document, for the most part, is a variation of the depth-alchemical hermeneutic method he describes.[1]

Over the years I have become aware that there is an interest in comparing Jung's opus with Eastern and other spiritual paths. I have become convinced that the comparison is usually not fair to Jung and

---

1   Robert Romanyshyn, 2013 passim.

his path, as he is often seen as not having attained the transcendent non-dual Reality and his critics judge his path to be comparatively deficient. In some cases today, I observe there is recognition by some writers that Jung's individuation process is a psychic phenomenon that is usually not adequately dealt with in most Eastern and other spiritual paths. But, their contention is that Eastern and other spiritual paths still have the advantage of aiming at and attaining the Transcendent, which Jung tends to repudiate as a legitimate goal. There is more to the issue than is generally understood, and one does not get a true picture of the significance and uniqueness of Jung's path with either of these two approaches just described.

On the other hand, by comparing Jung's way to the integral path of Sri Aurobindo and the Mother, where, as with Jung, the psyche or one's nature and culture are fully embraced, as is the immanent and transcendent God, one can get a much clearer picture of Jung's spiritual truth. This is precisely what I endeavor to do here. Especially with regard to the immanent and manifest God, I feel the need to acknowledge here that I was first introduced to Jung, along with the *I Ching*, in the summer of 1961 when I was a naïve 21-year-old university student and working as a bell hop at Jasper Park Lodge in the Canadian Rockies. An eccentric-looking man by the name of Joseph Murphy sidled up to the bellhop's desk and asked me if I had ever heard of the *I Ching*. I replied that I hadn't. We went into the bellhop's room for privacy and he showed me how it worked; and I asked a question about going to Europe. The answer given was that I should "pass over the great waters." Although I took it all as a kind of joke at the time, as did all my friends, I was impressed with the answer, which affirmed my travelling to Europe, which actually transpired at the end of the summer. In hindsight, I also realize that, at that time, I was being initiated into Jung's teachings and their direct relationship to the East. I later discovered that, some nine years later, Murphy published a commentary on the *I Ching*, entitled *Secrets of the I Ching*, using Judeo-Christian teachings,

JUNG'S GLOBAL VISION: WESTERN PSYCHE EASTERN MIND

and that he had had a strong association with India.[2] In the forward he extolled Jung and his commentary on the book of changes.

My present observation is that right from the outset I had the good fortune of connecting with Jung synchronistically (meaningfully) in relationship to India and the East. In fact, in 1967, I was posted as a Canadian diplomat to Switzerland, Jung's home country, when I began my studies of both Jung, and Sri Aurobindo and the Mother. I was invited for a dinner at the Indian embassy and was introduced to the latter's teachings by a woman invitee, who lived at the Sri Aurobinbdo Ashram for part of the year and otherwise lived in Berne, her home city. I was coincidentally reading Jung's popular autobiography, which gripped me with enthusiasm.

In 1969 I obtained an assignment to teach business at Xavier Institute in Jamshedpur, India, through CUSO (Canadian University Services Overseas), the Canadian equivalent to the American Peace Corps. I visited the Sri Aurobindo Ashram in Pondicherry, a former French colony, several times, subsequently to reside there for about 3 years including 1972, Sri Aurobindo's centenary. While in Pondicherry, by chance, I lived across from a German woman disciple of Sri Aurobindo and the Mother, who had studied at the Jung Institute in Zurich, and she helped me with my dreams. I was also initiated by the Mother and received her blessings every year on my birthday, which was a common practice for her disciples and devotees.

I spent 1975, Jung's centenary, at the Jung institute in Zurich, and when I was leaving to return to Canada, without knowing my background at the ashram in India the librarian gave me two books that were being discarded from the library. One was *The Adventure of Consciousness* by Satprem, a French disciple of Sri Aurobindo and the Mother, and the other entitled *The Hero with a Thousand Faces* by Joseph Campbell, whom I later briefly met in Montreal at a Jung

2   1977 passim.

Society meeting. As it turned out, these two books were symbolic in-
dicators for my subsequent life. Perhaps, at this point, I need to stress
that I have no formal theological or philosophic education and, in that
respect, I do not write critically of Jung's or Sri Aurobindo and the
Mother's positions. I write, rather, from an unsophisticated perspective, albeit of a person who has come under the direct and sustaining
influence of Jung, and Sri Aurobindo and the Mother.

We live in an age of extreme individualism, conspiracy theories,
breaches and invasions of privacy, and a great deal of confusion about
the proper way to proceed in our individual and collective lives. In a
letter to the Dominican Victor White, on November 24, 1953, Jung
writes: "We are still in the Christian aeon and just beginning to realize
the age of darkness (from the standpoint of history) where we shall
need Christian virtues to the *utmost*."[3] Although we live in a dark time,
Jung sees beyond the Christian aeon to the coming of the *"Oneness of
the Holy Spirit."*[4] Sri Aurobindo expresses the same sentiment in letters
to his disciples. In one letter, he writes: "I myself foresaw that the worst
would come, the darkness of night before the dawn: therefore I am not
discouraged. I know what is preparing behind the darkness and can see
and feel the first signs of morning."[5]

On February 19, 1956, Sri Aurobindo and the Mother declared that
the divine Will had become the Law on Earth, even if there still continues to be atrocities, tensions and difficulties that need resolution. In a
note on his elegantly written series on *The Hinges of [Western] History*,
Thomas Cahill writes that when darkness prevails and evolution seems
"frozen in death"—when there is a crisis of civilization—the "great
gift-givers" arrive bringing transformative art, thought, counsel, science and new ways of being and understanding, and leave behind a

---

3   As reported in Ann Conrad Lammers and Adrian Cunningham, eds., 2008, p. 220.
4   *Ibid.*
5   1970f, p. 1611.

more complex, awesome and, today, potentially truthful world.[6] I write from the perspective that Sri Aurobindo and the Mother, along with Jung, are major "gift-givers" in this protracted passing age of darkness, and that they point the way to a more luminous future. In the case of Jung, my main interest in this particular study, his global vision forms a psychological, spiritual and cultural bridge from the West to India and the East. It embraces the Western psyche in all its positive qualities and historical development, along with its blemishes and insults to life, while fully incorporating the Eastern mind.

6   1998, p. iii.

INTRODUCTION

> The Spirit of the East is really at our gates. ....the spirit of
> the East penetrates through all our pores and reaches the most
> vulnerable places....[1]
>
> — C.G. Jung

The sixteenth-seventeenth-century Christian mystic and theologian
Jacob Boehme writes: "For you must realize that Earth unfolds its
properties and powers in union with Heaven aloft above us, and there
is one Heart, one Being, one Will, one God, all in all."[2] Should what
he writes be true, divine intelligence supports all life and life on Earth
is significant and meaningful. This is Jung's view, although the question remains how one can justify and reconcile this perspective, given
the current well-documented and widespread phenomena of psychological pathologies and perversions and present cultural dysfunctions
and vulgarities, and clash of civilizations. The lack of meaning and
apparent intelligent unfolding and conscious individuation in both the
collective psyche and the majority of contemporary individual lives
today, rather, seem to be the rule, although the intuitive historian of
culture may see it otherwise.

According to the Gospel of St. Thomas, there is a need to "see"
with the spiritual heart and align one's life with the Self, one's wholeness and true nature. Otherwise one lives a fragmented and alienated
life. In the Gospel of Mary Magdalene, Jesus is reported as saying
that sin is merely the result of acting in a perverted fashion and that

---

1   C.G. Jung, 1962, p. 146
2   As reported in C. Bourgeault, 2010, p. 49.

"the Good has come among you pursuing its own essence in nature in order to reunite everything to its origin."[3] Reminiscent of Boehme, Jesus is also quoted as saying: "All of nature with its forms and creatures exist together and are interwoven with each other."[4] In these two Gnostic Gospels there is no sense that the world is unreal or illusory. Rather, the message is that the incarnated Good can find its essential truth in nature, which is interwoven in its wholeness, and consciously unite with the Self, although this requires coming to terms with misleading Satanic temptations. According to this advice, the psychological task, then, becomes to search for the Good, and by consciously uniting with one's origins one becomes the whole person one always was. In the language of Sri Aurobindo and the Mother, in order to attain truth of being, one needs to become conscious of the psychic being, the evolutionary portion of the incarnated aspect of the Self that knows and discerns through feeling.

At this point it is worthwhile noting that, throughout the study, I constantly refer to the works and experiences of Sri Aurobindo and the Mother as my hermeneutical reference point for discussing Jung. According to my research and reflections, they are individual incarnations of the Avatar and Divine Mother, respectively, and worthwhile protagonists to help put Jung's experiences into perspective. When Sri Aurobindo writes about Savitri in his magnum opus, *Savitri,* he is referring to his spiritual companion, the Mother, the individual incarnation of the Divine Mother. In his epic poem, he also refers to the cosmic Mother, who is the cosmic aspect of the same Divine Mother.

From Jung's point of view, there is first a need to deal with the "powers of darkness" and, for the contemporary Westerner, that requires all the Christian virtues one can muster.[5] In the postmodern world, where Christian morality seems to have slipped into the unconscious, Jung's

---

3   *Ibid.*, p. 46.
4   *Ibid.*
5   As reported in Edward F. Edinger, 1996a, p. 148.

counsel seems prescient. But, for Jung, the conflict with Satan is "only the first step on the way to the faraway goal of unity of the self in God."[6] There is a further development, which requires making peace with one's personal shadow as well as one's relationship with the anima/animus and subsequently the collective or archetypal Shadow. The unity of the Self in God involves assimilation of a relationship to the Shadow side of God; in order to attain transcendent unity, that means there is a need for a relationship to not only God as Good, but God as Shadow, at least insofar as the world of duality is concerned. Not only does the Good God seek incarnation, but so does the Devil. According to Jung, "This requires going beyond the Christian aeon to the *Oneness of the Holy Spirit* .... He is the experience of every individual that has undergone the complete abolition of his ego through the absolute opposition expressed by the symbol Christ versus Satan."[7] When faced with such irreconcilable opposites, there is resolution in what Jung refers to as the transcendent function, the attainment of which requires suspending the conscious ego and its perspective. It is clear from these statements as well as from Jung's later writings, especially *Aion* and *Mysterium Coniunctionis,* that Jung himself had gone beyond the Age of Pisces to the Age of the Holy Spirit.

The individuation process involves integration of one's basic nature as well as becoming conscious of a relationship to the eternal and infinite. It is based on the experience that the world is essentially real, even if there are antagonistic forces here that tempt, mislead and/or drive one away from one's essential truth. These forces, however, cannot be simply repressed; they have to be related to and understood for the truth they camouflage or pervert. They are an aspect of one's nature that needs to be transformed—necessitating, on the one hand, accepting qualities that challenge conscious values and beliefs belonging to the repressed shadow and anima/animus, which, when made conscious,

---

6   *Ibid.*
7   *Ibid.*

can add immeasurably to one's personality. There is also a need to reject qualities that effectively limit and pervert personality, also attributable to the unconscious shadow and anima/animus. These latter qualities, for example, can manifest as the seven deadly sins of medieval Europe: laziness/aimlessness, lust, greed, avarice, unconscious anger and pride, as well as other excesses, obsessions, compulsions, and drivenness.

In Tolkien's *The Lord of the Rings*, an important dwelling and work-space of Dwarves, Khazad-dûm, a mountain cave, was taken over by Orcs, who were reputed to have been Elves or humans who were grossly perverted to the point of serving Sauron, the presiding Lord of Darkness.[8] They are self-serving, angry, suspicious, mistrustful and quarrelsome, with harsh-sounding voices, and they hate nature, humans and Elves. Rather than bringing into the world the good, the beautiful and the true, they serve evil, falsehood and the ugly, and generate fear. In other words, destructive Orc-like energy needs to be replaced by the creative and productive energies of transformed hardworking Dwarves, also reputed to be mistrustful, quarrelsome and haters of vegetative life, but essentially, dutiful children of the Great Mother.

In Tolkien's cosmology documented in *The Silmarillion* and elsewhere, Aulë is Lord of material substance and, like the Greek Haephaestus and the Roman Vulcan, he is the smith for the gods and creator of the Dwarves.[9] Sauron, the Lord of darkness, was originally a Maiar, an angelic being subservient to Aulë who, through hubris, rebelled for his own Asuric and Luciferian power-directed purpose. The relationship between the Dwarves and Orcs is evident in that they are both ultimately related to the god Aulë; although the Orcs' relationship is perverted and unconscious, while the Dwarves' relationship is an important conscious aspect of their legendary origins.

Dynamics involving Orc-like harshness, to be rejected, and the

---

8   1983.
9   1998.

need to relate to productive energy residing in the inferior sensation function, requiring acceptance and transformation, appear in dreams of contemporary individuals. A middle-aged woman dreamt of needing to cleanse herself with black soap inscribed with what she believed was a nefarious symbol belonging to a male figure she thought was evil. He, in fact, has attributes of her inferior sensation function that need to become more conscious. Fear, the spirit of negativity, was also instilled in her by a harsh-sounding croaking voice on the telephone. The male figure in question came to her door and, although his smile was crooked, he gave her a helpful message and did not show any ill will toward her or act in a bad way at all. He had two energetic children that the dreamer subsequently drove home. Transformation requires cleansing of the ego with the black soap and developing a relationship with the inferior function, here the sensation function, which comes with new-found vitality. The inferior function is the problematic inferior aspect of one's nature, which is usually rejected but ultimately needs acceptance for the sake of transformation as what seems evil becomes a bearer of light and source of energy.

By way of a brief explanation of Jung's theory of the functions of consciousness, I will now attempt to adumbrate their significance, especially the importance of the inferior function. There are, according to his theory, four functions of consciousness: thinking, feeling, intuition and sensation. Sensation is what is, intuition refers to possibilities, thinking informs one about what is as well as future possibilities, and feeling puts value on both what is and future possibilities. In individual psychology, typically one or two functions are conscious, while the third and fourth functions reside in the unconscious.

For reasons of personal history and natural predisposition, exacerbated by material ambition, individuals tend to specialize in their superior function and develop it excessively, while devaluing the innate drive for wholeness. Although this tendency can lead to material success in one's chosen occupation and other avenues of interest, it also tends to foster one-sided personality development. The most conscious

THE FOUR FUNCTIONS OF CONSCIOUSNESS

2 RATIONAL FUNCTIONS: THINKING AND FEELING
2 NON-RATIONAL FUNCTIONS: INTUITION AND SENSATION

SUPERIOR FUNCTION

```
S                              F
E                              I
C                              R
O                              S
N                              T
D
|
A          _____|_____          A
U                     |                      U
X                     |                      X
I                     |                      I
L                     |                      L
I                     |                      I
A                     |                      A
R                     |                      R
Y                     |                      Y
```

INFERIOR FUNCTION

Superior thinking > Inferior feeling: Superior feeling > Inferior thinking:
Auxiliary functions > intuition, sensation

Superior intuition > Inferior sensation: Superior sensation > Inferior intuition:
Auxiliary functions > thinking, feeling

function is referred to as the superior function, while the second most conscious function is called the first auxiliary function, and the third most conscious function is the second auxiliary function. The least conscious function, generally shrouded in darkness and very unconscious, is called the inferior function. Because it is so undeveloped and awkward, and divorced from conscious ego determinations, the inferior function is the doorway to the archetypes of the collective unconscious, effective meaning and both the archetypal Shadow and God.

Thinking and feeling are both rational functions, while sensation and intuition are non-rational; the rational functions, thinking and feeling, are depicted lying opposite to each other, as are the two non-rational functions, sensation and intuition; together these axes form a cross. According to Jung's Theory of Psychological Types, the inferior function is relatively unconscious and is always depicted as lying on the opposite pole from the superior function, suggesting its inferior status. In the case of superior thinking, the feeling function is inferior and relatively unconscious and is shown to lie at the opposite pole from the thinking function; while in the case of superior feeling, thinking is inferior and relatively unconscious and is depicted as lying at the opposite pole from the feeling function. In the case of superior intuition, it is sensation, the reality function, that is relatively unconscious, and it is shown residing at the opposite pole from intuition, and vice versa in the case of superior sensation and inferior intuition. Everything one does, including research and writing style reflect one's personality type.

One of the primary goals of the individuation process is to become conscious of all four functions of consciousness, meaning that, in addition to the superior function, the second and third auxiliary functions and, to a not insignificant degree, the problematic inferior function are all assimilated to consciousness. The path of integration typically moves from the superior function through conscious assimilation of the first auxiliary function, following which, the second auxiliary function requires conscious assimilation and, finally, the inferior function calls for one's attention for the sake of assimilation and wholeness. This process ends in psychological wholeness, the attainment of which leads to functioning out of wholeness rather than more one-sidedly out of one, two or three functions of consciousness. Although one functions out of wholeness while being organized around the Self (the center of being, a psychologically desirable state), there is, at the same time, a collapse of the functional structure of personality. There is, in other words, sacrifice of qualities attributed to superior and relatively superior aspects of the personality, whether it be the thinking function, the feeling function, the sensation function or the intuitive function, as functioning out of wholeness takes over.

The Jungian enterprise is fundamentally based on the understanding that there is divine intelligence at the core of life and that all life is interrelated, including the shadow side. Therapy is done by accepting people where they are, including their pathologies, and following the empirically proven, intelligent interweaving of life back to the unitary Self. Jung first discovered this truth of the goal of psychological development on completion of his initial confrontation with the unconscious in 1917–1918. This realization was fully confirmed in 1928 with a compelling dream where, with six Swiss companions, Jung found himself in Liverpool at night in the winter. It was dirty and dark and obscured by rain, smoke and fog. The city was organized radially around a square in the center of which was a small island in a round pool. In sharp contrast to the surroundings, sunlight lit up the island on which stood a single tree, a magnolia tree with reddish blossoms. The tree was illumined by the sunlight, but it was also the source of light. At the time of the dream, Jung felt opaque and depressed and this wonderful image during the dream *lysis* gave him hope for life.

Reference to Liverpool suggests the "pool of life," the liver symbolically being that which "makes to live."[10] In Jung's case, there is, first, full acceptance of where one is, in this case, in dark shadow-land, which eventually leads to the light-filled center. "The centre is the goal," Jung realized, "and everything is directed toward that centre."[11] Jung writes, "Through this dream I understood that the self is the principle and archetype of orientation and meaning."[12] The individuation process is a path of continual circumambulation of the Self, the unitary center of being and "God within us."[13]

Unlike most contemporary spiritual paths, the Integral Yoga of Sri Aurobindo and the Mother has the unique qualification of fully accepting life and the body for the sake of their psychic, spiritual and

---

10   C.G. Jung, 1983, p. 198.
11   *Ibid.*, pp. 197,198.
12   *Ibid.*, p. 198.
13   Jung, 1975d, p. 238.

supramental transformations—the latter being a far-reaching mutation that goes beyond even spiritual transformation, to the unitary truth of being. Their writings consistently promote the need to fully embrace life and the passions of life and the material world, and not to prematurely seek release into non-dual Reality or nirvana. Their perspective adds support to the understanding that the Divine is at the center of life and the material world; as with Jung there is a need to not shy away from shadow conditions, behind which resides the hidden truth of being.

In her dialogue with the arch sophist, Death, in Sri Aurobindo's magnum opus, *Savitri*, the heroine, Savitri, says: "Even in all that life and man have marred, / A whisper of divinity still is heard, / A breath is felt from the eternal spheres."[14] Later on, in the debate of Love and Death, she responds to Death's ingenious arguments, proclaiming:

> The Mighty Mother her creation wrought,
> ...
> The Eternal's face was seen through the drifts of Time.
> His knowledge he disguised as ignorance,
> His Good he sowed in Evil's monstrous bed.
> Made error a door by which Truth could enter in.
> His plant of bliss watered with Sorrow's tears.
> A thousand aspects point back to the One;
> A dual Nature covered the Unique.[15]

Here, Sri Aurobindo eloquently captures the significance of fully accepting all aspects of life, including the Shadow side.

The difficult journey that Jung refers to as the individuation process requires full acceptance of life in the material world. It demands repudiating ambitious longings for non-dual Reality or nirvana or, for that matter, the ambiguous belief that the world is merely a relative reality,

---

14   1970a, p. 612.
15   *Ibid.*, pp. 624, 625.

or the world is not spiritually worthy of in-depth psychological exploration. The individuation process makes this demand, with experiential understanding that divine Unity is at the core of the material world and life, and it is both the guiding light and goal. The manifestation is the world of the creative Cosmic Mother and integrating the feminine means fully embracing Her existence.

After his visions in 1944, where he experienced eternal bliss, Jung returned to this world with great difficulty, recognizing this life as merely "a segment of existence" running its course in a "three-dimensional boxlike universe."[16] Yet, from his experiences, he learned to adopt an attitude of unconditionally accepting the things of existence, including his own nature, as they are. This path of individuation means fully accepting one's nature even while there is never any guarantee that one is making the optimum choice, as error and mistakes must be taken as part of the package. In subjective and psychological terms, this is what is meant by accepting the Divine Mother's manifestation and the feminine.

Although I compare Jung to Sri Aurobindo and the Mother throughout the study, in Part I, I am especially concerned with establishing Jung's understanding and appreciation of the intelligence embedded in nature. Jung's appreciation of intelligence found throughout nature, in fact, draws his psychology close to the Integral Yoga of Sri Aurobindo and the Mother, who recognize the Divine or the Supermind at the core of matter and nature in general. In Part II, I make more direct comparisons between Jung, and Sri Aurobindo and the Mother.

In Part I, I examine the case for essential intelligence behind life in the world at both a macrocosmic and microcosmic level. I begin with a personal touch, by examining Jung's relationship with the natural world and his psychological evolution. I then summarize the story of the intelligent unfolding of the universe, followed with a look at what

---

16   1983, p. 295.

astrology has to teach us regarding archetypal intelligence informing
life at both the cosmic and individual levels of being. Subsequently, I
study evolutionary evidence of intrinsic intelligence from biology and
the science of the brain.

In Part II, I return to Jung's personal narrative and demonstrate how
his life unfolded intelligently from below as well as under the direct
influence of a descent of the spirit from above. The descent of the spirit
should be taken as a literal felt-experience that, in Jung's case, was, in
part, symbolized by the figure of an angelic being he called Philemon
as well as the descent of a dove recorded in a dream. Intelligent unfolding from below refers to consciousness of the movement of the dynamic and instinctive psyche, symbolized by animals, serpents, worms and
vegetation. I emphasize how his personal consciousness of this double
action is a measure of his greatness and importance as a guide for the
contemporary seeker.

My original interest in comparing Jung's psychology to the yoga
of Sri Aurobindo and the Mother was initiated by a significant dream I
had in 1973, when I was living at the Sri Aurobindo Ashram in India.
Here is the dream:

> *I am with Jung, who is wearing a navy blue blazer and tie,*
> *looking strong and very impressive. I have Sri Aurobindo's*
> *book, The Synthesis of Yoga, which looks like the popular edi-*
> *tion of a book in Sri Aurobindo's Birth Centenary Library. The*
> *title of book, The Synthesis of Yoga, is clearly marked on the*
> *book cover in the dream. In reality, at that time, I owned the*
> *complete works of Sri Aurobindo, including The Synthesis of*
> *Yoga. I pass my book over to Jung, who flips through the pages.*
> *He turns to me and says: "This is exactly what I have written."*
> *Then, holding our hands to his heart center, my left hand and*
> *my woman therapist's right hand, Jung takes my therapist on*
> *his left hand and me on his right hand, and guides us through*
> *the city.*

I take the dream to indicate that my direct guide is Jung, who takes me through the city within, connecting me and my inner therapist, my *soror mystica*, to the Self behind the heart center or psychic being. In practice, this means fully accepting my Western background and roots. The nature of the Western psyche including its problematic shadow side and the rejected feminine, as well as phenomena compensatory to the West's conscious cultural and religious values and beliefs, such as Gnosticism and alchemy, is highly differentiated in Jung's writings. Sri Aurobindo is also highly articulate about the nature of Western culture as well as Indian culture. Interest in Western culture and its psychological relevance can be seen by the many references I make to Western traditions and history, and Western science as well as some of Jung's concerns about the Western psyche per se. According to the dream, this path is fully in harmony with Sri Aurobindo's Integral Yoga as presented in *The Synthesis of Yoga*.

As a matter of fact, in a letter to a disciple, Sri Aurobindo writes that he had originally intended to write more on the subject but "these latter chapters were not written."[17] These latter chapters were meant to delineate the complications of determining the supramental Truth when it descends to other planes of the human mind, including the Overmind. What he does write about in the last chapters of the published book concerns the transformation of the overmind plane, a plane of global awareness and dynamic action, through the workings of the more integral Supermind or Truth-Mind. From these indications, it seems reasonable to infer that Sri Aurobindo's yogic experience and knowledge goes beyond what is presented in *The Synthesis of Yoga*, although the core of his teaching remains as written and published, and that is what is most relevant for consideration as amplification for the dream. The dream, in any event, has assigned me the task of discerning Jung's approach to psychology (which he contends has "got as far as yoga"), in

---

17   1970e, p. 262.

relationship to the Integral Yoga of Sri Aurobindo and the Mother, a mission I have been attempting to understand ever since.[18]

In order to put this challenge in perspective, it is worthwhile observing Jung's experience of Indians in relationship with his psychology after his journey there in 1937–38. Prior to his visit he had read a great deal of Indian spiritual literature, including parts of the Upanishads and the Vedas, Tantra and the *Bhagavad Gita* and he had a deep appreciation of its wisdom. While in India, however, he realized that, for the most part, Indians had difficulty appreciating his approach to psychology and the symbolic nature of the archetypal unconscious. Thus, he writes:

> In India there is no psychology in our sense of the word. India is "pre-psychological": when it speaks of the "self," it posits such a thing as existing. Psychology does not do this. It does not in any sense deny the existence of the dramatic conflict, but reserves the right to the poverty, or the riches, of not knowing about the self.[19]

Jung is referring to the fact that he believes India is pre-Kantian and has not developed the critical intellect necessary to objectively study one's subjective states of mind. From my experience, I am in full sympathy with Jung's observations, even to this day. Spiritually inclined Indians tend to posit concepts and beliefs like the Self and God, whereas, for Jung, it is essential to know through experience and self-scrutiny. Moreover, there are many Westerners who are pre-Kantian as well, without relationship to subjectivity and critical realism. Yet, given his appreciation of traditional Hindu wisdom, he might have been surprised to learn about contemporary Hindu spiritual practices that ignore and virtually bypass the psyche in their elevated, but one-sided goal of achieving liberation and attaining non-dual Reality.

---

18   1975c-2, p. 573.
19   C.G. Jung, 1975 c-3, p. 580.

I sympathize with Jung's view notwithstanding the fact that the yoga of Sri Aurobindo and the Mother is fully psychological in Jung's meaning of the word—to the point of working with the creative imagination and dreams, and insisting on transformation of all levels of the psyche including one's engagement with shadow factors, and differentiating between good and evil forces. Knowing through experience is essential for their path as well. Meanwhile, contemporary India has also evolved to the point of integrating Western intellectual values as well as American consumerism and materialism, for better and for worse.

There is, nonetheless, a difference between the two cultural psychologies that needs accounting for, especially given India's spiritual legacy and less violent history in comparison to the West. Jung was particularly preoccupied with the difference between the Christian West and Hindu philosophy. The Hindu has apparently no identification with either good or evil and aspires spiritually for liberation from any conflict, in contrast to the Christian aspiration to identify with good over evil. Jung appreciates the difference and, as a therapist, he notes, he approaches the problem of good and evil empirically and needs to contend with the paradoxical fact that what is good or evil may vary according to individuals, their stage of development, situation, time and place. He believes the Hindu approach leads to a moral lassitude, whereas his psychological approach ultimately leads to dealing with conflicts of duty, which furthers individuation.

As a caveat to the above, I am aware of institutions in India today that teach a contemporary Western ethical approach to decision-making. Yet, it seems to me that in contemporary India, which is living far from the laws of the *sanatan dharma*, or the way of eternal truth, there is something to be said for Jung's position. According to Sri Aurobindo's path, in his reference to the spiritual age of the *sanatan dharma*, individual character development depends on fitting into one's appropriate place in the order of society, which today also demands integral development of personality, similar to the requirements found in Jung's psychology of individuation.

The Hindu ability to observe opposites can be seen in and on the outside of their temples, with their plethora of exotic and erotic images that depict life in all its richness, including the dance of desires. It depicts holy men and women, various gods and mother goddesses, as well as seductive dancing apsaras, and asuras, rakshakas and pisachas (manipulative, brutal, and impulsive hostile forces respectively). Jung recognizes the psychological value and wisdom of this approach to religion and spiritual life, which contrasts widely from the more repressive, less inclusive, Judeo-Christian way. He also delighted in Indian dance of the Kathakali school from south India, where he writes the dancers do not resemble anything from the world of the senses, but rather as realities from an inner dimension of being that could step over the threshold into life. Jung was also appreciative of the different way India civilized man "the way without suppression, without violence, without rationalism."[20] Although there is violence and suppression in India today and it has existed at a significant level, at least since the partition of British India into two countries, India and Pakistan in 1947, in the overall picture, I believe, Jung is correct.

For the record, with partition there were reportedly at least one million deaths, along with riots, rapes and other atrocities on both sides, as some 12.5 million Hindus, Sikhs and Muslims were displaced and migrated to the region where they found support from the community of the majority religion (Hindu and Sikh in India, or Muslim in Pakistan). To this day, from time to time, there continue to be riots and killings in India between Hindus and Muslims, who are still a sizable minority in India, some 140 million strong, 13.4 percent of the population. Kashmir, with a majority Muslim population, belongs to India, but is disputed by Pakistan and the source of border tensions between the two countries. Recently, there have also been several reported incidences of violence toward women as well as, from the Western perspective, a

---

20   Jung, as reported in Sulagna Sengupta, 2013, p. 185.

tradition of a culture of oppression of women, despite the ubiquitous presence of the Goddess.

Jung's observation that life is organized without rationalism is invaluable, as it points to the fact that Indian culture is essentially organized on intuition and Eros and feeling values. Indians are, consequently, more readily oriented to fulfilling their duties in life, their dharma, while being naturally religious, rather than being motivated by intellectual ideals and unnaturally forcing a spiritual life with a repressed nature. Following a spiritual path in this way seems more easily accessible to Hindus than Westerners, as it is generally based on a natural religious or spiritual instinct rather than intellectual or moral conversion and idealism, the Western tendency. Similarly, Sri Aurobindo and the Mother encourage their disciples to concentrate on and bring forward the psychic being, the incarnated soul found behind the heart center, which knows through feeling. With Jung there is a distinct parallel in his efforts to re-establish Eros and the feeling function, and their importance in the individuation process. His enthusiasm for Meister Eckhart's observation, which Jung refers to throughout his life, "The soul is not blissful because she is in God, she is blissful because God is in her," reflects his realization of its significance.[21]

Despite his reservations, Jung has great respect for Indian wisdom and spirituality, observing that the Easterner's greater accessibility to non-judgmentally observe opposites allows him "an ability to contemplate the world of reality and illusion together, giving him an awareness of *Atman*."[22] This teaching from the East, with its more introverted attitude and interiority, as well as its greater sense of Eros and feeling, is of considerable value to the Westerner, who is one-sidedly oriented to extraverted intellectual education at the expense of introversion, feeling and Eros. It is the intellect that divides and sets up impenetrable barriers of differences, and the extraversion that orientates the psyche

---

21   1974, p. 240.
22   *Ibid.*, p. 183.

outwards to the material world, with an obsessive disposition to "scientific objectivity" which misses the beauty of life. Despite the fact that there are aspects of Hindu spirituality that Jung admires and that harmonizes with his own experiences, he differentiates traditional Hindu spirituality, as he witnessed it, from his path of individuation. In fact, with Sri Aurobindo and the Mother, the parallels with Jung go much further than with any traditional Hindu spiritual path such as Advaita Vedanta. In Part I, before I delve into the comparison of Jung to Sri Aurobindo and the Mother in Part II, I explore Jung's connection with nature and the evidence for the intelligence of nature, appreciation of which is essential to understanding Jung's path.

PART I

INTELLIGENCE IN NATURE

God is always specific and always locally valid, otherwise he would be ineffectual. The Western God-image is the valid one for me, whether I assent to it intellectually or not... There is no place for Gnosis or the Midrashim in this image, for there is nothing of them in it. Only my intellect has anything to do with purusha-atman or Tao, but not my living thralldom. This is local, barbaric, infantile, and abysmally unscientific.[1]

– C.G. Jung

---

1   C.G. Jung, as reported in Adler, Editor, 1975.

CHAPTER 1

Jung and the Spirit of the Natural World

Since childhood, when he lived in the Swiss countryside in Laufen, situated above the Rhine Falls, and at the age of four, moving to Klein-Hünigen, near Basel, Jung resided in deep harmony with nature, loving all warm-blooded animals with a feeling of kinship, while regarding them as having a soul like humans. He felt that they experience in common with humans a plethora of similar emotions including "joy and sorrow, love and hate, hunger and thirst, and fear and trust."[1] His unconscious identification with animals was so intense that only by the age of sixteen to nineteen did he realize that he was gradually differentiating himself from the animal. He regarded plants as the beauty and thoughts of God and trees as the embodiment of the mystery and meaning of life. Between the ages of seven and nine, Jung sat for hours on a stone that he identified with to the extent that, in his imagination, he wondered if he was sitting on the stone or whether he was the stone being sat on. Meanwhile, God's world for the young Jung was not always edifying and included everything that transcended human reach, including the uncanny play of chance, light and darkness, and the apparent infinity of space and eternal time. His lifetime preoccupation of coming to terms with the opposites in the God-image was already a vivid concern.

Later in life he writes, "At times I feel as if I am spread out over the landscape and inside things, and am myself living in every tree, in the splashing of the waves, in the clouds and the animals that come

---

1   C.G. Jung, 1983, p. 67.

and go, in the procession of the seasons."[2] Given his early life and his kinship with nature, along with his spiritual inclinations and multiple spiritual realizations, his later experiences of nature are perfectly understandable. However, the following self-disclosure as a "force of nature" may require some commentary. In a letter about himself he writes:

> It is the truth, a force of nature that expresses itself through me—I am only a channel—I can imagine in many instances where I would become sinister to you …. By my very presence I crystallize, I am a ferment. The unconscious of people who live in an artificial manner senses me as a danger. Everything about me irritates them, my way of speaking, my way of laughing. They sense nature.[3]

There can be no doubt about Jung's intense inner relatedness to the natural world and assimilation of its spirit. But that does not lead to social correctness or a kind of undisturbed and diplomatic peaceful co-existence as some might imagine. It insists, rather, on authenticity, both of oneself and others.

As he warns above, by the force of his relationship to the spirit or soul of nature, his very presence has a fermenting effect on others. Jung's purity of being and naturalness cuts through the persona and can disturb the unconscious of those who identify with their persona and live artificially. In fact, his personal assimilation of the spirit of nature and his fermenting presence may well explain his reputed irascibility and perceived inability to relate with some people as is reported by several of his biographers. Jung realized that he offended some people because of his relationship with the voice of instinctual nature, describing the "natural mind" as being "absolutely straight and ruthless," yet "spring[ing] from natural sources" and "bringing with it the peculiar

---

2   *Ibid.*, pp. 225, 226.
3   C.G. Jung, as reported in Meredith Sabini, ed., 2008, p. xiii.

wisdom of nature."⁴ He learned about the "natural mind" from his mother as a child, and integrated the archaic quality of seeing through the persona and "seeing people and things as they are."⁵

In Jung's retreat in Bollingen, he writes that "silence surrounds me almost audibly."⁶ An important goal of life is to rediscover the natural person within, which does not mean a return to nature à la Rousseau; rather it refers to the natural person who lives in harmony with the instincts. For primal people the world of nature was animated by gods, spirits and demons of various descriptions depending on the locale and its ambience, whether it be forest, lake, pool, stream, river or cave, where there is no cleavage between the inner and outer worlds. First Christianity, then science dethroned the gods and demons of the natural world and excised the soul from nature. Jung found the solution by consciously revitalizing his relationship to the inner world of the psyche as well as the external natural world, living in what he humbly refers to as "modest harmony with nature."⁷

He attained this level of conscious harmony, along with the experiences described above, thanks to his consistent efforts to follow the intelligence of the natural unconscious and unify the objective psyche, that is, the archetypal psyche, with consciousness. He found his way, in other words, to live like primal people, only with a differentiated contemporary consciousness, where consciousness can be defined as being mindfully present. Even as a child he experienced living in a way that was alien to others in "God's world"; and he came to realize that people were generally unconscious about dwelling, like him, "in a unified consciousness, in God's world, in eternity where everything is already born and everything has already died."⁸

Jung insists there is one world, where humans are "in nature and we

---

4   *Ibid.*, p. 27.
5   *Ibid.*
6   1983, p. 226.
7   *Ibid.*
8   *Ibid.*, pp. 66, 67.

think exactly like nature." This world of nature needs to be understood as a violent play of opposites, with beauty, harmony and also light and storm, darkness and violently destructive forces.[9] With the advent of science and its emphasis on objectification, a huge abyss awoke between the world of nature and human beings. The spirits, gods and demons that previously populated the woods, rivers, hills and springs and the sunlight, sky and storms, and the darkness of night, became complexes in the human psyche. When nature is abused or neglected, as we are learning to our chagrin, it eventually responds or reacts with devastating long-term effects.

As an aspect of nature, humans too are affected by being separated from the natural rhythm of life with all its polarities. Thus, Jung writes, "the world hangs by a thin thread, and the thread is the psyche of man.... We are ... the great danger. The psyche is the great danger."[10] Not only can we be affected by catastrophic psychic epidemics, which in the twentieth and twenty-first centuries have taken the form of wars and dictatorial oppression; but also in the ongoing play of life there has been a gradual degeneration of culture, as Christianity and its values become a less effective force in a world ruled by economic interests. There is, concomitantly, an increase in local-level violence, as witnessed by senseless mass killings by psychologically troubled individuals.

There is today a deep-felt need for wholeness and a return to nature, to find there the living truth behind the symbolic projections of archaic people prior to the advent of science and the objectification of nature and, earlier, the establishment of Christianity, whose spirit opposed the worship of nature that was prevalent in Europe during its early years, as well as with primal people throughout the world. "Nature is not matter only," observes Jung, "she is also spirit."[11] To support his assertion he

---

9   *Ibid.*, p. 165
10   As reported in Meredith Sabini, ed., 2008, p. 164.
11   *Ibid.*, p. 80.

often refers to the alchemical *lumen naturae,* the light of nature, and the *anima mundi* or world soul. Jung observes that "psyche is a quality that appears in matter," and that the world seen from within is psyche or spirit, while seen externally, it is matter.[12]

These considerations urge the contemporary person on the path of individuation to find an inner connection to the spirit of nature, the animal soul and the spirit behind the projected gods of the primal people. That requires looking inward, into the eyes of the psychic animal, the eyes that have experienced and emanate the primal pleasures and pains, joys and sufferings of existence. Jung writes that having a living connection with the animal mind, with the truth of the natural mind, "alienates him from the cultural or spiritual mind," but he recommends it as an essential panacea for the one-sided modern mind.[13] The reason he encourages it is that "earth has a spirit of her own, a beauty of its own," and "the natural mind has a world of earthly beauty to itself."[14] Moreover, it is likely that, although unconscious, animals follow the archetypal patterns of life and are more instinctively knowledgeable than humans about the will of the deity.

The problem of being divorced from nature is Western and contemporary in its extraverted one-sidedness and propensity to conquer, control and harness and manage the natural world including human nature itself. Western and contemporary consciousness is highly educated and disciplined while the natural psyche is repressed; thus non-causal thinking and the laws of chance, which play a prominent role in the archaic world and are consciously experienced today as synchronicity (thanks to Jung, who coined the term), have no recognized value in the Newtonian scientific paradigm, which includes contemporary mainline psychology.[15] The introverted East has likewise shown

---

12   *Ibid.*, p. 82.
13   *Ibid.*, p. 171.
14   *Ibid.*
15   C.G. Jung, 1975, pp.419–531 passim.

a marked tendency to dominate human nature, although in a different way, by some yogic methods that lead to ascetic retreat from the natural world. Jung puts it that "both make desperate efforts to conquer mere naturalness."[16]

According to Jung's generalizations, which I believe still have some merit, for the Oriental in general, the extraverted world of nature lies in shadow, neglected to an appalling extent that is visible in rampant slums and paucity of vegetation everywhere, to sick and undernourished animals that wander the streets of urban India, for instance, and a population of humans that continues to grow at an unsustainable rate. Although India and the Orient in general have always produced brilliant minds, including people of science and commerce, and well-rounded spiritual leaders, the tendency in the spiritually inclined Eastern mind to devalue the extraverted demands of life needs to be seen for what it is in order for its different paths of spiritual liberation to be put into proper perspective in relationship to the plight of nature. Only a path that fully embraces the manifest world, including its potential transformation, has validity today and on into the future.

"Aren't we the carriers of the entire history of mankind?" Jung once asked rhetorically. His reply was that "when a man is fifty years old, only one part of his being has existed for half a century. The other part, which also lives in his psyche, may be a million years old."[17] At another time, when talking to students at the C.G. Jung Institute in Zurich, he suggested that when one has reached a blind alley, by paying attention to one's dreams, "the Great Man, the 2,000,000-year-old man, will speak."[18] Healing comes from our dreams, a product of the natural psyche, which by way of protracted dialogue with the unconscious, takes us back to ancient wisdom. Jung was here metaphorically pointing back toward psychic relatedness with early human ancestors. These

16   *Ibid.*, p. 128.
17   *Ibid.*, p. 196.
18   *Ibid.*, p. 215.

first humans are often identified as *homo habilis* and *homo erectus*. The former emerged some 2.33 million years ago and existed until 1.44 million years ago. The latter lived from 1.9 million to 143,000 years ago, long before the modern *homo sapiens sapiens,* our more direct ancestors, for whose existence there is evidence dating back 71,000 years.

Jung contends that for a healthy culture as well as healthy individuals, we need a consciousness that not only expands horizontally, with the typical concerns of the contemporary world, but one with "a more living sense of history." Our consciousness is not only of today, embedded in the spirit of the times; we have also a profound relationship with the wisdom of other times through what older cultures refer to as ancestral knowledge.[19] Not only would this expansion allow for a critical perspective on contemporary issues, but it would open up consciousness to a mythic perspective and the need to assimilate values that are repressed in the present one-sided scientific and consumer-driven world.

These comments go back to a well-known dream Jung had in 1909 of a multilevel house to which he sometimes refers when explaining modern consciousness and the need to descend to deeper levels of being in order to recapture the psyche's natural foundations. The top floor in his dream refers to the present and more recent times, the ground floor to the sixteenth century and the cellar to Roman times. Below that, there is a cave with Neolithic and Upper Paleolithic tools, dating back at least some seventy-one thousand years to modern *homo sapiens sapiens*. The cave also relates to the animal soul, given the psycho-biological closeness of these early human cave dwellers to animals and the fact that animals occupied these caves prior to them. Although it may have been necessary to become dissociated from the instinctual psyche for the sake of the development of consciousness, Jung believes that

---

19   *Ibid.*, p. 71.

now there is a need to consciously recapture our phylogenetic foundation, our relationship with nature and its rhythm and timing.

In point of fact, according to his grandson, Andreas Jung, Jung's house in Küsnacht, which Jung played an active role in designing and where he lived with his family and engaged in his professional activities, is reminiscent of the top floor of his dream.[20] Jung described the top floor in the dream as being like a salon, with fine rococo furniture and valuable old paintings hung on the walls, suggesting the home of an accomplished European man of Jung's time. Otherwise, the house in Küsnacht, one can surmise, is a concrete symbolic expression, with the strong phallic presence of its central tower, of the early Jung. He not only had a successful career in psychiatry at the world-famous Bürghölzi hospital, but the director, Eugen Bleuler, chose him as his deputy director. Jung was also a successful leader in the psychoanalytic movement and Freud's chosen "crown prince." In addition, he had other multiple interests and sensitivities, including psychiatry, theology, philosophy, mythology, anthropology, architecture, parapsychology, painting, the study of art, sailing and the exploration of nature and the outdoors. He was an accomplished artist and already had several publications on psychiatry to his credit.

Jung was influenced by his maternal grandfather, a theologian and student of Hebrew, and his second wife, a clairvoyant; and his paternal grandfather, a physician and Grandmaster of the Swiss Freemasons, playwright and scientist, with an interest in mental illness. Voltaire, Goethe, Nietzsche, von Schelling, Hegel, Schopenhauer, Bergson, Lamprecht, Kraft-Ebbing, Wundt, von Hartmann, Carus, Levy-Bruhl, Charcot, Janet, Kraepelin, Theodore Flournoy, William James, Freud, Haeckel, Bergson, Swedenborg, Burckhardt and others can all be considered Jung's intellectual and cultural ancestors and reflected in his

20   2009.

house in Küsnacht by his library and busts of Voltaire, Nietzsche and Scipio, the Roman general during the second Punic war.

Jung was a genuine Renaissance man, the quintessential Northern European male with extensive ego consciousness, who towered over his contemporaries. As he says in amplifying a significant dream he had on December 18, 1913, he had a secret identity with Siegfried, the Nordic mythological hero, who, in the dream, was shot dead by a little primal man, "a personification of the collective unconscious."[21] He writes: "This identity and my heroic idealism had to be abandoned" as one must bow to a higher will.[22] In a 1925 seminar he is recorded as saying; "I must then have had a hero I did not appreciate, and it was my ideal of force and efficiency I had killed. I had killed my intellect."[23] Jung sacrificed his superior function as the axis had begun to shift in earnest from the ego to the Self. This shift is reflected in his country house in Bollingen, which relates to the deeper layers of the archetypal psyche, and which grew organically with Jung's watchful participation.

In 1922, when he was forty-seven years old, Jung acquired another piece of property, about which he writes: "I had to achieve a kind of representation in stone of my innermost thoughts and of the knowledge I had acquired …. I had to make a confession of faith in stone. That was the beginning of the "Tower," the house which I built for myself at Bollingen."[24] The older Jung became the more time he spent at Bollingen, the move from Küsnacht to Bollingen symbolizing the transformation from the ego to the Self, which is the natural trajectory of the individuation process. Thus, regarding the latter, Jung writes: "In the Tower at Bollingen it is as if one lived in many centuries simultaneously. The place will outlive me, and in its location and style it points backward to things of long ago."[25] As an old man, he observes: "At

---

21   Jung, 1989, p. 57.
22   Jung, 1983, p. 181.
23   Jung, 1989, p. 57.
24   *Ibid.*, p. 223.
25   As reported in Andreas Jung, 2008, p. 26.

Bollingen I am in the midst of my true life, I am most deeply myself. Here I am, as it were, the age old son of the mother."[26]

Here personality number 2, whom he experienced as a child and who later took the form of Philemon, the timeless and ancient one, was at ease. After his wife died in 1955, Jung felt impelled to add an upper storey to the central section, which represented the extension of consciousness and ego personality achieved in later life. This extended consciousness is a reflection of his conscious assimilation of experiences of the Self. His relationship to Bollingen also unfolded during the time he became conscious of his spiritual ancestors, the Gnostics and alchemists, especially the latter. In Jung's case it is not a question of atavism, which refers to habits learned through family, education and cultural and racial heritage or a regression to earlier ways of being, but living according to a deeper truth. In fact, the answer to atavism is forming a living connection to the archetypal psyche just as Jung did and replacing atavistic behavior with behavior emanating from the truth of being.

It is quite extraordinary how Jung found ways to express his inner life so concretely. Both properties were, characteristically, built on Lake Zurich, with Bollingen in the country on the remote Obersee (Upper-lake) part, and Küsnacht closer to Zurich. On the entrance gates to the houses at both locations Jung had the words of the Delphic Oracle (*'Called or not Called, God will be Present'*) chiseled in Latin:

VOCATUS ATQUE NON

VOCATUS DEUS ADERIT

Over the entrance to the second tower at Bollingen, Jung also had inscribed *'Philemon Sacrum – Fausti Poenitentia'* ('Shrine of Philemon – Repentance of Faust'). The reference here is to Philemon and his wife Baucis as recounted in Ovid's *Metamorphosis* and in Goethe's *Faust*. According to the original story they were a humble old couple who

---

26   Jung, 1983, p. 225.

welcomed the gods, Jupiter and Mercury, disguised as mortals, when no one else would. Their modest dwelling was consequently transformed into a temple with columns of marble and a roof of gold; and to repay them for their hospitality, the god's offered them any wish they desired. Their wish was to become priests to lovingly serve in their shrine.

In Goethe's *Faust*, Part II, which reflects the consciousness of the late eighteenth and early nineteenth century, land was reclaimed from the sea and, to Faust's shock, Philemon and Baucis were burnt in their cottage by Mephistopheles. Jung felt a personal kinship with Goethe through their mutual interest in alchemy and was early on moved by his play, finding that the main figure Faust, who was comfortable in the Middle Ages, was like his number 2 personality. He felt personally implicated by the murder of Philemon and Baucis and felt it to be his responsibility to atone for their untimely death and bring healing to the Faustian split in the Western soul. Indeed, Jung and his psychology reflects this atonement in his loving service to the objective psyche and in his inviting the conflicting archetypes of the collective unconscious to find their home in the conscious human instrument.

Therefore, therapeutically, Jung promotes the need to be guided by "the patients' own irrationalities."[27] "Here," he says, "we must follow nature as a guide, and what the Doctor then does is less a question of treatment than of developing the creative possibilities latent in the patient himself."[28] Jung is suggesting that even in human pathology there is hidden divine intelligence that needs to be uncovered and not repressed or suppressed. Jung's personal life was fully attuned to the natural world, both inwardly and outwardly. His cure for the Western soul involves a conscious return to nature, the healing powers of which he found in alchemy, alchemical images and treatises as well as Gnosticism and mythology. He discovered that messages from the natural world of dream, fantasy and vision carry a similar significance.

---

27   1970b, p. 41.
28   *Ibid.*

In 1960, a year prior to his death, Jung had a significant dream that symbolizes the enormous psychic task he has accomplished for humankind, as follows:

> *I am at an unknown place at an unknown time, as though standing on air. I am with a primitive chieftain who might just as well lived 50,000 years ago. We both know that at last the great event has occurred: the primeval boar, a gigantic mythological beast, has finally been hunted down and killed. It has been skinned, its head cut off, the body divided lengthwise like a slaughtered pig, the two halves only just hanging together at the neck.*
>
> *We are occupied with the task of bringing the huge mass of meat to our tribe. The task is difficult. Once the meat fell into a roaring torrent that swept it into the sea. We had to fetch it back again. Finally we reached our tribe. The camp or settlement is laid out in a triangle, either in the middle of a primeval forest or in an island in the sea. A great ritual feast is going to be celebrated.*[29]

In this dream, Jung is symbolically participating in an important ritual event that dates back to the Middle to Upper Paleolithic where there is already evidence of the existence of our species, modern *homo sapiens sapiens, as* a hunter–gatherer. He is co-operating with a leading direct primal ancestor, a chieftain, who is intimately embedded in the natural world, with which it is un-self-consciously in magic interrelatedness. At that primal level of being, the completion of the task brings fundamental nourishment to the collective psyche. The primeval boar is a rich source of protein that, as the basic ingredient of life, builds and repair cells. Jung's contribution to recapturing this natural human embeddedness in nature is highly significant, with implications for the future of human evolutionary development.

---

29   As reported in Meredith Sabini, ed., 2008, p. 8.

In a letter to Peter Birkaüser in 1960, a Swiss artist, who sent him a picture of one of his paintings depicting a white boar-like horse ridden by a youth involved in creating new life, he refers to his dream and amplifies it. He relates a Hindu Puranic story about creation of the world and a Kabbalistic story about a meal for the righteous. In the Hindu myth, at the beginning of the *Kalpa* or cosmic age, Vishnu created the world in the form of a beautiful maiden floating on the waters of life. A great serpent dragged the new creation into the depths of the sea, but Vishnu retrieved it, diving down in the shape of a boar. In the Kabbalistic teaching, at the end of time, Yahweh will slay the Leviathan and serve it as a meal for the righteous.

More in amplification of the painting than his dream, although the two were evidently related, Jung then notes that, according to the Puranic myth, there will be a new creation at this end of the cosmic age, through Vishnu embodied as a white horse. Jung writes, "This refers to Pegasus, who ushers in the Aquarian Age."[30] Jung's psychological discoveries not only bring a cure to the Faustian split, but point forward to the Age of the Holy Ghost, where individuals become conscious vessels for the down-pouring of the Spirit, also referred to by disciples of Sri Aurobindo and the Mother as the Force.

Jung's intimate relationship with nature eventually led him to the natural philosophers of the middle ages, where he found kinship with alchemy and the alchemists. I examine Jung's relationship with alchemy in chapter 5. Prior to that and immediately following this discussion on Jung's personal equation with nature and its healing energy, in chapters 2, 3 and 4, I examine contemporary evidence for the intelligence in nature in cosmology, astrology and the contemporary sciences of neurobiology and the mind respectively. Inasmuch as alchemical praxis involves seizing the energy of nature for psychological and spiritual

---

30   1975, p. 607.

transformation, these amplifications are fully supportive of Jung's psycho-alchemical enterprise.

CHAPTER 2

The Intelligent Unfolding of the Universe

We live in "one world" as a minute but integral part of the unfolding
Universe, and not simply as outside observers, but as subjective participants. While acknowledging that the future may bring discoveries
that will modify or change their reading, mathematical cosmologist
Brian Swimme and cultural historian Thomas Berry give a compelling rendition of the story of the unfolding of the Universe over time
that appeals both intuitively and to sufficient reason.[1] What follows
immediately below is a highly simplified summary of Swimme and
Berry's account.

The story of the universe is that of an intelligent energy-field of
light, particles and antiparticles, hence both creative and destructrive
dynamics that began some fifteen billion years ago with a primordial
eruption of fiery energy. It eventually differentiated itself from a state
of chaos into four fundamental laws: the law of gravity, electromagnetism and strong and weak nuclear interactions. The blazing heavens
eventually stabilized enough to allow for the emergence of hydrogen
and then helium atoms, followed by a million years of turbulence.
Subsequently, there was dissolution of the primal field of energy as
cosmic night and virtual nonexistence blanketed the universe, leaving
only a few surviving particles.

There was continual darkness for the following billion years,
which prepared the way for the formation of one hundred billion galaxies including the Milky Way. These galaxies, each uniquely con-
figured with diverse interacting force-fields, formed systems from

---

1   1992.

which emerged multiple billions of primal stars. A billion years of nucleo-synthesis subsequently gave form to one hundred elements including carbon, nitrogen, oxygen and calcium. Exploding supernova disbursed these elements, creating second-generation stars, which were more complex and structurally intricate than those of the first generation. Some five billion years after it all began, a star now referred to as Tiamat came into being; it eventually exploded as a supernova, spreading its substance throughout the universe. Then, some five billion years ago, the Milky Way distributed remnants of Tiamat, forming ten thousand new stars, some of which became stable, including our Sun. The Sun dispersed the surrounding dust clouds and produced material bodies that became ten planets, each, like the Sun, with its own inherent intelligence.

Some four billion years ago, Earth generated the first living cell. The intrinsically intelligent primal cells, the prokaryotes, had the capacity to absorb energy from the Sun. They also drew hydrogen from the ocean, thereby releasing oxygen that gradually permeated everything, forming highly unstable conditions. Eventually the oxygen-laden prokaryotes spontaneously combusted, as the first eukaryotic cell, a single cell with a central nucleus, appeared. Unlike the prokaryotic cell, the eukaryotic cell had the ability to both endure the oxygen levels and shape itself purposefully. Meiotic sex through cell division and the production of gametes (eggs and sperm) for genetically different beings emerged that, with fertilization, produced unique cellular offsprings. Their individual existence terminated when an innumerable quantity of them merged to form the first multi-cellular animal.

Some six hundred million years ago a variety of multi-cellular organisms existed as both vertebrates (e.g. amphibians and reptiles), and invertebrates (e.g. corals, spiders, clams, starfish, insects, etc.). Sea plants that washed up onto rocks gave form to the wood cell, which developed into trees that gradually accumulated to form forests. The forests attracted insects, amphibians, and reptiles (including the dinosaurs). All this was made possible by a stable environment, to wit, the

Earth's repetitive circling around the Sun, the Sun burning hydrogen and the countless chemical bonds in the atmosphere.

This stable environment was rudely interrupted with asteroid collisions some sixty-seven million years ago, which radically changed the atmosphere and climate. There were mass extinctions of dinosaurs and other animals, while those that endured underwent creative renewal. In our own day, there is 100 percent probability of another potentially devastating asteroid collision with the Earth, although there is scientific tracking of the asteroids and various methods of preventing a disaster are being studied

Some two hundred million years ago, mammals emerged with the ability to relate to intense existential moments with emotional sensitivity as well as to form mother–infant bonds. There were, by then, new varieties of animals on Earth that we are familiar with today. Eventually humans, with the capacity for conscious self-awareness, entered the scene.

The story of the universe as recounted by Swimme and Berry gives compelling evidence for self-organizing intelligence operating at all levels of the universe, where consciousness-force and truth permeate the manifest creation. Since the beginning of time, along with periods of destruction and regression, new developments have occurred unaccountably as if out of nothing, creative acausal moments, with casual spinoffs. With the advent of the human being the intelligent nature of the unfolding universe took a major step forward, given the presence of an important agent of self-aware moral intelligence.

The specifically human adventure began some four million years ago as early humans stood on two feet in order to survey the scene before them. An exciting recent discovery (2013) in the depths of a single cave in South Africa unearthed a new species called Homo *Niledi*, where niledi means star. At the moment, this ape-man is classified as Homo, having feet and hands like a human, and a small ape-like brain. One and a half million years ago humans discovered fire, used for various purposes, both practical and ritualistic. Some thirty-five to forty-two thousand years ago, during the Upper Paleolithic time, the first cave paintings appeared as a central aspect of ritual events. Twenty thousand years ago humans became aware of seasonal rhythms and the cycle of plants basic to the nourishment of life. Twelve thousand years ago saw the beginning of the domestication of different plants and animals, which varied according to the geography.

Thanks to a steady food supply, some ten thousand years ago, populations grew and the first Neolithic villages appeared. Life underwent radical social transformation from the hunter-gatherer ethos to settled village life and greater cultural and religious sensibility that included rituals and shrines dedicated to the Great Mother. From five to ten thousand years ago language and religion developed richness and complexity, with art, music and dance serving as natural symbolic expressions.

Five thousand years ago saw life evolved to the point of being organized around an urban population and sacred kingship. Specialization and bureaucracy allowed the efficient management of human and natural resources, including irrigation systems, ship building, fortifications, palaces and numinous monuments and structures of worship. International trade grew dramatically, wealth increased and populations multiplied. Territories expanded through war, conquest and public proclamation. War gods replaced the Great Mother as the principal deity. Three universal religions, Christianity, Islam and Buddhism, put down roots in Europe, the Middle East, Southeast Asia, and China.

There have been three significant human migrations along with several subsidiary movements. The first of these involved *homo erectus* who left Africa and travelled north to Eurasia some 1.8 million years ago. The second migration involved *homo sapiens sapiens*, modern humans, who found their way to Australia some forty thousand years ago, and to the Americas fourteen to thirty thousand years ago. The third began roughly five hundred years ago, when Europeans colonized other peoples around the world, especially the Americas and Australia. In the nineteenth century, Europeans colonized India, while Japan and China became trading partners. Colonization resulted in much oppression and cultural genocide, although, eventually, the realization of a common humanity and a sizeable ongoing migration. In 2016, some 50 million and growing individuals are either international refugees or have suffered internal displacement.[2]

The nation-state was formed as the collective glue for wide populations of cities, villages and tribal peoples. In the West, it eventually integrated the ennobling ideals of liberal democracy and individual freedom, along with the rights to own private property, nationalism and progress. Although liberty has gained something of a sacred status in the West, the implementation of equality has generally been more confused and brotherhood relegated to the drawer. National will-to-power and ideological tensions, e.g. Communism vs. Capitalism, have given birth to a conflicted world. There are changing dynamics, however, as rapidly accumulating connectivity of "supply chains" unite various resources and infrastructure that cross national and state borders, as mega cities have become nodal points of political and economic power, regardless of political ideology.[3] This evolutionary development is based on functional exigencies, is largely unconscious, and comes with a massive materialistic shadow.

Meanwhile, the contemporary relationship between the West and post-Soviet Union Russia is complex and, with regard to the Middle East, for instance, currently (2016) with Syria, sometimes tense. With Russia's 2014–15 aggressive initiatives in the Ukraine, the Russia–West relationship took a turn for the worse. There are other areas of present or potential tension, for example, between the West and North Korea, with its repressive and unstable political ethos, and increasing belligerence, e.g. by testing several nuclear missiles. China is a growing economic power with sizeable global investments, including in North America, Africa, Europe and South America. Given its communist political organization and dismal human rights record, this economic

---

2   Parag Khanna, 2016, p. 66.
3   *Ibid.*, passim.

entanglement, however economically advantageous for Western countries, South America and Africa, comes with tensions and uncertainties.

The European Union, consisting of 28 member countries, initially established in order to encourage economic stability along with potential political integration, is presently (in 2016) showing signs of fragility. A major blow was delivered to the EU on June 23, 2016 when Great Britain voted in a referendum to leave the union. Greece is heavily in debt and potentially facing bankruptcy, while other countries, e.g. Italy, are also in economically precarious positions. Otherwise, there are increasing international trade agreements that encourage a duty free global economy, which favor large corporations to the detriment of local production. The most significant of these is the impending Trans Pacific Partnership that affects some 40 percent of the global economy.

Contemporary Western civilization has given birth to high idealism, a multi-sided intellect increasingly open to the intuition, and a wide-ranging inquiring scientific mind with extraordinary instrumentation, while virtually relegating Eros and feeling, the religious spirit and spirituality to isolated pockets of life. The sense of beauty and inquiring intellect of the ancient Greeks, with ideals that found application in life, have all but disappeared as the vital or life energy has made a long descent to embrace a vulgar economic barbarism. The most dominant institution today is the multinational corporation, which mobilizes wealth, power, practical knowledge, and technological and administrative capacity, while cajoling science to invest in its one-sided economic interests. The result, noble ideals aside, is a utilitarian and mechanical, materialistically oriented culture that enchants and seduces the world with constant change and an ever growing range of technologically advanced consumer products.

Although appealing and with perceived value, the accumulated effect distracts individuals from broadening their cultural horizon and searching within. Capitalism, and the promotion of self-interest of the corporation or individuals in senior positions, has another destructive shadow. The corporation is narrowly focused on economic profitability and power, while still, for the most part, being less than responsible in its relationship to the natural world and humanity, to the great detriment of ecological balance and psychological well-being. There are, nonetheless, significant advances being made in empathic understanding of the environment and greatly improved ecologically friendly technology. In fact, advances in technology itself and its products are extraordinary and becoming increasingly "spiritualized," if I may be permitted to use the word. The science of psychology is also making notable advances even though the most significant psychologist of all, C.G. Jung, who redeems and advances contemporary Western culture by incorporating spiritual values, the inner person and the heart-Self and wholeness of personality, is not, for the most part, understood, while being dismissed and relegated to the margins. Although much has been lost or diminished from the past and life is presently ruled by a vulgar vital force, there have been significant gains made during the times we live in that can enrich the future.

India and the East, with India having the most fulfilled and pervasive spiritual, cultural and material history, are going through a renaissance that promises to eventually recapture their past glories. At this point in time the main effort is being placed on gaining econonomic and political power in a world driven by utilitarian and materialistic values. In the long run, signs of renewing spiritual ways, recast in contemporary form, with reliance on the heart-Self (psychic being) and the inner person harmoniously integrated with the external world are gaining ground, even if haltingly. In the meantime, there is the distinct danger of being inundated with Western materialistic values and forms. Auroville, which I discuss later on in this study, is potentially an exception. It is an experimental international city located in South India, which is attempting to integrate both Western, and Indian and Eastern values. Should it fulfill its envisioned destiny, it will be a harbinger for the future not only for India, but for the world.

The story of the universe includes the phenomenon of what Swimme refers to as "centration" or the evolutionary development of multiple centers of purposeful self-organizing intelligences at different levels of being, from the original point of creation down to the individual human being and beyond to all aspects of nature.[4] As he articulates it, the universe itself courses through individuals, who, as centers of self-organization, through conscious self-awareness, now have the potential to creatively participate in its unfolding. However dark the situation may seem to some people today, there are signs of radical change.

Swimme is convinced that we are at the end of the Cenozoic era in the history of the universe that began some sixty-five million years ago. The universe itself, as he sees it, is presently urging a new much broader focus and organization in all fields of life, which demands humans' creative participation. He exults in the fact that there are forces of allurement in the universe, or Eros, that naturally draws systems, ideas and people together for creative solutions and their propagation.

In 2016, the global human population adds up to roughly 7.5 billion human souls, and growing daily. Given the serious psychological and economic repercussions of overpopulation, especially evident in places like India and China, this is a significant concern. Severe ecological problems that reduce the diversity in nature and upset weather patterns carry human implications that need to be immediately addressed. Humans are beginning to realize that they are embedded in the natural world, while belonging to a global community. They are beginning to understand that they are important participants and members of a community that includes not only humans and animals, but organic and inorganic life, with moral obligations to the global ecology. This is one side of the equation regarding life in the subjective age that we are in the early stages of uncovering. The other side is the need for an inner search and authentic spirituality that not only seeks transcendence but transformation of the psyche at all levels of being.

---

4   2004.

The Fundamental Unitary Fourfold Law of Life

The Universe's story is one of intelligent unfolding and of the teleological purposefulness, over an immense period of time, of a living Universe that comprises both creation and destruction. In contemplating this phenomenon the image of the Hindu deity Shiva, creator and destroyer, comes to mind. The differentiation of the initial primordial oneness into the four fundamental laws of the physical world—gravity, electromagnetism and strong and weak nuclear interactions—points to a fundamental law of life that is fourfold with an underlying unity.

In pre-Socratic thought the physical Universe devolved from a single substance, primal matter, which differentiated into the four elements, air, fire, water and earth, which in turn recombined variously to produce the objects of the Universe. Alchemy later picked up on these ideas and reversed the process, reasoning that in order for there to be a transformation of base-substances into the philosopher's stone and to complete the opus, there was, first, a need for the substances to return to their undifferentiated state. Given the alchemist's animistic view of the natural world and belief in the spirit in matter, the original elements had a spirit and could be perfected, thus, potentially re-composed to form the desired substance, the *elixir vitae,* the *lapis,* the uncommon gold and the philosopher's stone. In both pre-Socratic thought and alchemy, then, the fundamental law of differentiated life is also that of fourfold unity.

Archetypal Intelligence and the Unfolding Future

The self-organizing archetypal intelligence around the Sun and its planets adds a further dimension to the active intelligence involved in creation of the Universe. From the beginning, and then, specifically, from the creation of the Sun and planets, there have been statistically improbable developments at every step of the way: from the appearance of the single cell, and primitive wood plants to mammals with emotional bonding, and trees, then a long line of different species of human beings until the modern *homo sapiens sapiens*. Life also took unexpected and unforeseen turns of organization, when it developed from nomadic hunter-gatherer bands to settled Neolithic villages and, from there, urban civilization and finally the nation-state, and now the present emerging global society and the current planetary ecological crisis, which requires a creative solution.

The story of the Universe to date, in other words, relates a tale of living intelligence that informs life at all level of being including consciously self-aware humans. And there are no signs that the intelligent evolutionary unfolding stops here. Cosmologist Brian Swimme observes that, with twenty to forty thousand species being destroyed every year, the planet is "withering" in a way that has had no precedence for "tens of millions of years," demanding a creative response and human transformation.[5]

Jung foresees a coming Age of the Holy Spirit, where the conscious and unconscious minds will be in complete harmony and life will be spontaneous and open to the descent of the spiritual Force and its motivating Will, an age of Truth. Sri Aurobindo and the Mother bring clarity to the evolutionary future and see *homo sapiens sapiens* as a transitional being. In their vision, the present crisis of civilization is potentially a harbinger for a new species of being beyond the human, the Superman, the Divine Person who lives in harmony with the Truth-Mind. Presently, in order to bring evidence to how the cosmos and humans meaningfully interrelate, I examine the macrocosmic signature of the self-organizing archetypal intelligence and its functions in the microcosm through human beings, both individually and collectively.

---

5   2004.

CHAPTER 3

The Cosmic Dimension and
the Human Equation

According to the macrocosmic view of evolutionary life, there is a profound interrelatedness between the cosmos and human nature, while the Universe is an interconnected whole. The self-organizing archetypal intelligence evident in the complete planetary system is directly related to life on Earth and is especially relevant to self-reflecting human life and its unfolding. This phenomenon is recorded in astrological charts as applied to individuals, social organizations and institutions, and objects, and is explained in books, essays on astrology and astrological readings. What is often not properly understood is the fact that it is highly unlikely that there is a causal influence such as a subtle energy flow between the planetary bodies and humans or other phenomena of interest. It is, rather, a question of different archetypal influences that are reflected in the planets and their positions at any particular moment in time, where archetypes refer to fundamental ways of apprehending life and the dynamic readiness for action.

Jung describes the qualitative significance of time in particularly poignant terms. He writes that "time, far from being an abstraction, is a concrete continuum which contains qualities or fundamentals which can manifest themselves in relative simultaneousness in different places and in a parallelism which cannot be explained, as in cases of simultaneous appearance of identical thoughts, symbols or psychic conditions .... Whatever is born or done at this particular moment of time has the quality of this moment of time."[1] Jung seems to be saying that all phenomena are qualitatively imprinted with the nature of the archetypal constellation at any given moment of phenomenological time. Over a long life, one cannot help but be impressed by the changing nature of the collective *zeitgeist* that is reflected individually and culturally in people's lives and thoughts, as one epoch gives way to another in ways that, in the concrete meaning of the word, are unpredictable.

The archetypes are decisive principles and forces and give form to life, yet they are not the whole story. Individuals are eminently important and play a significant participatory and potentially creative role in their interface with archetypal principles. Every individual is unique, each having a different moral capacity, truth of being and beckoning destiny. For this reason two people can have very similar horoscopes and lead very different lives. Personalities with vastly different destinies and character, for example, yet with similar natal charts are Charlie Chaplin, the comedian, and Hitler, the Nazi Führer, who were born within four days of each other. Despite their widely different lives and places in history, the archetypal forces at play in each case were similar. It is, consequently, not surprising that Chaplin did such a superb job of mockingly portraying Hitler in the movie *The Great Dictator*.

The importance of the individual and the individuation process or individualization for creative social change is central to the teaching of both Sri Aurobindo and Jung. In the case of Jung, this is evident throughout his writings. It is vividly portrayed early on, in his active imaginations as illustrated in *The Red Book,* where an emotional ego is constantly confronting, challenging and coming to terms with archetypal figures from his rich fantasy life. In fact, with individuation, Jung's ego gains in authority and strength in the face of these figures as the fantasies unfold.

In keeping with the importance Jung put on the development of ego

---

1   C.G. Jung, 1966, pp. 56, 57.

consciousness, in *Memories, Dreams, Reflections*,[2] his popular autobiography, an intricate dream is described where his father, depicted as a
learned theologian, knelt down and touched the floor with his forehead
in full submission to "the highest presence," while Jung was only able
to bring his forehead to a millimeter of the floor.[3] Jung's comment is
that one cannot submit as "a dumb fish," but that, for the sake of consciousness, there is a need to maintain some "mental reservation."[4]
One cannot surrender unconsciously; there is a need, rather, to surrender consciously. That's one valid way of understanding the dream.
Another possible understanding is that Jung's inner father principle
was fully surrendered (his father being a learned theologian), but such
a complete surrender was still consciously resisted by Jung's attitudes
and beliefs at the time.

At any rate, Jung's point is that the ego has a divine responsibility to act as consciously as possible and that assumptions, implicit or
otherwise, including about one's relationship to the divine, can skew
one's approach to life and submission to the divine. His attitude, as
expressed here, does not abrogate in the slightest his appeal to relate
to the center of being as "the spiritus rector of everyday life," where
every "experience of the Self is a defeat for the ego."[5] In this case, he is
not referring to an attitude or belief but to experiential phenomena that
are well attested to by anybody with an understanding of the symbolic
language of dreams and visions, who pays respectful attention to them,
along with synchronicities.

Aniela Jaffé recounts a later dream of Jung's, which suggests a
more complete surrender that involves his being charged with an ardu-
ous task. Here, below, is the dream as recorded in her book entitled:

---

2   The book was recorded and highly edited by Aniela Jaffé to the point that Jung
    often referred to it as her project. I still refer to it as Jung's autobiography, as it is
    popularly perceived.
3   1983, p. 219.
4   *Ibid.*, p. 220.
5   C.G. Jung, 1974c, pp. 544, 546.

Was Jung a Mystic? And Other Essays. In this dream, Jung's head is at the level of his father's feet, suggesting Logos and discriminating consciousness of the latter's perspective, and not, in any way, resistance to it. His mother's feet seem to be at his heart level, implying Eros-based feeling as well.

> *I am on a journey, or at least at a train station .... I am somehow in a foreign country and there is a large building. Perhaps the hall of a train station, or a hangar at the edge of an airfield. But there are no airplanes. A broad field stretches away in front of me at colossal distance to the horizon. A dark distance. It stretches into the infinite. There is awareness in me that I am on a journey.*
>
> *In the background there was a train on a track. We, a crowd of people, are standing near the locomotive, and I am with Father and Mother. I knew that they were there without seeing them exactly. So I was on a journey with Father and Mother and, in addition, we were in festive clothing. I know that we were coming back from a wedding that had taken place in a foreign country, far away. Father wore a top hat, and I had one too; that is I held it in the hand in which I was also carrying my suitcase. Somewhat uncomfortable, I am thinking: how stupid, why didn't I bring a hatbox with me? I look at the top hat, which indeed looks somewhat ruffled. Mother was rather more distant than my father ....*
>
> *Suddenly, it struck me: my sister was missing! Of course, she is the one who celebrated the wedding! So, the land from which we came must have been the beyond, or whatever that is called .... My sister died in her thirties. I never had a close relationship to her. I have told you about her and her marvelous attitude. I always admired her.*
>
> *The top hat ... makes the man appear taller. That is its purpose. One becomes more important because one is taller. That is, right "there," in the place we designate as the beyond. Here, it is a hindrance, an impediment. It is really very disagreeable when one again returns to earthly conditions.*
>
> *So we are standing on the platform beside the locomotive. I don't know. Had we gotten out of the train? We walked alongside the train away from the locomotive. Presumably, we*

wanted to find a carriage into which we could climb. It was not as if we were boarding the train in Paris or Vienna, in order to go home, but at the same time as if we had actually come from much further away.

Now, here again, was something astonishing: Father was walking on my left and he was, or was walking much higher than I, as if his feet were about at the height of my head. Mother was walking on my right and her feet were half as high as my father's feet. I myself had the feeling of being rather short.

The great área of the airfield, which apparently bordered on the train station, or was identical with it, had something terrifying about it. It was dark, the beginning of night, or rather, a night-like darkness, and a space of monstrous breadth, an emptiness, a colossal emptiness. I stood just on the very edge of the field, and in front of me lay this colossal expanse, and I was engaged in "departing" or "arriving."[6]

Jung has this to say about the dream: "I have the feeling that my tiredness during the last few days is connected with this dream experience, with this enormous distance from which I had to return. I have the feeling of a great task: I must return, must reduce the distance, 'take off the top hat,' get my feet back on the ground. My father had his feet at the height of my head. But somehow that was not in the air: it simply was so."[7]

Perhaps there is nothing more that needs to be said about the dream as, in addition to what Jung is recorded as saying about it, it speaks for itself as an unusually difficult divinely invested task that, I assume, given the magnitude of Jung's opus, he was capable of fulfilling. The fact his head is where his father's feet are suggests that he is conscious of the former's standpoint through Logos discernment. That his mother's feet are half the height as his father's feet suggests that they are close to his heart center and that he knows her standpoint through feeling and Eros. Evidently his sister's marriage in the beyond indicates a newly

---

6   Jung, as recorded in Jaffé, 1989, pp. 114–117 passim.
7   *Ibid.*, p. 117.

formed bond of a remarkable and sensitive personification of the unconscious, with a masculine element of discernment that presumably opens up Jung to the nature of the enormous task ahead of him. Overall, the dream seems to suggest that Jung has a discriminating soul, sensitive to the "beyond," as well as the qualities of both Logos and Eros-based feeling, which will allow him to bring home his new-found consciousness of the "beyond." That requires humility, being connected to the Earth and removing the top hat and any feeling of importance. It requires an unusually intense relationship to wholeness and, in Sri Aurobindo and the Mother's nomenclature, the psychic being, the feeling center of individual life.

To put these comments in the proper perspective, Jung asserts that the goal of psychological development is wholeness of being, the Self, and a connection to the infinite. Although the ego is a psychological complex and, in everyday functioning, typically contaminated by the shadow and/or anima/animus, it is a delegate from the Self and center of conscious awareness. In its essential nature, the ego is connected to self-knowledge and, therefore, potentially to a point of view superior to archetypal exigencies. In the Hindu way of seeing things, what Jung refers to as the ego is ultimately grounded on the *purusha* that, when connected to Eros and feeling, becomes the *caitya purusha,* the conscious incarnated soul or what Sri Aurobindo and the Mother refer to as the psychic being, which knows through feeling. A disciple of Sri Aurobindo and the Mother, Professor Indra Sen, an Indian psychologist, refers to the following quote from Jung: "The centre of personality acts like a magnet upon the disparate materials and processes of the unconscious and like a crystal grating, catches them one by one," equating Jung's description of the center of personality with Sri Aurobindo and the Mother's understanding of the psychic being.[8]

In order to amplify Sen's important observations, I now quote

8   1986, p. 183.

directly from Jung's unparalleled description of the center [the psychic being]; its functioning as an attractive magnet, and the fear of truth that disturbs the flow to the central point:

> What is particularly noteworthy here is the consistent develop-
> ment of the central symbol. We can hardly escape the feeling
> that the unconscious process moves spiral-wise round a centre
> gradually getting closer, while the characteristics of the centre
> grow more and more distinct. Or perhaps we could put it the
> other way round and say that the centre—itself virtually un-
> knowable—acts like a magnet on the disparate materials and
> processes of the unconscious and gradually captures them as in
> a crystal lattice. For this reason the centre ... is often pictured as
> a spider in a web ... especially when the consciousness attitude
> is still dominated by fear of unconscious processes. But if the
> process is allowed to take its course ... then the central symbol,
> constantly renewing itself, will steadily and consistently force
> its way through the apparent chaos of the of the personal psyche
> and its dramatic entanglements ....[9]

Professor Sen makes the following observations on the parallel between Jung's psychology and the practice of the Integral Yoga of Sri
Aurobindo and the Mother, especially regarding the important place of
the psychic being, the evolving soul:

> The Integral Yoga of Sri Aurobindo and the Mother as prac-
> ticed at the Sri Aurobindo Ashram, Pondicherry, of which the
> writer had personal experience, bears out happy parallelisms
> with Jungian psychology and its practice, in many respects. The
> soul is here too the unitary and the unique centre in man, which
> commands body, life and mind and their dualities or divided
> opposing reactions and their seekings. This soul is the evolving
> soul which they call the psychic being to distinguish it from
> the soul, which is the abiding individual spiritual reality as held
> by religions and philosophical systems. The psychic being is a

---

9   1977, p. 217

spiritual principle, a representative of the metaphysical soul, involved in man's evolutionary history. Ordinarily, it stands apart
acting from behind, whereas body, life and mind constitute the
apparent personality of man.[10]

Professor Sen then goes on to write: "The yogic pursuit consists of
seeking a contact with the psychic being and making it the dynamic and
dominant principle of life .... The parallelisms between the practice of
Integral Yoga and that of Jungian psychology," he says, "are evident.
Jung's approach is that of an empirical scientist and, as such, he went
the farthest one could go. And indeed he achieved the highest truths."[11]

Sen then examines the nature of the collective unconscious, quoting directly from Jung as follows: (1) "In talking about the unconscious
we have always to talk in paradoxes .... We know just as well, and can
rely on the fact, that the unconscious is not only chaos but also order"
and, further, (2) "the ever deeper descent into the unconscious suddenly becomes illumination from above," to which Sen adds a third
statement from Jung, (3) "Is there anything more fundamental than the
realization 'This is what I am'? It reveals a unity which nevertheless
is—or was a diversity."[12] The psychic being is directly related to the
archetypal psyche and has the psychological challenge of integrating
both light and dark aspects of the psyche to consciousness, allowing for
both unity and diversity.

It is perfectly evident from the foregoing quotes and comments that
Professor Sen endorses the fact of the central role of the psychic being in Jung's approach to psychology. Unfortunately, he believes that
the Jungian approach is only based on "empirical science," while the
yogic method involves "inner exploration."[13] This is an odd misreading
of the Jungian approach, which can be explained by the fact that Prof.

---

10   1986, p. 143.
11   *Ibid.*, pp. 143, 144.
12   *Ibid.*,
13   *Ibid.*, pp. 144, 145.

Sen never worked therapeutically with Jung's approach to psychology, where inner exploration is equally as important as it is in yogic enterprises. His comment, however, doesn't take away from his recognition of the importance of the psychic being in Jungian psychology. If the psychic being is implicated in Jung's approach to healing, it works according to its own logic and the individual's *uniquely unfolding life*, so it does not matter whether one calls it the individuation process or the psychic transformation of personality, as is the case in Integral Yoga.

Comments made by astrologer Richard Tarnas, in his convincing book *Cosmos and Psyche,* are relevant at this point in the discussion. In response to many popular astrologers who make life predictions based on the horoscope, he asserts that the archetypal patterns as indicated in the horoscope are "not concretely predictive" in the way suggested by these astrologers, "but archetypally predictive."[14] He acknowledges both the full power of the archetypal constellation at birth as well as the archetypal influence over time according to the planetary transits, but also, their extensive variability in application to life experience.

Tarnas refers to Jung in order to account for the mistake often made in astrological commentaries that define the role of the planets, by which I mean archetypal dynamics, too narrowly and rigidly. Thus, he quotes Jung as follows:

> "The ground principles, the *archai*, of the unconscious are indescribable because of their wealth of references, although in themselves, recognizable. The discriminating intellect naturally keeps on trying to establish their singleness of meaning and thus misses the essential point, for what we can above all establish as the one thing consistent with their nature is their manifold meaning, their almost wealth of reference, which makes any unilateral formulation impossible."[15]

14   Richard Tarnas, 2006, p. 128.
15   *Ibid.*, p. 87.

Tarnas quotes Jung further on in order to emphasis the vast range of meaning potentially linked to each archetypal pattern according to the individual, the overall life context, culture and the time.

> "A kind of fluid interpenetration belongs to the very nature of all archetypes. They can only be roughly circumscribed at best. Their living meaning comes out more from their presentation as a whole than from a single formulation. Every attempt to focus them more sharply is immediately punished by the intangible core of meaning losing its luminosity. No archetype can be reduced to a single formula. It is a vessel that we can never empty, and never fill … it persists throughout the ages and requires interpreting ever anew. The archetypes are indispensable elements of the unconscious but they change their shapes continually."[16]

Archetypes are multivalent with widely ranging feeling values and with both positive and negative vectors from the point of view of the conscious ego and the cultural setting. They are also multidimensional and cannot be pigeonholed into too narrow a meaning.

Archetypes need to be understood in relationship to the qualitative value of the time, their own particular subjective dynamics and the cultural milieu. Given the unique soul angle and spiritual development of each and every individual and their different moral refinement and capacity, along with the fluidity of the archetypes, an authentic interpretation of astrological dynamics recognizes essential free will and the indeterminate nature of human experience. Such an approach does not invalidate astrology and its fundamental assumptions, but opens it up to more nuance and complexity in interpretation. It does not suggest the spiritual need to go beyond "the compulsions of the stars" but suggests, rather, the exigency to open up to increasing individuation, differentiation and refinement of one's relationship to archetypal powers.

Jung is particularly charming in this observation on the qualitative

---

16   Jung, *Ibid.*, p. 89.

importance of time and place of birth: "We are," he says, "born at a given moment, in a given place, and we have, like celebrated vintages, the same qualities of the year and of the season that saw our birth."[17] The planetary positions at the moment of birth are especially relevant in that the natal chart depicts the basic nature of the individual personality, while personal planetary transits over time in relationship to the natal chart are a reflection of changing archetypal influences throughout a lifetime. World transits, in the meantime, are a record of the planets in relationship to the Earth at any given moment in time and depict archetypal influences and patterns involving collective historical and cultural phenomena.

From an astrological point of view, the most significant planetary cycles involve the five outer planets, Jupiter (11.88-year transits), Saturn (29.42-year transits), Uranus (83.75-year transits), Neptune (163.72-year transits), and Pluto (247.7- year transits), as they are relatively slow-moving, each circuit lasting many years. In *Cosmos and Psyche,* Richard Tarnas studies the implications to both personal biographies and cultural shifts reflected in the cycles of Neptune, Uranus and Pluto, the three most recent planetary discoveries (Uranus in 1781, Neptune in 1846 and Pluto in 1930). The archetypal significance of the Sun and Moon, and the five innermost planets, Mercury, Venus, Mars, Jupiter and Saturn, are appropriately indicated by their names, suggesting the names were chosen advisedly by ancient experts in the sacred, mythology and the gods. With the exception of Pluto, this is not the case regarding the three outer planets, which were discovered relatively recently and named by scientists with a less imaginative, more secular orientation to life.

Regarding Uranus, Tarnas argues that the story of Ouranos, the god of the starry sky, does not fit with the archetypal dynamics reflected in empirical studies of the nature of this planet. Empirical research

---

17   *Ibid.,* p. 103.

indicates that the phenomena of liberation, rebellion, intuitive insights, the unexpected, structural breakups, breakthroughs and creative originality are relevant. Tarnas argues that these attributes point to the story from Greek mythology of Prometheus, the "cosmic trickster," as being more indicative of the archetypal dynamics at play.[18]

Neptune is god of the sea and, as such, in many ways, it fits the qualitative nature of the consensual findings around the archetypal energies reflected in the planet of that name; yet in other ways the name is not apt at all. Thus, inasmuch as Neptune, the god, is described as tempestuous, belligerent and vengeful, this characterization bears no relationship to astrological findings. Otherwise, the planet Neptune refers to ideals, the imaginative, the dissolution of boundaries, dreams and visions, spiritual transcendence and the infinite and the eternal. Inasmuch as he is associated with the ocean and other bodies of water, mists and fogs, where dissolution and fluidity is suggested, as is divine love and mercy, the mythological Neptune is highly relevant to the meaning of the archetypal dynamics reflected by the planet Neptune.

Unlike the other two planets and their names, the story and character of Pluto, god of the underworld, as well as Dionysus, a close associate to the point of sometimes being considered identical, show extensive consensually agreed-upon parallels to the archetypal qualities empirically recorded concerning the planet of the same name. Astrologically, the planet Pluto is associated with depth and primal power, volcanic eruption, creation and destruction, primal transformation, birth and death and the elemental underground reality below the surface of life, the collective unconscious. The twentieth-century discovery of the planet Pluto, the splitting of the atom, the increasing utilization of nuclear energy and the growth of industrial organizational power, in this light, is no coincidence.

Tarnas has documented many historical events that demonstrate

---

18   *Ibid.*, p. 93.

the relevance of planetary configurations involving the three outer planets on individuals, cultural movements and epochs. In some cases the patterns demonstrated are *synchronic,* where events of the same archetypal nature occur simultaneously in different societies and culturally significant individuals. There were, for instance, a multiple of *synchronic* patterns related to a Uranus–Neptune opposition between 1899 and 1918 in almost every category of culture, including painting, literature, music, dance, psychology, spiritually and science. In common to all categories of cultural expression there was a major archetypal shift of cultural vision, which is characteristic of Uranus – Neptune alignments. Jung's *Symbols of Transformation,* which led to his break from Freud, was written in 1911–12. Between 1912 and 1928 Jung was immersed in *The Red Book,* where the seeds of all his later work were planted "and everything essential was decided."[19] Meanwhile, Sri Aurobindo was producing revolutionary 64-page articles monthly, later published in seven volumes in book form, on his integral spiritual path for a periodical called the *Arya* between August 15, 1914 and January 15, 1921.

In other cases, Tarnas shows *diachronic* patterns, where archetypally related events occur in different periods of time with similar planetary alignments. By way of example, Feminism developed in stages over the last 250 years, with major impetuses taking place in four pulses relating to Uranus–Pluto alignments, which refer to in-depth breakthroughs of some magnitude. The women's movement began while Uranus and Pluto were in opposition in 1787–1798, with a major boost from the publication of Mary Wollstonecraft's *A Vindication of the Rights of Women* in 1792. The second major Feminist thrust developed in 1845–1856 during the following Uranus–Pluto opposition.

Tarnas makes a highly significant observation when he draws a parallel between the almost identical configuration of Uranus, Neptune

---

19   1983, p. 199.

and Pluto in the natal charts of St. Augustine and Jung. This indicates that the operative archetypal principles and dynamics were similar in each case, although at different times and with different historical precedence. Along with St. Paul, St. Augustine was the major architect of early Western Christianity and he was concerned about how the Church could attract pagans to its fold, while establishing its own truth. This led to repression of the gods of nature and instinctual life, while the Church offered freedom from fate and superstition. One of St. Augustine's beliefs, which became Church doctrine, was that evil has no substance in its own right but is a *privatio boni* or deprivation of the Good.

Jung felt a need to bring a psychological corrective to what was discarded and repressed in Christianity, as well as the notion of evil as *privatio boni,* which he found odious, given the phenomenological reality of great evil and destructive forces operative in the world. He believed that the *privatio boni* argument devalues evil and the need to responsibly come to terms with the shadow side of life. The archetypal dynamics and polarities were similar for St. Augustine and Jung, but the psychological consciousness and moral vector of these two men were decidedly different. Whereas St. Augustine had the important role of establishing Christianity in the Age of Pisces, Jung had the psychologically significant vocation of reasserting the pagan relationship with the natural world and instinctual life, and healing the schism in the modern psyche, without losing the gains of Christianity and reason. Encouraging this important retrieval, without losing the gains of reason and Christianity that "educated man to a higher consciousness and responsibility," he advocates "love combined with insight and understanding."[20]

Jung is an important guiding light in pointing the way forward to the Age of Aquarius, which, following the medieval Christian monk Gioacchino de Fiore, Jung refers to as the Age of the Holy Spirit. It can

---

20   Jung, 1970 a-2, p. 297.

be understood as a fulfillment of the Christian message and initiation into the new way, where each individual potentially becomes a conscious receptacle of truth through a Christification process, by which Jung means living one's life as fully as Christ lived his, and not imitating his life. The Age of Pisces is characterized by Christ as fish, the devil as a second fish, and the disciples as fishers of men, where the two fish symbolically imply the differentiation of good and evil, although unconsciously. It took Jung and his psychology to make it conscious. The Age of Aquarius is reflected in the fact that the emphasis is on the individual human being, the individuated person as water carrier or conscious human receptacle of the Holy Spirit and a potential water pourer as one who can transmit the spirit.

Jung's daughter, Greta Baumann-Jung, an astrologer, wrote a reflective paper on the horoscope of her father, showing how he experienced the archetypal dynamics associated with progressed and transiting planets during his life.[21] She observes that Jung's Rising Sign or Ascendant is Aquarius, which is ruled by Uranus and Saturn. The Ascendant refers to the way one interacts with the world and the ruling Ascendant's ruling planets are considered important enough to be considered the chart's ruler. The significance of Uranus and Saturn for Jung, then, goes beyond the usual meaning attributed to either of these two planets taken alone. Baumann-Jung emphasizes that Uranus highly constellates the unconscious and, especially when transiting the Ascendant, imposes a new conscious attitude on the individual or organization. She relates Uranus to intuition and John the Baptist, in that he "bears witness to the light" and connects to Christ, as the Self.[22]

With this background in mind I will now examine some interesting comments Baumann-Jung makes regarding one of Jung's dreams during a creative period of his life that shows the relevance of transiting Uranus. Here is the dream that took place on December 18–19, 1947,

---

21   1975.
22   *Ibid.*, p. 35.

during a period when he was seventy-two years old and in correspondence with the Dominican Victor White:

> *Last night I dreamt of at least 3 Catholic priests who were quite*
> *friendly and one had a remarkable library. I was the whole time*
> *under a sort of military order and I had to sleep in the barracks.*
> *There was a scarcity of beds, so that two men had to share one*
> *bed. My partner had already gone to bed. The bed was clean,*
> *white, and fresh and he was a most venerable looking very old*
> *man with white locks and a long flowing white beard. He offered*
> *me graciously one half of the bed and I woke up just as I was*
> *slipping into it.²³*

In a letter to Father Victor White, dated January 30, 1948, Jung refers
to this old man as *senex venerabilis* and, a month later, as Philemon.
For Baumann-Jung, Uranus is the wise old man with a white beard,
what Jung often refers to as his number 2 personality, ultimately the
Intuitive Mind and, through it, direct relationship to the archetypal
unconscious. Natal Uranus is on the opposite side of the chart to his
Aquarius Ascendant, and in Jung's seventh house, the house of partner-
ships. Natal Saturn, which defines destiny or fate, is in his first house,
which rules the formation of the conscious ego, what Jung refers to as
his personality number 1.

On studying Jung's horoscope, Baumann-Jung found that all his
major creative writings were especially related to transits of Saturn and
Uranus. This is implicitly acknowledged by Jung, when he writes: "All
my writings may be considered tasks imposed from within [reflected
by Uranus]: their source was a fateful compulsion [reflected by Saturn].
What I wrote were things that assailed me from within myself [reflected
by Uranus]."²⁴ On the day of the dream indicated above, Uranus was at
24° Gemini, making a grand airy trine with Saturn and Jupiter suggest-

---

23   *Ibid.*, p. 46.
24   As recorded in Baumann-Jung, 1975, p. 53.

ing, according to Baumann-Jung, a harmonious relationship between personalities numbers 1 and 2, the conscious and the unconscious, as reflected in the Uranus–Saturn trine. The Uranus–Saturn trine, meanwhile, emphasizes the religious and philosophical/theological dimension. Spiritual knowledge is reflected in the dream by the priestly figures, especially the one with a "remarkable library."[25]

Taken on its own, the horoscope reveals nothing of an individual's unique combination of genes or quality of soul, moral capacity, and evolutionary development of the psychic being or heart-Self. These brief reflections, however, do indicate that Jung had a particularly conscious relationship with the macrocosm and archetypal psyche as reflected in his dreams, his creative work and his life story. The creative outpouring of his psyche reflects its advanced evolutionary status and a highly developed moral and creative capacity.

Answering his own Cartesian reflections on the nature of humans in relationship to the Universe, Richard Tarnas writes: "Is it not more plausible that human nature, in all its creative multidimensional depths and heights, emerges from the very essence of the cosmos, and that the human spirit is *the spirit of the cosmos itself* as inflected through us and enacted by us? … And … that this larger spirit, intelligence and imagination all live within and act through the self-reflective human being who serves as a unique vessel and embodiment of the cosmos."[26] From an astrological perspective, the testimony of Jung's life reveals that he embodies the truth of this statement as a unique vessel of differentiated archetypal energy in an exemplary fashion, particularly conscious and responsible.

After this look at indications of archetypal intelligence reflected in the cosmos and the interrelationship between the macrocosm and the human, in particular Jung, the trajectory of my study now descends in search of signs of intelligence in the natural world. In the following

---

25   *Ibid.*, p. 48.
26   2006, p. 492.

discussion I emphasize the evolution of nature as well as the relation-ship between the mind and the functioning of the brain. My purpose for this apparent diversion is to reinforce the truth that the laws of nature are intelligent and unitary, and that the mind and the brain are ulti-mately one. It is part of my effort to establish the intelligence of nature as a basic building block for Jung's approach to psychology, drawing it close to the Integral Yoga of Sri Aurobindo and the Mother, who posit the existence of the Divine or the Supermind at the core of matter. This line of thinking finds its earlier parallel in the *Corpus Hermeticum*, attributed to the legendary father of alchemy, Hermes Trismegistus, where God's essence is "pregnant with all things," and the cosmos has been created for purposes of God's self-knowledge.[27] Humans, in this account, have been appointed the task of gaining knowledge of God, which is God's knowledge of Himself, and completing God.

---

27   Glenn Alexander Magee, 2008, p. 9.

CHAPTER 4

Laws of Nature and Neurobiology
and the Development of Mind

In the spirit of inquiring into the intelligence of nature, in this chapter I briefly examine Rupert Sheldrake's hypothesis of morphic resonance, the habits of nature and the role of creative development in nature. He demonstrates how the laws of nature are shaped through cumulative experiences of specific morphic fields in a process of morphic resonance involving formative causal influences. He argues that there is both soft-creativity, which involves intelligent adaptive change, and strong or hard-creativity, where there are creative new formations. I also briefly examine the work of Daniel J. Siegel on the relationship between the brain and the mind or psyche, and its implications for psychology. His conceptual framework is based on complexity theory, a position that is very similar to Sheldrake's hypothesis of formative causation. In both cases there is evidence of intelligence in nature as well as parallels with Jung's thinking. There are also differences. These differences are significant and, from my perspective, what is important is that they indicate the shift in viewpoint that is necessary in order to appropriate Jung's findings for a truly unitary approach to the laws of nature, on the one hand, and between the brain and the psyche or mind, on the other.

Rupert Sheldrake: Habits in Nature and Creative Change

The biologist Rupert Sheldrake formulates the hypothesis of formative causation whereby memory is inherent in all levels of nature.[1] According to this hypothesis, specific morphic fields, which can be described as "fields of information," shape each natural system, from subatomic particles to atoms to crystals, to snowflakes, to societies, to cultural ideas and to the organization of the cosmos.[2] Morphic fields are non-material centers that organize patterns of structure and activity with influences that enter space and persist over time. It functions through the conceptual existence of chreodes or developmental pathways and morphogenetic attractors, which I discuss below. Through a process referred to as morphic resonance, which involves the transmission of formative causal influences through collective memory, the past becomes present within each morphic field, while acknowledging that there may be formative influences from the "presence" of the future as well. Complexity is accounted for by assuming a hierarchical nesting of morphic fields within fields. For example, there is a fundamental crystal morphic field and then morphic fields for different versions of crystals, such as a rose crystal that nests within the fundamental crystal field. It is noteworthy here that Sheldrake acknowledges the similarity between this hypothesis and his understanding of Jung's thinking on the archetypes, at least inasmuch as they are conceived as being contained in the collective unconscious in a hierarchical organization. Jung, in fact, writes that tendencies in the direction of attempting to establish "a hierarchy of archetypes ... can be shown to exist in the unconscious."[3]

Morphic resonance functions through oscillation and vibrations by way of characteristic rhythmic patterns. Memory depends on morphic resonance, which functions according to similarity; the more a natural form resembles previous organisms, cultural life-forms or ideas, the greater the influence of morphic resonance from the past. There

---

1   2009 passim.
2   *Ibid,* p. 113.
3   1975b-3, p. 495.

is, in addition, a cumulative effect of the memory of any specific type of past form. The concept of chreodes and morphogenetic attractors help explain how morphogenesis and the creation of forms take place. Chreodes are conceived as channels in morphogenetic fields that guide development, whereas future patterns of organization are determined by morphogenetic attractors. For example, a developing acorn is influenced by morphic resonance from countless previous oak trees and guided by chreodes toward the morphogenetic attractor, its final form as an oak tree. The morphogenetic field becomes stabilized accordingly.

As memory is cumulative, each system of nature becomes increasingly habitual over time and therefore enduring, although only as a probability. The probability factor accounts for the variation in nature of any particular organism, cultural life-form and life process or mental formulation. The structure of each morphic field depends on what happened before and the development of a collective memory. Despite this dependence on the past, there are indications of creative evolution. As I elaborate below, thanks to mutual interactive influences between each morphic field and the existential natural form (organism, cultural life-form and life process, mental idea, atom, etc.), morphic fields emerge and evolve over space and time. Thus, despite the tendency of organisms, ways of organizing life, and ruling ideas to become habitual, the cosmos seems to act not as a mechanical universe, but rather more like a purposeful, living, evolving and growing organism as Swimme and Berry demonstrate.

Formative Causation and Soft and Strong Creativity

Formative causation explains the regular and repetitive patterns of organization, found in nature as dependent on habit. The causal nature of this process, however, does not explain the development of new patterns of organization, such as a new crystal, new scientific theory or new, more comprehensive, creative thinking in any given field of study or across fields. Sheldrake, in fact, believes that nature is manifestly not a mechanical machine or illusory, but that there is intelligence in nature, with morphic fields being intrinsically creative. He consequently hypothesizes that the immanent organizing principles of nature, the morphic fields, with their inherent memory, evolve along with the evolution of physical organisms, cultural life-forms and life-processes, and ruling archetypal ideas.

In Sheldrake's own words: "The organizing principles of nature are not beyond it, in a transcendent reality but within it. Not only does the world evolve in space and time, but the immanent organizing principles themselves evolve. These organizing principles are morphic fields, which contain inherent memory."[4] This reading of morphic fields is reminiscent of Jung's understanding of the archetype except that, according to Jung's later formulation, the archetype is psychoid, with spiritual and material poles that are ultimately transcendent. Thus, Jung writes: "Matter and spirit both appear in the psychic realm as distinctive qualities of conscious content. The ultimate nature of both is transcendental, that is irrepresentable, since the psyche and its contents are the only reality which is given to us *without a medium*."[5] As I demonstrate below, Jung's appreciation of the ultimate transcendental nature of the psychoid archetype, as well as related phenomenological experiences of synchronicity, allows for an appreciation of new creation in time in a way that Sheldrake has some difficulty explaining, except through open-ended metaphysical speculations.

Sheldrake argues that an adjustment to new conditions in nature is made possible by the tendency to strive toward the morphic attractor, as I illustrate above with respect to the acorn becoming an oak tree. With humans, he surmises, the new integration comes through consciousness, although the creative process itself works through the unconscious. Examples are solving social or cultural problems and the results of calamities, where social integrity is re-established with a new

4   1995, p. 313.
5   *Ibid.*, p. 216.

social or cultural order, and/or, where appropriate, the construction of new physical dwellings and public buildings, along with appropriate infratructure. In terms of human psychological development, the process is described below in my discussion of Daniel Siegel's complexity theory of the mind. In the case of social insects, like bees or ants, overcoming disasters or obstacles to nest construction, and re-establishing harmony and nest integrity, a similar creative process ensues. This kind of creativity is the normal type of insect, animal and human creativity, which Sheldrake calls weak or soft-creativity. It works within existing morphic fields and their habitual patterns, and does not refer to the riddle of new patterns of organization altogether. In addition to habit, however, there is a creative element involved in soft-creativity in the sense of being intelligent, resourceful and flexible in the process of adapting to new circumstances.

The appearance of a new morphic field and organizing pattern, for example a new crystal, a new philosophic theory or art form, or a new pattern of behavior, requires a quantum jump and a higher order of organization through what Sheldrake refers to as hard or strong-creativity. Sheldrake examines this kind of creativity in two ways, as emerging from below and emanating from the top down. From the former point of view, evolution gives birth to the "emergence" of increasingly complex forms with "higher levels of organization."[6] There seems to be a creative principle inherent in the primal energy basic to matter and life as well as the evolutionary process itself that generates a bottom-up dynamic of emergence. From the top-down perspective, new morphic fields may come into being as emanations from "a pre-existing field" at a higher, "more inclusive level of organization" that promotes creative evolutionary development.[7] Thus, new kinds of proteins arise from the morphic field of cells, new formations of stars and galaxies in an expanding universe and ongoing terrestrial developments unaccountably

---

6   *Ibid.*, p. 216.
7   *Ibid*, p. 322.

come into being. For another example closer to home that actually happened relatively recently; the blue tit bird adapted a compelely new habit of feeding behavior by opening milk-bottle tops.

These are all examples of hard-creativity. The creative process depicted above, either as below-up or top-down, is interactive and higher level morphic fields develop greater complexity thanks to the new morphic fields that are contained within them. Moreover, morphic fields are influenced by what has happened in the past as well as by what is happening in them presently in the creative evolutionary process. The creation of new more compex fields with a higher level organization, therefore, can be understood to involve either an ascending process or a descending process, or understood as involving a combination of these processes.

Sheldrake speculates metaphysically that the creative process depicted here points to both the primal unified field of contemporary physics, as well as to the Platonic *anima mundi* (world soul), the primal order of becoming. The unified field, according to some physicists, relates to eternal laws, while the *anima mundi* consists of eternal ideas. In these speculations, Sheldrake is hesitatingly groping towards a solution like Jung's *unus mundus,* which I allude to below. According to Sheldrake, however, there can only be metaphysical speculation and no satisfactory answer to the question of origin and source of activity, fundamental laws and ideas. He then observes that the question as to the source of these transcendental laws and how they give rise to the physical universe, therefore, needs to be open-ended.

It is worthy of mention here that Jung postulates the principle of synchronicity or meaningful coincidences, where the human subject consciously experiences acausal or non-dual Reality in a new act of creation in time. The experience of synchronicity is a phenomenological function of the medieval idea adapted by Jung of a transcendent *unus mundus,* a non-dual one world or Mind of God, consisting of both unity, which points to a transcendent Beyond, and multiplicity, while being based on the principle of non-locality or nonlocal interactions, as understood in quantum physics. This helps explain the workings of an evolutionary creative force and its source that is confused in Sheldrake's opus, who, in his theory of formative causation, does not go beyond causal thinking, however subtle.

Sheldrake, in fact, posits three possible explanations for the effects and speed of morphic resonance over astronomical distances: (1) causal influences that function faster or slower than the speed of light: (2) causal influences that travel at the speed of light, and: (3) some analogy to "the non-local correlations in quantum theory, which are in some sense instantaneous."[8] Sheldrake, the biologist, cannot make a choice between these possibilities. He does not consider acausal phenomena, like Jung does in his hypotheses, which assumes a non-dual unitary world or *unus mundus* and non-locality as well as full embededdness of the psychoid archetypes or morphic fields in nature.

Sheldrake's theory of formative causation, in fact, seems to separate morphic fields from living forms and processes inherent in nature itself, despite their material influences. This, at least, is John Haule's view, which is also my understanding. Regarding Jung's perspective, where the subjective psychic sphere may be prevalent, yet the psychoid nature of the archetype reflects the non-dual unitary world and full embededdness in nature, Haule argues that "our more subtle and universal vision of a psychoid field locates it in the process that is the flower's or the mouse's living, organic being."[9] In contrast, with Sheldrake, the morphic fields seem to exist independently of embodied forms and life processes in a non-material subtle realm, although they bring influence to bear in the material world.

Every authentic experience of synchronicity, which involves the constellation of a psychoid field of archetypal energy through, in Sheldrake's terms, either soft or hard-creative energy expressed through a morphic field, contributes to the creative transformation of

---

8   *Ibid*, p. 302.
9   2011, p. 186.

the individual human psyche. In addition to strong-creativity, I include adaptive soft-creativity because, even though there are obvious casual factors involved, the underlying deeper truth, in my estimation, may at times also be acausal, especially given the intelligent, ingenous and flexible nature of any given soft-creative response. Meanwhile, the testimony of Jung's own life, as recorded through dreams and visions as well as his theoretical writings on psychology, indicates that there is both a top-down and bottom-up process involved in the creative transformation of being, that I will explore later on.

Daniel J. Siegel: the Brain, the Mind and Healthy Integration

Daniel J. Siegel uses ideas and a line of reasoning similar to Sheldrake's in order to formulate his complexity theory hypotheses on the development of the mind, meaning psyche, where he observes that *"a driving force of development is the movement from simplicity toward complexity,"* as its first principle.[10] Stability comes from the maximization of complexity, where old patterns are applied in similar, but not identical situations. These patterns emerge from specific brain neurons interacting with its surrounding conditions and, through reinforcement, gain in probability as they become more ingrained and habitual. Patterns can be healthy or pathological and, by way of self-organization, the activated aspect of the brain draws in other neuronal groups "to create a sense of ordered complexity."[11] Reinforced patterns are known as "attractor states" that promote self-organization and engender stability and continuity.

The goal of mental health is healthy integration, which allows for a balance between continuity and flexibility and maximum complexity. By integration, Siegel is referring both to various levels of processes within the mind and between minds in relationship, where there are

---

10   1999, p. 217.
11   *Ibid.,* p.218.

potentially increasing levels of neuronal integration and differentiation over a lifetime. In reference to the brain, integration is both horizontal, involving the right and left hemispheres and vertical involving the neo-cortex down to the limbic system and the autonomic nervous systems. In terms of verticality there is some parallel here with Jung's approach, inasmuch as archetypal images are understood as having a violet, men-tal (and spiritual) pole, as well as a red instinctive or dynamic pole. The need to integrate anima/animus and the shadow in Jung's approach to psychology are relevant to both vertical and horizontal brain inte-gration. Stuck relationships and pathological states of mind, perhaps resulting from early trauma, create rigid and/or chaotic thought pro-cesses, styles of communication and behavior.

Like Sheldrake, Siegel's thinking is causal and, like him, he al-lows for both determinant and predicable, and indeterminate and non-predictable responses based on the principle of non-linearity and the observation that small changes in one part of the brain, for instance as expressed through either mental dysfunction or healthy integration, can lead to a series of unpredictable reactions. These reactions are some-times huge, emanating from other components of the brain and the brain and the mind as a whole, and manifest in behavior. In addition to the principle of non-linearity, another principle of complexity theory is that dynamic complex systems have both emergent and recursive pat-terns of organization. Regarding the mind, emergent patterns mean that patterns of the mind unfold over time, while recursive patterns mean that a state of mind resulting from any given neuronal activity returns to further influence the emergence of that state of mind. One source of dysfunction, from a neuro-biological point of view, is that different states of mind can be in conflict, and healthy integration requires their reconciliation. This principle has similarity to Jung's understanding of psychic energy, archetypal patterns and psychic processes that unfold over time and which can be in conflict with each other, but ultimately need reconciliation.

Noteworthy, however, is the difference in views regarding brain and mind or the psyche. In Siegel's case, mind is an emergent property of the brain that functions recursively, while, for Jung, the archetype as he later defined it, is psychoid, transcending spirit and matter, rendering the psyche, now extended to include a psychoid base, and brain are a unity, two aspects of the same thing. Rather than the mind emerging from the brain, they both devolve as a unity from a transcendent phenomenon. Despite the intrinsic unity of the psyche and the brain for Jung, his view reflects the greater emphasis in his psychology on the play of the imaginal or archetypal psyche and the psychological benefits of entering into a dialogue with it, while keeping the conscious ego intact, as well as the principle of synchronicity. Siegel's interest in guided imagery, an external intervention by the therapist, reflects his more causally oriented perspective.

Siegel does acknowledge the importance of dreams for integrating "memory and emotion," but he has an undifferentiated and limited understanding of their nature, seeing them as consisting of memories requiring assimilation, memories from experiences during the day, multiple sensations during sleep and, what he refers to, as random images from REM states.[12] Dreams, for Jung, in contrast, are highly differentiated and can be primarily subjective, as is usually the case, while, simultaneously being objective, referring to external events and people as well as the collective unconscious and the objective psyche. In all cases, they are compensatory to conscious attitudes and values and play the role of potentially bringing the unconscious to consciousness—essential for conscious individuation, the process of moving toward wholeness. There are both a personal unconscious and a collective unconscious, the former referring to unconscious aspects of the personality related to one's personal history that can be assimilated to consciousness relatively easily, the latter referring to universal archetypes, with values which are more difficult to assimilate to consciousness.

---

12   Daniel J. Siegel, 2011, p. 141.

Whereas becoming conscious of the personal unconscious enhances one's personal life, assimilating aspects of the archetypal unconscious has a major transformative effect on the personality.

Another similarity between Jung and Siegel is the emphasis the latter places on both neuronal differentiation and differentiation of emotional states, as well as his recognition of the logical interpretive function of the left brain and the nonverbal primary emotions mediated by the right brain, mirroring the former's call for Eros relatedness and Logos differentiation. According to Siegel, emotions and the experience of emotion play a central regulating role in self-organization both synchronically (at the same moment in time) and diachronically (across time). Emotions are essential ingredients in cognitive and relational development as "emotion, meaning and social interaction are mediated by the same circuitry in the brain."[13]

Emotions are central to self-organization because they reflect value given to inner and external events and, consequently, the regulation of energy and the discernment of knowledge, showing a parallel with Jung's position regarding feeling-toned complexes and the flow of archetypal patterns. Siegel defines emotions as "a subjective experience involving neurobiological, experiential, and behavioral components," indicating that "it is 'in fact' the essence of mind."[14] Inasmuch as emotions have a behavioral component, they involve movement into action. Such a definition directly relates emotions to archetypes as understood by Jung, where they form the essential contents of the psyche. From a Jungian point of view, emotions are the essence of the psyche inasmuch as they are connected to the dynamic energy portion of the archetypal image, which also has a spiritual component involving a mode of apprehension. In practical experience, Jung observes that "in their original form—they are images and at the same time emotions."[15]

---

13   Siegel, 1999, p. 258.
14   *Ibid.*, p. 275.
15   1976b, p. 257.

Siegel understands "resonance" as describing the nature of mutually co-regulating influences, interpersonally between brains, and intrapersonally between different subcomponents of the brain, which become effectively linked.[16] Functional integration results from the resonance of various subsystems, achieving cohesive states and their coherent flow across time. Feeling attunement between caregiver and child form an affirmative resonance between mutually regulating states of mind and secure attachment between them. It allows for the transfer of emotional energy and the flow of discrete packets of consciousness (information) between caregiver and child, facilitating the movement from emotion to behavior. Misattunement creates dysregulation that impedes integration due to blockages to neuronal linkage and differentiation. Secure attachment between caregiver and child are ideal, evoking curiosity, openness, acceptance and love in the child. Later in life, "interpersonal integration" is essential and interpersonal attunement is a "requirement for the individual to survive and to thrive."[17] Healthy interpersonal integration is essential for a healthy mind and secure relationships, and it opens up the possibility for healthy intrapersonal dynamics as well, given that the same neuronal circuits are involved.

Mindfulness, being aware of the present moment without judgment, requires intrapersonal or internal attunement. It involves attunement to one's authentic identity, love of oneself, and integrative influences on different aspects of the mind, including one's social and regulatory neuronal circuitry. Mindfulness allows for increased receptivity and "the ability to perceive the mental state of others" with empathic receptivity to them.[18] In fact, the brain circuits involved in both self-reflection and empathy overlap, inducing Siegel to refer to mindsight as contemplative self-knowledge and empathy.

The self, according to Siegel, has a public aspect, similar to Jung's

---

16   Siegel, 1999, p. 321.
17   Siegel, 2007, p. 317.
18   Siegel, 1999, p. 140.

persona, as well as a core self that refers to one's essential identity. Here Jung is more differentiated with his understanding of the ego as a delegate from the Self as totality of being; of personal shadow as qualities that are rejected by the ego, but often of value to life when integrated to consciousness and of anima/animus, the contra-sexual side of the psyche that potentially relates one to the collective unconscious and the archetypes including the Self of wholeness. As with secure attachment and secure interpersonal relationships, mindfulness evokes well-being and seems to stimulate similar neuronal circuits in others. Likewise, in Jungian terms, extraverted relatedness or Eros along with Logos corresponds to differentiated interpersonal dynamics, while introverted relatedness or Eros along with Logos corresponds to differentiated intrapersonal dynamics and love of oneself. One's state of mind, whether pathological or healthy, can affect others; advancement in the individuation process is silently contagious.

Siegel recommends an exercise involving what he refers to as the wheel of awareness for developing mindful awareness. Of central importance is the hub, which he sees as a space of tranquility and infinite possibilities. It is the 'inner place of the mind from which we become aware," and "a visual metaphor for our prefrontal cortex."[19] The prefrontal cortex has important regulatory functions with links to the cortex, limbic system and brain stem as well as the nervous system of the body itself. It also links those neuronal circuits to inter-relational communication that is sent and received. It is highly integrative. Siegel refers to the hub as the curve of infinite possibilities and a place of tranquility that, when accessed, can increase mindful awareness and mindful choices that avoid both chaos and rigidity.

Again there is a characteristic difference between this and Jung's approach to awareness. With Jung the parallel practice involves engaging in a dialogue with figures from the collective unconscious in

19   Siegel, 2011, p. 89.

a dynamic meditative process he calls active imagination. Here, not only is the hub or prefrontal cortex the central focus, but one also directly engages the psyche and comes to terms with the figures of the collective unconscious for the sake of transformation of both the ego and the archetypal unconscious. An approach that involves a direct engagement of the psyche involves the whole person rather than just the prefrontal cortex in the dialogue and vastly extends Siegel's brand of unity of the brain/mind or psyche.

Siegel's scientific approach to the study of the mind brings interesting elucidation of relational behavior and of functional and dysfunctional relationships, involving different parts of the brain. Although his healing approach and goals of integration have real value and promote clarity of insight and well-being, it always involves conscious ego directedness, which tends to devalue the unconscious, even if it is mindful and receptive. Jung's active imagination and goal of realization of the Self are potentially far more transformative, and this realization involves not ego directedness but sacrifice of the ego. According to him, psychological transformation requires that experience of the center of being "proves to be the spiritus rector of everyday life," where every "experience of the Self is a defeat for the ego."[20] Experience of the Self may bring a feeling of infinite freedom, but it also binds one to the limitations of one's nature. The process of individuation takes one on a journey through psychic places that promote a feeling of well-being, but also to places of disturbing feelings and chaos, not to be avoided, as they are also essential for the sake of greater differentiation and integration.

Given the dynamics expressed above, Siegel, observes: "We are always in a perpetual state of being created and creating ourselves," … with "an underlying sense of an incredible amount of freedom and cohesion within the system at any given moment."[21] Despite his use of

---

20   C.G. Jung, 1974c, pp. 544, 546.
21   2007, p. 221.

superlatives to describe the feeling of freedom and self-creation when advancing toward healthy integration, what Siegel is referring to here sounds like what Sheldrake calls soft-creativity, which functions within the normal range of healthy patterns of the mind, with flexible adaptation, and not strong-creativity, with development of new patterns of mental or psychic organization. New patterns, as I mean it here, involve a relationship to the archetypal psyche and the Self as the guiding spirit of everyday life.

Although both Sheldrake and Siegel make significant contributions to the study of the laws of nature and the mind or psyche/brain interface respectively, they fall short because they do not include acknowledgement of either the individual or cosmic Self in their calculations. Nor do they bring in synchronicity and acausal thinking in their scientific equations. Although they acknowledge a kind of indeterminacy, it involves a form of causality, however much it allows for unknowable effects. In the case of Jung, experiences of synchronicity are acausal and indeterminate in a truer sense of the word. There is no cause and effect at all, except as secondary factors, just meaningful coincidences between inner and outer events as an experience of the *unus mundus* or one world of unity and multiplicity. Appropriating Jung's view to their thinking would result in a more unitary view of nature and of the brain/mind dynamic. Indeed, Jung's continual insistence that his psychology is firmly grounded empirically finds support from a comparative study of the research and thought of Siegel and Sheldrake, as well as Berry and Swimme, discussed in chapter 2.

CHAPTER 5

Jung's Natural Affiliation with Alchemy

Alchemy, Jung proposes, developed in compensatory relationship to medieval Christianity, where, through faith, humans believed in a God that actively redeems them from their sins through grace. In contrast, the alchemical *opus* requires the human adept to continue "the divine work of redemption" and to redeem both the divine soul from the chains of *heimarmené* or worldly fate as well as *the anima mundi* or world soul dormant in matter.[1] Putting this process and its consequences in perspective, Jung writes: "His attention is not directed to his own salvation through God's grace, but to the liberation of God from the darkness of matter. By applying himself to the miraculous work he benefits from its salutary effect, but only incidentally."[2] In order to achieve their goal, alchemists devised several chemical operations such as *solutio, sublimatio, separatio, calcinatio, mortificatio* and *putrefactio,* that they believed reduced base-substances to their original elements, along with *coagulatio* and *coniunctio,* which brought the new substance into consciousness and being. Also required for the transformation of the substances was a discovery of a catalyst, the miraculous Mercurius, the penetrating spirit and transforming agent, which was, according to the alchemical literature, elusive.

In addition, alchemists also differentiated the alchemical process

---

1   C.G. Jung, 1977, p. 375.
2   *Ibid.*, p. 312.

leading to the goal into four stages and states of mind, such as the *nigredo* (blackness), *albedo* (whitening), *rubedo* (reddening), and *citrinitas* (yellowing)—referred to as the quartering of the philosophy. In the fifteenth and sixteenth century, *citrinitas* was gradually dropped. Psychologically, *nigredo* refers to depression, melancholia, and psychological and spiritual death; *albedo* to receptivity and insight, innocence, an abstract state of waiting and daybreak; and *rubedo* refers to quickening, life involvement and the rising dawn. *Citrinatis* refers to illumination and enlightenment, and the full light of day. Originally the four colors corresponded to the four elements (earth, air, fire and water) and four qualities (hot, cold, dry and moist), but subsequently there were only three, creating a certain disharmony. The change to three colors seems to have been due to a lack of procedural standardization, uncertainty about how to attain the goal, related psychological reasons and the symbolic significance of the quaternity and the trinity. Whereas the quaternity symbolizes wholeness and completeness, the trinity not only draws from the Christian Trinity, but it symbolizes process and insight. Despite this confusion, the fundamental fourfold nature of reality consisting of the four elements remained a basic tenet of alchemy.

Alchemy predates chemistry; these chemical operations were not scientific in the contemporary sense of the word, and there was little knowledge of the nature of matter. They were, instead, related to the practitioner's *meditatio* and *imaginatio*, where *meditatio* involves an inner dialogue between the adept and God or the "other," and *imaginatio vera*, true imagination, the key to the opus, was related to the symbolic world of subtle bodies or archetypal images. Not faith, as in Christianity, but knowledge based on laboratory experience, constitutes the alchemical path. Alchemists held to the Aristotelian belief in the unity of matter and understood that what they witnessed transpiring in the chemical solutions was also taking place in their own psyches. They believed that their own psychic and spiritual processes coincided with the chemical phenomena they saw in the chemical retort and their alchemical reference texts.

In this regard and with reference to the third-century CE mystic, Zosimos of Panopolis, a Gnostic and alchemist and, perhaps, the earliest writer of Greek alchemical texts, Jung writes: "The identity [with the behaviour of matter] was unconscious," for which reason Zosimos "is no more able than the rest of them to make any pronouncement about it."[3] The identity is simply there, without understanding, serving as a bridge uniting inner psychic and external material events into one. But the psychic contents continue to reside in the unconscious as autonomous complexes split off from consciousness. Although their *meditatios* and *imaginatios* gave some of them access to inner knowledge, there were a considerable amount of projections from the unconscious psyche into matter, about which the alchemists were, by and large, unaware.

In an interview with the mythologist and student of alchemy Mircea Eliade, Jung is recorded as making the following observations regarding the alchemical opus, which puts it into proper perspective: "Alchemy represents the projection of a drama both cosmic and spiritual in laboratory terms. The *opus magnum* had two aims: the rescue of the human soul and the salvation of the cosmos. What the alchemists called 'matter' was in reality the [unconscious] self. The 'soul of the world,' the *anima mundi*, which was identified with the *spiritus mercurius,* was imprisoned in matter. It is for this reason that the alchemists believed in the *truth* of 'matter,' because 'matter' was actually their own psychic life. But it was a question of freeing this 'matter,' of saving it—in a word, of finding the philosopher's stone, the *corpus glorificationis.*"[4] When the projections are withdrawn from the external world of matter, the philosopher's stone is recognized as nothing other than the transformed individual human personality, with the center of consciousness having shifted from the ego to the Self, to the point of assuming a glorified body.

3   1977, p. 30.
4   As reported in William McGuire and R. F. C. Hull, eds., 1980, p. 221

It was not until the twentieth century, thanks mainly to the work of C.G. Jung and some of his disciples, most notably Edward Edinger, Marie-Louise von Franz and now, some of her students and others, that the belief in the fact of inner psychic and spiritual processes coinciding with chemical phenomena seen in the laboratory reports have been clearly understood to be mixed with projections from the unconscious of the alchemical adepts themselves. The relevance for today is that the same kinds of projections occur in contemporary people and take on image and feeling in their dreams, visions and authentic fantasy or active imagination, which are directly related to their psychological state of mind and personality mutations. The sought-for transformation that was projected into matter, with the somewhat clouded understanding that it was also happening in the adept's psyche, actually concerns the psychological and spiritual transformation of being—to the extent of realizing the glorified body, and not that of external substances at all.

Jung's natural affiliation with alchemy was born with his "first systematic fantasy," as he refers to it, when he was still a boy walking to school along the Rhine.[5] First, in his fantasy, a great sailing ship appeared and he wondered about the possibility of Basel becoming a port, connecting him to a different time and different world. Then, he visualized a small medieval city of several hundred inhabitants, built on the slopes of a rocky hill emerging from the lake. There was a watchtower and fortified castle, which the child, Jung, took to be his house. The rooms were simple and small, and there was, in addition, an attractive library with books containing valuable knowledge. There are weapons and a garrison of soldiers, and two powerful cannon. A mayor and a council of old men governed, and Jung was justice of the peace, with arbitration and counseling duties.

The specific alchemical imagery involved the center of operations and purpose for its existence, an important secret of nature, which, in

5   1983, p. 80.

his fantasy, Jung alone knew. It consisted of thick wire copper cable which, at the top, emanated very fine branches that extended into the air. From the air a mysterious substance is drawn that was conducted down to the cellar, where the spiritual essence drawn from the air became gold coins. This fantasy lasted several months after which Jung tired of it.

Jung had no idea of the nature or meaning of his fantasy or its affinity with alchemy, where copper is considered to be the metal of Venus. Its purification refers to shadow cleansing and eventual transformation into gold, the philosopher's stone or wisdom. Theodor Abt reports that for the Arab Ibn Umail and earlier Greek alchemists, copper is symbolic of the "god-man" in need of purification.[6] Basel becoming a great port refers to potential traffic of new (alchemical) symbols from the unconscious.

The second part of a dream that presaged Jung's break from Freud is related to alchemy, although more directly to the Grail tradition and the Knights Templars. They were warrior monks sanctioned by the Church during the Council of Troyes in 1129, with Bernard of Clairvaux as their patron. A fighting force, the Templars were charged with the responsibility of protecting European pilgrims during the Crusades of the Middle Ages.

The dream was situated in Basel, although it appeared as an Italian city.[7] It was summer, between noon and 1:00 p.m., and the sun was at its zenith and a city square was lit up with intense light. There was a crowd of people advancing toward Jung, in the midst of which ambled an armored knight. Over his chain armor he wore a white tunic with a large red cross on both the front and back. Jung was the only one who saw him. A voice informed him that the procession of the knight took place every day at the same time that he had been doing it for centuries; and although invisible to all but Jung, everyone was aware of it. Jung

6   2009, p. 80.
7   Jung, 1983, p. 165.

recounts that the dream was highly numinous and that he knew the knight came from the twelfth century, the time of the beginning of alchemy and the quest for the Holy Grail in Europe, with which he identified. The knight was fully alive and real. In retrospect, given Jung's life and the challenge to realize his brand of psychology, the dream is understandable as referring to his attitude as a spiritual warrior, required to incarnate and champion his psychology in everyday reality. The need for a warrior attitude and to defend his position is also evident in his early fantasy reported above. The knight in his dream, with the large Red Cross on front and back, is naturally amplified by reference to the Knights Templars, the Grail tradition and the search for truth.

Around Christmas in 1912, while Jung was struggling with finding his own myth, he had a remarkable dream with direct alchemical overtones. The setting was an Italian loggia, situated high in a castle tower, and appointed with a marble floor, balustrade and pillars. Jung was sitting on a golden Renaissance chair, in front of a beautiful table of emerald or green stone, and looking out into the distance. Jung's children were also sitting at the table. A white seagull or dove descended and alighted on the table, inciting Jung to motion to the children to be still. Immediately the bird transformed into an eight-year-old blonde girl, who went off with his children to play amongst the pillars. Jung was musing about the situation when the little girl returned, gently put her arm around his neck and then disappeared. Meanwhile, the white bird had returned and spoke, saying: "Only in the first hour of the night can I transform myself into a human being, while the male dove is busy with the twelve dead."[8]

Although Jung doesn't give a clear interpretation or amplifications of the dream, subsequent developments and interests give a clue. The obvious alchemical reference to the dream is the emerald table, which Jung relates to the legend of Hermes Trismegistus and the *Tabula*

---

8   *Ibid.*, p. 172.

Smaragdina, an emerald table on which the wisdom of alchemy is engraved in Greek, beginning with the postulate, "As above, so below."[9] Sitting on a gold Renaissance chair suggests Jung's "seat" and his reflections have the high value of truth, wisdom and spiritual and psychological rebirth. The twelve dead may refer to potential ancestral wisdom becoming conscious through an inner alchemy.

The number twelve can be amplified as being related to devotion to the Self and wholeness, like the twelve Apostles devoted to Christ, the twelve pillars of the Matrimandir in Auroville and the twelve months of Vedic knowledge, where each month symbolizes an aspect of knowledge as a part of the whole. The Mother's symbol is a mandala with a unifying center, four inner petals, symbolizing four aspects of the Mother, and twelve outer petals, representing differentiated qualities of manifest being. Perhaps the most relevant and direct amplification is the Egyptian Amduat or underworld, with its twelve gates, each of which refers to one of the twelve hours of the night and opens to a specific region of the Amduat related to the hour in question.[10]

The ancient quest for immortality requires a journey through the netherworld or Amduat, which Jung refers to as the collective unconscious. There, most importantly, one gains liberty of movement by associating with the ba-soul, a prefiguration of the psychic being, which is given great importance by Sri Aurobindo, and which takes one through the Amduat to the beyond with the possibility of attaining permanent residence in Heaven. One also meets the gods, the archetypal energies, including the Sun god, the archetype of consciousness, while gaining knowledge of their transmutations. These images and their expressive powers correspond to Jung's discoveries regarding the individuation process; they include a vision of paradise, healing, reconciliation of

---

9   Glenn Alexander Magee, 2008, p. 13.
10   Theodore Abt and Eril Hornung, 2003, pp. 16-21 passim.

opposites, initiation into a new way of being, regeneration and rebirth, all related to psychological transformation and renewal.[11]

The white dove can be understood as a theriomorphic symbol of Sophia, wisdom, who, according to the dream, alights on the table of wisdom to which she is drawn, and becomes consciously humanized at the onset of every attempt to enter the unconscious, symbolized by the night. The pillars, around which the children play, including the humanized dove as a little blonde girl, could refer to becoming conscious of the unfolding process through the Logos principle of discernment and meaning.

Before discovering alchemy, Jung had several other interesting dreams about the subject. In them, there was an annex attached to his house of which he was unaware, which had, apparently, always existed. Eventually, a dream surfaced where he found himself in the unknown wing. There was a fine library with books mostly dating from the sixteenth and seventeenth centuries. Against the walls were fat volumes with pigskin covers. A number of them had strange copper engravings and illustrations of arcane symbols. Jung was fascinated by the library and the symbols he found there. About the dream, Jung recounts, "only much later did I recognize them as alchemical symbols."[12] He writes that the annex represents an aspect of his personality of which he was not yet conscious. The wing and library refer to alchemy of which, at the time, he was ignorant. In real life, Jung reports, "Some fifteen years later, I had assembled a library very much like the one in the dream."[13]

In 1926, Jung had another highly numinous dream that anticipated his direct involvement with alchemy. In the dream Jung was in the South Tyrol region of Italy during war time, returning from the front with a peasant, with his horse and carriage. It was dangerous as bombs were exploding all around them. They made their way through

---

11   Andreas Schweizer, 1994, pp. 195-209 passim.
12   *Ibid.*, p. 202.
13   *Ibid.*, p. 202.

a partially destroyed tunnel, to find a sunlit space of green Lombard planes and Verona lit up by the rays of the sun. They travelled down a lovely countryside with rice fields, vineyards and olive trees. Then they saw a grand manor house with many annexes. The road continued through a large courtyard and on past the building. Jung and the peasant coachman drove in through the front gate and saw a second gate in the distance through which they could see the sunlit plains once again. On his left Jung could see servants' quarters, stables, barns, and so on. When they reached the middle of the courtyard, both gates shut with a dull clang. The coachman leaped down exclaiming, "Now we are caught in the seventeenth century."[14]

Jung remarks that only when reading *The Secret of the Golden Flower*, sent to him by Richard Wilhelm in 1928, did he begin to realize the value of alchemy, which he understood was actually the significance of *The Red Book*. Thus, he writes, "The experiences of the alchemists were, in a sense, my experiences, and their world was my world."[15] He was subsequently stimulated to investigate in depth the subject, which stopped being a vital force in Europe in the seventeenth century, the time Jung was locked away in the Italian manor house in the dream. He writes that he had found the historical counterpart of his psychology and that "he was condemned to study alchemy from the beginning" in order to realize the meaning of his dream.[16] He became absorbed in the task for over a decade.

Jung's interest in alchemy culminated in his 1944 experience of the *mysterium coniunctionis*. As Jung observes in his interview with Mircea Eliade that I refer to above, in order to arrive at this point of spiritual self-realization, the process culminates in "the mystery of the *coniunctio*, the central mystery of alchemy ... the synthesis of opposites,

---

14   *Ibid.*, p. 203.
15   *Ibid.*, p. 205.
16   *Ibid.*

the assimilation of the blackness, the integration of the devil."[17] Once again, for contemporary Jungian depth psychology, the fundamental law of differentiated life is based on the drive for the integration of the opposites and the same fourfold unity as found in alchemy, as well as in Gnosticism and various religions and spiritual systems. The trinity also has value in psychological terms in that it can refer to individual insight into the unfolding archetypal process. The fourth principle, however, which is related to the devil and the divine feminine, is required to bring insights fully into embodied life. As with alchemy, yet now consciously, the psychological opus involves individual human participation in the redemption of the Cosmic Mother and the archetypal psyche in its fourfold nature. In the most direct and simple terms, psychologically the quaternity is expressed as the four functions of consciousness, thinking, feeling, intuition and sensation.

Western alchemists wavered between realization of the three and the four, suggesting the difficulty they experienced in realization of the fourth principle. That difficulty is mirrored today in contemporary depth psychology, where very few individuals seem to be capable of integrating qualities of the fourth function to consciousness. The primordial nature of the difficulty is recognized in the Vedas of India and stories about the creator god, Prajapati. Typically the stories involve "three worlds": "the sky, the earth and atmospheric space," in other words, spirit, matter and the archetypal psyche.[18] There is also recognition, although uncertain, of a fourth world, which turns out to be Prajapati himself, the progenitor of the manifest world. What this means is that integrating the fourth to consciousness takes one beyond process, insight and aesthetic or imaginal psychology to realization of reality itself in its fourfoldedness, which is a monumental achievement of the Self.

The fourfold order of society, the *caturvarna*, consisting of priest,

---

17   *Ibid.*, p. 222
18   Roberto Calasso, 2014, p. 93

leader, trader and servant, and the similar fourfold soul-force structuring human nature originally devolved from the Original Man or *Anthropos* according to Sri Aurobindo's articulation of ancient Vedantic teachings. "That system corresponds," says the *Gita*, to a divine law; it "was created by Me according to the divisions of the Gunas and works"— created from the beginning by the Master of existence."[19] In this light, the Mother is recorded as saying that, in a vision she saw a Being, the "origin of all Avatars," at the edge of "form and the formless ... in a golden crimson glory."[20] She notes that He is "the first universal Avatar," who eventually manifested as a line of embodied avatars to this day for purposes of perfecting the Universe.[21] As remarkable as it may seem to those unfamiliar with the work of Sri Aurobindo and the Mother, the Mother is claiming to have had firsthand visionary experience of the *Anthropos,* the Original Being and initiating source of the fourfold order of society.

Attributing the number four to god figures and truth permeates religious literature throughout the world. In ancient Babylonia there was a four-faced god with a goddess consort with four faces.[22] In Judaism, the divine is represented by the Tetragrammaton consisting of four letters, *yod he wav he.* The symbol of the cross consists of four directions and the sacrifice of Christ on the cross refers to the fourfold nature of the incarnation of the divine. There are many other references to the fourfold nature of reality in Christianity, including the selection of four gospels for the New Testament, and the four horsemen of the Apocalypse described in the *Book of Revelation.*

The Mother, who had extraordinary occult knowledge, remarked that prior to the gods there were emanations of four beings of light with great formative power.[23] They separated from the Source and became

19   Sri Aurobindo, 1970b, p. 492.
20   2004b, p. 333.
21   *Ibid.*
22   Heinz Westman, 1983, pp. 253, 262.
23   2003a, p. 188.

its opposite as asuras of Hindu and occult tradition and became known as Lords of Falsehood, Death, Ignorance and Suffering, the qualitative opposites of Truth, Existence (Sat), Consciousness (Chit) with Force, and Bliss (Ananda). They became Shadow beings, hostile forces that subvert the Divine Will that, however perverse, are still aspects of four-fold reality.

The fundamental fourfold nature of Truth is reflected in Sri Aurobindo's choice of the number four as symbol of the Supermind or Truth-Mind, where the One is differentiated into Being, Consciousness, Force and Bliss and the Supermind contributes the fourth. According to Jung's later writings, four is the symbolic value for the Self and psychological completeness, which is both static and dynamic and ultimately embraces the wholeness of the Original Man—the *Anthropos* and its apparent opposite, the alchemical Rotundum, "the heavy darkness of the earth," with which it is, in reality, in intimate occult partnership of oneness.[24] In fact, according to ancient accounts, the body of the *Anthropos* consists of metals or metals were created from his body. As I discuss below, in his later work *Aion*, Jung elaborates on the nature of the Self as consisting of fourfold quaternities. In more popular psychological terms, wholeness includes conscious integration of the four functions of consciousness, thinking, feeling, intuition and sensation. Similarly, for Sri Aurobindo it means integration of the four soul-types to consciousness. All in all, the relevant point is that the fundamental fourfold nature of reality can be apprehended at all levels of being.

At this point it is worthwhile noting that chemistry and the physical sciences evolved out of alchemical laboratory techniques and methods. Ignoring the alchemist's projections on matter went along with a more objective and scientific study of the material world. Jung realized that the alchemists were projecting their psyche into matter, which he did not ignore, but regarded as having symbolic value. He realized the

---

24   1975a, p. 246.

same projective phenomena are happening with contemporary people, as indicated in their dreams, as with the alchemists, where similar symbols occur projected into their chemical solutions. Jung's approach to psychology is fully empirical, although, unlike with the physical sciences, he relies on dreams and comparative symbols from alchemy, Gnosticism, religion and mythology and elsewhere, as his field of scientific study of the human psyche, in relationship with the individual's contextual circumstances.

One could say his science of depth psychology developed from alchemy as did the physical sciences, but his field of study requires empirically examining the individual's unique situation, along with various subtle realms of the symbolic and objective psyche, where the statistical methods of the physical sciences prove to be completely inadequate. From this perspective, the approach of most contemporary psychology is misguided inasmuch as it applies methods natural to the physical sciences. According to Jonathan Shedler, the science behind "evidence-based therapies" such as CBT (Cognitive Behavioral Therapy) is dubious at best and its highly touted claims for being scientific are fraudulent.[25] For a worldview that sheds light on Jung's position, it can be helpful to now turn to Part II and the integral thinking of Sri Aurobindo and the Mother, beginning with an exploration of the involution and evolution of consciousness from their perspective.

25   Jonathan Shedler, 2015. pp. 47-59 passim.

PART II

Jung's Vision and
the Yoga of Sri Aurobindo and the Mother

(In the West) "mind" has lost its universal character altogether. It has become a more or less individualized affair, with no trace of its former universal aspect as the *anima rationalis*... In the East, mind is a cosmic factor, the very essence of Existence.[1]

– C.G. Jung

By an inevitable decree of fate the West is becoming acquainted with the peculiar facts of Eastern Spirituality.[2]

– C.G. Jung

---

1   C.G. Jung, 1975c-7, p.479, 480.
2   C.G. Jung, 1975 c-7, p. 483.

CHAPTER 6

Involution and Evolution of Consciousness:
Sri Aurobindo and the Mother

The most comprehensive understanding of the nature of life and the evolving universe is that articulated by Sri Aurobindo. He begins with creation, which he posits as beginning with the involution of Divine Reality or Supermind, as Existence-Consciousness with Force-Bliss, into its opposite, the Inconscient, traditionally referred to as Non-Being, the last dark cavern of the Ignorance caused by separation from unitary consciousness. Here, it is worthwhile to note that, according to Sri Aurobindo's spiritual colleague the Mother, in addition to consciousness, the presence of Divine Love is everywhere, in plants, metal and stone, anywhere there is any "organization of atoms."[1] The attractive power of Divine Love is at the foundation of all things, emanating from the depths and all corners of the material world, and it is the reason for there to be consciousness there at all. "It might be said," observes the Mother, "that forms in general are the efforts of Love to bring consciousness into matter."[2]

Subsequent to the involutionary plunge of Supermind, Sri Aurobindo argues that there has been a slow process of evolution, first with the formation of Matter, then Life in Matter, then the Mind in Living Matter, and presently into what Sri Aurobindo refers to as the Supermind itself, which is both established in unity while also being the creative source of the becoming. Evolution, according to him,

---

1   2003a, p. 240.
2   *Ibid.*

involves a double action of an emerging evolutionary consciousness from below and an involutionary descent from above of the appropriate archetypal formation for Matter, then Life and then Mind and presently the Supermind, with a corresponding emergence of the supramental consciousness from below.

The Mother is recorded as saying that there are involutionary be-ings "from the overmind plane or elsewhere" that descend from above and incarnate by uniting with a "fully formed" psychic being, by which she means a fully evolved soul.[3] The individual subsequently has ex-panded capacities according to the nature of the incarnated being that are potentially used to enhance Earth life and further the evolution-ary process. In this case there is a "supreme man," "the human be-ing at the peak of humanity ... human consciousness that has attained perfection."[4] In the case of Sri Aurobindo and the Mother, the former is regarded by his disciples to be the avatar of our time, the incarnation of Supreme Truth charged with the task of manifesting Divine Grace; and the latter, the Divine Mother, is considered to be "the great dispen-satrix—through identity—of Divine Grace with a perfect knowledge—through identity—of the Absolute mechanism of Universal Justice."[5] Here it is a question of the incarnation of God in human bodies.

Sri Aurobindo openly acknowledges that the Mother is an incarna-tion of the Divine Shakti, the Divine Mother, and indirectly alludes to the fact that he is the avatar of our time, a contention supported by the Mother.[6] In fact, she says: "What Sri Aurobindo represents in the world's history is not a teaching, not even a revelation; it is a de-cisive action from the Supreme."[7] The knowledge and mantric qual-ity of Sri Aurobindo's writings (especially in *Savitri*), the unparal-leled authority with which he writes, and the vastness of his vision, all

---

3   2003b, pp. 323, 324.
4   The Mother, 2004a, p. 375.
5   *Ibid.*, p. 360.
6   1972a, 1972b.
7   As recorded in Kishor Gandhi, 1965, p. 216.

point to him being an embodiment of the Avatar. In fact, the Mother is recorded as acknowledging that Savitri, with whom she identifies, in Sri Aurobindo's poem *Savitri,* represents "the Mother's conscious-ness," and Satyavan, with whom Sri Aurobindo identifies, is the Avatar, "the incarnation of the Supreme."[8] Their mutually avowed purpose was to incarnate the Supermind and initiate the supramental transformation of being in order to take evolution to its next level.

In this regard, there is a fundamental need to make a significant differentiation between different spiritual paths and the path of Integral Yoga. Sri Aurobindo writes,

> I am concerned with the Earth, not with worlds beyond for their own sake; it is terrestrial realization that I seek and not a flight to distant summits. All other Yogas regard this life as an illu-sion or a passing phase; the supramental Yoga alone regards it as a thing created by the Divine for a progressive manifestation and takes the fulfillment of the life and the body for its object. The Supramental is simply the Truth-consciousness and what it brings in its descent is the full truth of life, the full truth of consciousness in Matter.[9]

In this statement, Sri Aurobindo clearly embraces the complex reality of life and physical nature, while asserting that is not the case in other yogas.

Jung does not make such extensive claims about his path of indi-viduation as Sri Aurobindo does regarding Integral Yoga. Generally speaking, he does not define a major spiritual or psychological goal for individuals, except to consciously individuate, discover and live by the Self and to find one's unique truth. After his experiences of the *myste-rium coniunctionis* in 1944, he fully realized the psychological need to "affirm one's destiny" and forge an ego "that endures the truth, and that

8   The Mother, 2003b, p. 390.
9   1972b, p. 124.

is capable of coping with the world and with fate."[10] By accepting fate and not meddling with it, Jung argues that "even to experience defeat is also to experience victory, as "one's own continuity has withstood the current of life and time."[11] While his path of individuation is not as far-reaching as that of Sri Aurobindo's supramental yoga, unlike other recognized religious and spiritual paths including Christianity (which tend to minimize psychological factors if not ignore them as irrelevant), it does establish the ideal of realization of a completely individuated life with distinct allusions to the spiritualization of the body.

Definitions: Sri Aurobindo, Jung and Evolutionary Psychiatry

Even if one has difficulty accepting the reality of an incarnated Avatar and Divine Mother, the logic of the process articulated by Sri Aurobindo and the involutionary phenomenon described above appeals to sufficient reason. It encourages acceptance of the fact that life, at all levels of being including matter, is penetrated by creative Reality and, therefore, is not simply an illusion or some kind of relative reality, as propagated by many spiritual paths today. Thus, spiritually, at the level of the Cosmic Mind below the Supermind or realm of Truth, according to Sri Aurobindo, life works through Ignorance and self-limiting Knowledge—"limitative but not necessarily falsificative"—while, materially, it is a suppressed Consciousness or hidden God that seeks unveiling as transformative Knowledge at the foundation of existence.[12]

These observations support Jung's depth psychology enterprise and his frequent references to the hidden God or *deus absconditus* in matter, which he relates to the alchemical philosopher's stone and Mercurius as *deus terrestris*, "an essential element of the psychological

---

10   Jung, 1983, p. 297.
11   *Ibid.*
12   1970c, p. 286.

self."[13] According to the alchemists, Mercurius is "the prima materia of the lowly beginning as well as the lapis as the highest goal [and] the process which lies between, and the means by which it is affected, an emanation of the divine and 'harmonious with God's own being.'"[14] The alchemical task was to free God from the embrace of matter, as depicted in the Gnostic legend of Sophia's decent to *Physis,* while becoming lost in her embrace.

Taking this line of thought further, Sri Aurobindo writes that "even in the Inconscient there seems to be at least an urge of inherent necessity producing the evolution of forms and in the forms a developing Consciousness, and it may well be held that this urge is the evolutionary will of a secret Conscious-Being and its push of progressive manifestation the evidence of an innate intention in the evolution. This is a teleological element."[15] The intentional workings of nature can be explained by the existence of a secret intelligence, the *Purusha* or Conscious Being that lies behind the activities of the Inconscient as the self-oblivious form of Prakriti. Thus, Sri Aurobindo observes that, thanks to the self-absorbed trance of the infinite Superconscient, which produces the Inconscient, an "ordered world is created."[16] The spiritual and psychological task, thus, involves bringing light to the obscure darkness of the Inconscient in order to form a "mould and lower basis of the spirit."[17]

As I allude to above, Jung turns to the alchemical Mercurius to find an ambiguous phenomenon that, from the psychological perspective, answers Sri Aurobindo's observations about a secret Conscious Being pushing for progressive manifestation. Mercurius is a unity although he consists of all possible opposites. Jung quotes from the alchemist Michael Maier, who had the Erythraean Sibyl say: "He will make you a

13   1970a, p. 241.
14   *Ibid.*, p. 235.
15   1970d, p. 834.
16   1970c, p. 344.
17   Sri Aurobindo, 1970d, p. 930.

witness to the mysteries of God and the secrets of nature…. Mercurius is the revealer of Divine secrets … the soul of the arcane substance."[18]

He is the *principium individuationis,* "both material and spiritual and the process where "the lower and material" interacts with "the higher and spiritual" and transform each other. He is a psychopomp, the devil and trickster and "God's reflection in matter."[19] Mercurius is the *lumen naturae,* the light in nature, "the self," "the individuation process" and "the collective unconscious."[20] He is the friend of the knight errant, the wandering knight, and weaves a labyrinthine path through ignorance to the Self. The etymological meaning of errant/error is suggestive; it is based on the prefix "er," meaning "wandering about," eventually progressing to mean "making mistakes."[21]

Mercurius is the god of individuation who takes error for the handmaid of truth and as essential for a self-fulfilled life. Given the mixture of opposites in the world, of truth and falsehood, and right and wrong, when one does not know the right way or right choice to make, which can often be the case in a life of conscious individuation, there is a need to consider different possibilities, or "wander about" and make a choice that could be mistaken or in error. As Jung writes: "But when one follows the path of individuation, when one lives one's own life, one must take mistakes into the bargain. There is no guarantee—not for a single moment—that we will not fall into error or stumble into deadly peril. We may think there is a sure road. But that would be the road of death. Then nothing happens any longer—at any rate, not the right things. Anyone who takes the sure road is as good as dead."[22] When there is Ignorance and Inconscience there is bound to be error; consequently, the vocation of individuation and the defeat of evil involve bringing more and more of the unconscious to consciousness.

---

18   1970a, p. 230.
19   *Ibid.*
20   *Ibid.*, p. 237.
21   Word-Origins.com.
22   1983, p. 297.

Thus, Sri Aurobindo writes: "God is infinite possibility. Therefore Truth is never at rest; therefore, also, Error is fine [justified] of her children."[23] The Mother interprets this aphorism to mean that, in fact, there is no error from the point of view of the Divine and that it is a relative phenomenon of space and time. There is no error, but, in space and time, nothing is in its proper place. According to Sri Aurobindo,

> the whole world and every particle of it is ... nothing but the divine force in action and that divine force determines and governs its every movement, inhabits its every form, possesses here every soul and mind; all is in God and in him moves and has its being, in all he is, acts and displays his being; every creature is the disguised Naryana [Divine].[24]

Here, Sri Aurobindo and Jung speak the same truth from slightly different perspectives.

Like Sri Aurobindo, Jung believes that the essence of the Self is in the duality itself, particularly evident in archetypal experiences, where archetypes are "a priori structural forms of the stuff of consciousness," not only as ways of perceiving the world, but as containers of active energy that compel behavior.[25] Given the significant amount of error, falsehood and ignorance in the world, one could argue that there is considerable illusion that ought to be avoided. But, from a psychological point of view, Jung observes: "What we are pleased to call illusion may be for the psyche an extremely important life-factor ... a psychic factor of overwhelming significance.... What we call illusion is very real for the psyche."[26] The challenge psychologically, therefore, is not to be caught by dogmatic judgments but to listen to the intimations of the heart-Self or psychic being and follow the threads of life in order to

23   As reported in the Mother, 2001, p. 145.
24   1970b, p. 143.
25   1983, p. 347.
26   1970b, p. 51, 52.

deepen one's relationship to the archetypal psyche for healthy integration of being.

Evolutionary psychiatry, as presented by Jungian analyst Anthony Stevens and John Price, looks at mental disorders and symptoms from the point of view of age old natural adaptive patterns of the mammalian and reptilian minds, dating back to early human behavior.[27] They argue that all psychological pathologies are perversions of two fundamental archetypal patterns, where the archetypal intent, specifically of affiliation and dominance–submission patterns, are frustrated. For example, depression, from this point of view, can be seen as an adaptive submissive response to loss of rank and self-esteem. In the animal kingdom, animals that are forced to submit do so to avoid further attacks by the more dominant animal, in the process, adapting to a relatively lower status in the pack or herd. Although the contemporary spirit of the times discourages it, in human society, depression can be an adaptive inner turn to seek new ways of being and a potentially creative renaissance in the way one lives. Depression is a relatively introverted adaptive solution to life's problems.

Mania is a relatively extraverted adaptive solution to the problems of life. It can be understood as an adaptive response to finding one's position in the social order by a tactic of dominance, like that of the alpha male animal who, in the field of sexual mating, is rewarded with increased opportunities to pass on his genes. Passed-on genes, even when expressed pathologically as in mania or depression, indicate that the inherent appraisal process that encourages genes to be passed on evaluates the behavior as helpful for survival. The obsessive nature of mania points to the need for self-reflection in order to discover and direct one's energies toward an appropriate place in the social order in harmony with healthy inner dynamics.

---

27   2000.

Eros affiliation and discovering one's natural vocation bring one closer to living one's truth of being. Emphasis on status and other so-called needs, as defined by the zeitgeist and socio-cultural context, can be very misleading and, ideally, seen through with discernment. It is not a question of repressing engagement with contemporary life, but relating to it with discernment.

Stevens and Price note that "symptoms according to Jung always serve a purpose."[28] Jung writes: "The values which the individual lacks are to be found in the neurosis itself."[29] Like dreams, symptoms are symbolic and meaningful responses to life problems, and bring a compensatory message to encourage an appropriate adjustment in one's conscious beliefs, values, attitudes, and adaptive choices. They do not drive one to unrealistic and idealistic solutions but, if understood, nudge one forward toward the distant goal of living according to the truth of being. Anyone who has led a creative life of conscious individuation, in old age, can look back and see the meaning behind the unfolding sequence of life events, even when in apparent error, in light of the teleological drive toward the Self and completeness.

The symbolic truth behind psychiatric symptoms is nicely elucidated in an observation Jung makes regarding catatonia. He writes:

> One could say that the classical catatonic condition is a fixed or congealed Yoga mechanism, i.e., a natural tendency released under pathological circumstances. This is to be interpreted as a teleological attempt at self-cure, as it is a compensatory process produced under the stress of the schizophrenic dissociation of the mind. The dissociation leads to a sort of chaotic disrupture of the mental order and the catatonic tendency tries to bring about an order, however pathological, creating fixed positions over against the relentless flow of associations.[30]

28   *Ibid.*, p. 231.
29   C.G. Jung, 1975d, p. 61.
30   C.G. Jung, as recorded in Adler, 1973, p. 498.

From these examples, one can conclude that not only is life essentially real and not an illusion, but truth can be found behind all life, including all psychological pathologies as perversions of Logos and the social order, and Eros affiliation; they are a reflection of both an unconscious relationship to the Time spirit and individual mental disorders. In the following chapter, I examine the nature of the Unconscious and Circumconscient in Sri Aurobindo's yoga and the alchemical Rotundum and archetypal psyche in Jung's depth psychology, giving the foregoing considerations added substance.

CHAPTER 7

Sri Aurobindo's Unconscious and Circumconscient: Jung's Rotundum and Archetypal Psyche

Metaphysically, the Inconscient is the end result of ignorance, "darkness veiled within darkness … a consciousness plunged into an abyss of self-oblivion, inherent in being but not awake in being."[1] "It is," Sri Aurobindo writes, "an inverse reproduction of the supreme superconscience" equally absolute, although involved in a trance.[2] Like the Superconsient the Inconscient is infinite. Despite its opaque nature, "this involved consciousness [is] still a concealed knowledge by identity."[3] It acts primarily as energy and not consciousness, yet "with the precision and action of an intrinsic consciousness," thanks to the workings of a "secret intelligence."[4] Sri Aurobindo and Jung have similar understanding: in the former case, expressed metaphysically as concealed knowledge by identity; in the latter case, as discussed below, a reflection of the alchemical Rotundum, the foundation of the Self.

The Inconscient of Sri Aurobindo is faithfully reflected in Jung's study of the Self in *Aion* as the Rotundum, found at the nadir of the *Lapis quaternio* and out of which the four elements (air, water, earth and fire, the common denominator being energy) are discriminated and then synthesized. It is the chaos, the original state of conflict, and

---

1   Sri Aurobindo, 1970c, p. 550.
2   *Ibid.*
3   *Ibid.*
4   *Ibid.*, p. 588.

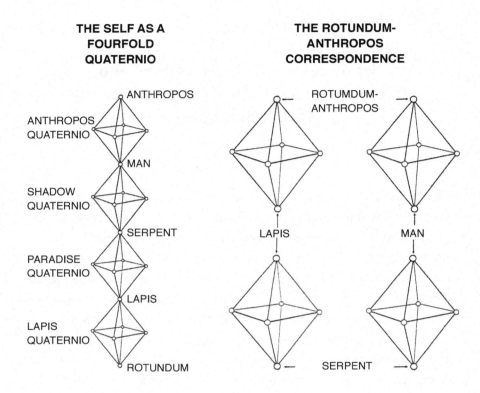

THE SELF AS A FOURFOLD QUATERNIO

THE ROTUNDUM-ANTHROPOS CORRESPONDENCE

prima materia, the primary substance, referred to by Paracelsus as the *increatum,* meaning uncreated being, or non-existence, the Inconscient, and "regarded as co-eternal with God."[5] Yet, it is round and "the world soul and world substance in one," and corresponds to the archetype of the Original Man, the *Anthropos,* the superconscient bridge to the transcendent *That,* suggesting a secret relationship between the lowest, the darkness of the earth and metal, and the highest, the spiritual *Anthropos,* that exists between matter and spirit.[6] The *Anthropos-Rotundum* correspondence is parallel to the *Uroborous,* the serpent biting its tail.

The round nature of the Rotundum as chaos is reflected by the

---

5   Jung, 1975a, p. 237.
6   *Ibid.*

"preconscious Self," and is experienced psychologically in the realization of unconscious material aspects of the Self.[7] In everyday psychological terms, Marie-Louise von Franz observes: "If one has served this earthly heavy matter humbly enough, at the end of his life matter and spirit will link and become one. And the contrast between the inner and outer, matter and spirit no longer exists."[8] Matter, including the physical body as well as external experiences, becomes spiritual and symbolic.

In Jung's correspondence with the Dominican Victor White, on May 21, 1948, he sent a rough sketch of four interlocking *quaternios* with the Higher Adam (*Anthropos*) on top and the Sphere (Rotundum) below, with "Chaos" written on the bottom below the word "Sphere."[9] Here, Jung is in the relatively early stages of formulating his equation for the Self, which later appeared at the end of *Aion*. Below the Sphere (Rotundum) and "Chaos" he wrote "Formlessness" and above the Higher Adam (*Anthropos*) he also wrote "Formlessness." Jung is drawing from the Formlessness of the primal state or Pleroma of Gnosticism, and giving a parallel image to Sri Aurobindo's understanding that both the Inconscient and the Superconscient are absolute and infinite, with the Inconscient being the inverse reproduction of the Superconscient. Given this background, the Chaos of the Sphere (Rotundum) grounded on the Formless seems to more accurately fit the nature of the Inconscient of Sri Aurobindo than the Rotundum alone. With this image, it becomes more readily understandable that full transformation of the infinite Inconscient requires the infinite of the Supermind with its direct relationship with *Tat* or *That*, and that the Overmind, which is more cosmic in nature, is insufficient for the task. This is Sri Aurobindo's contention.

Understood psychologically, the Inconscient is an obscure region of

---

7   Marie-Louise von Franz, 2004, p. 160.
8   *Ibid.*, p. 172.
9   Ann Conrad Lammers and Adrian Cunningham, eds., 2008, p. 122, figure 4.2.

the psyche, the source of inertia or *tamas* and the principle of resistance to the light of consciousness. It is, as well, the foundation for the fixed habits, good or bad, of mind, life and body, mechanical repetitiveness, irrationalities, and automatic and impulsive reactions to the challenges of existence, and it can be found expressed in incoherent and jumbled dreams. It is the main support for death and disease and the abode of many fears and anxieties. It is a region of the psyche where opening to light "is a Herculean task."[10] There is, in addition to the Inconscient, a space between consciousness and the Inconscient that Sri Aurobindo refers to as the Subconscient. He identifies the Subconscient, with personal as well as universal aspects, as a gateway for the Inconscient to enter consciousness, as well as a repository of repressed elements that were formerly conscious.

The Subconscient is sub-mental and below waking consciousness, esoterically located underneath the *muladhara chakra*, the center of physical consciousness, and below the feet. It contains obscure impressions from past experiences of external life as well as aspects of the psyche that were conscious but, through repression and denial, have fallen into the Subconscient. It is also the region for things emerging from the chaos of the Inconscient, still indeterminate as an ill-differentiated turgid swirl of energy with the potential for differentiation. The Subconscient itself is the operational basis of what Sri Aurobindo calls "the Ignorance," while its contents are both individual and universal; yet they are false impositions on the truth of one's being. They mainly affect the sex center, what Sri Aurobindo refers to as the lower vital, with its sexual and petty impulses, and the external physical nature, which, in turn, influence the mind and its thoughts and speculations.

According to Sri Aurobindo, like the animal mind, the human lives "largely in impressions rising up from the Subconscient;" and the ordinary natural being lives a great deal of the time in habitual vital and

---

10   Sri Aurobindo, 1970f, p. 1609.

mental movements that arise from "the Subconscient physical," where they are stored. In Jung's psychology, the Inconscient and Subconscient are accounted for, on the one hand, by the repressions of the personal unconscious, and on the other, by dreams and fantasies containing universal images and themes that can find amplification in mythology and alchemy (especially the latter, with its states of chaos, *putrefactio, mortificatio* and *nigredo*).

Here it is worthwhile to draw some distinction between Jung's treatment of psychoid processes and Sri Aurobindo's Inconscient. To begin with, Jung differentiates between the psyche and psychoid processes. He argues that the psyche can be emancipated from instinctive functioning and become accessible to consciousness and the will. The psychoid nature, in contrast, cannot be accessed, as it is both unknown as a direct phenomena and unknowable. He refers to psychoid processes as "quasi psychic," for example the "reflex processes."[11] The psyche is accessible to the will by becoming conscious, where the unconscious refers to the "unknown psychic" and not the psychoid unconscious.[12] The psychoid processes, in contrast, are tied to physiology, have the compulsive "all-or-none" character of a drive and, in Jung's view, "are not capable of consciousness and of whose existence we have only indirect knowledge."[13]

Jung writes in a letter to Enrique Butleman in July, 1956: "The archetype itself ... is psychoid, i.e., transcendental and thus relatively beyond the categories of number, space and time. That means, it approximates to oneness and immutability."[14] Thus, the psychoid is transcendent both in the direction of the unknown instinctual and material and the unknown spiritual. It is, accordingly, the source of grace and the 'voice of God,' as well as the unknown instinctive and physical

---

11   Jung, 1975, p. 177.
12   *Ibid.*
13   1975, p. 185.
14   As reported in Adler, ed., 1975, p. 318.

base. I owe this line of thinking to John Dourley, who demonstrates how Jung relates the psychoid to the *unus mundus,* the unitary world that embraces multiplicity.[15] As a point of confirmation, on August 30, 1951, Jung writes in a letter to Dr. H. about the transcendental and psychoid nature of the archetype as "an 'arranger' of psychic forms inside and outside of the psyche."[16] As arranger of psychic forms, the psychoid core of the archetype may not be representable or expressible, but it can be known indirectly through synchronistic occurrences.

Dourley argues that Jung was struggling with the nature of the psychoid functions and makes the excellent observation that it would be logical and advantageous to integrate the psyche and psychoid for the sake of simplification. He also notes that differentiating the psychic from psychoid processes was probably due to the mature Jung, especially in his work with the Nobel Prize-winning physicist, Wolfgang Pauli, vastly extending the nature of the unconscious. But, argues, Dourley, there is no reason not to extend "the conception of the psyche and the role of the divinity within the amplification of the immensity of the psyche taken in its totality."[17] In fact, according to the Mother, with direct influence from the supramental Light and Force, a felt experience—the physical nature itself, along with instinctive aspects of the psychoid functions—can become conscious and transformed, as she demonstrates in her undergoing a transformation of the bodily cells.

With these considerations, I fully concur with Dourley and suggest that unifying the concepts of psyche and psychoid would align Jung with the thought of Sri Aurobindo on the nature of the Subconscient and Inconscient, as well as upper spiritual planes like Sri Aurobindo's Intuitive Mind, Overmind and possibly even the Supermind, to the profit of the Jungian model. As I indicate above, the deeper transformation of the Inconscient requires the light and power of the Supermind

---

15   2014, p. 29–33 passim.
16   As reported in Adler, ed., 1975, p. 22.
17   2014, p. 33.

or Truth-Mind. As Jung understands it, the psychoid functions, which are unknowable, inexpressible and irrepresentable, are tied up with the *unus mundus*, which, with some reservation, I argue throughout this study is equivalent to Sri Aurobindo's Overmind. However an exalted state and global in its scope, it is still part of the Ignorance and, from that perspective, Jung is right in determining it to be unknowable and, therefore, not transformable. This fits Sri Aurobindo's understanding of the Inconscient which he regards as a product of the Ignorance, where only a superior Truth plane can bring adequate transformative light and power. By aligning Jung's concept of the psychoid process with Sri Aurobindo's Inconscient and Subconscient, as well as the unknown regions of spiritual phenomena, there would be recognition of potential transformation of the psychoid functions, like all other aspects of the psyche, although requiring the supramental Light and Force to be effective, at least for its deeper reaches.

Sri Aurobindo's Circumconscient and Jung's Archetypal Psyche

In addition to the Inconscient and Subconscient, Sri Aurobindo also describes a subliminal and Circumconscient or environmental consciousness that relates the individual to others as well as to universal forces—in Jungian terms, archetypal energies—of all kinds. Sri Aurobindo writes:

> The subliminal forms a circumconscient, an environing part of itself, through which it receives the contacts of the world .... The subliminal is able to widen indefinitely this circumconscient envelope and more and more enlarge its self-projection into the cosmic existence around it. A point comes where it can break through the separation altogether, unite, identify with cosmic being, feel itself universal, one with all existence.[18]

---

18   1970c, p. 541.

The Circumconscient includes typal mental, vital and subtle physical planes of being, potentially integrated around the psychic being, the incarnated aspect of the soul that goes through evolutionary development.

What Sri Aurobindo describes here as the Circumconscient is similar to the archetypes and the collective unconscious in Jung's psychology. Thus, in a letter to Fritz Kunkel in July, 1946, Jung observes:

> Your view that the collective unconscious surrounds us on all sides is in complete agreement with the way I explain it to my pupils. It is more like an atmosphere in which we live than something that is found in us. It is simply the unknown quantity in the world. Also it does not by any means behave merely psychologically; in the case of so-called synchronicity it proves to be a universal substrate present in the environment rather than a psychological premise. Wherever we come into contact with an archetype we enter into relationship with transconscious, metaphysic factors, which underlie the spiritualistic hypothesis as well as those of magical actions.[19]

As with Sri Aurobindo, the archetypes, as understood by Jung, are also related to the Self in the depth of the heart, the integrative center of being which, in psychological terms, functions like the psychic being. In fact, according to Jung, the soul has both a "living" "relation to the unconscious" and is "a personification of unconscious contents." John Dourley correctly attributes the latter to the ever-recurring mediation of archetypal symbols from the unconscious to consciousness.[20] Regarding Jung's reference to magic, this operation, for Jung, does not refer to doing magic on others, black or white, but of inner transformation through engaging in an active dialogue with the archetypal unconscious.

---

19   Jung, as recorded in Gerhard Adler, ed., 1973, p. 433.
20   As reported in Dourely, 2014, p. 101.

CHAPTER 8

Sri Aurobindo and
the Evolution of Human Consciousness

Whereas Sheldrake emphasizes the evolution of form, with Sri Aurobindo the primary concern is the evolution of consciousness. Human consciousness, according to Sri Aurobindo, has gone through a developmental course that begins with the *Symbolic Age*, for instance in Vedic India, when the elite attained unprecedented levels of consciousness and the ordinary people lived according to a direct relationship with high mythological symbols and rituals.[1] Thanks to their emotional and bodily participation in the symbols and rituals, they learned about their place in the cosmos and the relevance of the gods and goddesses in their collective lives. They were instinctually and spiritually rooted and lived according to one of four sanctioned soul-types—priest, leader, trader and servant—in a similarly ordered society. There was a gradual degeneration of consciousness to the next age, the *Typal Age*, when the spiritual urge was less dominant and people lived according to an ethical pattern and determination grounded on their soul-types.

There was a further degeneration to the *Conventional Age*, when not only the original symbolic truth of life was repressed, but so was the natural ethical instinct, as life took on a conventional pattern based on inflexible and fixed dogma, doctrine and tradition that protected the status quo. The injustice and inequality of convention was subsequently challenged and disabled by thought and an upward surge

---

1   1971a.

of consciousness that began with the *Age of Reason*. But reason alone does not suffice, and its narrowness and limitations in recognizing truth and determining codes of conduct is increasingly acknowledged to the point that it is presently giving way, with considerable resistance, to the *Subjective Age* and an inner turn.

Given the development of the intellect and growing self-awareness, humans have become more aware and knowledgeable about the potential for a growth in consciousness, which presently requires a turn within and the development of an inner foundation. But the Subjective Age has a shadow side, which is all too apparent today. Reason is giving way and is being replaced by a solipsistic subjectivity, aided and abetted by the advent of the Internet, video games, iPads and the like, along with considerably less interest in reading. This conclusion is based on the research of S. Jacoby, who writes that "Americans are in serious intellectual trouble—in danger of losing our hard-won cultural capital to a virulent mixture of ant-intellectualism, anti-rationalism and low expectations."[2] In support of this observation, Jean Twenge and Keith Campbell, authors of *The Narcisssm Epidemic,* argue forcefully that we live in the age of entitlement, that is with core narcissistic cultural values, which began in earnest in the 1970s, with seeds having been planted in the 1960s.[3] The actual evolutionary need of the Subjective Age, observes Sri Aurobindo, is to progress toward a triple transformation of being and an integral transformation of consciousness. There is, here, a double movement: an aspiration and ascent from below through the psychic being, the evolved expression of the incarnated aspect of the soul; and a descent from above, as in the original act of creation.

Thus, Sri Aurobindo writes, "At present mankind is undergoing an evolutionary crisis in which is concealed the choice of destiny."[4] Later, the Mother refers to humanity having "arrived at a certain state

2   2008.
3   2013.
4   As recorded in Kishor Gandhi, 1965, p. 250.

of general tension."[5] "This tension," she goes on to say, "is so entire and general that something obviously has to break up. That cannot continue in this way."[6] This state of general tension continues until this day (2016), although the focus of attention has shifted since the time Sri Aurobindo and the Mother were alive.

The present general malaise not withstanding, the evolution of consciousness today can be seen in a positive light, despite the present darkness and uneasy tension that continues to assail us. On February 29, 1956, Sri Aurobindo and the Mother announced that the Supermind or creative Truth-Mind had "manifested in the Earth-consciousness," as a result of their intense yogic efforts over some forty years.[7] Since that time a New World has descended to the subtle physical plane and its effects can occasionally be openly seen, sometimes only after intense global conflict and tension. Although, as the Mother said: the event "was not proclaimed by the beat of drum," the fate of humanity is no longer hanging by a thin thread, as the divine Will has become the presiding world Law.[8] Still, according to the Mother's teaching, from the point of view of humankind, there is a need for individual participation and disciplined effort by engaging in a process of psychic, spiritual and supramental transformation.

The Way of the Triple Transformation

The first transformation Sri Aurobindo refers to is the psychic transformation, which involves a transformation of the mind, heart and vital or life being in the direction of the True, the Beautiful, and the Good.[9] The psychic being, which is formed through evolution and an expression of the incarnated aspect of the soul behind the heart, knows through feel-

5   *Ibid.*
6   *Ibid.*, p. 251.
7   Kishor Gandhi, 1965, p. 270.
8   *Ibid.*, p. 195.
9   1970d.

ing. The goal of the psychic transformation is for increasing psychic purity and strength, as well as the growing exertion of control over the inferior aspects of one's nature, requiring some of the Subconscient and Inconscient to become conscious, as well as gaining more consciousness of the Circumconscient and one's relationship to typal planes of being and the guidance of the psychic being. In Jungian language this means becoming more conscious of the shadow, the anima/animus and one's relationship with the archetypal psyche, as well as the coalescing and directing quality of the heart-Self.

Sri Aurobindo and the Mother refer to the sunlit path, which requires bringing the psychic being forward and allowing for its direct guidance in everyday life.[10] This path necessitates surrender to the Divine Mother, meaning following inner and outer influences from the Self, especially the feminine Self, and advancing in yoga without ego struggle or fear. In Jung's path of individuation there is a similar process reflected in alchemy as the third stage of the work, the *rubedo* or reddening, where the ego serves the philosopher's stone, the Self. At the beginning of the opus the ego is required to work hard, represented by the first two stages of the alchemical work, the *nigredo* or blackening, a time of depression and confusion, and the *albedo* or whitening, a time of waiting, reflection and insight. According to the alchemists, with the reddening "the hard work is over," the sun rises, the sunlit path takes over and the Self becomes experientially real in life.[11] There is a fourth stage known as *citrinatis* or yellowing, also referred to as the *multiplicatio*, where there is a multiplication effect and the Self as *unus mundus* is realized through synchronicities in harmony with the world and the inner and outer cosmos.

The second transformation in Sri Aurobindo and the Mother's yoga is the spiritual transformation of being, which eventually necessitates the full dissolution of the ego and identity with *Tat* or *That*, non-dual

10   1997 passim.
11   Marie-Louise von Franz, 1992d, p. 180.

Reality. That is one side of the equation. From Sri Aurobindo's perspective, given the fact that the Universe is permeated with divine Reality, there is also a need to widen one's consciousness to include cosmic nature and the cosmic Self. There are several levels of consciousness prior to the Supermind or Truth-Mind that can potentially be progressively attained in one's spiritual ascent; from the Higher Mind, to the Illumined Mind, through the Intuitive Mind and then the Overmind. In the order of creation, there is a descending order based on the self-limitation of the powers of the Supermind, beginning with the Overmind down to the Higher Mind and then the ordinary mind. The bridge to human consciousness for each of these statuses of Mind is the psychic being, which is indicative of the importance of having a fully formed psychic being and going through the psychic transformation before engaging in the spiritual ascent, although it is not advisable to define this development too rigidly.

The Higher Mind is the philosophic mind and a mind of Thought that works through the idea. The Illumined Mind is a revelatory mind of spiritual light, the visionary and creative mind of the Seer that comes with energy, enthusiasm and power. Experiences of the Illumined Mind include the infusion of consciousness and light in the cells of the body, emphasizing the fact that the body is involved in the process of enlightenment. Both the Higher Mind and the Illumined Mind are dependent on the Intuitive Mind, the source of their knowledge. Intuition functions in a way nearer to knowledge by identity. It involves penetration of the object and its consciousness by the subject's consciousness, with the revealing insight bursting forth like a flash of lighting. Intuition, according to Sri Aurobindo, consists of the fourfold power of "truth-seeing," "truth-hearing," "truth-touch" or understanding the significance of things, and "truth-discrimination."[12]

The next level of ascending consciousness is the Overmind,

12   1970d, p. 949.

which is a delegated light from the Truth-Mind or supramental gnosis and the principle of global or universal knowledge. Here the ego is subordinated to the cosmic vastness and eventually disappears to be replaced by the true individual, the Self. It is still an aspect of the Mind in the Ignorance and, therefore, takes its stand on multiplicity and division, and the play of possibilities. It is a creator of truths but not Truth. It functions on the basis of an implicit unity, with knowledge of the truth of each possibility, but it needs to work each possibility through according to its own evolutionary impetus. It can individualize the cosmic Mind and, on its highest plane, observes Sri Aurobindo, the individual Self identifies with the cosmic Self and acts with universality.

But the Overmind cannot take the Mind beyond itself; nor can it incarnate the Transcendent in the dynamic play of life. Nor can the Inconscient be totally transformed, as the rays of overmind consciousness do not penetrate all areas of being, and the play of possibilities allows for the continual re-entry of the Shadow of darkness. There is a need for the Overmind to transform into Supermind, requiring the soul and psychic being to leave the cosmic formation of Overmind in order to form a conscious relationship with the Transcendent. The Supermind is integral Truth-Consciousness and Truth-power, and the creative source of life, where the multiplicity is taken up into unity and the Inconscient has been transformed into consciousness. Only with the Supermind and its supramental gnosis is there the infinite Self-organizing Truth-power of the Supreme that can fully illuminate the Inconscient, also infinite, and replace it with effective Truth.

"The *Supermind*," writes Sri Aurobindo, "is a Truth-Consciousness that knows by its own inherent light of nature; it has not to arrive at knowledge but possesses it."[13] But it is not only "power of knowledge," it is a luminous play of "consciousness and knowledge" po-

---

13   1971b*, p. 70.

tentially consisting of "spiritual feeling" and "spiritual sensation," as
well as omniscient knowing and revealing spiritual substance with
effective and omnipotent power of acting and manifesting.[14] The
Supermind allows the "secret truth in things" that has always been
there to emerge and manifest itself, divinizing life and giving meaning
to our existence.[15] In later life, Sri Aurobindo defines an involutionary
borderline state below the Supermind on the summit of the Overmind,
which he refers to as the "Mind of Light," where the Supermind veils
and limits itself, although it still acts in relationship to its source, in
light, truth and knowledge, while proceeding "from knowledge to
knowledge."[16] Although in the Mind of Light there has been a descent from Supermind into the Mind, the "inherent connection with
the supramental principle" is not severed and "it is still an agent of
the Truth-Consciousness," where there is no place for "inconscience,
ignorance and error."[17]

In evolutionary terms, attaining the Mind of Light is the necessary
stage that, when achieved, will transform present humans into a new
type of divinized human being. Sri Aurobindo perceives two stages in
the birth and full establishment of the Mind of Light. The first stage
involves self-gathering out of the Ignorance until it finds itself established in its own Light. In the second stage, the Mind of Light develops
itself in this Light of nature, further defining itself until it "joins the
Supermind and lives as its subordinate portion or its delegate."[18] Thus,
Sri Aurobindo perceives the transformation of the human being into a
"gnostic mentality" with "an illumined divine life" prior to the supramental transformation itself.[19]

14   *Ibid.*
15   *Ibid.*, p. 74.
16   *Ibid.*, p. 71.
17   *Ibid.*
18   *Ibid.*, p. 69.
19   *Ibid.*

Later on in this study, I refer to Sri Aurobindo's categories of the Mind and the Supermind in relation to Jung. In the following two chapters I discuss Jung's understanding of the objective psyche and then his particular take on the evolution of human consciousness. Then I examine the role of creative individuals and the transformation of the community.

CHAPTER 9

Jung, the Archetypal Psyche and the Evolution of Consciousness

Sri Aurobindo and the Mother offer the most comprehensive understanding of the nature of the evolution of consciousness and the transformation of human nature required today to take evolution to its next step, through what is essentially the intensification of a natural process through yogic methodology. C.G. Jung makes a remarkably similar proposition, although with relatively less differentiation and more loose ends, where he, too, emphasizes the evolution of consciousness and the need, today, to become more conscious. As with Sri Aurobindo's understanding of yoga, Jung regards individuation to be a natural process that can be made more conscious through psychological methods.

Archetype and Instinct

Central to Jung's thinking is the phenomenon of the archetype, which, according to experience, has formative power and orders life. The archetype can be accessed through the image, although in itself, that is, in its essence, it is unknowable. Etymologically the word *arche* means origin, rule and command, suggesting it is a dominant factor in ordering the world. The word *type* means model, blow and mark of the blow, for instance, as form, image, imprint, pattern underlying form and so on.[1] The added suggestion is that the archetype is the

---

1   Douglas Harper, 2001–2010.

essential product of a power higher than itself, a Being that strikes a blow to make an imprint, image and form, and that it is through the archetype that the created world is experienced, perceived and ordered. In Sri Aurobindo and the Mother's terms, the source of the imprint would be the Supermind.

Before I examine the nature of the archetype along with its companion instinct, it may be helpful to realize that archetypes are organized in a series of hierarchies. Rather than functioning completely independently of each other, each archetype in a hierarchy is nested within another according to the degree of differentiation, from the most highly differentiated down to the more general. By way of example, the priestly archetype, the leadership archetype, the trader archetype and the servant archetype are nested in the archetypes of the Goddesses of Wisdom, Strength, Beauty and Relationship, and Service, respectively. They, in turn, are nested in the Great Mother archetype as the archetype of the order of society. Otherwise, archetypes from different hierarchies are contaminated with each other, making it nearly impossible to clearly differentiate the precise archetype that has been constellated at any given time.

At a deeper level than the personal unconscious Jung hypothesized the existence of the collective unconscious. The former relates to one's personal psychological history and complexes; the latter consists of archetypal and instinctive factors, where both archetype and instinct transcend the human ego. The archetypes, which have coalesced over time, refer to "the ruling powers, the gods, images of the dominant laws and principles, and of typical regularly occurring events in the soul's cycle of experience."[2] "The animal symbol" also points to "the transpersonal" psyche, as the collective unconscious contains not only "residues of archaic, specifically human modes of functioning, but

---

2   Jung, 1975d-3, p. 95.

also the residues of functions from man's animal ancestry."[3] The symbolic animal functions in the human in a material and dynamic way.

Archetypes are typical inborn blueprints that determine "regular and uniform" human patterns of perception and apprehension, whether one recognizes their archetypal nature or not.[4] Instincts are "uniform and regular modes of action and reaction" under specific conditions, whether conscious or not.[5] Thus, instincts compel one to naturally act in a human way, and the archetypes coerce perception and apprehension according to specific human patterns. In fact, for Jung, the instinct and the archetype intermingle as two poles of the same functional dynamic. Thus, Jung writes, the archetype is *the instinct's perception of itself* or "the self portrait of the instinct, in exactly the same way as consciousness is an inward perception of the objective life-process."[6] The question of what comes first, "apprehension of the situation or impulse to act," is not clear, and, yet, Jung seems to lean toward giving priority to the archetype.[7] Hence, he continues: "Just as conscious apprehension gives our actions form and direction, so unconscious apprehension through the archetype determines the form and direction of instinct."[8] Apprehension through the archetype is determinative of the instinctual dynamic according to this statement.

The archetype is self-activating and generative and "expresses the unique and un-conditioned creative power of the psyche."[9] The archetype itself, as distinguished from the archetypal image, is the condition for bringing order and determining meaning for both outer sensuous perceptions and inner perceptions and apprehensions. Consciously participating in an individual relationship with an emerging archetypal

---

3   Ibid, p. 98.
4   Jung, 1975f, p. 135.
5   *Ibid.*, p. 137
6   *Ibid.*, p. 136, 137.
7   *Ibid.*, p. 138.
8   Ibid, p. 137.
9   Jung, 1974b, p.445.

image connects the archetype to life and meaning. When an archetypal image emerges into consciousness, notably through dreams and visions, it is inevitably charged with emotion and experienced as fascinating, magical and numinous. Such a conscious experience is felt to be meaningful, and it can have a significant transformative impact on one's life. Thus, according to Jung:

> When a distressing situation arises, the corresponding archetype will be constellated in the unconscious. Since the archetype is numinous, i.e., possesses a specific energy, it will attract to itself the contents of consciousness—conscious ideas that render it perceptible and hence capable of conscious realization. Its passing over into consciousness is felt as an illumination, a revelation or a "saving idea."[10]

In this case, the archetype acts through the archetypal image in such a way as to bring acceptable complementary life affirming ideas, values and emotions to consciousness that answer to and transcend the stressful circumstances. Otherwise, writes Jung, the fascinating power of the autonomous archetype can enter "into active opposition to the conscious mind, and may be said to mould, in the long run, the destiny of individuals by unconsciously influencing their thinking, feeling and behavior, even if this influence is not recognized until long afterwards … without the cooperation of the conscious personality."[11] An unconscious relationship to the archetype is also expressed in every manner of unrealistic projections by both ordinary people as well as neurotics with psychological disorders, on those with whom one is in intimate connection as well as others, individuals or communities. This phenomenon is at the origin of many conflicts. Conscious cooperation with the unconscious is essential to become consciously aware of the flow of archetypal dynamics in one's life; and becoming conscious of the

---

10   1974a, p. 294.
11   *Ibid.*, p. 309.

emerging archetype is imperative for a meaningful relationship to life. Becoming aware of the archetype through an external event or a series of synchronistic events can also be awe-inspiring, although the ability to feel its numinous power depends on having an inner relationship to the archetype in question.

In 1927, near the end of a sixteen-year personal engagement and in-depth dialogue with the collective unconscious as illustrated in *The Red Book*, Jung notes that "the collective unconscious contains the whole spiritual heritage of man's evolution born anew in the brain structure of every individual. His conscious mind is an ephemeral phenomenon that accomplishes all provisional adaptations and orientations .... The unconscious, on the other hand, is the source of the instinctual forces of the psyche and of the forms and categories that regulate them, namely the archetypes."[12] Here, Jung differentiates the conscious mind from the unconscious, specifically the collective unconscious, the container of the archetypes and instincts. Although the conscious mind has the important function of orientation and adaptation to the everyday world of conscious concerns, the collective unconscious has the more pro-found function of connecting humans to their spiritual and instinctive heritage, which was Jung's conscious realization gained from his en-counter with the collective unconscious and the archetypal psyche.

Jung's conception of the archetype is metaphysical and, accord-ing to Marilyn Nagy, it has a direct parallel in the primal Will of Schopenhauer.[13] For Schopenhauer, images, ideas and psychic process-es are all secondary phenomena, dependent on the Will, the sole source of psychic energy. The primal Will is the only essential reality in the universe; it is a transcendent phenomenon, while material phenomena including the body, the "will to live" and the rhythm of life, with its positive and negative polarities, are its subjective representations.

Although Jung's archetypal theory is a lot more differentiated, the

---

12   1975b, p. 158.
13   1991, p. 144.

similarity between Schopenhauer's primal Will and Jung's archetype is readily apparent. Like the primal Will, the archetype-in-itself is directly related to a transcendent source, the primary intelligence and force behind the manifest universe. In Sri Aurobindo's terms, the archetype embodies Consciousness-Force, the second moment of the Trinity of *Sat Chit Ananda* along with the prime moving Force of the manifestation, where Consciousness-Force is the Shakti or Divine Mother. This understanding is in harmony with Jung's dedication to the Goddess, which I discuss below.

The Reality of the Psyche

From early on Jung recognizes a relationship between the archetype and evolution. Even as a twenty-three-year-old medical student in 1898, he discusses the evolutionary natural history embodied in human beings in a talk, entitled "Thoughts on Speculative Inquiry," that he delivered to his fellow Zofingia fraternity brothers. He says: "The world of the amoeba is, roughly speaking, contained in that of the worm, the world of both in that of the mammal; and all three in that of man .... At bottom, ... everything that exists moves within one and the same world .... All is one."[14] With this early interest, it is not surprising that, throughout his writings, there are several references to humankind's inherent evolutionary nature. Thus, in 1912, Jung writes: "Just as the body has an evolutionary history and shows clear traces of the various evolutionary stages, so too does the psyche."[15] It is noteworthy that, in this case, he stresses the fact that the psyche—in other words, the psychological and cultural constitution of humankind—potentially made conscious, partakes in this evolutionary unfolding.

Jung was not convinced by Freud's biological explanation of the origin of the psyche and sought for other explanations. He initially

---

14   C.G. Jung, 1983, p. 77.
15   1974a, p. 29.

resorted to an explanation borrowed from the phylogenetic theories of Ernst Haeckel's "biogenic law," where ontogeny, the psychological development of the individual, recaptures phylogeny, the evolutionary development of the race.[16] Haeckel meant that adult forms of evolutionary development are seen in individual human developmental recapitulation. According to this assumption, evolution proceeds in stages, the traces of which individuals carry in their brain structure and, presumably, their psychological makeup. The cornerstone of Haeckel's theory is faith in Lamarck and his theory of the selective inheritance of acquired characteristics, where individuals can pass on characteristics acquired during their lifetime to their offspring. His theory was also based on the postulates that nature is evolving from lower and simpler forms to higher, more complex manifestations, and that there are fundamental bonds of unity in nature.

Along came Mendel who based his Mendelaen laws of inheritance on the transmission of genes (published in 1865–66 and rediscovered in 1900); Mendel's work challenged Lamarck's scientific credibility and Haeckel's theory that ontogeny recaptures phylogeny. Although Jung continued to speak in terms of phylogenetic cultural development, it is not clear whether, regarding the brain, he continued to speak metaphorically or literally referred to the development of the brain structure. Nagy believes that evidence points to his thought on this subject developing toward his speaking metaphorically. Yet, there continued to be evidence of Jung referring to phylogenetic development in terms of traces being found in physiological bodily and brain structures as well as a priori archetypal patterns in the mind. In support of Jung's thinking regarding phylogenetic development, the contemporary discipline of epigenetics has garnered increasing scientific evidence for heritable changes in gene expression at the level of the phenotype, which involves biochemical attributes and physical traits.

---

16   Nagy, 1991, p.132.

In 1916, Jung refers to dream thinking as "a phylogenetically older form of thought" putting the priority on the psyche and psychic experiences, although implying that structural changes in the brain develop over time.[17] In the 1928 edition of his essay on "The Archetypes of the Collective Unconscious," Jung writes:

> The collective unconscious, being the repository of man's experience, is an image of the world which has taken aeons to form. In this image certain features, the archetypes or dominants, have crystallized out in the course of time. They are the ruling powers, the gods, images of the dominant laws and principles, and of typical regularly occurring events in the soul's cycle of experience, in so far as these images *laid down in the brain* are more or less faithful replicas of psychic events, their archetypes, that is, their general characteristics which have been emphasized through the accumulation of similar experiences, also correspond to certain general characteristics of the physical world. Archetypal images can therefore be taken metaphorically as intuitive concepts for physical phenomena.[18]

With reference to accumulated psychic experiences over time, there is clear evidence of a material Haeckelian and Lamarckian influence on the brain and the physical world. Yet, in the final edition of the essay, the phrase "*laid down in the brain*" was deleted.[19] It appears, then, that Jung may have developed some questions about the nature of the actual relationship between the psyche's activities and a parallel formation in the brain. Otherwise he is emphasizing the development over time of recurring archetypal ideas and patterns.

Despite any reservations he may have had, further on in the same essay, Jung wrote more on the archetypal image in relationship to

17   1975c-5, p. 247.
18   1975d-3, p. 98.
19   Nagy, 1991, p. 134.

phylogenetic development, here especially regarding the bodily instincts. He writes:

> The animal symbol points specifically to the extra-human, the
> transpersonal, for the contents of the collective unconscious are
> not only the residues of archaic, specifically human modes of
> functioning, but also the residues of functions from man's ani-
> mal ancestry, whose duration in time was infinitely greater than
> the relatively brief epoch of specifically human experience ....
> If we take the figures of the unconscious as collective psychic
> phenomena or functions, this hypothesis in no way violates our
> intellectual conscience. It offers a rationally acceptable solution,
> and at the same time a possible method of effecting a settlement
> with the activated residues of our racial history.[20]

In the above two quotations, Jung is establishing an argument for a
theory of the subjective evolution of consciousness, as well as there
being a direct relationship between the mind and the body, including
the brain.

In 1918, Jung observes: "We receive along with our body a highly
differentiated brain which brings with it its entire history that age old
natural history which has been transmitted in living form since the re-
motest times .... And this structure tells its own story, which is the story
of mankind: .... This unconscious buried in the structure of the brain
and disclosing its living presence ... through the medium of creative
fantasy, is the *suprapersonal unconscious*."[21] Here, again, he lays stress
on the psyche, observing that the brain, with its natural history, is directly related to the living psyche, which can be accessed through the
unconscious by way of true fantasy.

At this juncture it is worthwhile to examine the nature of what Jung
means by the psyche, along with the psychological implications. To
begin with, it is an objective phenomenon that requires it be referred

---

20   Jung, 1975d-3, p. 98.
21   1970d-1, p. 10.

to as *the* psyche, in which "man ... is enclosed," and not *my* psyche.[22] The etymology of the word is based on Latin *psyche*, Greek, *psyckhe,* meaning "the soul, mind, spirit, breath, life, the invisible animating spirit which occupies and directs the physical body."[23] Jung alludes to the ancient meaning of psyche in order to amplify the significance of his postulate of a "psychology with the psyche," by which he means "the psyche based on an autonomous spiritual principle."[24] He observes that, according to the ancient view, the psyche-in-itself is without extension, that it is moving force or life-force and that it suggests moving air and breath-body.

Jung relates the experience of synchronicity to the ultimate nature of the psyche. He writes:

> Synchronistic phenomena prove the simultaneous occurrence of meaningful equivalences in heterogeneous, causally unrelated processes; in other words, they prove that a content perceived by an observer, at the same time, be represented by an outside event, without any causal connection. From this it follows either that the psyche cannot be localized in space, or that space is relative to the "psyche." The same applies to the temporal determination of the psyche and the psychic relativity of "time." I do not need to emphasize that the verification of these findings must have far-reaching consequences.[25]

Experiences of synchronicity reflect a meaningful intersection of non-dual Reality with time and space.

Jung understands the psyche to be purposive, "as an arrangement not merely of matter *ready for life,* but of *living matter* or, more precisely, of *living processes.*"[26] Psyche is for him, he writes in a letter dated 1951, "an inclusive term for the totality of all so-called psychic

---

22   Jung, as reported in Adler, 1973, p. 556.
23   Harper.
24   1975b-2, p. 344.
25   Jung, 1975b-3, p. 531.
26   *Ibid.*, p. 321.

processes." Jung also indicates that spirit is a qualitative designation for certain psychic contents (rather than "material" or "physical").[27] Not only is the psyche a living process in space-time that includes spiritual phenomena, considerable parapsychological and depth-psychological evidence suggests that it is relatively trans-temporal and trans-spatial.[28] In fact, in a letter written in 1952, Jung writes:

> Shouldn't we give up the time-space categories altogether when we are dealing with psychic existence? ... [Perhaps] psyche should be understood as *unextended intensity* and not as a body moving with time. One might assume the psychic gradually rising from minute extensity to infinite intensity, transcending the velocity of light and thus irrealizing the body. [He continues his speculative observations writing that] the brain might be a transformer station, in which the relatively infinite tension or intensity of the psyche proper is transformed into perceptible frequencies or 'extensions.' Conversely, the fading of introspective perception of the body explains itself as due to 'psychification,' i.e., intensification at the expense of extension. Psyche = highest intensity in the smallest space.[29]

Jung's speculations here come eight years after his major *coniunctio* experience in 1944 when he experienced a heightened suprarational non-temporal state, and have considerable intuitive appeal. He suggests that this understanding of the nature of the psyche explains the elasticity of space and time in ESP and synchronistic experiences. In experiences of synchronicity that seem to originate from a multidimensional form of relative spatio-temporal existence, where inner and outer reality coincide meaningfully, Jung states: "Psychic contents ... act as much *outside* me as in *me,* just as much outside time as in time."[30] They include the material world.

---

27   Jung, as reported in Adler, 1975, p. 4.
28   *Ibid.*, p. 413.
29   *Ibid.*, p. 45.
30   Jung, as reported in Adler, 1973, p. 522.

Ultimately, the determinants of all psychic processes are the archetypes, including the archetype of the Self; they emerge from the unconscious into consciousness as archetypal images with feeling value, and not in their essence as archetypes per se, which are unknowable. They are perceived and apprehended both inwardly through dreams and fantasy and perceptively in external sensuous experiences in the physical world. Jung writes: "The archetype itself ... is psychoid, i.e., transcendental and thus relatively beyond the categories of number, space, time. That means it approximates to oneness and immutability."[31] Elsewhere he writes: "The archetypal world is 'eternal,' i.e., outside time, and it is everywhere, as there is no space under psychic, that is archetypal conditions."[32] Consistent with the metaphysical nature of the archetype, the psyche per se, as an *ousia* or a pure essence, the essential and divine depths of being, transcends all dualities, including spirit and matter.[33] Including the psychoid functions in the contents of the psyche further emphasizes the depth and height of being, referred to here.

My comments above show that the psyche defies hard definition. From what Jung writes, however, one can glean his sensitivity to the nature of the psyche, and the way it can be experienced. The psyche can be experienced both inwardly and outwardly in time as well as outside time; it is experienced as a living process that includes the material world. The contents of the psyche are archetypal, the ground determinants of all psychic processes, which have both a spiritual and instinctual dimension. Thus, archetypes are modes of apprehending the world; they are instincts of self-perception, while being blueprints for action.

In a letter dated March 15, 1954, Jung writes: "I am personally convinced that our mind corresponds with the physiological life of the body, but the way in which it is connected with the body is unintelligible."[34]

---

31   As reported in Adler, 1975, p. 318.
32   *Ibid.*, p. 46.
33   Jung, as recorded in Adler, 1973, p. 540.
34   as reported in Adler, 1975, p. 160

Yet, he goes on to observe that with vertebrates, the archetype is presumably "based upon the brain and its annexes," while with insects, one can assume it is found "in the sympathetic nervous system."[35] The archetype as "psychological representation of Instinctual patterns" in humans, he conjectures, is likewise found in "the sympathicus."[36] Jung then argues that if an aspect of the brain is destroyed, there is the likelihood of destruction of the transmitter of a psychological function and not the function itself. Having written the above, Jung ends the letter writing that localization talk is foolishness and a "remnant of old brain mythology,"[37] suggesting the difficulty of determining the exact correspondence between the mind and the brain.

Yet, reference to the brain as a transformer or transmitter station suggests that brain structures and their extensions into the body correlate with archetypal modes of apprehension and dynamic expression, and the brain and psyche are ultimately one. The equation of psyche as *living matter* and matter *ready for life,* suggests psyche and matter are two sides of the same coin, although the psyche-in-itself is immaterial and pure intensity without extension. Although the psyche-in-itself including the psychoid transcend spirit and matter, and is, ultimately, non-dual Reality and oneness, in extension, the psyche is one with the brain and the body. In fact, whether the psyche is studied through visions, dreams, fantasy and synchronistic experiences, as does Jung and his school of psychology, or through contemporary brain science and neuro-biology, it involves acceptance of the functional reality of the brain and its direct relationship to the mind or psyche.

In 1921, when Jung wrote *Psychological Types*, he refers to the medieval theologian and mystic Meister Eckhart favorably regarding the fact that "God is a psychological or, to be more accurate, *a*

35   *Ibid.*
36   *Ibid.*
37   *Ibid.*, p. 161.

psychodynamic state."[38] Of particular interest to understanding Jung is the following statement attributed to Eckhart: "The soul is not blissful because she is in God, she is blissful because God is in her."[39] Jung explains that, psychologically, this means that normally God, as the dynamic principle or libido, is projected outside the psyche onto external objects. When this projection is recognized through introversion and withdrawal of libido, objects are no longer autonomous phenomena, but God has become an inner reality in the psyche or soul. Thus, the determining factors of life now emanate from the collective unconscious within, most deeply, the incarnate God-image, representative of the Self or Sri Aurobindo's and the Mother's psychic being as the principle of individuation.

For Eckhart the soul now functions in an intermediate position as a symbolic image relating the subject to the unconscious, which it symbolizes. This, writes Jung, is a fortuitous and *"creative* state ... when God is in the soul, i.e., when the soul becomes a vessel for the unconscious and makes itself an image or symbol of it."[40] The soul functions creatively and gives birth to God's *"dynamism* in the form of a symbol."[41] Jung insists on the fact that "the soul must contain in itself the faculty of relationship to God, i.e., a correspondence .... *This correspondence is, in psychological terms,"* he writes, *"the archetype of the God-image."*[42] Thus, Jung is referring to a potentially creative relationship between the soul and the symbolic archetypal images that emerge from the unconscious, bringing new attitudes to life and conscious individuation.

These archetypal images not only embrace modes of apprehension but also instinctual *dynamism* and effective formative power. Eckhart foreshadows Jung in his psychological interests and involvement, which

38   1974b, p. 246.
39   *Ibid.*
40   *Ibid.*, p. 251.
41   *Ibid.*, p. 251.
42   1977, p. 11.

is a departure from most Western theology, and may be one reason for the Church's suspicion of his work. One could summarize Jung's life work and personal psychology by saying that it reflects, above all, the conscious realization of the birth of God's dynamic nature and ways of perceiving life and matter in the soul, which Jung generally refers to as the psyche. As far as the macrocosm is concerned, as discussed above in the section on astrology, the manifest deity traces its signature in the heavens that correlates with the individual microcosm and the archetypal psyche.

In his discussion on Eckhart, Jung observes: "It would be blasphemy to assert that God can manifest himself everywhere but in the human soul," going beyond his usual caution about being scientific and referring to the God-image and not God.[43] In a rejoinder to Martin Buber, who accused Jung of psychologisms with regard to human relationship to the Divine, he first explains the subjective nature of the human relationship to God, but then he writes: "Here, for once and as an exception, I shall indulge in transcendental speculation …. God has indeed made an inconceivable divine and mysteriously contradictory image of himself, without the help of man, and implanted it in man's unconscious as an archetype, an archetypal light … in order that the unpresumptuous man might glimpse an image in the stillness of his soul that is akin to him and is wrought up of his own psychic substances. This image contains everything he will ever imagine concerning his gods or concerning his psyche."[44] Here, Jung is asserting that the archetype-in-itself is the manifest Divine, which incarnates in the human soul as a multifarious contradiction of opposites.

As a psychiatrist, Jung was always concerned about human anthropomorphisms about God. But when he was eighty years old and, with greater circumspection than Meister Eckhart, who expresses the belief that man is God and God, man, Jung writes: "[The human being] has

---

43   *Ibid.*, p. 10.
44   1976b, p. 667.

and holds a mystery in his hands and at the same time is contained in his mystery. What can he proclaim? Himself or God? or neither? The truth is that he doesn't know who he is talking of, God or Himself."[45] With this observation and the statements indicated in the previous paragraph, it is clear to me that, in Jung's personal convictions, it is God who becomes manifest through the archetypal images, and that, by realizing the archetypal image born in the psyche, humans can become conscious of their relationship to God, at least the dynamic immanent God.

Thus, Jung notes that "the true history of the mind is preserved in the living psychic organism of every individual."[46] Although there is a biological aspect to evolution as envisaged here, Jung is particularly interested in the evolution of consciousness. Hence, he writes that "man's task" is "to become conscious of the contents that push upward from the unconscious. Neither should he persist in his unconsciousness, nor remain identical with the unconscious elements in his being, thus evading his destiny, which is to create more and more consciousness."[47] The path of individuation, which involves gradual differentiation of the uniqueness of being, requires the development of consciousness, not as an intellectual extension of consciousness per se, but by way of the inner confrontation of opposites, which are ultimately experienced as superordinate to the ego. These considerations lead to the following exploration of Jung's take on the evolution of human consciousness.

---

45   As recorded in Adler, 1975, p. 255.
46   1975c, p. 35.
47   Jung, 1983, p. 326.

CHAPTER 10

Jung and the Evolution of Human Consciousness

Jung does not write systematically about the evolution of human consciousness, as did Sri Aurobindo. One can glean from his writings, however, reference to five different evolutionary stages: the primal or archaic, the ancient, the modern, the contemporary subjective age, and the Age of the Holy Spirit. Although Jung appears to be suggesting a progressive development, he, in fact, recognizes that the evolution of consciousness actually takes place in a spiral-like fashion. Jung's observation is based on empirical evidence of the psyche in that "dream-motifs always return after certain intervals to definite forms, whose characteristic is to define a centre."[1] Most deeply, he regards the evolution of consciousness as a drama of an *"Aurora Consurgens*—the dawning of consciousness in mankind ... that began in the grey mists of antiquity and continues through the centuries into a remote future."[2] Consciousness is fundamentally a phenomenon of the psyche and brain, and its outward expression and organization of life is the dynamic aspect of a unified inner and outer world.

Primal or archaic folk, according to Jung, live in *participation mystique,* unconscious identity, with their surroundings and project subjective contents of their psyche onto people, objects, and situations. There is, accordingly, little sense of individuality, but a collective orientation to life and psychological domination by the group or tribe. People live with a sense of unconscious wholeness and, through

---

1   1977, p. 28.
2   Jung, 1977, p. 476.

shamanic rituals and effective use of symbols a relationship is established with the archetypal roots of being, the instincts and the natural environment.

Between the primal mind and the mind of modernity Jung lumps civilizations from ancient Egypt to medieval Christendom in what can be characterized as the ancient mind. There is less unconsciousness compared to archaic peoples, as ancient civilizations live less in participation mystique and projections are no longer ubiquitous. Projections are now directed toward God or the gods, goddesses and lesser divine forces, experienced as separate and distinct from the individual. For the average person, religious ritual and the realization of the religious instinct, however, serve to bring a relative balance to life, connecting people to their spiritual roots of being. As with shamans in archaic cultures, during this period, mystics are significantly more conscious than the common person.

The next two stages in the evolution of consciousness, according to Jung, include the modern mind and what he refers to as the contemporary psyche. The modern mind is organized by scientific reason and technology, and the ego has been effectively separated from the natural mind and the unconscious, while rejecting it and its value. Although the Age of Reason was initially a liberation from convention, today the ego and causal thinking reign supreme, resulting in extreme one-sidedness and a dangerous severance from the instinctive and archetypal roots of being. In fact, the modern mind has an exceptionally wide-ranging mental consciousness that comes with a dynamic drive for successful realization on many fronts.

Considerable unconscious projection of shadow based on individual and collective stereotypes persists, along with weak attempts to deal with them through reason and rationalization. At a deeper level there continues to be projections on the opposite sex, despite efforts toward finding more harmonious relationships and equality. In fact the psyche has, by and large, moved from a modern into a postmodern mind, where reason and the standards of reason are being relativized, even devalued, without an apparent increase in moral judgment (or even with its degeneration). Society, for instance, is having great moral difficulty coming to terms with the Internet and other contemporary devices, which are opening up a multitude of options, some of which facilitate life, self-expression, creativity and the search for information and knowledge, while others are of questionable value, vulgar and degrading, and others, again, are of ambiguous value.

The difficulty stems from the fact that by allowing individual freedom and the potential to enrich one's sense of being and potential for discovery of the divine Will in life, there is increased temptation and license that is offered by the Internet in the privacy of one's dark corner of the home. Potentially, there are progressively weakened relational values and individual moral standards, and a distancing effect from the here and now. A relatively high percentage of Internet traffic, for instance, involves pornography, and Internet addiction is a recognized psychological problem.

At a deeper level the question is what are people looking for more deeply in their search for alternative life on the Internet. I would suggest integration of shadow and anima/animus qualities, true Eros and relational values and a connection to the heart-Self. At a deeper level the question is what are people looking for more deeply in their search for alternative life on the Internet. I would suggest integration of shadow and anima/animus qualities, true Eros and relational values and a connection to the heart-Self.

New Skins for New Wine

Jung believes that people living in the contemporary mind are a distinct minority. Reason and its insistence on experience can, however, open individuals to a symbolically oriented life and the individuation process.[3] One then lives subjectively in relationship with non-rational

---

3   1970b.

stirrings of the unconscious, as well as being more fully aware of the immediate present. The process involves integration of the personal shadow, assimilating values of the anima/animus as well as gaining a relationship to the archetypal psyche, including the collective shadow, the shadow side of the God-image. An examination of his writings prior to 1944 gives one the impression that Jung did not want to disturb or combat the truth of Christianity but bring fresh understanding to bear. In 1945, when he was seventy years old and early in his relationship to the Dominican Father Victor White, he writes: "It is a gigantic task indeed to create a new approach to an old truth. More than once I have put the question to my theological friends: what about new wine in old skins?"[4] He goes on to say that with the help of science he can interpret old truths anew and influence the modern mind, the locus of his argument.

But, fifteen years later in 1960, when he is eighty-four years old, Jung writes to Father White from a transformed perspective: "Things had to be moved in the great crisis of our time. New wine needs new skins."[5] Given all the resistance to Jung including from Christian and other quarters, one cannot help forming the opinion that traditional Jungian psychology, with its appeal to Gnostic, mythological and alchemical truths, without invalidating the truths of Christ and Christianity, is already new wine with new skins. As he writes Father White, some of his analysands need to be helped out of the Church: "It is their destiny and adventure."[6] But Jung actually takes the metaphor further and, no doubt based on his own vast experience of bringing the unconscious to consciousness, foresees an evolution of consciousness to a new aeon. Indeed, he writes that it requires the complete abolition

---

4   C.G. Jung as reported in Adler, 1973, p. 387.
5   As reported in Adler, 1975, p. 555.
6   *Ibid.*, p. 136.

of [the] ego through the experience of the divine opposites as "expressed by the symbol of Christ versus Satan."[7]

He writes this in an earlier letter to Victor White in 1953, when he is seventy-seven years old, as he tries to educate him on what he foresees transpiring. First, Jung observes that it is a time of darkness, where Christian virtues are essential and the symbol of Christ valid. When this time has passed and the shadow fully assimilated, however, he believes a new orientation will be essential. Here Jung looks forward to the Age of the Holy Spirit as anticipated by Gioacchino de Fiore, a medieval monk, and predicted by Christ's reference to the coming of the Paraclete. Jung elucidates that this means going "beyond the Christian aeon to the *Oneness of the Holy Spirit,*" which refers to "a restitution of the original oneness of the unconscious on the level of consciousness."[8] I will discuss below the significance of these reflections in relationship to Jung's realization of a feeling experience of the *unus mundus*, one world, in light of Sri Aurobindo's Integral Yoga. At this point I will only remark that he writes as a farsighted prophet with considerable embodied visionary experience, and not as the Messiah or Avatar, who is an actual incarnation of the New Way of the Spirit as Jung articulates it here.

Jung never tires of insisting that it is important psychologically not to identify with Christ and his path in a blind imitation of Christ. This, in fact, was the recommendation of Thomas à Kempis, a late medieval monk, who writes: "Anyone who wishes to understand and to savor the words of Christ to the full must try to make his whole life conform to the pattern of Christ's life."[9] I recently enjoyed an inspiring Cannes Festival Grand Prix-winning movie based on real-life events, entitled *Of Gods and Men (Des Dieux et des Hommes),* where this is basically what transpired. Eight French Trappist friars in Algeria felt they had no

---

7   *Ibid.*, p. 135.
8   *Ibid.*, p. 135.
9   1996, p. 33.

choice but to stay in terrorist-ridden Algeria as servants of Christ and as a Christian model for the villagers. They were eventually joined by a ninth friar, who brought needed supplies. Their discussion centered on what Christ would want them to do, based on their reading of the Bible and collective self-reflection, and, as a group, they all decided to stay despite the danger they faced. Although each friar was given the liberty to make up his own mind, in the end, group morality prevailed. One can admire their courage, as the danger was real; it led to seven of them being beheaded in an untimely martyrdom.

Only two friars survive, one being the oldest friar, Amédés (a name meaning "Love of God"), who hid under the bed on arrival of the terrorists. Following Christ's path externally and as a collective, without truly encouraging individual differences, comes with not having a psychological perspective and understanding the possibility of realizing God in the individual soul or psyche. The two surviving friars may, nonetheless, reflect this potential. Amédés' name and its meaning, in this light, are intriguing and worthy of some reflection.

Today, Jung contends, it is psychologically necessary for self-directed individuals to live their own unique life as fully as Christ lived his. The life of Christ is both personal and archetypal; it is the archetype of the hero and the mythological dying and resurrecting sun-god as lived in the individual embodied life, as the incarnation of the Self. As Jung experiences it, "what happens in the life of Christ happens always and everywhere. In the Christian archetype all lives of this kind are prefigured and are expressed over and over again or once and for all."[10] The way Christ lived his life, according to Jung, is "the example of how a human life should be lived."[11] Since, from a psychological vantage point, this is the case, Jung observes: "We can't receive the Holy Spirit unless we have accepted our own individual life as Christ

---

10   1975c, p. 89.
11   As recorded in Shamdasani, 1998, p. 54.

accepted his."[12] "Thus," he says, "we become the "sons of god" fated to experience the conflict of the divine opposites represented by the crucifixion."[13] Birth of God in the soul requires experiencing the paradoxical God within and the realization of all the opposites at an archetypal level in a *complexio oppositorum*. This means fully living one's myth, where, according to Jung, myth "speaks to us as the Word of God" and is "the revelation of a divine life in man."[14] This realization is in keeping with living one's own life as truthfully as did Christ, where, in the Christian universe, he is the Logos made flesh, the incarnation of the Word of God.

In a seminar held in 1939, Jung clarifies what the incarnation of Christ means in psychological terms. He is recorded as saying: "The dogma claims that Christ was God who became man. In psychological terms this means that the Self approached the consciousness of man or that human consciousness began to realize the Self, as a real human fact."[15] The fact that Jung recognizes other incarnations as symbols of the Self besides Christ—for instance, Buddha, Krishna and Lao Tse—suggests that the individuation process eventually involves the "imitation" of the archetype of the Self and its realization and not an externally defined path per se. The Western symbol for the image of the incarnation of the Self, nonetheless, has historically resembled that of the life of Christ.

New bottles for new wine in Jung's teachings are the intricate scientific study of the psyche and a full psychological perspective that leads to its spiritual transformation in the incarnation of the Word of God and a divine life. Here Jung once again shows his harmony with Sri Aurobindo, who describes the dynamics of Universal Activity as the play of Vidya and Avidya, Science and Nescience, where "Vidya

---

12   1976c, p. 688.
13   *Ibid.*
14   1983, p. 340.
15   Jung, as recorded in Sonu Shamdasani, 1998, p. 54.

or Science is (Parabrahaman's) power of shaking off His own imagination and returning upon His real and eternal Self."[16] This understanding
of depth psychology as a science is expressed in psychological terms
by Jung, when he writes: "The aim of individuation is nothing less
than to divest the soul of the false wrappings of the persona on the one
hand and of the suggestive power of primordial images on the other."[17]
Etymologically, the word *science* refers to knowledge, and the purpose
of science is the unveiling of knowledge. In fact, science, as it is normally understood, as well as the science of depth psychology, functions
through inner discovery by way of dreams and/or intuitions and not
human invention or inventiveness, as is often thought to be the case.

We live in a subjective age, with an ability to self-reflect that has
hitherto not been possible. What is new is the discovery of the tools
and method for unprecedented psychological self-reflection of the personal and archetypal psyches, as well as a world picture (painted by
Jung) that includes the addition of acausality and synchronicity to the
tripartite scheme of causality and space and time, giving a quaternity.[18] The significance of this scientific model is that, being a quaternity,
it has the quality of wholeness and it adds dimensions not found in
the Newtonian models, acausality and synchronicity. Jung's scientific
worldview also includes a second quaternity involving spirit and matter as opposites, and the Transcendent as opposite to the psyche.[19] The
value of this model is that spirit and matter are included as opposites,
as are the Transcendent and the psyche, opening up a psychological
perspective that goes beyond the purely material Universe. The dualities represented in this model are indicative of the nature of the task
required for psychological integration. New, too, is the scientific study
of the relational quality of the psyche, especially the inevitable exis-

---

16   1972d, p. 29.
17   1975d-1, p. 174.
18   David Lindorff, 2009, pp. 105–107 passim.
19   *Ibid.*, pp. 145–149 passim.

tence of transference and counter-transference between patient and therapist (consisting of a series of projections and counter-projections). When aware of the nature of the transference and counter-transference responses and reactions in any given healing situation, therapists can bring this awareness to bear for both self-knowledge and for the creative psychological healing of the patient.

In the West, the Gnostic tradition, which influenced Jung considerably, allows for the birth of God in the soul, although it was limited in that, not in all Gnostic paths but, for the most part, the world was seen as evil and "the emergence of consciousness a mistake of creation."[20] In alchemy, which had an even more powerful and enduring influence on Jung, most practitioners did not realize that their visions related to them personally. Meister Eckhart, as I indicate above, realized the virtue of giving birth to God in the soul, but he was a rare figure in Christianity, which still, typically, neglects the divine reality of the psyche. Nobody in the West or, outside of Sri Aurobindo and the Mother, in the East, has taken the psyche so seriously and scientifically studied it in its full complexity as thoroughly and intensely as did Jung, followed by his students.

With publication of *Mysterium Coniunctionis* in 1955/1956, Jung believed his work was solidly grounded on historical reality and that he had "reached the bounds of scientific understanding, the transcendental, the nature of the archetype per se, *concerning* which no further scientific statements can be made."[21] This is an extraordinary statement that will stir up considerable controversy once people realize what he is saying. It is a different kind of science than that generally understood as science today. But it is based on conscious experience and scientific scrutiny of the objective psyche by both him and his students. In his visionary *coniunctio* experiences he had, in fact, feelingly realized the

---

20   Alfred Ribi, 2013, p. 200.
21   1983, p. 221.

transcendent source of the *anima mundi* or world soul, the undivided and cosmic psyche, the container of all the archetypes.

The psyche has been obliged to go through an evolutionary process, the development of reason and the possibility of detachment and enhanced individual self-reflection, in order to appreciate this new potential. Von Franz lived this new method of psychological self-reflection; and early on in her work as a therapist, she is reported to have dreamt that she was walking on new ground, where "no one" had previously trodden.[22] What Jung brings is truly new, so new that it is still not accepted by mainstream psychology or different religious and spiritual paths, some fifty years after his death on June 26, 1961 and 136 years after his birth on July 26, 1875. His psychological insights, however, are influencing a growing number of ordinary folk in different walks of life.

Judaism and the Christian Myth

After the separation from Freud and prior to his serious confrontation with the unconscious that began in 1912, Jung lived in a state of considerable uncertainty. In his self-reflections he understood that he did not have a living myth, where myth is understood as a guiding truth. He realized that he and the modern person of his time did not live by any myth, including the Christian myth. That is when he voluntarily engaged "the unconscious as a scientific experiment," although in late life he remarks: "Today I might equally well say that it was an experiment which was being conducted on me."[23] Jung's personality number 1, his conscious ego, and the Self conducted the original experiment that led to the formation of his brand of depth psychology. In retrospect Jung's life and psychology can be seen as a fulfillment of the evolutionary curve of the Western psyche that has become dominated by the

---

22   Anne Maguire, 2006.
23   C.G. Jung, 1983, p. 178.

scientific spirit. But it is much more than that, being a fulfillment of Western culture and religion, for the past two millennia largely driven by Judeo-Christianity.

There is a great difference between Judaism and Christianity despite the fact that Christianity developed out of Judaism and the first "people of the way" were Jewish as was Jesus himself. It is relevant that Jesus spoke to his disciples as a way-shower and not as a leader of an institutionalized religion. Noteworthy, too, is the fact that God's revelation to Moses is directed to a nation of people, and not to an individual or individuals. That, according to Rabbi Neusner, is one of the two key differences between Judaism and Christianity, the other being the fact that Christ speaks as an individual who has replaced the Torah.[24] He has become, observes the rabbi, not only master of the Sabbath, as indicated in *Matthew* 12:8, where "the Son of Man is master of the Sabbath," but master of the Torah, where, in the Judaic tradition, Torah refers to "God's revelation to Moses," and *torah* means "the instruction of a master—in the context of the teaching of the Torah."[25] Despite what Christ says about him coming "not to abolish the Law or the Prophets ... but to complete them," in fact, the rabbi feels, he speaks with authority as the Word of God, as if he personally replaces the Torah (as in *Matthew* 5: 18).

Christ is the Messiah, the incarnation of the Lord, the Logos made flesh, and he speaks as the individual Divine Son to individuals, as indicated in the Beatitudes. From Pope Benedict XVI's perspective, Christ's words comprise the "Torah of the Messiah, that is "totally new and different" and as such truly "fulfills the Torah of Moses."[26] Moreover, the "I" of Jesus speaks to and reflects the divinity of the individual ego which can be in harmony with the divine Will, and not the contaminated ego of self-will. It seems to me self-evident that, as

---

24   1993.
25   *Ibid.*, p. 4.
26   2007, p. 100.

God-man, Jesus is showing the way for his disciples, as People of the Way, to find spiritual freedom beyond the Law by following his path of truth, and not establishing an institutionalized religion. Jung's interpretation of the psychological meaning of Christ's incarnation in this light makes infinite sense. He observes: "The dogma claims that Christ was God who became man. In psychological terms this means that the Self approached the consciousness of man or that human consciousness began to realize the Self, as a real human fact."[27]

Although Christ is a particularly significant example for the Western mind, Jung's path of conscious individuation in its deeper meaning involves relating to the Self as the regulating spirit of everyday life. Not only Christ but others, such as Krishna, Buddha and Lao Tse, are all symbols of the Self. For the contemporary person, following intimations of the Self are what is truly important and not any specific representation, although one or more symbolic personage may have special relevance for the individual.

Rabbi Neusner, however, does not see Christ in that way, as an incarnation of God with the particular mission to bring greater individual consciousness to humanity. What troubles him is that not only does Jesus not speak to the people of "eternal Israel," but he encourages individuals to leave their family and community and follow him, as he is the way, the life and the truth. The rabbi is especially referring to the fact that Christ said to a young man who assiduously followed the Torah: "If you wish to be perfect, go and sell what you own and give money to the poor, and you will have treasures in heaven; then come, follow me" (*Matthew* 19: 21, 22). The rabbi believes that this commandment contradicts the teachings of the Torah of Moses, which emphasizes the here and now, the social order and family and community with a Covenant with God.

Rabbi Neusner claims that he respects Christ but does not accept

---

27   Jung, as reported in Shamdasani, 1998, p. 54.

him as the incarnation of the Divine. Thus, he interprets the above passage as meaning that Christ tempts individuals away from "eternal Israel" and the Torah of Moses. A Christian way of understanding the incarnation of Christ is that he is the Messiah, the anointed one, with a particular mission from God, and that he did fulfill the Torah as I indicate above. As Benedict XVI points out, from the beginning, the emerging Church does encourage the social order based on strong families in harmony with the Torah. If, indeed, there was an initial disruption of Israel's social order, Christianity, he argues, was given the task of universalizing the teachings of the Old Testament and spreading them beyond the nation of Israel to embrace the world.

Moreover, he believes that the fact that Christ brings freedom from the Law is one important reason that led the Church to embrace the separation of Church and State. Secularization of society gives humans the opportunity to find ways for fulfilling God's unfolding Will according to their own intrinsic truth and emerging community. "The decisive thing," observes Benedict XVI, is the underlying communion of the Will with God, as given by Jesus."[28] This means referral to Christian truth, although this is far from the way secular society has developed in its contemporary, highly individualistic, postmodern, liberal, humanistic thinking that finds Christian teaching limiting and repressive.

The incarnation of divine Love in the individual God-man, Jesus Christ, brings the possibility of enhancing individual human consciousness both in terms of a vertical aspiration to the Beyond and in terms of relational values and "brotherly love" with one's fellow human beings. Jesus' first commandment after entering Jerusalem was: "*You must love the Lord your God with all your heart, with all your soul, and with all your mind*" (*Matthew* 22: 37, 38), which, according to Rabbi Neusner, is a reflection of the Hebraic S*hema,* "the prayer proclaiming God's unity and Israel's submission."[29] The second commandment, "You

---

28   2007, p. 118.
29   1993, p. 82.

must love your neighbor as yourself," is also found word for word in *Leviticus* 19: 17–18, along with other practical counsel on how to relate with one's neighbors, including if they are offensive (*Matthew* 22: 40).

Despite these parallels with the Hebrew Testament, thanks to the incarnation of Christ, Christianity represents a development of consciousness that emphasizes the spiritual reality of the Beyond and the aspiration to the Beyond, the kingdom of God, whether in this life or after death. Unlike Judaism, which is concerned with sanctification and holiness in the here and now, Christ brings the message of potential redemption through grace for individuals who follow his way. In its unfolding, Christianity emphasizes individual perfection with the help of reason, a phenomenon that, in Europe, began with the classical Greek philosophers, and was given further definition in the Renaissance, leading up to today, where the individual's intellectual ego has taken on monumental proportions.

At any rate, with Christ's teachings there was emancipation from strict adherence to the Law and individual freedom to make personal choices in life; by following Christ, one follows the perfection of the divine Will. Along with its lofty ethics, the Church enlists the help of reason, based on the belief that Christ is the Logos itself, where Logos is the light of Reason. Spiritually gifted individuals can still profit from the Christian mystery by realizing the need for their individual and personal participation in this process. Christianity attributes an immutable soul to the individual, formerly projected onto the king and royal family, and fostered an advance in individual consciousness and culture. Thus, Father Cantalamessa, preacher of the Pontifical Household in the Vatican, emphasizes the effective importance of the individual, by saying, "The influence of the Gospels on society comes about through the individual, not through the community or ecclesial institution."[30]

In the Jewish tradition, the development of the Kabbala is

---

30   2011.

psychologically a parallel movement to the Christian truth and, according to Jung, even more comprehensive in its extensive inclusion of the shadow.[31] At the same time, what for the most part transpired psychologically and sociologically was that Christian teachings, as propagated by institutionalized Christianity, led to severe collective and individual repression and, eventually, to contemporary secular society and the forceful dominance of an extensive proactive ego, not particularly interested in Christian truths in themselves. Missing in institutional Christianity is an emphasis on the need for individuals to participate in furthering God's redemptive process as understood by medieval alchemists.

Perfection *vs.* Completeness, Jung's Act of Seeing and Freedom

As lauded in the Hebraic tradition, Jung engages in an extended dialogue with the Self as an argument with God, very evident in his book, *Answer to Job*, and with God's Word, incarnated as archetypal phenomena, evident in *The Red Book*. Also, in harmony with Judaism, he does not encourage perfection as it is commonly understood, as being without flaw or error, but rather emphasizes wholeness or holiness, while giving it psychological definition. Hence, he writes; "The individual may strive after perfection ('Be ye therefore perfect as your heavenly Father is perfect') but must suffer from the opposite of his intention for the sake of his completeness."[32] Here Jung acknowledges that striving for perfection in the Greek sense of the word *teleiosis*, meaning "a completing, perfecting fulfillment," is inborn.[33] But he continuously warns against a narrowly defined search for moral perfection that has

---

31   As reported in Adler, 1975, p. 92.
32   Jung, 1975, p. 69.
33   Thayer and Smith.

become central to Christian ethical teaching, which he believes, results in repression and one-sidedness.

One could argue that Christian ethics are "lofty" and "the height of moral greatness," as does Benedict XVI, but they are, for most people, a difficult burden to bear and, psychologically unrealistic, based on the Christian notion of a God that is all-Good and all-Light.[34] The dogma of God as *Summun Bonum*, all-Good, and the doctrine that evil is merely *privatio boni*, deprivation of Good, and not substantial in its own right—which led to the corollary, that *omne bonum a Deo, omne malum ab homine, all good to God, all evil to man*—put humankind, in its imperfection, in a humanly impossible position of moral inferiority. In contrast to the Christian God, the God of the Hebrews is ambiguous, expressing many opposite tendencies such as anger, jealousy and revenge as well as mercy, caring and loyalty. Jung felt the psychological need to compensate the one-sidedness of the Christian God with the God of the Hebrews in order to give a more complete picture of the manifest God.

Commenting on one of Sri Aurobindo's aphorisms, the Mother makes the same point as Jung:

> All the believers, all the faithful (those from the West in particular) think in terms of "something else." When they speak of God—He cannot be weak, ugly, imperfect. He is something immaculate—but this is wrong thinking. They are dividing, separating—The divine perfection is the whole of the Divine with nothing subtracted from it.[35]

Understanding God as a complex of opposites rather than as all-Good and all-Light makes an enormous difference in one's personal moral vector and the collective moral equation. In fact, the old Hebrews lived in a highly ethical social order, where village, home and family, and the

---

34   2007, p. 123.
35   1978, pp. 280–81.

here and now, were the place to live a holy life and follow God's Will, as revealed in the Torah of Moses. Indeed, their collective Covenant with God and commandments are all directed to becoming sanctified as "a kingdom of priests, a consecrated nation," through the practice of ritual, ethical codes, prayer and engaging in sincere debates with God (*Exodus* 19: 6–7).

Jung concludes his imaginative argument with the God-image in *Answer to Job*, by noting that Job proves himself to be morally superior to Yahweh, the amoral Jewish God-image, who lacks self-reflection and any recourse to absolute knowledge, which Jung finds in the unconscious. In Jung's subjective reading, this is the proximate cause of the incarnation of Christ, the purpose being "the differentiation of Yahweh's consciousness."[36] The aspiration from below was answered with the descent of the Messiah, the Divine Son and incarnation of Love, an expression of the love God has for the world.

This is a kind of Gnostic treatment of the Christian myth and suggests a unified world, where all is One, in that the Divine is not only in the Heavens or Pleroma but revealed as incarnated in a living body with a mission to lead individuals to the kingdom of God. In fact, in the Gnostic Gospel according to Thomas, the kingdom is both within one and outside, indicating a *unus mundus* or one world, where the inner and outer worlds are one. In the Christian mysteries, following Jesus takes one to the kingdom, which is a parallel notion to Meister Eckhart's appreciation of the birth of God in the soul. An extension of this kind of logic permits Jung to make the surprisingly metaphysical statement that "all creation *ex nihilo* is God's and consists of nothing but God, with the result that man, like the rest of creation, is simply God become concrete .... God is reality itself and therefore—last but not least, man."[37] In this point of view, all is One: both inside, within the psyche, and outside, in the external world, suggesting that the

---

36   1975g, p. 406.
37   *Ibid.*, p.402.

immanent God can be known from his creation. Realistic Advaita, the path of Sri Aurobindo, has an identical world view.

In Jung's mind, the answer to Job is not the incarnation of Christ per se but the moment of despair on the Cross when Jesus felt forsaken by God. Jung sees this empathetically as a moment of intense suffering when Christ's "human nature attains divinity."[38] It is the moment when the Divine knows what it is to suffer in the way Job suffered under the rule of the paradoxical God. Otherwise, in Jung's estimation, Christ shows "a manifest lack of self-reflection."[39] He was who he was, an incarnation of Divine Love, who lived according to the archetypal pattern of the dying-resurrecting sun-god. For Christ, transfixed on the Cross and feeling abandoned by God the Father, is the fulfillment of Yahweh's intention to become man after his encounter with Job, and the realization of his archetypal destiny. As fully human and fully divine, the life of Christ is inevitably a symbol, its mythological character previously depicted in the early death of a "light" son in Abel, Adam and Eve's second son, a shepherd, or in the early demise of the dying-resurrecting sun-god, expressing its universal validity.

Jung points to the declaration in 1950 of the dogma of the Assumption of the Virgin Mary, where she is now in the nuptial chamber with Christ, as being highly significant. He notes that it signifies the *hieros gamos,* the sacred marriage in the Pleroma and a future child, which following the trend of divine incarnation, will incarnate in humankind. As a religious phenomenon Jung observes that: "I consider it to be the most important religious event since the Reformation."[40] In his way of thinking, this refers to individuation, which, when a conscious process, leads to the integration of opposites, the divine child being a symbol of wholeness. The "indwelling of the Holy Ghost, the third Divine Person, in man," declares Jung, "brings about a Christification

38   *Ibid.*, p. 408.
39   *Ibid.*
40   *Ibid.*, p. 464.

of many."[41] Since Christ, for Jung, is a symbol of the Self, Christification does not mean imitating Christ's external life but a fully Self-directed, uniquely lived life.

The mythological nature of the incarnated life of Christ as God-man and symbol of the Self, over time, can be potentially internalized by normal human beings and realized as a goal of individuation. Christ on the Cross, suffering the opposites, with emphasis on the heart center, the point of juncture of the human and divine, is paradigmatic for the process of individuation. In fact, conscious individuation is the result of facing and realizing life's conflicts in the context of the Self and wholeness. In Sri Aurobindo and the Mother's terms it refers to the incarnated aspect of the soul and psychic being in relationship with, on the one hand, the mental, vital and physical natures, and on the other, the *Jivatman*, the un-incarnated individual soul, a delegate of the universal and transcendent *Atman*.

Jung writes that "psychology is concerned with the act of seeing and not with the construction of new religious truths, when even the existing truths have not been perceived and understood."[42] It is about the growth of consciousness and not the development of a new dogma, doctrine or tradition. He is interested in Christ not only because Christ's life is paradigmatic of the path toward individual wholeness and spiritual well-being, but because people are blind to the truths of Christianity that have not been properly understood. Unlike Christ himself, Jung brings a highly self-reflective consciousness which, historically, may not have been possible until after the development of the modern mind. Jung's approach to psychology brings to consciousness and fills out the meaning of freedom from the Law, and new creation, as alluded to and initiated by Christ.

Freedom is not license but requires self-discipline and a responsible life. Freedom is reflected in experiences of the Self as a blissful

---

41   *Ibid.*, p. 470.
42   1977, p. 13.

"window" into eternity.[43] It is reflected in the transcendent function as a source of creative solutions to real-life conflicts of opposites, and in experiences of synchronicity as moments of grace, when non-dual Reality embraces life in the physical world in a new act of creation in time. Freedom is experienced in realizations of the *unus mundus,* one world, where multiplicity is contained in an underlying unity. For Jung's spiritual ancestors, the alchemists, matter has a divine aspect; either God was imprisoned there as "the *anima mundi* or *anima media natura,* or matter represented God's 'reality.'"[44] In his psychological opus, the intervention of the spirit in life and matter generates a tendency to spiritualize the "body" in the formation of the "*corpus glorificationis,* the resurrected body."[45] There is, in other words, a sublimation of matter and concretization of the spirit, which, at a more practical level, refers to seeing material events as synchronistic and symbolic, while psychological and spiritual realizations become incarnated in life.

Jung's *coniunctio* experiences in 1944 involved the whole person in an elevated spiritualization process that included a feeling relationship with the *unus mundus.* It seems to follow his discussion in *Mysterium Coniunctionis* and elsewhere, that the whole person includes the subtle body. It is not without significance that his visions involve images from Greek, Jewish and Christian mysticism. There were celebrations as the Greek All-Father Zeus and Hera consummated the *hierosgamos*; there was the marriage of Malkuth with Tifereth as indicated in the Kabbalistic tradition, where, Jung recounts: "At bottom it was I myself. I was the marriage. And my beatitude was that of a blissful wedding;" and, further, he writes, "I was the 'Marriage of the Lamb' of the Christian Book of Revelation."[46] There were "ineffable states of joy. Angels were present and light."[47] Meanwhile, Jung was enthralled by

---

43   Jung, 1974, p. 535.
44   *Ibid.*, p. 537.
45   *Ibid.*, pp. 535, 536.
46   Jung, 1983, p. 294.
47   *Ibid.*

the magic of his environment, while his nurse took on the glamor of a saintly, old Jewish woman charged with the responsibility of preparing ritual kosher dishes for him. In keeping with the meaning behind the enchantment, at times, Jung identified with Rabbi Simon Ben Jochai, the Kabbalist of the early nineteenth century; for whom there is a legend about his mystic marriage being celebrated in the afterlife.

It is as if to say that, in Jung's wholeness, he brought to fulfillment all three spiritual traditions that are ultimately intrinsic to the unfolding Western culture. These three traditions are integral to Christianity: the Jewish heritage and Christianity itself being self-evident; the Greek heritage including the Stoics through Paul, neo-Platonism through Augustus and others, and Aristotle through Aquinas. Prior to these visions Jung suffered a heart attack and broke his foot, suggesting a kinship with the astrological Pisces, which is bodily related to the feet.

These wounds, which require healing, also point to the archetype of the wounded healer, especially Chiron, the original wounded healer, whose foot was poisoned with the blood of the hydra from an arrow launched by the bow of the hero, Hercules, which Chiron purposely dropped on his left foot. His healing took the form of trading immortality for the right to die and mortality, which allowed Prometheus to release fire from the Underworld for the benefit of humankind. This legend suggests the deepest healing, which is in service to humanity and cannot evade the reality of physical death. In fact, Jung's aforementioned experiences are often referred to as his death experiences. He wrote: "I hung on the edge of death … I was close to death"; and his subsequent works, especially, are the result of surrender to a greater power and are in service to God and humanity.[48]

The Christian aeon took place during the Age of Pisces and involves two fishes, according to astrological speculation: the good fish as Christ and the evil fish as the devil. It involves the differentiation

---

48   *Ibid.*, p. 289

of good and evil, but at an unconscious level. Jung's mission, it is fair to say, is to bring healing to the modern and postmodern minds at the end of the Age of Pisces. It involves achieving conscious wholeness by integrating the *complexio oppositorum*, the complex of opposites, to conscious awareness. By bringing consciousness and differentiated fulfillment to the Christian aeon in his own person, where healing the heart and the foot can be taken to symbolize healing of the Piscean psyche, Jung shows the way to healing the heart of the split modern and postmodern minds, while demonstrating the way forward to the Age of Aquarius, the Age of the Holy Spirit. The Age of Aquarius is reflected in his work inasmuch as it is dedicated to the formation of individuated individuals as conscious receptacles of truth, capable of receiving and emanating the spirit, water carriers and water pourers of Aquarius iconography.

If attaining wholeness is the goal of life, then how is it that Christ counsels his disciples to be perfect? The meaning of the word *perfect* as it is normally understood today is "without flaw or error." With this understanding, the commandment "You must therefore be perfect just as your Father in Heaven is perfect" (*Matthew* 5: 48) is impossible to fulfill. The language of the people at the time of Jesus was Aramaic, and the word used for perfect was "*gĕmar*," a verb meaning "to complete."[49] The Hebrew equivalent is *tam*, and it normally means perfect, complete, wholesome.[50] The Greek word used in Matthew 5:48 is *teleios*, which means perfect, complete.[51] When the word *perfect* is understood in terms of becoming complete and whole, then it makes more sense and harmonizes with the goal of the individuation process as presented by Jung. Completeness in this way ultimately refers to the realization of the archetypal psyche as a complex of opposites.

The Christian path emphasizes the individual finding the treasure

---

49   Heartlight, Inc., 2001–2011.
50   *Ibid.*
51   Kypros-net, Inc.

in his soul, immortality and the Kingdom of Heaven. If that is the case, then the question arises: what about the collective, the society, the family, the here and now of the nation of people, which was the major concern of the ancient Hebrews in their Covenant with God, and which Rabbi Neusner finds missing in Jesus's message? Benedict XVI's response is that, with Christ, the Covenant with Israel was universalized and the new family is based on "adherence to Jesus himself to his Torah."[52] Specifically, universalization of the Covenant and the creation of a new family is the result of following Christ's command to his disciples to "go, therefore, make disciples of all the nations" (*Matthew* 28: 19).

The new family consists of individuals who belong to a community of faithful, who "call God Father" through communion with Jesus in God's Will.[53] Although one can appreciate the significance of universalizing a spiritual truth, nonetheless, the emphasis on the here and now of the Jewish tradition does seem to have become somewhat relativized in the process. Opening up the Judaic truth of submission to the Will of a monotheistic God to the spirit of universalization eventually led to the separation of Church and State. Given the spread of Christianity across different communities and cultures, there was a need to overcome the inevitable problems caused by the imposition of theocratic rule, which can be overly narrow, conservative and repressive, on different cultural complexes, values and attitudes. And given the complexity of the unfolding nature of the manifest deity over time, this requirement has become an unending evolutionary issue, requiring considerable vigilance. Yet, universalization of Christian teaching also offers a widened field for the expression of human freedom and the search for individual truth to be accommodated within the collective; in the long run, it fosters individuation of both the individual and the community.

Although Jesus felt it necessary to rail against the hypocrisy of

---

52   2007, p. 115.
53   *Ibid.*, p. 117.

the Pharisees in their application of the Law, the dogma, tradition and doctrine of the Church can also be repressive to the contemporary individual. From a psychological point of view, religious institutions have their place and educational value, but for those destined for more conscious individuation, there is a need to find their own unique path that may carry them outside of any institutional authority. At any rate, in the contemporary West, a large percentage of people do not find the Church answers to their spiritual needs. Although the incarnation of Christ defines the spiritual value of individuals and their need to participate in their own redemption, by and large, institutionalized Christianity encourages the humanization of life, while repressing the natural psyche. The result has been a split between the mind and the body with its healthy instincts, a phenomenon that contemporary Roman Catholicism is trying to come to terms with in Jean-Paul II's theology of the body, which Thomas Cahill finds "painfully abstract."[54]

The teachings attempt to make sexuality and sexual desire sacred in the context of Christianity by emphasizing that we are all, male and female, made in the image of God.[55] We can give ourselves as a gift in love to our spouse through the body, which makes visible the divine. By way of exemplary prototypes, the teachings allude to the marriage of Adam and Eve at the beginning of time and later, Jesus, styled as the Groom with his bride, the Church. Through original sin, and the contemporary influence of popular media and present-day societal values, people have moved away from this simple truth that requires sincere giving and receiving in mutual love. The theology of the body stresses the sacred and the need to relate the body and sexual desire to the divine—in Jung's terms, the Self.

These teachings may well have a healing effect for some people. However, were the Church ever able to accept Mary Magdalene as the spouse of Christ, as is recorded in The [Gnostic] Gospel according to

---

54   2013, p. 281n.
55   God, Sex, and the Meaning of Life Ministry, 2014.

Mary Magdalene and in various legends, there would be a much more embodied and humanized example for people to emulate. Even if understood as legendary, its truth would shine through. It would be much less abstract and would have the effect of minimizing theory and ideology, making the divine image of the *mysterium coniunctionis* readily available to each and every marriage, while empowering sexuality with sacred potential.

A major challenge to the Western psyche, in fact, involves a return to the Goddess tradition and the pagan psyche, without losing the humanization of culture and growth in consciousness brought about through the advance of Christianity. According to Thomas Cahill, the unique contribution of Judaism to the West includes the value of individuals as images of God, democracy, responsible engagement with time and history which has a beginning and an end, and the value of worldly freedom.[56] Yet, as Joseph Campbell writes, in Europe, Judeo-Christianity was "pasted on top" of the nature-oriented mythology that was already there.[57]

The imposition of a patriarchal Jewish culture with its emphasis on social order rather than nature led to repression of the natural psyche, the Goddess and the pagan world. Campbell also shows how in Judaism the Goddess and her wisdom was covered up, although, as he observes, she always returns, as is evident in the ongoing transformation to near-Goddess status of the Virgin Mary in Christianity. There is a need, for individuals and the culture as a whole, to assist in her return. This difficulty must not be underestimated, since the repression of the Western psyche involves enhancing Christian and related aesthetic values and decorum that it believes admirable and subduing qualities it considers undesirable. What needs acceptance are values and qualities that sympathetically relate, on the one hand, with the ecology of the natural world and, on the other hand, the archetypal and instinctive

---

56   1998, pp. 245–252 passim.
57   2013, p. 234.

psyche that, for the most part, have been rejected. As is evident in the foregoing example of a dream of Jung's, the natural psyche has exigencies that may seem frightening to people raised to always be pleasant and socially adapted.

Marie-Louise von Franz reports a dream of Jung's, where "Wotan, Tiw and Thor (a triad of the same god) had entered the country demanding that a house should be built for them."[58] Jung said, "They are among other things the dark, murderous side of God."[59] Here is a living example of an important demand from the pagan collective unconscious for realization in the contemporary material world. There is a need for conscious assimilation of this triad of a god, along with its values and qualities, without which there is potential disaster.

Here we have three aspects of the same god, Wotan, who can be said to embody "the spirit of the unconscious psyche, the spirit of nature."[60] When there is no conscious dialogue with this archetypal personality, it acts autonomously and can carry people away in a dangerous and destructive frenzy as happened with Nazi Germany or occurs with possessed individuals. When related to consciously, the same god brings understanding of how to deal with the perils of the unconscious on both a collective and an individual basis. As a *mercurius-duplex* figure, he is also a *psychopompos* that potentially weaves a full life of conscious individuation and the embodiment of wisdom.

An excellent literary example of the embodiment of a positive Wotan figure is Gandalf of *The Lord of the Rings*, where Wotan's destructive shadow is depicted by Gandalf's knowledgeable colleague, Saruman, with all his murderous and destructive ambitions. Gandalf is

---

58   As reported in Wertenschlagg-Birkhauser, 2009, p. 68.
59   *Ibid.*
60   *Ibid.*, p. 69.

the architect of the drama and he has the knowledge and sensibility to deal with all the dark forces. He is able to resist the cunning temptations of his direct counterpart, Saruman, who, through pride, became a psychopathic black magician. Gandalf is also the guiding intelligence and force behind the four hobbits' heroic quest and maturation, and the return of Aragorn to his rightful seat of power as King, the governing ruler of life and the community. In the following three chapters I discuss the current status of the evolutionary impetus, first, by examining contemporary society, then, the individual and the transformation of community and, finally, the creation of Auroville, an international society based on the ideal of human unity in south India.

CHAPTER 11

Contemporary Society

Contemporary society is organized on very different principles altogether than those discussed below regarding the creation of Auroville; its principles have nothing to do with becoming more conscious of the group-soul or adopting that as a guiding cultural matrix. Global capitalism, with profits as the main goal, is the principal engine of cultural formation today, frankly based on satisfying needs of all kinds, some fundamental, and others stimulated desires; alongside it is science, largely propelled by the requirements of the military-industrial complex and consumer-based operations. Technological research and production for military purposes in the United States and other countries has attained a level of sophistication that borders on science fiction in its robotic capacity and micro technology that is frightening to contemplate. Such technology is also fast becoming accessible to individuals and terrorist groups, its destructive capability and effectiveness far surpassing human moral capacity and understanding. The consumer society has encouraged hedonistic goals and narcissistic attitudes and values as, for instance, exemplified in the startling fact that pornography and pornography-related messages constitute some 33 percent of Internet and e-mail traffic.

Although there is little room for the expression of the group-soul, humanistic concerns and liberal ideas, including the exercise of individual human rights, have a background influence. Western classical and romantic traditions have also receded into the background, as has Christianity as a dominant cultural influence. Popular culture highlights not the group-soul, nor individuals in touch with the psychic being or individual soul, but sports heroes and heroines along with entertainers, more often than not living in a vulgar manner. Yet, they have an inordinately large influence on contemporary life and culture.

People today are generally driven by narrow ambition for economic success according to what the culture and the economy make available, rather than by noble ideals or aspiration for psychic transformation and conscious individuation. The gods of the contemporary secular culture are science, the application of science for the sake of commercial gain, and consumerism. As early as *The Red Book,* Jung decries science as a "prison master who binds the soul and imprisons it in a lifeless cell."[1] Consumerism is driven by desires and worship of inferior gods, and not true needs; and whereas in a more spiritual society, there is self-discipline, in today's secular society, there is license and psychic confusion.

The paucity of religious and spiritual values has been filled by increasing street-drug consumption and growth in gangs, as a locus of identity, and gang violence. As unemployment rates in the developed world suggest, while there is greater wealth amongst a select few at the top, with outrageous levels of remuneration, there is a growing population of disenfranchised individuals. In some Third World countries, an increasing need for the expression of a popular demand for democracy is often, on the one hand, aided by a Western coalition military presence and, on the other, by the computer social network. We are also beginning to witness an outburst of mindless violence throughout the world including in wealthy nations, thanks to aimlessness and a meaningless existence, again, assisted by social media.

In either case, an undercurrent of explosive chaos seems to float under an apparent, if somewhat dubious or tenuous social order without a meaningful center. These sometimes senseless actions against the social order are aided by computer images along with mobile phone texting, which puts people in a light trance or otherwise bypasses the intellect and moral order by directly stimulating the desire nature,

---

1   2009, p. 238.

including the desire to destroy for its own sake and pleasure in looting. Meanwhile, Africa often boils in rebellious turmoil, along with horrible existential conditions of drought and the tragic reality of endless poverty and hunger.

Social media also lends itself to the possibility of interpersonal indignities of all kinds. Moreover, in addition to the undeniably positive value of the computer, for instance for ease of research and communication, it tends to promote and facilitate different modes of escapism and narcissistic manipulations, affecting contemporary cultural values and attitudes and, more ominously, democratic elections. Societies that believe in freedom of expression do not know how to handle this new personal technology, nor are they cognizant enough of the difference between license and ethical freedom, or how to implement adequate disciplinary measures without being oppressive. Widespread surveillance by governments, allegedly for security purposes, and by other bodies, like Google, with manipulative commercial interests, violates codes of privacy with impunity. There are other more personal breaches of individual privacy, further reflecting the present moral confusion.

The danger of these trends is dramatized in a book by Dave Eggers called *The Circle*. Individual privacy is systematically removed for the sake of transparency, purportedly for security purposes and, otherwise, for the well-being of the community.[2] In the process individual and cultural history are effectively deleted from the psychological equation. Neglected are the rights of privacy and confidentiality, the needs of the natural person and the place of the cultural complex in self-understanding. Otherwise, in his book *The End of Absence,* Michael Harris argues that our need for solitude is assaulted by the constant stream of messages that fill the computer screen.[3] Neither personal morality nor collective morality has caught up with the psychological and social effects

---

2   2014.

3   Harris, Michael. "Are we connected, or are we chained?" *National Post*, Toronto. August 15, 2014, p. A9.

of often trance-inducing contemporary technology and issues of how to deal with it. Rather, crass individualism, without Eros and the true laws of relatedness, is promoted in a postmodern culture that lacks a center.

Out of the mist of this social and cultural disorientation, however, are signs of religious, spiritual and cultural rebirth, including Christianity itself as a cultural force, and a deep yearning in the hearts and souls of people everywhere for life to be organized more meaningfully. The state funeral for the Honourable Jack Layton, Leader of the Opposition in the Canadian federal parliament and party head of the New Democratic Party, which elicited an unprecedented and unexpected outpouring of heartfelt emotions from ordinary members of the public, is indicative of this yearning. He touched his fellow Canadians in a letter written to them from his deathbed, where he recommends love, hope and optimism in place of anger, fear and despair, as a path toward the future. What seems to have most moved people was Jack's genuine goodness, lack of guile and inclusiveness. However, as Layton was a politician, who functioned in the extraverted world of political exigencies, his message can easily become lost in the political arena and the river of time. Layton died on August 22, 2011, and his sentiments already seem to reflect another age and another zeitgeist.

A Jungian perspective on the future is in fundamental agreement with the Mother's position, which I discuss below. Edward Edinger observes that "Jung has penetrated to the root-source of all religion and culture and thus has discovered the basis for a new organic syncretism of human knowledge and experience."[4] He goes on to note that "the revolutionary consequences" for humans and their view of themselves and the world are immense.[5] Dourley argues on the basis of Jungian assumptions that there is a need to realize the creative source behind religion, secular society and culture.

Following Jung's observation, this realization requires individuals

---

4   1972, p. xiii.
5   *Ibid.*

being highly self-organized and whole in their individuality, a monumental task that demands serious dedication to the individuation process and the symbolic life. It requires a living relationship with the Self
and the collective unconscious. According to Dourley, Jung envisages
the "archetypal unconscious ever seeking greater historical incarnation
in individual and collectivity progressively enriched by such expression and the more universal compassion it carries with it."[6] Any abiding change in society comes through creative individuals, who, on a
personified level, have earned some relationship with the *Anthropos*,
the source of the archetypal unconscious for both individuals and society. A far-reaching solution for the rebirth of individual and society,
for Jung, ultimately requires lonely individuals forging a relationship
with the *unus mundus*, "the eternal ground of all empirical being." and
creative matrix of life.[7]

With considerable cogency, Dourley argues that, given their affinity to the mystic Jacob Boehme, "Hegel is Jung's philosopher" and
Jung can be considered the former's "psychologist."[8] Hegel is Jung's
philosopher, that is, as long as one detaches his thought from his one-
sided championing of a victorious Christianity. Of particular relevance
here is the fact that both Hegel and Jung understand the identity between humans and the divine, that humans are the divine's eyes and
ears of self-conscious discriminating consciousness, and that unfolding
consciousness reflects the progressive incarnation of the deity. In this
light, Hegel, Dourley observes, is more precise than Jung in declaring
that "the movement of the mind is to its identity with its origins, an
origin itself ever active in the movement toward its full expression in
conscious humanity."[9]

Rather than calling Hegel Jung's philosopher and Jung, Hegel's

---

6   2014, p. 16.
7   1974c, p. 534.
8   2014, 135, 108–169 passim.
9   *Ibid.*, p. 133.

psychologist, I would rather say that Jung brings Hegel's thought to fulfillment. This is reflected both in the former's conceptual thinking as well as in his developed psychological praxis, which, from a spiritual point of view, amounts to yoga. In alchemical terms, evidence suggests that although there is tension in Hegel's writings between the three and the four, which is typical for alchemists, he remained predominantly a trinitarian thinker, which, from Jung's perspective, is deficient. Hegel's philosopher's stone, the Self, for instance, is triadic whereas for Jung it is symbolized as both a circle and a quaternity.[10]

Throughout this study, I demonstrate the spiritual and psychological relevance of the number four for the realization of wholeness and truth. Jung, in contrast to Hegel, shows evidence of having realized the four and did not just waver between three and four, conceptually, especially marked in his book *Aion* in the chapter "The Structure and Dynamics of the Self."[11] In his psychology the movement from three to four is essential for embodying wholeness. Thus, he writes: "Psychologically, however, three—if the context indicates that it refers to the self—should be understood as a defective quaternity, or as a stepping-stone towards it …. From the circle and quaternity motif is derived the symbol of … wonder working stone."[12] According to Jung, the philosopher's stone arises from both the circle and the quaternity and not the triad as Hegel proposes.

Given Jung's recognition of the *unus mundus* as the creative womb of life and his own recorded feeling experiences of the *unus mundus*, which I discuss below, I also think that it is fairer to Jung to emphasize that his experiences reflect the psyche's movement to its near-identity with its origins. In this light, the fact that Hegel's thought seems more precise than Jung's in defining the movement of the mind to its identity with its origins, as Dourley claims, is of relative merit only

---

10   Glenn Magee, 2008, p. 212.
11   1975a, p. 222–269 passim.
12   *Ibid.*, p. 224.

in comparison with Jung's documented experiences with the *unus mundus*. I use the expression *near-identity* rather than *identity* given the differentiation I make, using Sri Aurobindo's classification of the mind, between the Overmind, which I relate to the *unus mundus*, and the Supermind, the true creative source of life. I reflect on this distinction further in chapter 19.

Given the Mother's relationship with the creative source of life, the Supermind, her vision for the future is a genuine antidote for an imploding culture. The development of the soul, both individual and group, is in the forefront of her concerns. She envisions neither a hierarchy based on top-down authoritarianism nor living in a sea of chaos or rebelliousness, but a quest to live in harmony with both the individual and group souls, through relationship with the Avatar and Divine Mother as emanations of the *Anthropos*. This vision is her answer to contemporary woes and is essential to bring in the true culture of the future. The unfolding creative process involves progressive transformation beginning with the psychic being, through the different levels of the spiritual mind, and then the Supermind, the Truth-Mind. The importance of the creative individual in the transformation of the community, which I examine in the following chapter, cannot be overestimated.

CHAPTER 12

Individuals and the
Transformation of Community

Jung's psychology has a healing message for contemporary people
with modern and postmodern minds who feel they have nowhere to
go. It contains a message that synthesizes the essence of both the
Jewish and Christian paths, although it requires a turning within and
intentional engagement in the individuation process to find it. As with
Christianity, there is emphasis on the individual; and, as with Judaism,
although defined psychologically, the goal is holiness or wholeness
and completeness, and not perfection in the narrow sense of the word.
Following the Judaic emphasis on the here and now, the individuation
process and the goal of wholeness does not involve identifying with
optimistic ideals but living consciously within the bounds of one's
nature, for the simple reason that only by accepting the limits of one's
fate is there individuation and the potentiality to discover the inborn
law of life.

Thus, according to Jung "every individual has the law of his life
inborn in him"; the individuation process requires one to consciously
follow this law in order to fulfill one's unique life, "become a personality," and achieve wholeness.[1] Becoming a personality does not require genius but the ability to cope with the changing demands of life
and, in that way, to become a leader and guide to others. Requirements
for individuation are detachment from collective institutional beliefs,
values and standards, and shifting focus from the ego and the adap-

---

1   1974d, p. 179.

tive persona to the Self. Individuation means individual distinctiveness and differentiation from the collectivity, while overcoming identity with the unconscious, which is mythologically depicted as deliverance from the mother. Since it requires separation from both the unconscious and the collective, a feeling of isolation arises which in turn requires having fidelity in the sense of "trustful loyalty" to the law of one's being and to psychological development through psychic integration.[2] Individuation ultimately involves finding one's vocation that, writes Jung, "acts like the law of God from which there is no escape."[3] The individuation process carries one naturally to the Self as the goal of life, where the individual Self is the Self of all.

The goal of the individuation process is the Self, which, according to Jung, is eternal and infinite and comes with a feeling of immortality. He refers to the Hindu *Atman* in its individual and cosmic aspects, which, he says, "form an exact parallel to the idea of the self and the *filius philosophorum.* "[4] He writes, "The self as such is timeless and existed before any birth."[5] Elsewhere, he observes that the "urge to individuation gathers together what is scattered and multifarious, and exalts it to the original form of the One, of the Primordial Man."[6] Jung's choice of language here suggests he is referring to experience of the *unus mundus*, which I discuss below, rather than dissolution in the transcendent non-dual Reality. The approximation to the reconstitution of the primordial condition results from the "incorruptible" or "eternal" character of the Self, which, notes Jung, is "pre-existent to consciousness."[7] Thus, the individuation process potentially involves far-reaching transformation and divinization. To be more explicit, in

---

2   *Ibid.*, p. 173.
3   *Ibid.*, p. 178.
4   Jung, 1970d, p. 265.
5   *Ibid.*, p. 184.
6   Jung, 1975c-6, p. 265.
7   *Ibid.*

an exegesis on Simon Magus, Jung refers to the 'transformation of the vital spirit in man into the Divine'."[8]

The individuation process involves an intensified effort to become more conscious, where new consciousness emerges from the unconscious. When an archetype is unconscious, there is no differentiation and no potential for an abiding change of personality. It is only latent with a potential to become conscious, as opposites contained in the Pleroma cancel each other out. Archetypes require conscious perception in order to be differentiated as an archetypal image, which initiates a concomitant transformation of consciousness. Jung writes that consciousness is "something like perception" and that, with a shift in consciousness, *"It is not that something different is seen, but that one sees differently."*[9] Consciousness occurs at various levels, at different depths of being and over a field of vision of greater or lesser breadth. There are, consequently, both differences of degree and differences of kind in consciousness, as Jung asserts, "since they depend on the development of personality, that is to say, the perceiving subject."[10] Ultimately, then, it is the subjective individual and not his thoughts or feelings per se that are relevant to consciousness and individuation.

The goal of individuation is the discovery of one's unique being, and not achieving a virtuous life or worshiping at the altar of culturally and collectively defined beauty or truth, since these qualities always coexist with their shadow opposites. The greater the ardor spent on the one-sided effort to be virtuous or aesthetic, virtuous or aesthetic, or defending one's truth, the more likely is one afflicted by evil, falsehood and ugliness. By following the urges put forth by the principal of individuation, the Self, one potentially attains wholeness and a proper balance between the many opposites that have become conscious for the individual. Since some of the opposites are conscious and no longer

8   *Ibid.*, p. 237.
9   1975 c-4, p. 546.
10   *Ibid.*, p. 547.

latent in the collective unconscious, there is potential for consciousness of an inner division which requires the realization that virtue and an aesthetic disposition attain value only when exercised against the background interplay of their shadow.

To keep the foregoing statements in perspective, the following observation made by Jung is relevant: "The unconscious is an irrepresentable totality of all subliminal psychic functions, a 'total vision' *in potentia*."[11] "It constitutes," he argues, "the total disposition from which consciousness singles out fragments from time to time."[12] Although this statement seems to suggest that there will always be more material to emerge from the unconscious into consciousness, Jung also sees the coming age of the Holy Spirit as a time when the original oneness of the unconscious is brought to consciousness. Oneness of the unconscious brought to consciousness does not preclude the fact of their always being more emergent consciousness, although it does suggest a very different perceptive subject, operating out of genuine wholeness and unitary being, no longer in thrall to ignorance.

The following excerpt from a letter, dated June 3, 1957, from Jung to his foremost disciple, Erich Neumann, helps to differentiate Jung's position regarding sin, the shadow and good and evil.[13] Neumann proposes a new ethic to replace the Judeo-Christian code, which he feels is ineffectual and, given the findings of depth psychology, out of date. Jung's view is more realistic and psychologically nuanced than Neumann's, which Jung believes overestimates the capacity of consciousness and undervalues the compensatory nature of the unconscious. He writes:

> For it is not really a question of a "new ethic." Evil is and remains what you know you shouldn't do. But unfortunately, man overestimates himself in this respect: he thinks he is free

11   *Ibid.*, p. 551.
12   *Ibid.*
13   As reported in Gerhard Adler, ed., 1975.

to choose evil or good. He may imagine he can, but in reality, considering the magnitude of these opposites, he is too small and impotent to choose either the one or the other voluntarily and under all circumstances. It is rather that for reasons stronger than himself, he does not do the good he would like, in exactly the same way that evil comes upon him as a misfortune.

An ethic is that which makes it impossible for him deliberately to do evil and urges him—often with scant success—to do good. That is to say, he can do good but cannot avoid evil even though his ethic impels him to test his strength of his will in this regard. In reality he is the victim of these powers. He is forced to admit that under no circumstances can he avoid doing evil absolutely, just as on the other side he may cherish the hope of being able to do good. Since evil is unavoidable, he never quite gets out of sinning and this is the fact that has to be recognized. It gives rise not to a new ethic but to differentiated ethical reflections such as the question: How do I relate to the fact that I cannot escape sin?[14]

Jung calls for holding fast to Judeo-Christian virtues along with differentiated ethical reflections, requiring conscious Eros and feeling, in order to come to terms with evil and not simply an ethic that includes conscious recognition of the shadow. Reflection is the human cultural instinct par excellence that can stand against any meaningless and disturbing drive such as sexual and other drivenness, power ambition, greed, excessive aggressiveness and so on.

Good and evil, and beauty and ugliness are human value judgments that vary according to historical time and culture. Perceptive subjects are conscious according to the status of their personality and no more. That means that in the present world of ignorance, one has to always contend with the intrusive phenomena of unconscious complexes of various kinds and, in many cases, personality disorders, mood disorders and other disorders of personality, or worse. There are also the well-known phenomena of psychic epidemics that can overcome entire

---

14   *Ibid.*, p. 364.

populations, taking advantage of peoples' ignorance. In addition to the virtues and a sense of beauty, and the capacity for self-reflection, recognizing the shadow side of life helps come to terms with evil. At least, its integration into consciousness is essential for individuation and achieving a balanced personality and wholeness, and dealing with evil. But, integration of shadow aspects to consciousness does not mean one acts out unconsciously, but that the formerly unsavory shadow becomes transformed and the personality enhanced, or, at the least, one consciously bears and suffers the shadow aspect of one's personality. From the point of view of increasing consciousness (the integration of personality and uniqueness of being), the opposite of consciousness (Ignorance, as well as non-being and the annihilation of being) can be regarded as evil. Becoming increasingly conscious in the sense of bringing more of the unconscious to consciousness is a *sine qua non* for dealing with shadow and other projections, ignorance and evil. Self-reflection and adherence to Christian and/or other virtues are essential to the process of integration and the transformation of shadow.

The individuation process is not only dependent on emerging new consciousness, but also on the formation of distinctive being and a differentiated conscious personality. This realization requires relationship with the transcendent function that syntheses the opposites as a third point, ultimately leading to the self-creative individuated personality. Jung goes so far as to foresee a far-reaching transformation of personality as an intrinsic creative aspect of the Age of Aquarius. He writes: "A new man, a completely transformed man, is to appear on the scene, one who has broken the shell of the old and who not only looks upon a new heaven and a new earth, but has created them."[15] This remarkable statement is in complete harmony with the goal of Sri Aurobindo and the Mother's Integral Yoga.

Not surprisingly, Sri Aurobindo's views are identical to Jung's

---

15   Jung, 1975, p. 547.

on the need for individual transformation in line with one's unique truth, and are beautifully expressed in his book, *Essays on the Gita.* According to chapter 18, verse 47 of the *Bhagavad Gita:* "Better is one's *Swadharma*, one's self-law, though in itself faulty, than an alien law well wrought out. When one does the work regulated by one's self-nature one does not incur sin."[16] Following one's inner law, declares Sri Aurobindo, means doing work "according to the truth within us" and "should not be an accommodation with outward and artificial standards, it must be a living and sincere expression of the soul and its inborn powers."[17] To follow one's *Swadharma* according to one's soul-force and inner truth of being is the path to living "in oneness with God and our true self."[18]

Both Jung and Sri Aurobindo recognize the primary importance of the creative individual and individual transformation with regard to the transformation of culture and the community. Here there is full recognition of the Hebrew concern for the here and now and community, although the response is more psychological, inwardly directed and creative than in contemporary Judaism. Thus, writes Jung, "The psychology of masses is always inferior, even in the most idealistic enterprises."[19] Although idealism can motivate an interest in a creative new way of life, it can actually get in the way of genuine transformation, unless it is grounded in practical reality. Otherwise, the group-mind always functions in a way that is inferior to that of the progressive individual.

Jung is wary of the regressive pull of the mass-mind and stresses the importance of the individual's relationship with the Self and the numinous, the only genuine agent of psychological transformation. He writes: "The approach to the numinous is the real therapy and inasmuch

16   Jhunjhunwala, 1974, p. 225.
17   1970b, p. 507.
18   *Ibid.*
19   1976d, p. 571.

as you attain to the numinous experiences you are released from the curse of pathology."[20] Rather than causing disturbances to others because of unassimilated shadow and unconscious psychological complexes of various kinds, the individual becomes a potentially creative contributor to the community. To be realized, individuation needs to proceed along the lines of increasing individual distinctiveness in opposition to collective values. Thus, according to Jung, "resistance to the mass can be effected only by the individual which is as well organized in his individuality as the mass itself."[21] There is a continuous and challenging need to deflect societal and institutional pressures, and to align oneself to the Self, with all its power of forming unique and distinctive personalities and relational connectedness.

Elsewhere, stressing the importance of the creative individual, Jung makes the following observation: "The sole and natural carrier of life is the individual, and that is so throughout nature."[22] It is, in fact, an accurate observation that changes in animal life are initiated by a single individual and then transmitted to other individual animals of the same species in the environs, as the observed example of the first potato-cleaning monkeys attests. It is evident in the animal kingdom that the individual does not function apart from the herd. For humans, too, the whole purpose of life is not to form a conscious personality apart from the community, even if individuation forces external isolation. Although, from one point of view, the community is merely an agglomeration of individuals, it is an important formative container that conditions life, with which the creative individual can develop a conscious relationship.

The process of individuation itself "brings to birth consciousness of human community," since it makes one aware of the archetypal unconscious, which is universal and common to humankind, to both

---

20   Jung 1973, p. 377.
21   1972e, p. 278.
22   1970c, p. 106.

individuals and the community.[23] Hence, "the organized accumulation
of [conscious] individuals," observes Jung, "will result in the formation no longer of an anonymous mass but of a conscious community,"[24]
where individuals develop a conscious relationship to the community
soul.

Regarding the formation of a conscious community, Sri Aurobindo
writes: "A change of this kind, the change from the mental and vital to
the spiritual order of life, must necessarily be accomplished in a great
number of individuals before it can lay any effective hold upon the community .... It is through the progressive and formative individual that
it offers the discovery and the chance of a new self-creation."[25] For the
communal mind holds things subconsciously at first or, if consciously,
then in a confused chaotic manner."[26] Both Jung and Sri Aurobindo are
in agreement that individuated individuals, individuals having undergone some psychic and spiritual transformation, are required to bring
to birth new creative formations and conscious community. By forming
individual relationships to the soul of the community through the Self,
the energy, ideas and creative formations of individuals can break the
tendency toward the uniformity of the collective ego.

Jung makes astute observations that bring some understanding to
bear on how this transformation from collective thinking to becoming
a more individuated, unique personality can transpire and how personal
psychological issues relate to social concerns. Like Sri Aurobindo, he
observes that "it is always single individuals who are moved by the collective problem," and not the mass, which can only follow the progressive and form-creating individual.[27] Individuals of destiny are drawn
by their nature to suffer societal problems as a matter of fate, and, having suffered the problem, they may find creative solutions. Here, I am

23   *Ibid.*, p. 108.
24   *Ibid.*
25   1971a, p. 231.
26   *Ibid.*
27   Jung, as quoted in Jacobi & Hull, 1974, p. 296.

particularly referring to people who have been drawn into the individuation process, which involves being subjected to meaningful suffering. Others suffer mental disorders, which, from a psychological perspective, are unsuccessful individual attempts to solve collective problems.

The individual, observes Jung, is the "makeweight that tips the scales," and it is in the individual human being that, "if we read the Christian message aright, even God seeks his goal."[28] Everything depends on the individual, for better and for worse, and therefore the significance of the potential accumulation of conscious individuals with their creative resolution of the collective problem is immense. Although it is evident that politically powerful individuals can have a direct effect on the life of the community either positively or negatively, and creative geniuses can move the collective psyche in new directions, what is less appreciated is that, through the individuation process, more ordinary folk can have a positive and creative transformative effect on the community as well.

From the point of view of the individuation process there is discernible psychological development that includes assimilation of the personal shadow, then the anima/animus and the collective shadow, and, finally, the formation of a conscious relationship with the Self. Integration of the shadow means one stops projecting rejected inferior qualities on others, while assimilating their values, often positive, to conscious awareness in oneself. This growth alone not only enhances one's personal life but improves relationship with others. Otherwise, individuals can contribute to the collective shadow that gives birth to countries or communities that become possessed with evil forces (like Nazi Germany), or harden to the point of exhibiting radical intolerance of differences. Individual contribution to the formation of the collective shadow results from ignorance and the undifferentiated individual shadow, for instance, through arrogance, greed, ambition, lust and fear.

---

28   1970e, pp. 304, 305.

The integration of the anima/animus opens one up to contra-sexual values as well as aspects of the archetypal unconscious, enriching consciousness and, potentially, relationships with members of the opposite sex. The psychological work of withdrawing anima/animus projections and enriching consciousness, as indicated here, is already a boon to the community, not only relationally but also in creative terms.

The Individual and Relationship to the Anthropos

Developing an individual relationship to the Self, eventually as the regulating principle of life, is the most significant factor in terms of formative transformation of both the individual and the community. The individual is the sole self-reflective and responsible moral agent; the individual Self is ultimately identical to the universal Self and is, therefore, the creative source of being and profoundly relational. As the Self is the source of psychological wholeness, integration of a relationship with the Self also involves assimilation of a relationship with the collective shadow, the shadow side of the God-image. This effectively means that individuals with a relationship to the Self are not only aware of their own personal shadow, but also their relationship to the collective shadow and, in addition to seeing the positive side of others with whom they are in relationship, they are aware of those individuals' personal shadows and relationship to the collective shadow as well. Conscious awareness of these phenomena is an important ingredient in developing community harmony and creative relationships between people with different backgrounds and predispositions.

As I mention above in the section on *The Unfolding of the Universe*, according to Vedantic teachings of the *Gita*, the *Anthropos* gives birth to the fourfold social order. In Christian Gnosticism, Christ was understood to be the *Archanthropos*, the Original Man and the second Adam. He is androgynous, the inner God-man and goal of gnosis, the "kingdom of heaven within you."[29] "As the *Anthropos*," Jung writes, "he corresponds to the most important archetype and, as judge of the living and the dead and king of glory, to the real organizing principle of the unconscious, the quaternity, or squared circle of the self."[30] Here, Jung refers to the Gnostic Christ figure in light of the importance of Gnosticism for Western culture, as it brings clarity and definition to the prophecies about the coming Messiah, Christ's actual incarnation, and synchronicities around the archetype of his incarnation. He recognizes that the Christ figure is a symbol of the Self and not the other way around; and that can be taken to mean that he sees Christ, the God-man, as an incarnation of the *Anthropos*, the Original Man, whom the Mother calls the "origin of all the Avatars," or "the universal Avatar"—where the Avatar is an incarnation of the Supreme Lord,[31] and the Divine Mother is his *Shakti*, "the Consciousness and Force of the Divine."[32]

In fact, in the Jewish tradition, Saturday is the Sabbath and taken as a celebration of the day that God rested after the creation; it is an opportunity for the believing Jew to rest in holiness, in imitation of God. The Resurrection of Jesus on the first day of the week, Sunday, is the Sabbath for Christians; it is for them the first day, the beginning of creation, the Lord's Day. In a Gnostic myth, as the second Adam and androgynous, similar to the Vedic *Anthropos*, Christ produces from his side a woman, with whom he later unites. This association of Christ with the God of creation suggests Christ was an important avatar in world history. Sri Aurobindo, in fact, argues that "the death of Christ was the starting-point of a new stage in the evolution of human civilization," a point of view that would find no opposition from believing Christians.[33]

---

29   C.G. Jung, 1975a, p. 203, 204.
30   *Ibid.*, p. 204.
31   The Mother, 2004b, p. 333.
32   Sri Aurobindo, 1972a, p. 63.
33   *Ibid.*

The Mother is recorded as indicating that she heard Sri Aurobindo say that Christ was "an emanation of the Lord's aspect of Love" and she observes he is "the concrete and dramatic enactment of the divine sacrifice." In Christianity the original enactment is known as *kenosis*, from Greek meaning "emptying," referring to the relinquishing of the divine attributes for the sake of uplifting humanity through the Incarnation.[34] The Mother sees those attributes of the Supreme Lord as "All-Light, All-Knowledge, All-Power, All-Beauty, All-Love, All-Bliss"; according to her, Christ's holocaust involves "accepting to assume human ignorance and suffering in matter, in order to help men to emerge from the falsehood in which they live and because of which they die."[35] What the Mother says here fully resonates with Christian teaching.

Given the above amplifications, it is evident that, in terms of the potential transformative influence of the individual on society, experience and relationship to the Self as *Anthropos* is of prime significance. All human relatedness is based on the archetype of the Self, the *Anthropos*, which, according to Marie-Louise von Franz, may be the personification of Eros, the principle of relatedness par excellence. She writes:

> The symbol of the Anthropos appears in the individual as their Self, as the very unique inner-most core of his or her individuality, yet at the same time he is represented in myths and religious systems as the "totem" of mankind as the archetypal factor which actively creates all forms of positive human relatedness.[36]

With consciously realized individuation, usual bonds of relationship such as family kinship or common interest are replaced by connectedness through the Self. The bonds of relatedness through the Self connect individuals with others, without discriminating on the basis of cultural differentiation, from the less conscious to the highly

34   Farlex, 2011.
35   2001, p. 61.
36   1975b, p. 35.

individuated. Individuation doesn't divorce one from the world, but realigns one's world around the Self.

CHAPTER 13

Creation of Auroville

I saw the Omnipotent's flaming pioneers
Over the heavenly verge which turns towards life
Come crowding down the amber stairs of birth;
Forerunners of a divine multitude
...
I saw them cross the twilight of an age,
The sun-eyed children of a marvelous dawn,
The great creators with wide brows of calm,
The massive barrier-breakers of the world
...
The architects of immortality.[1]

– Sri Aurobindo

The original creation myth which involves the direct emanation of the *Anthropos,* the Original Person and primary organizing principle of life and society, is once again being enacted, this time thanks to the vision and work of the avatars of our time, Sri Aurobindo and the Mother. I refer to the development of Auroville, an international township and ideal society based on human unity, located in Tamil Nadu, South India. This ideal city is not meant to be a flattened society without a hierarchy, nor one based on external evaluation or family background as is presently the case throughout the world, but a hierarchy based on inner worth and soul-type.

Auroville's immense significance in human history is evident in

---

1   1970a*, pp. 343, 344.

the Mother's message, recorded in 1968, about its reality and purpose and what, in her view, is required to live there. Her message later became the Charter of Auroville. She notes that she didn't write it but that she transcribed what came to her as an imperative:

1. Auroville belongs to nobody in particular. Auroville belongs to humanity as a whole. But to live in Auroville one must be a willing servitor of the Divine Consciousness.
2. Auroville will be the place of an unending education, of constant progress, and a youth that never ages.
3. Auroville wants to be the bridge between the past and the future. Taking advantage of all discoveries from without and from within, Auroville will boldly spring towards future realisations.
4. Auroville will be a site of material and spiritual researches for a living embodiment of an actual human unity. [2]

The wisdom of the Supramental Parashakti, known in the West as *Sophia*, is expressed in these words, describing the way for the realization of the long-sought-for Kingdom of God on Earth. From the point of view of individual psychology, it requires individuals aspiring to live according to the Self as the regulating spirit in the practice of everyday life. It requires becoming conscious of psychological completeness, involving all aspects of one's nature. It involves conscious relatedness to the central temple, the Matrimandir, representing Divine Consciousness and Force, along with connection to the *Anthropos,* the Original Being and origin of all Avatars, the source of wisdom and infinite creativity. It requires becoming conscious of the group-soul.

2   1981a, pp. 51–54.

In harmony with the observations made above on the origins and creation of the fourfold order of society that corresponds to a divine law, the Mother is recorded as saying: "Even if you don't believe it, even if all the circumstances seem quite unfavorable, I KNOW THAT AUROVILLE WILL BE.[3] It may take a hundred years, it may take a thousand years, but Auroville will be because it is DECREED." The city and the appropriate individual and group consciousness to establish Auroville is decreed by a divine fiat. The Mother observes that individual inner discovery is essential for its realization; and beyond desire, she assures us, "At the centre there is a being, free and vast and knowing, who awaits our discovery and who should become the active centre of our being and our life in Auroville."[4] This being is the *Anthropos,* the Original Being and origin of all the Avatars, the source of absolute knowledge and infinitely creative—now, thanks to the work of Sri Aurobindo and the Mother, consciously accessible to aspiring human beings.

Realization of Divine Law and Auroville, the City of the Dawn

As I indicate above, according to ancient Vedantic teachings, the fourfold order of society and the similar fourfold soul-force structuring human nature originally devolved from the *Anthropos*, the Original Being. One learns from the Gita that the Manifestation itself along with the fourfold order of life was "created from the beginning by the Master of existence."[5] According to the *Rig Veda*, the fourfold order of being was derived from the thousand-eyed *Purusha* and later, when sacrificed by the gods, his mind gave forth the Moon, his eye the Sun, his navel the air, and his skull the sky. This teaching asserts: "He is everything that was and everything that will be .... Verily he is the inner Self of

3　　1980, p. 210.
4　　As recorded by Sonia Dyne, 2006.
5　　Sri Aurobindo, 1970b, p. 492.

all sentient beings."⁶ Realization of divine law, accordingly, requires an intimate relationship with the *Anthropos* through the individual Self.

With regard to forming an intimate relationship with the creative *Anthropos* by both individual souls and the group-soul, there is a significant psychological caution. Individual and collective identification with the *Anthropos* that when conscious, can result in inflation and megalomania and, when unconscious, to feelings of inferiority, needs to be an ever-present concern. Essential in such situations is sufficient differentiation of the individual ego personality from the *Anthropos*. According to a letter from Jung to his disciple, James Kirsch, in response to the latter's dream vision of finding himself face to face with the *Anthropos* it requires assiduously defining one's values, especially in relationship to a "stronger will."⁷ It demands scrutinizing and eliminating "pretexts, false reasons and illusions," which often requires suspending answers to questions for a long time, until they are answered "beyond a doubt."⁸ Although Jung is referring to the individual as the carrier of meaning in relationship to the *Anthropos*, the group can be affected by individuals, either in the direction of inflation or towards feelings of inferiority as well.

The Anthropos and the Matrimandir

Accessing the *Anthropos* relates creative individuals to the living truth and the potential for its cultural embodiment. In this regard, it is noteworthy that the Matrimandir, the temple at the center of Auroville, according to the Mother in 1970, "wants to symbolize the Divine's answer to man's aspiration for perfection." It is a "symbol for human aspiration for the Divine," at least as the Mother originally perceived

---

6   As recorded by Marie-Louise von Franz, 1997a, p. 253.
7   As reported in Ann Conrad Lammer's, editor, 2011, pp 261, 262.
8   *Ibid,* 262.

THE MOTHER'S ORIGINAL VISION
FOR THE CENTER OF THE INNER CHAMBER

it.[9] In the same year, she writes further that it "wants to be the symbol of the universal Mother according to Sri Aurobindo's teachings."[10] Again, in 1970, she noted that "the Matrimandir will be the soul of Auroville."[11] These observations by the Mother indicate the importance of the Matrimandir being embodied according to her original vision and not by human aesthetic judgment or other calculations; while a close reading of the Mother's dialogues on the temple suggest the latter is what actually happened.[12]

The Mother's original vision of the inner chamber includes at the center a symbol of the incarnation of the Avatars of our time, Sri Aurobindo and the Divine Mother, in addition to the receptive individual soul in direct relationship to them. When properly realized according to the Mother's actual vision it is a perfect symbol, especially in the context of the inner chamber, with its unadorned walls and

9   2004, p. 223.
10   *Ibid.*
11   *Ibid.*
12   1981a, 1981b.

twelve surrounding pillars, representing the twelve months of the year. Sri Aurobindo and the Mother were embodiments of the *Anthropos,* in its male and female personifications. They are ultimately one, and, together, they are creating the New World, along with participation of the individual soul.

This central configuration consists of Sri Aurobindo's symbol embossed in gold on white marble on each of four sides, placed as if emerging from the Mother's symbol below it, while supporting a translucent globe. It rests on the creative central point and the inner four petals of the Mother's symbol, which refer to four essential aspects of the Mother, *Mahashwari, Mahakali, Mahalakshmi*, and *Mahasaraswati*, each of whom presides over a different soul-type, *brahmin* (priest), *kshatriya* (leader), *vaishya* (trader) and *sudra* (servant), respectively. The individual soul is represented as a translucent globe that is positioned to continually absorb a ray of (supramental) light descending from above. Of considerable interest is the fact that, in addition to the globe receiving and absorbing the light from above, the globe is penetrated from below by the upper apex of the upward-directed triangle of each of the four symbols of Sri Aurobindo. Not only is there a descent from above of the new supramental consciousness, there is a fourfold symbolic penetration from below of the Avatar of our time, in full union with the Divine Mother. There is, in other words, a descent of the new consciousness from above and the upward penetration of the evolutionary dynamis from below, which includes integration of the divine secret hidden in matter, now realized and unveiled.

For the individual and the community, these symbols signify the fourfold psychic, spiritual and supramental transformations of the individual soul according to primary soul-type, as priest, leader, trader and servant, which includes the integration of each of the other soul-types to consciousness. I can't imagine a more complete and perfect symbol of what is essential today in order to create a New World in the present age, the receptive individual soul in relationship with the *Anthropos*. This is the symbol for the New World in the Age of Aquarius, superseding the image of the God-man transfixed to the Cross and the two fishes of the Age of Pisces or even the image of Christ Victorious descended from the Cross. The full significance of the inner chamber and this configuration is esoterically examined in detail by Patrizia Norelli-Bachelet in her document entitled "Chronicles of the Inner Chamber" and elsewhere.

Since the individual soul and the soul of the city are ultimately one, individual self-discovery is essential for the formation of the group-soul. Individual transmutation initially involves what Sri Aurobindo and the Mother refer to as psychic transformation and the emergence of the psychic being, the personal and historical representative of the soul, as the regulating center of one's daily life. In the language of C.G. Jung, such a metamorphosis requires conscious involvement in the individuation process to the point that the Self behind the heart becomes the *spiritus rector* of everyday life. When individuals attain this level of individuation there has been far-reaching personality transformation that can have an inevitably salutary effect on the culture of the community. Such a transformation of individual being and individuation requires personality engagement and transformation at all levels of being—the supramental, the spiritual and the psychic being in relationship to the mental, vital and physical natures—in order to realize psychological completeness and perfection. Many individuals involved in the psychic transformation alone, which, perforce, puts them in direct contact with the archetypal psyche and the divine presence, contribute to the formation of a creative cultural matrix. A direct inner relationship of many individuals with the soul of Auroville and the wisdom of the Self as the all-knowing creative *Anthropos,* however, are required for the full formation of the group-soul as a cultural phenomenon. The group-soul, which otherwise remains an unlived potential, can only then become a conscious living reality.

The influential study of the nature of freedom and its potential betrayal by the liberal philosopher, Sir Isaiah Berlin, is particularly noteworthy in light of the creation of an ideal society.[13] Berlin holds that there are two concepts of liberty, what he refers to as "negative liberty," by which he means the absence of interference with an individual's field of action, and "positive liberty," which refers to self-mastery and mastery over one's environment. Negative liberty is the absence of external obstacles or constraints on an individual's actions. Positive liberty refers to acting in such a way as to enhance an individual's or collectivities' purpose and individuation. Berlin demonstrates that these two definitions of liberty can be incompatible.

Liberal thought generally supports negative liberty, with the argument that individual liberty is best attained by severely limiting the regulating and censorship role of the state. The sacrosanct nature of the Western cry for freedom of speech, with some restraint, is the best example of this form of liberty. Those critical of negative freedom argue that true freedom is the realization of individual and/or collective fulfillment and that this, paradoxically, may require state intervention. This concept of freedom finds support amongst leaders of communist and other totalitarian states as well as well- meaning idealists.

Liberal thinkers look back at the twentieth century and the course of events and totalitarian systems, where individual and collective liberty was severely curtailed, often with a devastating impact. They, therefore, fervently, support the concept of freedom as negatively defined. Isaiah Berlin belongs to this category of liberal thinkers and, after his exhaustive study of liberty, he comes down in full support of the value of plurality and negative freedom, given the destructive history of the twentieth century, with its line of communist and other dictatorships, and their imposition of obstacles to individual freedom, justified by it being done for the sake of uplifting their population with their definition of positive freedom.

In contrast, the liberal solution to general ignorance is through

13   1958, pp. 1-27 passim.

education rather than impositions, ensuring freedom for both individuals and collectivities. Hence, for the sake of demystifying certain beliefs and values, contemporary liberal thinkers support the French satirical weekly magazine *Charlie Hebdo* and its right to publish cartoons, some of which are crude and mocking of Islam, as well as, for that matter, Christianity.[14] Freedom of speech includes the right to insult, whether it is one's own collectivity or others, both individuals and groups.[15] When a radical portion of the outraged target of ridicule reacts by massacring 10 staff members of *Charlie Hebdo* and two police officers, the response is both one of confusion and outrage, although with fervent resolve to defend freedom of speech, no matter how it may affect others who do not share in this belief.

Given the nature of the contemporary global world and the growing proximity of peoples with different beliefs, values, attitudes, traditions and histories, it would be of value to rethink the Western way and the absolute priority it gives to individual freedom. Some people hold brotherhood or equality, or status and recognition as more important than liberty. Sri Aurobindo proposes the religion of humanity, with the triple pillar of liberty, equality and fraternity as essential ingredients, to counteract human egoism, its enemy.[16] The key, he insists, is the power of brotherhood, which can unite equality and liberty. He defines brotherhood as existing in the soul and for the soul and not by any external parameter, whether it be intellectual affinity, physical kinship or vital association. Likewise, freedom and equality are external attributes of the spirit and natural expressions of the soul. The claim for freedom in the soul refers to the freedom for individuation teleologically directed by the Self. The claim for equality in the soul means equality for all, where the individual Self, is the Self of all. By brotherhood in the soul, freedom and equality are based on a common aspiration and the recog-

14   Christopher Hitchens, 2015.
15   Mark Steyn, 2015.
16   1971, p. 541-547 passim.

nition of a common mind and feeling, and spiritual unity. By placing brotherhood at the center of the triumvirate, Sri Aurobindo is promoting the need for recognition of human unity and our common destiny, where aspiration for living in the soul and not the ego is the only way it can be achieved.

In Jungian language, living in the soul, what he refers to as the Self, and genuine brotherhood and fellow feeling requires both Logos and Eros. According to Jung, despite Christ and his message of love and brotherhood, Christianity is "based on Logos" and, despite the force wielded by Islam and the sword of Allah, Islam is "based on Eros."[17] These observations are reflected in the fact that the Logos of Reason, bequeathed from the Greek tradition and the Logos of military might and administrative acumen inherited from the Romans, are highly developed for the former, whereas brotherhood and equality, albeit in the context of a single religion, are more relevant to the latter. Sri Aurobindo writes: "All men are equal in Islam" and "All men are brothers in Islam," although it is limited since exclusive to Islam, and imperfect, since it embraced "rude and undeveloped races."[18] In fact, there are long standing tensions in Middle Eastern, North African and Pakistani Islam that divide Shiite and Sunni as well as different Islamic states and ethnic groups. In the Christian West, keeping with its Logos orientation, there is political equality and attempts to create social equality, but not equality in the soul. The ideal of liberty and freedom of speech is powerful, but "there is no fraternity in this liberty," a perspective that deserves pondering given the strong conflicting emotions apparent in the West with regard to Islamic refugees, some welcoming, although risking sentimental coloration, as well as some harshly rejecting and defensive.[19]

Logos, the Word, refers to the principle of discrimination and

---

17   Barbara Hannah, 2011, p. 193.
18   1972e, p. 757, 758.
19   Sri Aurobindo, 1972f, p. 84.

understanding, while brotherhood and equality require feeling and Eros, the principle of relatedness. The present skirmishing between Christianity and Islam, the West and the Middle East and Pakistan, much more than is normally understood, reflects the challenge for Christianity and the West to assimilate Eros and its values of brotherhood and equality, and Islam to integrate the value of Logos, meaning Reason, and the power of discrimination. A noteworthy fact is that Christianity is a religion concerned with the incarnation of the son of God, where God becomes man, whereas, in the Islamic spiritual (Sufi) tradition, one is encouraged to ascend from the material world to become God. The two religions emphasize opposing spiritual tendencies. The difficulty facing Islam and the West and Christianity is exacerbated by the fact that these two religions and civilizations shadow each other, with much mutual unconsciousness.

True Eros includes the discriminating sword of Logos, without which it is blind and works on the power principle. Contemporary Islam is a culture of the "after-life," where energy and interpretation of the Koran and Sharia law are fully directed toward post-mortem pleasures, the opposite of the here and now life emphasis of secular liberalism that currently rules the West. The deeper truth of Islam understands time as ahistorical and mythic; where historical events are understood *"sub species aeternitatis, "* under the eyes of eternity.[20] In comparison, since the incarnation of Christ, Western history moves in "exterior, literal, material Time" and "quantitative space," without a vertical or mythic dimension.[21] The contrast between these two metaphysical positions cannot be sharper, whereas effective truth enacted in the material world requires their reconciliation.

True Logos, the guiding principle of life, includes Eros, without which there is no heart and, potentially, no active engagement in life, especially with feeling values, as the world is experienced as soulless.

---

20   Tom Cheetham, 2003, p. 10, 11, 1–15 passim.
21   Henry Corbin, as recorded in Tom Cheetham, 2003, 118–140 passim, 134, 135.

The contemporary West is individualistic and separated from the living source. Despite its liberal humanism, Western culture is currently organized according to narcissistic values that clash with religious values of whatever stripe.[22] Recognizing the importance of the relational aspect of learning, authentic dialogue between the West and Islam is essential for mutual education about these different perspectives. In either case, aspiration toward human unity is required; which means, first and foremost, non-exclusive brotherhood in the soul, then freedom and equality, while working through unconscious projections of a collective nature.

The United States and its allies meet contemporary Islam with science and overwhelming military might, and as Gwynne Dyer forcefully argues, America (and the West) has become drawn into the fray in the Middle East as "far enemy" in a terrorist strategy to get Muslims upset with Americans, resistant to occupying forces and supportive of radical Islam. Hundreds of millions of Muslims—Jihadists, Islamists and Fundamentalists, especially from the Middle East, Africa and Pakistan—are implicated.[23] The principal architect of this strategy, at least at the beginning, was Osama bin Laden and (Sunni) Al-Qaeda. Meanwhile, Islamists are fighting the "near enemy" in the Middle East for Islamist dominance and the (2016) establishment of a so-called Sunni Caliphate in Syria and Iraq.[24] The struggle is principally between Sunni and Shiite factions and potentially involves massive structural re-organization. Meanwhile, minions of radical Islam, living abroad, respond to the perceived affront of America and its allies against Islam, with inhuman atrocities that elicit personal feelings of disgust.

Given these considerations, I now return to the subject of Auroville, its goal and purpose and the Mother's guidelines for attaining them. The city is an international township based on the ideal of human unity,

---

22   Anne Manne, 2014.
23   2015, p. 45, 46.
24   *Ibid.*

on the values of brotherhood, out of which emanates equality and freedom. It is open to people from India and all over the world, including
neighboring Tamil villagers, whom the Mother called "Auroville's first
inhabitants."[25] It is meant to be self-supporting and includes an industrial zone in addition to sectors for all activities common to humankind
in the twenty-first century. In order to join Auroville, the single requirement is goodwill and aspiration for human unity.

Organization of Auroville is based on minimum needs, which mean
basic life-needs, such as food, basic shelter, cleaning products, clothes,
recreation, transportation such as bicycle and electrical vehicles, and
other products that are uniquely required for practical and functional
reasons. Minimum needs do not include all the desires, which are commonly miscalled needs in the consumer culture. The Mother established
an in-kind system, where people trade their manufactured products or
services for being taken care of by Auroville who provides all their
basic needs and requirements. She described Auroville as being based
on the communist model, but without the leveling—without the leveling of democracy as well. Thus, nothing personally belongs to anybody
but only to the collective, and, although there is no external hierarchy,
people work according to their inner capacity, where the aristocracy of
nature is honored.

The Mother regards Auroville to be "the meeting point between the
inner and outer worlds" and "the concrete proof that spirit and matter
are one."[26] The purpose of Auroville is to create a "group-soul" and
"communal mind" capable of receiving, assimilating and putting into
practice the higher wisdom worked out inwardly by Sri Aurobindo and
the Mother.[27] There is at work in Auroville, in effect, a very different
organizing principle, potentially conscious, than in other urban centers
and settlements around the world.

---

25   2012, p. XXXIII
26   *Ibid.,* pp. XXIV, XXV
27   *Ibid.,* pp. XXIV, XXV

In present communist states and totalitarian regimes there are severe obstacles to negative liberty, along with the pretense of fostering
positive liberty and ideal conditions for superior human development.
Under the mother's guidelines, in contrast, there are essentially no obstacles to negative liberty at all, although, today, individual sacrificial
effort is required to reach Auroville's aim of achieving the greatest
possible freedom.[28] There is, at the same time, maximum freedom for
the development of positive freedom in a climate where understanding
its meaning, at least mentally, is accessible to everybody, including
through the writings of Sri Aurobindo and the Mother. Although their
teachings are easily available, Aurovilians are not coerced or required
to adopt their path or, for that matter, any specific spiritual path.

Initially, goodwill and aspiration toward human unity and its nur-
turing are the only requirements to become accepted as a citizen of
Auroville. Yet, in her later years, the Mother indicated that the high
purpose of Auroville is to be "the cradle of the superman," preparing
the field for the incarnation of a supramental society.[29] Her actual guidelines for individuals in order for Auroville to become realized, contain
several principles, the first being the "inner discovery," by which she
means the opening of the psychic being.[30] The decisive difference between Auroville and the democratic world is that, for Auroville to be
successful, there is a need for individuals to aspire toward and achieve
a psychic opening, and this inner discovery is facilitated by living according to minimum needs and being a willing serviteur of the Divine.
This amounts to maximizing positive freedom in the sense of individuation within a culture, where the group-soul is open to the wisdom
incarnated by individuals and develops accordingly in the process.

For Western democracies, there is no such requirement and, within
limits that are increasingly breached by the internet culture, all kinds of

---

28   *Ibid.,* p. XXV
29   *Ibid.,* p. XIII
30   *Ibid.,* p. XIX

so-called needs, in medieval Christendom known as the seven deadly sins (pride, envy, greed, anger, sloth, lust and gluttony) are encouraged by the consumer society, while, again within limits, freedom of expression and the removal of most obstacles to negative freedom is considered to be a significant sign of societal maturity. How much Aurovilians, who are comprised of ordinary folk of our time, many raised in or influenced by consumer oriented cultures, are able to follow the Mother's guidelines is therefore an open question. Evidence suggests that there is considerable disparity between the way many Aurovilians conduct their lives and the life the Mother envisioned. Knowledge of and truly understanding the Mother's guidelines and the implications of following or not following them are also debatable.

Given the pivotal role of Sri Aurobindo and the Mother in the lives of many people throughout the world, including in Auroville, the integral nature of their teachings and embodied wisdom, there is danger of the formation of a religion and a religious attitude toward them. They strongly discourage such an eventuality, inspiring individuals to make their own self-discovery instead. Institutionalized religion, with its dogma, doctrine and tradition, eventuality simply kills the living God and forms ultimately antagonistic divisions between individuals and between different groups, as we witness in today's clash of civilizations. The realization of the New World, rather, requires both the incarnation of the divine and humans becoming divine—in the Mother's words, humans finding perfection. Jung is fully convinced of this requirement and writes that in the forthcoming Age of the Holy Spirit, religious (and spiritual) formations will be superseded by a situation where "man will be essentially God and God man."[31] Along with the teachings of Sri Aurobindo and the Mother, the manifest reality of Auroville, the Matrimandir and its central symbol need to be understood aright, not as static symbols that represent a new religion, with

---

31   As reported in G. Adler, ed., 1975, p. 167.

all the implied exclusivity, but living symbols that belong to humanity and which refer to a conscious process of divine incarnation in receptive individuals.

CHAPTER 14

Creative Individuals and the Group-Soul

The ascent of the human soul to the supreme Spirit is that soul's highest aim and necessity, for that is the supreme reality; but there can be too the descent of the Spirit and its powers into the world and that would justify the existence of the material world also, give a meaning, a divine purpose to the creation and solve its riddle. East and West could be reconciled in the pursuit of the highest and largest ideal, Spirit embrace Matter and Matter find its own true reality and the hidden Reality in all things in the Spirit.[1]

– Sri Aurobindo

The Mother approved for publication in the Auroville Gazette the quotation indicated immediately below from Sri Aurobindo's *The Human Cycle,* followed by her comment to one of her disciples, an engineer by the name of Udar:

Therefore if the spiritual change of which we have been speaking is to be effected, it must unite two conditions which have to be simultaneously satisfied but are most difficult to bring together. There must be the individual and the individuals who are able to see, to develop, to re-create themselves in the image of the Spirit and to communicate both their idea and its power to the mass. And there must be at the same time a mass, a society, a communal mind or at least the constituents of a group-body, the possibility of a group-soul which is capable of receiving and effectively assimilating, ready to follow and

_____

1   2006, p. 553.

185

effectively arrive, not compelled by its own inherent deficien-
cies, its defect of preparation to stop on the way or fall back before the decisive change is made. Such a simultaneity has never
yet happened, although the appearance of it has sometimes been
created by the ardor of a moment. That the combination must
happen someday is a certainty.[2]

After reading the above quotation to the Mother, Udar asked her
if it was now the time for the realization referred to by Sri Aurobindo,
simultaneity between the teachings of chosen individuals and effective group fulfillment. Inasmuch as the first conditions regarding the
individual and individuals had been fulfilled with the communication
of the realizations and teachings of Sri Aurobindo and the Mother, the
question concerns the second condition, the development of a group-
soul capable of effectively receiving and assimilating the idea and its
power intrinsic to the teachings. The Mother replied: "This is exactly
what Auroville is for. But Auroville is still far from fulfilling the necessary conditions."[3] Auroville's specific *Swadharma* or vocation as a
collective body is to form and live by its group-soul, although that was
far from evident in the Mother's time, nor is it evident today.

Although the realization of the group-soul is the *raison d'être* of
Auroville and the original work has been done by Sri Aurobindo and
the Mother, without the inner discovery and work of creative individuals in relationship with the *Anthropos,* the formation of the group-
soul will not become a conscious and living cultural matrix. When
the group-soul is progressively embodied collectively in the Auroville
community culture, thanks to the work of spiritually creative individuals, it becomes an expression of the manifest group-soul that, in turn,
has a leading influence on the community, while educating individual
Aurovilians in the spirit of the Mother's vision. The ability of the conscious group-soul to discern and effectively assimilate the messages

2   1997, p. 247.
3   1971, p. 31.

of soul-gifted and creative individuals is, in itself, dependent on the group-soul being nourished, supported and brought forward as a guiding principle in the community consciousness by Aurovilians.

The Mother, Living Numbers and the New Creation

In this light, there are recorded comments made by the Mother on the Matrimandir on December 31, 1969, and January 3 and 10, 1970, as well as her vision of seeing herself manipulating numbers signifying the active working of the Superman in the new creation. These and related comments need to be appreciated as highly important phenomena pertaining to the realization of Auroville and the new world.[4] What follows are the Mother's vision and her comments on the vision:

On January 1, 1969, the Mother proclaimed the "arrival of the Superman consciousness," and went through a related process that lasted until January 1, 1970, when she revealed the measurements for the original plan of the Matrimandir.[5] In conversations throughout the year the Mother also observed that "the number 9 has something to do with this."[6] At the beginning of February, she indicated the nature of the symbolic workings of that new consciousness, which, as one will see, is intimately tied up with living numbers. Although highly edited, here is what she is reported to have said to a disciple:

> *I remember a vision when I was doing a work with numbers during the night, and I was putting ... groups of numbers ... in certain positions ....*
>
> *...*
>
> *Well, it is associated with ... groups of people spread out in the world and connected with ... what planet? Planets? I don't know ... I still see the arrangement of numbers I was making, which were totally living .... When it is like this (the Mother*

---

4   Norelli-Bachelet, 1985 passim
5   As reported in Norelli-Bachelet, 1985, pp. 5, 15.
6   *Ibid.*, p. 13.

indicates a certain arrangement) it expressed a certain thing, and when it was like that, it expressed a certain other thing. And at the same time I was saying: "It doesn't only express it, but it has a power to realise that thing ....

...

It was ... the numbered expression of the application to life in a coming realisation: Life to come, but not very far away; for example, in the next century which is beginning now.

...

A truer application, more universal, and with spiritual knowledge; the principle of the position (place) and the utilisation of individuals on Earth. Two columns here, one column there; but living columns. It was not on paper ... it was in the air, and these numbers were LIVING ...
And there were groups of numbers; those were blue, dark blue, and the others were golden yellow ....

...

But these were two principles ... the principle ... of conception (origination) (a gesture of descent from above) and the principle of realisation.

...

I DO, I ACT, and I am completely conscious ... all these numbers were organised and that they determine future events.

...

And it is only because you are present now that the contact with that memory is made.

...

It was not the "conception" of a work: it was the WORK itself .... It was the organisation of groups of numbers which determined the events and the ORDER of events (above all the order of events) and the place on earth.

...

I am active, ... in what is being prepared to manifest on earth... it is the creative zone of the physical ... , yesterday it was like that, but now it is necessary that it be like this, with the knowledge that tomorrow another change will be necessary. But it is this that determines the events. But the consciousness (the waking consciousness, or ordinary consciousness) MUST NOT know what is decided there. ... it is only because I had taken the decision to speak to you about it (the "dream") that I could make a connection with the memory of it .... It has no longer any meaning for me.

...

There was ... in the waking state ... a sort of application to know what the functioning, the action of the Superman Consciousness would be .... It is necessary to know what the changes will be in the body's functions, in the work and the method of the work. And then this experience (of the numbers) was a reply to teach me a bit how it is going to be .... Then I placed them in the arrangement like that. The arrangement in its wholeness was a continuity, but within which the details changed.

...

Last night I knew I was doing it regularly each night, but not since very long. This must have come with that Consciousness. This vision was like the application of certain scientific means ... it was a force that acted like this (gesture of descent that imposes itself), ... this force makes one act ... blue and golden numbers. And the priority for action was always with the golden numbers, while the blue ones came as if to fill in the holes. This had a form.

...

But this has a strong action ... it commands action on the Earth .... This constantly received the Will, and the Power from above ... it is not above, it is ... (a gesture signifying it is "everywhere inside") ... "superior" in the true sense of the word.
And this body RECEIVES things ... it felt the need to know what effect that Superman Consciousness would have on this consciousness here.[7]

There are several important points to make in regard to the Mother's "vision/dream." The first is that the Mother is revealing herself here as the Supramental Shakti, which is actively involved in giving birth to the new world by way of the principles of conception (origination) and realization. This birth involved the descent of a superior Will and Power that commands action on Earth. Her actions are not mechanical but involve making different arrangements depending on need on

---

7   *Ibid.*, pp. 5–10.

an ongoing basis. Secondly, her activities in the "visions/dreams" involved arranging and rearranging a series of living numbers over different nights. Golden yellow numbers and blue numbers were arranged in the air according to necessity, where the blue numbers filled in the holes according to the principle of conception or origination and the golden ones had a priority for action. Thirdly, the arrangement and rearrangement of numbers determine events, the order of events and their place on Earth. The Mother, as Supramental Shakti, insisted that, in these "visions," she was involved in "the WORK itself." Finally, because of the existence of her disciple on the physical plane, she could bring this memory into consciousness, suggesting the needed participation of the individual human being in the process.

Thus, according to the Mother, this arranging and rearranging of numbers that took place in the creative zone of the physical came with the new supramental consciousness. The process itself was not routine, but a living organizational phenomena requiring her active and conscious participation. Living numbers were involved, where the arrangement of numbers in its wholeness was laid out in continuity, although within the continuity, the details changed. These were manipulated by the Mother in order to realize events, the order of events and the place of realization, sometime in the twenty-first century on Earth. The presence of her disciple allowed her to bring this memory into consciousness, a fact that, in itself, alludes to synchronicity and acausal orderedness.

Arranging numbers based on a one-continuum and, as the Supramental Shakti, effecting events, their order and location in the material world are an extraordinary confirmation of Jung's and von Franz's observations on numbers as the most primordial expression of the archetype and the archetype of order made conscious. The involvement of the new supramental consciousness and projected realizations on the physical plane indicate numbers are symbolic of the Supermind, paralleling Jung's contention that numbers are symbolic of the *unus mundus* and the principle of order made conscious, unifying spirit, psyche and matter, and that they involve synchronicity and acts of creation in time. The outstanding difference between Jung's model and the experience of the Mother is that the Mother is depicted as consciously and actively involved in creating a new world; whereas the usual connection to the qualitative value of numbers comes via the unconscious in a dream or vision, where the individual plays a more passive or receptive role as a witness—along with the need for being actively engaged, however, in the awareness of synchronistic happenings.

Given the descent of the Supermind into the Earth's atmosphere on February 29, 1956, and the arrival of the new Supermind consciousness on January 1, 1969, individuals' conscious experiences of what Jung refers to as acts of creation in time through synchronicity surely contribute to or are an expression of the Mother's new creation in one way or another. Conscious awareness of synchronicities, when authentic, multiplies with an increasingly rigorous psychological and religious or spiritual attitude, and paying close attention to and reflecting on inner experiences and meaningful coincidences. People often mistakenly understand synchronicity to require some form of causal thinking, believing, for instance, that it was caused by a dream or some directed ritual. In fact, the experience of synchronicity is always an act of grace that goes beyond any form of causality and agency of the ego. In the example of the Mother, she was identified with the Supramental Shakti in her "vision," and, as such, she was depicted as the source of grace itself.

Whether one agrees with Norelli-Bachelet or not, her discussions regarding the measurements of the Matrimandir's inner chamber and the nature of the central symbol are based on what appears to be valid numerological assumptions as well as the Mother's comments.[8] Her arguments are ideally taken seriously by Aurovilians and not, as is now the case, rejected out of hand by those in decision-making positions. At stake is the fact that, according to the laws of a unitary world, where the

8   1986, 1987

inner and outer are in direct relationship, when the inner chamber and the central symbol of the Matrimandir are correctly rendered, then the outer expression of the temple and the city itself will also potentially be correctly realized, but not otherwise.

Thus, temple measurements (numbers), considered qualitatively, are an important ingredient in evaluating the Matrimandir's physical presence. For those unfamiliar with the science of numerology, it is noteworthy that Jung regards numbers as having, in addition to a quantitative dimension, a depth-qualitative aspect and as being the most primordial expression of the archetype, and related to the mystery of the unity of psyche and matter. He defines "number as *an archetype of order which has become conscious*," supporting Patrizia Norelli-Bachelet's basic assumption and giving an explanation for the significance of the Mother's manipulations of numbers.[9] Related to the qualitative value of numbers is an ongoing conflict around the accuracy in the construction of the inner chamber of the Matrimandir, the resolution of which may well prove to be the first and fundamental example of how the group-soul can be nurtured and begin to come forward. Conscious relationship to the Matrimandir, the soul of Auroville, as the Mother perceives it, where the inner and spiritual, as well as its physical embodiment both belong to a unitary world, is essential for discovery of the group-soul.

---

9   Jung, as recorded in J Gary Sparks, 2010, p. 47.

CHAPTER 15

Jung's Deification: Prophet and Vibhuti

Jung is a prime example of an individual whose works are exemplary of a creative force that is helping to bring in a new world. Here it is worthwhile noting, however, that, although Jung writes compellingly about the *Anthropos,* there is no suggestion that he identifies with this figure. Sri Aurobindo and the Mother, on the other hand, are, in all likelihood, the embodiments of the *Anthropos* as contemporary avatars. Whereas Sri Aurobindo accessed the Logos, notably as expressed in his writings, especially *Savitri,* the Mother, as the Parashakti, was the incarnated Word, and has left the legacy of a new township and city of the Dawn in Auroville, with its center, the Matrimandir. Although Jung is not an avatar, in his 1925 seminar, he did speak of experiencing being deified, implying a feeling of immortality; and, in his essay "Concerning Rebirth," he explains what the feeling of immortality refers to psychologically. In the latter, he writes that "there is ... something non-spatial and non-temporal attached to [the experience]" along with "the presentiment of immortality of a peculiar *feeling of an extension of space and time.*"[1] In the seminar, he amplifies his experience with reference to the Mithraic mysteries and the lion-headed god, Aion (derived from the Persian deity Zrwanakarana, meaning "the infinitely long duration"[2]).

In fact, in his deification experience, Jung identified with the Mithraic god, inasmuch as in his vision, like depictions of Aion, a

---

1   Jung, as reported in Shamdasani, 1998, p. 52.
2   C.G. Jung, 1989, p. 98.

AION: GOD OF ENDLESS TIME

snake coiled around him from his feet to the heart level and his face took on the shape of a lion or tiger. Jung went through his initiation, but was able to detach from his identification with the god by understanding the meaning of the experience.

Jung was always concerned with the feeling of "god-likeness" and psychological inflation that accompany such experiences, and with the need to understand their meaning in order to "remain in human society."[3] He went on to have other exceptional experiences that he assimilated to consciousness as well. Deification is not the divine incarnation itself; but, considering his other recorded experiences and

---

3   *Ibid.*, p. 99.

the extraordinary scope of his work, it can be said that Jung attained an unusual degree of completeness in his life and that he is a superior individual.

In the Western tradition, Jung is a prophet, in the sense that he writes with profound insight as an interpreter of the divine Will and, thanks to his own experiences and those of his disciples, his psychological work opens the way for the future. According to the Hindu tradition, Jung is a human Vibhuti of the Divine in that he expresses such highly differentiated powers of the Self as knowledge, strength of character, enterprising forcefulness, creative force and love, in his works and life. In the *Bhagavad Gita*, The Godhead tells Arjuna: "Those in whom My powers rise to the utmost heights are Myself always, My special vibhutis."[4] In a description that certainly fits Jung, Sri Aurobindo writes that "a pre-eminence in this inner and outer achievement, a greater power of divine quality, an effective energy, is always the sign (of the Vibhuti)."[5] Sri Aurobindo and the Mother, the incarnated Avatar and Divine Mother, are also supreme Vibhutis, pre-eminently expressing the power of God in their lives and works with unprecedented perfection.

Edinger believes that Jung was the first representative of the Age of Aquarius, based on his early initiatory experience and his highly differentiated understanding of the Christian aeon and the Self as presented in his book *Aion*.[6] He argues that Jung's differentiated consciousness of the Age of Pisces means that he had gone beyond the Christian aeon to the Age of Aquarius. I find Edinger's reasoning compelling, although, given the phenomenon of Sri Aurobindo and the Mother as both Vibhutis and incarnations of the Avatar and Divine Mother respectively, I see them as the most differentiated embodiments of the Divine and creators of the new world, and Jung as one of the first

---

4   Sri Aurobindo, 1970b, p. 350.
5   1978, p. 174.
6   1996b.

human individuals, if not the first, to consciously enter the new aeon as prophet and Vibhuti of the Divine.

Jung's Structure of the Self as Fourfold Quaternities

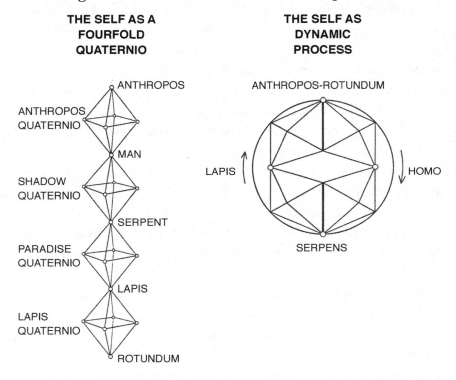

Jung's differentiation of the Self includes four quaternities, from the *Anthropos* through the human ego as intermediary between God and the world, to the chthonic and vegetative aspects of the psyche through inorganic matter, all as functions of the Self. In his model, the structure of the Self is static in form, but dynamic in process. Individuation involves a dynamic process of ascent and descent, where the descent from the spirit through different aspects of the psyche to matter transforms the original unconscious state to a conscious one. Noteworthy is the fact that the four elements (air, fire, water and earth) that unite as the *lapis*, which is comprised of inorganic matter, emerge from the Rotundum as an unknowable state of chaos and energy. Whereas the *Anthropos* relates to Sri Aurobindo's Superconscient realm, ultimately as Formless and the unknowable aspect of the spirit, the chaos of the Rotundum, also based on the Formless, has similarities to his Inconscient, out of which emerges the physical as well as the vital and mental aspects of human nature.[7]

Given the unitary nature of Jung's description of the Structure and Dynamics of the Self, and his referral to the early Christian Clementine creation myth, where the unitary God-image contains and does not split the opposites, there is little doubt that his presentation of the Self is an emanation of a unitary God and a reconciliation of opposites.[8] In the course of his discussion on the Self, appropriating Kant's epistemology on the subjective nature of space-time categories—where categories reside in the mind and not in the external world—Jung makes the highly insightful observation that the space-time quaternity, consisting of three dimensions of space and one dimension of time, or three dimensions of time and one of space, is an image of the fourfold Self in relationship to the physical world. Thus, it is the fourfold space-time Self that allows one to experience the physical world in an orderly fashion, forming a bridge between psyche and matter.[9] Jung's insight finds its parallel in Sri Aurobindo, who writes: "For it is this inner divine Self ... who is all the time evolving the mutations of our personality in Time and our sensational existence in Space —Time and Space that are the conceptual movement and extension of the Godhead in us. All is this self-seeing Soul, this self-representing spirit."[10] Unlike many spiritual paths which relativize the physical world or turn it into an illusion, both Jung and Sri Aurobindo are greatly concerned with the immanent God,

---

7   Ann Conrad Lammers and Adrian Cunningham, eds. (2008), p. 122, fig. 4.2.
8   Edinger, 1996b, pp. 184, 185.
9   *Ibid.*, pp. 183, 184.
10   1970b, p. 347.

and its fundamental direct penetration of the world. Even individual and cultural pathologies and their symptoms mask a truth that can be unveiled and prove meaningful. In the following chapter I examine more closely Jung's path of individuation per se, specifically as a spiritual path of yoga.

CHAPTER 16

Jung's Path of Individuation
as Ante-Integral Yoga

From the point of view of contemporary individuals divorced from
the ancestral psyche, Jung is an important guiding light, especially
for Westerners and modern and postmodern people everywhere. He
elucidates a path which can be seen as leading to or followed concomitantly with Integral Yoga of Sri Aurobindo and the Mother, more
closely allied with it than any other spiritual path of which I am aware,
for reasons that should become clear in what follows. In Jung's path
of individuation, the psyche is thoroughly accepted and scientifically
examined, and goes through a potentially far-reaching psychological
and spiritual transformation process.

Sri Aurobindo writes that his yoga begins where the others end
and that "the realization of this yoga is ... higher than Nirvana or
Nirvikalpa Samadhi."[1] He allows for the existence of many doors to
pass into the realization of the Absolute (Parabrahman), nirvana being one. He defines the "true spiritual individual which appears in
its complete truth when we get rid of the ego and our false separa-
tive sense of individuality, realize our oneness with the transcendent
and cosmic Divine and with all beings."[2] "It is this," he writes, "that
makes possible the Divine Life."[3] In terms of his triple transformation, this seems to refer to the culmination of the second, the spiritual

---

1   1970e, p. 59.
2   *Ibid.*, pp. 46, 47.
3   *Ibid.*, p. 47.

transformation, that leads on to the supramental transformation and Sri Aurobindo's yoga proper.

Sri Aurobindo contends that, in comparison to the old yogas, his yoga is new for the following reasons: There is an ascent and descent of consciousness, where "It is the descent of the new consciousness attained by the ascent that is the stamp and seal of the sadhana."[4] The object is "the divine fulfillment of life," whereas in the old yogas "the ascent is the real thing" and any descent incidental.[5] The object sought is not for divine realization for the sake of the individual, "but something to be gained for earth-consciousness here, a cosmic, not a solely supra-cosmic achievement."[6] The goal is to bring down the Supermind or Truth-Mind to be organized for earth use, which happened in 1956.

Jung's path of individuation is new for reasons similar to some of the comments articulated above; that is, there is ample evidence in Jung's opus for an ascent and descent of consciousness and the goal of life is the Self, or divine fulfillment. Moreover there is a strong emphasis on archetypal or cosmic realization, which relates individual transformation to the collective. Marie-Louise von Franz refers to "the great adventure of individuation,"[7] which is reminiscent of Sri Aurobindo's comment that "our yoga is not a retreading of old walks but a spiritual adventure."[8] What seems to be deficient in Jung's articulation of his path is the lack of any apparent emphasis on supra-cosmic achievement like non-dual Reality, nirvana or nirvikalpa samadhi, or bringing down the Truth-Mind or Supermind to Earth.

Yet, Jung had a visionary experience just prior to his death, where he saw the following words engraved on a great round stone: "And this shall be a sign unto you of Wholeness and Oneness."[9] He then

---

4   p. 109.
5   *Ibid.*
6   *Ibid.*
7   1975, p. 287.
8   1975, p. 287.
9   As reported in von Franz, 1975, p. 287.

saw "a quadrangle of trees whose roots reached around the earth and enveloped him and among the roots golden threads were glittering."[10] I report the full dream-vision and discuss its significance below. Having such a powerful experience, in my opinion, can only come to the true spiritual person as defined by Sri Aurobindo above, where spiritual realization involves the spiritual mutation of the roots of being, and a transformed relationship of the fully surrendered individual to the cosmic Self and the attainment of Wholeness and Oneness, a highly individuated reflection of the transcendent One.

Jung's lack of apparent concern—even, rather, his apparent disdain for the goal of attaining ego-dissolution in non-dual Reality—is based on his belief that without a separate ego, there cannot be any conscious-ness of the experience, but at best only a vague memory, Sri Aurobindo and the Mother actually have the same opinion, as indicated in the fol-lowing amusing exchange between the latter as a young woman and Sri Aurobindo regarding spiritual literature extolling the superiority of the samadhi-trance state. She said she wasn't sure that the fact she never had this experience was a sign of inferiority or not. Sri Aurobindo re-plied that with such an experience one actually enters into a region of being where there is no more consciousness, that it is a state of uncon-sciousness. The Mother said that reassured her, and she remarked to Sri Aurobindo: "Well, this has never happened to me," and he responded: "Nor to me!"[11] Sri Aurobindo and the Mother's experiences and posi-tion are similar to that of Jung in that what is of utmost importance is the spiritual transformation of consciousness and not experiences that are ultimately unrelated to consciousness, regardless of how exalted they may be. Jung's visionary experiences need to be understood in this light.

The Mother is also recorded as saying that in meditation one can experience samadhi trance, while "your waking consciousness remains

10   *Ibid.*
11   1978b, p. 314.

what it is, without ever changing."[12] The Mother went on to encourage her disciples to "develop your interior individuality, and you will be able to enter these same regions in full consciousness, and have the joy of communion with the highest of these regions, without losing all one's consciousness and returning with a zero instead of an experience."[13] Sri Aurobindo, similarly, writes that it is because of the uneducated psychic being that one returns from trance experiences with nothing but a general memory and, "as (the psychic being) becomes the master of its Samadhi, it is able to pass without any gulf of oblivion from the inner to the outer waking."[14]

The Mother and Sri Aurobindo recognize a luminous self-gathered waking state of samadhi as described in the *Bhagavad Gita*, and known as samadhishta or, in Vedanta, as nirvikalpa samadhi. This is an egoless state of the liberated *Jivanmukti*, where the center has been shifted upwards in oneness with the Transcendent and "established in God rather than Nature." The psychic being of the advanced soul has extended itself to the point of being able to bridge the gulf between non-dual Reality (which, according to the Mother, is beyond all forms, even the most subtle) and remain self-absorbed in samadhi—not in the transcendent Beyond, but while actively engaged in the world itself in divine service to society.[15] These advanced beings lean down to serve humanity, being instruments of "The will of God in action."[16] Attaining Supermind requires this realization, as well as the full transformation of being involving the individual, the cosmic and the Transcendent.

Ramana Maharshi, whose experiences are similar to the practitioners of the Advaita Vedanta school of Yoga, speaks of the state of "abiding permanently in *Samadhi,* either *samikalpa or nrvikalpa* as *sahaja (*the natural state)," while being "able to function naturally in

12   *Ibid.*
13   2008, p. 260.
14   1971d, p. 504.
15   1978a.
16   Sri Aurobindo, 1972c, p. 57.

the world" like the ordinary person."[17] He equates this state of being to Turiya, awareness of the Self, the fourth state, and supreme consciousness, which is beyond the three states known as "waking, dreaming and dreamless sleep."[18] The end goal of his yoga is the attainment of Turiya and the other states in themselves are deemed unworthy of attention and bypassed.

Sri Aurobindo's view is different. According to him, waking consciousness is the normal state of embodied being, "dominated by the physical mind" and the dream state refers to consciousness of "subtler life planes and mind planes."[19] Sri Aurobindo also notes that the "sleep-state" corresponds to the supramental plane, but is beyond experience because of lack of development of our "causal body or envelope of gnosis."[20] According to him, the Turiya beyond, "a certain fourth" state, "is the consciousness of our pure self-existence or our absolute being," only accessible by samadhi or yogic trance.[21] Sri Ramana Maharshi and Advaita adherents are aware of the reality of Turiya, but there is no evidence in their expressed beliefs or writings that I have seen that they know anything of the Supermind, which is "inherent in all cosmic force and existence," the creative and ordering principle that is "Sachidananda Himself" and infinite, or its function "to determine and combine and uphold relation and order and the great lines of the manifestation."[22] They seem to know nothing of Supermind because their intention from the beginning is to one-sidedly attain identification with the Supreme in Turiya and, consequently, to bypass the universal archetypal reality, the cosmic force and existence.

Although the Turiya can be understood as the fourth beyond, from the point of view of Sri Aurobindo's yoga, where transformation of

17   1985, pp. 155, 157.
18   *Ibid.*, p. 157.
19   1971d, p. 499.
20   Sri Aurobindo, *ibid.*
21   *Ibid.*, p. 499; 1970c, p. 267 n.
22   *Ibid.*, p. 267.

nature at all levels is essential, Supermind, as the Truth or Real Idea and "inherent in all cosmic force and existence," is the fourth name, after the trinity of Existence, Consciousness, Bliss, therefore the "fourth to *That* in descent."[23] It is also the fourth to "us in our ascension."[24] In Jungian language, there is a double interlocking *quaternio*, in that, in their cosmic being, humans consist of a lower trinity of Mind, Life and Physical nature, along with the magnetic glue of the incarnated soul and psychic being, its evolutionary and expressive aspect. Thus, Supermind, as the connecting link between the upper trinity of *Sat* (Existence), *Chit* (Consciousness) and *Ananda* (Bliss) and the lower trilogy of Mind, Life and the Physical, is fourth in descent and fourth in ascent between the two trinities. In Sri Aurobindo's cosmology, Mind is linked to Supermind, the Life plane or Vital is linked to Consciousness, coupled with Force, *Chit-Shakti*, and the Physical is linked to pure Existence or *Sat*, as a form of *Sat*. The incarnated psychic being relates to Bliss or *Ananda*.

Jung was fascinated by several Western mystics who attained a level of consciousness that involves total loss of ego and submersion in the source beyond any differentiation, yet they reported returning with enough of a general memory to affect their lives. Most notably Jung was enchanted by Meister Eckhart and Jacob Boehme. With Eckhart, Jung was primarily taken by the emphasis he put on the birth of God in the soul, relativizing the God-image, where God and man are "functions" of each other, and both are contained within the psyche. In Jung words, "man can be understood as a function of God and God as a psychological function of man."[25] By this, Jung means that "God's actions spring from one's own inner being."[26] Jung also acknowledges the

23   *Ibid.*
24   *Ibid.*
25   As reported in Dourley, 2010, p. 57.
26   *Ibid.*

value of Eckhart's breakthrough experience and the effect it can have on the conduct of life, given submersion in the creative Source itself.

Eckhart differentiates between the Godhead and God as Trinity and creator; the difference is between "doing and non-doing."[27] In Hindu terms, this means differentiating between the active and passive Brahmin, although not acknowledging a reconciling Supreme Being beyond both the active Divine and the passive Godhead, the *Purushottama* of the *Gita*. Regarding his own experience of the Godhead, Eckhart writes: "In this breaking through, I find that I and God are both the same. I am what I was, I neither wax nor wane, for I am motionless cause who is moving all things."[28] On return to life in the world, Eckhart recognizes his otherness and distinction from the divine source and, consequently, his alienation. There is no sense here of him abiding in the Godhead, as in samadhistha and nirvikalpa samadhi, as discussed above.

Jung's interest in Jacob Boehme is even more far-reaching. Like Eckhart, Boehme experiences a moment of total identity with the divine, then a return to what he refers to as the "very grossest and meanest matter of the earth."[29] Boehme's experience led him to believe that the opposites as experienced in the divine life "are not reconciled in eternity, as Christian orthodoxy contends."[30] Boehme believes that an unconscious divinity can neither perceive nor reconcile the inherent contradictions of its manifestation and the life of humanity, and He created humans for this purpose. In terms of Hindu differentiation, it appears that, unlike Eckhart, who seems to have experienced the passive Brahman, Boehme experienced the active Brahmin or, at least, emphasized it. According to Dourley's reflections, Jung believes Boehme's experiences describe the full self-realization of archetypal dynamics

---

27   *Ibid.*
28   *Ibid.*
29   *Ibid.*, p. 59.
30   Dourley, 2010, p. 59.

in both personal and collective historical consciousness, and not in the beyond, which is compatible with Jung's views. Boehme's fully embracing the world on his return in order to reconcile the opposites of life is what Jung found compelling and a precedent to his own psychological work.

In Boehme's return to consciousness of the world after experiencing the featureless nothingness of non-dual Reality, he found himself confronting two fundamental conflicting opposites, for one, God the Father as "a dark burning fire, an angry, masculine figure of immense power and based on the primacy of unrelated self-affirmation."[31] In contrast to this dark Shadow (Asuric) side of God, he also encountered "an androgynous Christ figure," whom he occasionally relates to as "Sophia ... the bride of Christ," who is communicable and emanates a warm light.[32] According to Boehme and in harmony with Jung, perception and reconciliation of the opposites, including the two divine opposites of Boehme's experience, require the historical field of human consciousness. Jung was influenced by Boehme not only directly but, also through the philosopher, Hegel, which he acknowledged in a letter late in his life.[33]

Thus, Boehme extends Eckhart's experience of identification with nothingness to include the world, in order to resolve God's contradictions in the historical play of consciousness. Dourley ingeniously forms an overlapping double *quaternio* consisting of Eckhart's experience of the Godhead as the fourth status beyond the Trinity, as in the Hindu Turiya, to include Boehme's extension from the Trinity to the fourth as humanity, a second *quaternio*. Inasmuch as both the Godhead and humanity are essential ingredients of this double *quaternio*, there is some relationship to Sri Aurobindo's double *quaternio,* although there would be more similarity if the center piece were Jung's *unus mundus,*

---

31   *Ibid.*, p. 61.
32   *Ibid.*, p. 62.
33   *Ibid.*, p. 61.

with the Trinity on the spiritual side and tripartite human nature consisting of the intellect, the vital or life plane, and the physical, on the
other side.

Dourley also writes about three women Christian mystics, Mechtild
of Magdeburg, who lived in the thirteenth century, whom Jung mentions several times in his works, and Hadewijch and Marguerite Porete,
who lived in the thirteenth and fourteenth centuries respectively, whom
he doesn't mention. Each of these women was a member of a lay group
of women known as the Beguines. They each in their own way had
mystic experiences of the nothing beyond differences that is the all. Of
particular significance for this study is the fact that Marguerite Porete
claims to not only have experienced nothingness that is the all, but that
she became "established" in the nothing as described above in nirvikalpa and samadhista samadhi, as a liberated soul.[34]

Jung's personal adventure of consciousness may simply reflect his
contemporary Western psyche, with its complicated history and am-
bivalent relationship to spiritual values. Westerners are more identified with nature in comparison to Indians, who have had a long and
conscious tradition of seeking non-dual Reality. For Westerners to aim
at the spirit per se without reference to the natural world can be a misguided pretention. Nonetheless, there is ample evidence to show that
Jung was attracted to mystics like Jacob Boehme, Meister Eckhart and
others, and their experiences of the transcendent non-dual Reality as I
relate above. Moreover, he sometimes uses very suggestive language
that indicates familiarity with such experiences. As early as 1928 Jung
writes, for instance, "Indeed, he is completely modern only when he
has come to the very edge of the world, leaving behind him all that
has been discarded and outgrown, and acknowledging that he stands
before the Nothing out of which the All may grow."[35] The question of
whether or not Jung himself attained such a level of spiritual realization

34   *Ibid.*, p. 215.
35   Jung, 1970f, p. 75.

and identity with non-dual Reality, however, remains something of a mystery, since he never makes it explicit in his formal writings. Yet, according to Jung's most numinous visionary experiences, he did attain a high level of conscious individuation and a differentiated ladder of being from which he could very well be said to stand on a high rung of the ladder, before "the Nothing out of which all may grow."[36]

Although with Sri Aurobindo, one might say that his sincerity rises to the absolute, what Jung has in common with him is the sincerity with which he took his inner experiences without a power drive or spiritual ambition to attain transcendent non-dual Reality or nirvana. As with Sri Aurobindo and the Mother, Jung's approach involves building a ladder of being, which the Mother recommends as "indispensable if you want to take part in the knowledge of your higher being."[37] In a letter to a Hindu disciple, Arwind Vasavada, on November 22, 1954, written some ten years after his major visionary experiences of the *mysterium coniunctionis*, Jung writes, "I can say that my consciousness is the same as the self, but that is nothing but words, since there is not the slightest evidence that I participate more or further in the self than my ego consciousness reaches."[38] In Jung's language, the ladder of being involves the extension of ego consciousness. In either case the intention is to engage in a transformation process that requires linking various levels of being and not seeking experiences of the Transcendent per se.

Regarding his experience of nirvana, for instance, Sri Aurobindo writes: "It came unasked, unsought for, though quite welcome."[39] Although he sometimes insists that Integral Yoga begins with the experience of nirvana, the Mother observes that, for their disciples, "If the Nirvana aim had been put before them more would have been fit for it, for the Nirvana aim is easier than the one we have put before us."[40]

---

36   *Ibid.*
37   2008, p. 224.
38   As reported in Spiegelman, 1987, p. 192.
39   1970e, p. 50.
40   2003c, p. 455.

In one exchange with a disciple, she is mostly concerned about the external being that requires a change in the physical nature and goes on to say that "many do not even seem to have awakened to a necessity of a change." [41] The Mother's emphasis on the external being may reflect the fact that the Hindu psyche tends to be introverted, with comparatively inferior extraversion that is both relatively unconscious and resists transformation. It more likely reflects the universal difficulty, reflected in alchemy, in moving psychologically from three to four, which I discuss below. The West's superior extraversion, on the other hand, is complemented with comparatively inferior introversion.

More specifically, one can have spiritual experiences through introverted intuition and have high ideals, and yet have difficulty actualizing the experience in the physical reality of everyday life. In medieval Christian ascetic practices such as the spiritual exercises of Saint Ignatius Loyola, there is an effort to overcome desires based on the belief that the body is evil and should be rejected. In many Eastern meditative practices there is also a rejection of the body and bodily desires, as worldliness is considered illusory or superficial and a distraction that needs to be transcended. These ascetic traditions encourage atavistic regressions that do not speak to the need of contemporary individuation and the potential transformation of being.

Like Sri Aurobindo and the Mother, and following the lead of the alchemists, Jung seeks transformation, not rejection. Jung writes that man's task is not to set the attainment of nirvana or a non-dual state as a goal per se but, whether introverted or extraverted, to "become conscious of the contents that press upward from the unconscious. Neither should he persist in his unconsciousness, nor remain identical with the unconscious elements of his being, thus evading his destiny, which is to create more and more consciousness."[42] Becoming more conscious includes more differentiated consciousness of the intuition, the intellect,

---

41   *Ibid.,* p. 456.
42   1983, p. 326.

the vital (dynamics of life), bodily desires and the body. It is not a question of manipulating the unconscious or using it to realize personal or collective ambitions, but of becoming more conscious according to the exigencies of the Self, which differs according to the unique disposition of the individual.

In fact, I was thrilled to discover during the final stages of the preparation for publication of this study, at the last moment, as it were, that in 1958 in a conversation with Zen master Sini'chi Hisamatsu in Zurich, Jung explicitly stated that "through liberation man must be brought to the point where he is free from the compulsion to chase after a myriad of things or from being controlled by the collective unconscious. Both are fundamentally the same: *Nirvana*."[43] Jung goes on to authoritatively affirm that it is possible to free oneself from the collective unconscious and attain this transcendent condition of freedom. In confirmation of Jung personally having had such an experience of liberation, the book he was reading on his deathbed was Charles Luk's *Chan and Zen Teachings* and, according to von Franz in a letter dated September 12, 1961, Jung asked his secretary to write Luk, saying that he was "enthusiastic" and sometimes felt that "he could have said exactly this!" i.e., as the zen master Hsu Yun was reported to have said.[44] The name Hsu Yun means "Empty Cloud," which refers to a state totally empty of ego without self-reference, functioning like a wild animal or vegetable.[45] His teachings are based on Buddhism grafted onto a Taoist alchemical ground. Like Sri Aurobindo, although later in life, it appears very likely that Jung actually did attain the non-dual state of nirvana.

At the same time, again, like Sri Aurobindo and the Mother, it is highly relevant that Jung speaks of freedom from the collective unconscious and not skirting around or ignoring the opposites of the collective unconscious as is the case in many, if not most, paths that aim

43   Murray Stein, March 15, 2015.
44   *Ibid.*
45   Jy Din Shakya, 1996, p.ii.

directly at non-dual reality as *nirvana* or *That*. In *Memories, Dreams Reflections*, he writes:

> To me there is no liberation *à tout prix*. I cannot be liberated from anything I do not possess, have not done or experienced. Real liberation becomes possible for me only when I have done all that I was able to do, when I have completely devoted myself to a thing and participated in it to the utmost. If I withdraw from participation, I am virtually amputating the corresponding part of my psyche.[46]

Jung's liberation, then, is along the lines of Sri Aurobindo's and the Mother's, where a ladder is built from the material psychoid level of being through the psyche to nirvana or non-dual Reality per se. The difference between the path that aims directly at the end goal of non-dual Reality by skirting around the psyche and Jung's path, where the psyche and its psychoid base are diligently worked through, is much larger than is normally assumed to be the case. As I try to demonstrate in this study, in this case, there is an intensive and extensive transformation of being, the potential for which is virtually ignored in most other spiritual paths that have attaining nirvana or Non-dual Reality as the primary goal. The following discussion on the nature of the psychoid archetype, the *unus mundus* and synchronicity help elucidate the distinctive quality of Jung's path of individuation.

---

46   C.G. Jung, 1983, p. 276.

CHAPTER 17

Archetype as Psychoid, the *Unus Mundus* and Synchronicity

> The ... third degree of conjunction (the *unus mundus*) is universal: it is the relation or identity of the personal with the suprapersonal atman, and of the individual tao with the universal tao.[1]
>
> – C.G. Jung

As I mention above, the most significant aspect of Jung's approach to psychology involve the archetypes of the collective unconscious, with the Self as the central archetype. Archetypes give form and order to life, being both the way the world is apprehended and an effective power of organization. Prior to 1944, Jung envisaged the archetypes as consisting of two antinomies or two poles: the spiritual pole that allows for apprehension of the object through feeling-toned images, and the dynamic or instinctive pole that is a blueprint for action. Jung attributed red to the instinctual pole of the archetype, and violet (which is a synthesis of blue and red) to the spiritual pole—instead of the blue often taken to be a spiritual color, in order to accentuate the fact that the true spiritual dimension of being incorporates the (red) dynamic instinct and is not divorced from it.

In fact, Jung eventually regarded spirit and matter or spirit and instinct less in oppositional terms, but as two sides of the same coin.

---

1   C.G. Jung, 1974c, p.535

He writes that "psyche and matter are two aspects of one and the same thing" and "the ultimate nature of both is transcendental, that is irrepresentable."[2] Jung suggests that "this living being [consisting of mind and body] appears outwardly as the material body and inwardly as a series of images of the vital activities taking place within it."[3] The dualistic separation of mind and body relates to the development and overriding dominance of the intellect, with its emphasis on differentiation. Thus, Jung writes that the division of mind and body "may finally prove to be a device of reason for the purpose of conscious differentiation."[4] As a systematic whole, there is only one stream of energy, with different velocities determining its density from pure spirit down through the intellect, then the vital or life realm, and finally the densest, the physical and material.

Thus, regarding the biological/organic aspect of the human psyche, with "development and structure that preserves elements that connect it to the invertebrates and ultimately the protozoa," Jung writes that "theoretically it should be possible to 'peel' the collective unconscious, layer by layer, until we came to the psychology of the worm, and even of the amoeba."[5] The amoeba acts psyche-like despite its unconsciousness and needs to be studied in relationship to its environment, where it has foreknowledge about where to obtain food and how to metabolize it, and so on. Such knowledge that is not ego-related and unconscious, encouraging Jung to refer to it as "absolute knowledge," can explain the amoeba's psyche-like intentionality, and its complete embeddedness in and "synchronistic" experiences with its environment.

Amplifying Jung's observation on the amoeba-like aspect of the psyche, John Ryan Haule observes that the molecules comprising an amoeba are constituted differently at each moment in time as a result

2   Jung, 1975b, pp. 215, 216.
3   *Ibid.*
4   *Ibid.*, p. 326.
5   *Ibid.*, p. 152.

of its interaction with its surrounding environment.[6] Each molecule is governed by the larger purpose of the wholeness of the amoeba and flows in an uninterrupted process of instantaneous choices. Haule suggests that the neuron in the brain functions in an essentially similar way, not in search of food like the amoeba, but in search of organismic balance. The surrounding environment in this case consists of the established neural networks of which it is a part, as well as any novel activity of the dendrites for the establishment of new neural pathways. The wholeness of the brain is the governing principle of the neuronal conglomerates in the brain, while the psyche functions as the agent of wholeness for the brain and other organs of the body.

Haule analyses the zygote's development in both physical terms and in terms of its psyche-like attributes and psyche as process. The zygote is a single-celled organism that comes into existence with the fertilization of the ovum by the sperm, followed by a process in which each cell divides into two cells through mitosis during a two-week period of rapid cell division to become the embryo. Although, originally, in terms of psyche-like attributes, the zygote is not more complicated than an amoeba, Haule sees its complex development as paradigmatic for the psyche's unfolding life.

Thus, he writes that "psyche is a process that is always changing, always growing, never the same from one moment to the next or one decade to the next."[7] Although psyche is a process, the question remains, how does it function as a unified phenomenon and not through pathological dissociation? In order to explain the unifying nature of the psyche, Haule resorts to the Jungian notion that "every living body is pervaded by psyche," with a unifying center, the Self. He then quotes Jung, who often emphasizes that "the self is a circle whose circumference is everywhere and centre, nowhere."[8] Such a definition of the Self

---

6   2011.
7   J. R. Haule, 2011, p. 154.
8   *Ibid.*, pp. 154, 155.

identifies a center that allows for a dynamic psyche that may be static in form, but is forever in process, at all levels of being, including the zygote.

In 1946, Jung made a decisive breakthrough with his postulate that the archetype is psychoid, drawing him closer to the unitary thinking of Sri Aurobindo and the Mother. By psychoid Jung means that both the spiritual and the biological/organic poles of the archetype are transcendent and essentially irrepresentable and unknowable. Thus, the psychoid archetype not only forms a bridge to the transcendent spirit but also to matter. Jung elaborates on the biological/organic side of the equation when he writes that "the archetype would be located beyond the psychic sphere, analogous to the position of physiological instincts, which is immediately rooted in the stuff of the organism, and, with its psychoid nature, forms the bridge to matter in general."[9] "Matter and spirit," observes Jung "appear in the psychic realm as having distinctive qualities of conscious content."[10] Thus, he argues, "the ultimate nature of both is transcendental, that is irrepresentable since the psyche and its contents are the only reality which is given to us *without a medium.*"[11]

As I allude to above, Jung's fullest and most intriguing treatment of the unity of spirit and matter can be found in his book, *Aion,* where both spirit and inorganic matter are each shown as a quaternity and a differentiated function of the Self. This means that the ability to perceive and relate to spirit and matter is, in both cases, a reflection of the Self as a quaternity, an image of order par excellence. The spiritual Anthropos Quaternio, which effectively comes with shadow and instinct as depicted in the Shadow Quaternio, emanates from an irrepresentable and unknowable spiritual reality, while the four elements, air, fire, water and earth of the material Lapis Quaternio emerge from the

---

9   1975b, p. 216.
10   *Ibid.*
11   *Ibid.*

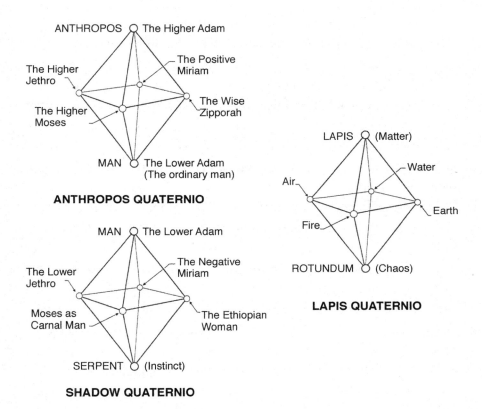

ANTHROPOS QUATERNIO

SHADOW QUATERNIO

LAPIS QUATERNIO

Rotundum or chaos as prima materia, which is also ultimately irrepresentable and unknowable—and, according to Paracelsus, "co-eternal with God."[12] In Aurobindian terminology, Jung is positing that, in addition to a Superconscient, there is an Inconscient, both of which, typically, transcend consciousness and that are, therefore, unconscious to the individual.

The psychoid nature of the archetype also helps explain synchronistic phenomena or meaningful coincidences as equivalencies of psychic and physical contingencies, in which there are no causal relationships. Not only is the psyche clearly involved in such experiences as,

---

12   C.G. Jung, 1975a, p. 237.

for instance, in inner and outer events coinciding meaningfully over space-time, but matter itself is part of the equation inasmuch as matter seems to move as a container of life. Thus, Jung writes: "Psyche cannot be totally different from matter, for how otherwise could it move matter? And matter cannot be alien to psyche, for how else could matter produce psyche? Psyche and matter exist in one and the same world, and each partakes of the other, otherwise any reciprocal action would be impossible."[13] Hence, the ultimate unity of psyche and matter is apparent in synchronistic experiences.

Synchronicities are not the result of causal manipulation; they are acausal, and their orderedness points to *acts of creation in time*. Jung, in fact, takes the position that synchronistic experiences are "particular instances of general acausal orderedness" where the individual is able to "recognize the *tertium comparationis,*" the quality held in common between the different phenomena.[14] Thus, according to Jung, since they are causeless acts, "we must regard them as *creative acts,* as the continuous creation of a pattern that exists from all eternity, repeats itself sporadically, and is not derivable from any known antecedents."[15] As a pattern that exists from all eternity, the phenomena are archetypal, ultimately contained in the archetype of the Self as *unus mundus*, the creative center of cosmic being.

Wolfgang Pauli, the Nobel Prize-winning physicist who collaborated with Jung on studying the nature of synchronicity, contends that Jung's psychoid archetypes function not only as "a bridge to matter in general" but more poignantly as a bridge to "a cosmic order independent of our choice and distinct from the world of phenomena."[16] This means that archetypes-in-themselves emanate from a transcendent objective order beyond both the external world of sense perceptions and

---

13   1975a, p. 261.
14   1975b-3, p. 516.
15   *Ibid.*, p. 518.
16   As reported in Anthony Stevens 2003, p. 83.

the mind and its ideas. Amongst the schoolmen of the Middle Ages this center of cosmic order is Sophia as the Mind of God, which contains all the archetypes. Following the alchemist Gerhard Dorn, Jung refers to this creative cosmic center as the *unus mundus* or one world.

Jung writes about the cosmic order in his discussion on the alchemical *unus mundus,* the potential world of the first day of creation and creative background for the empirical world. He understands the multiplicity of the phenomenal world to be based on this background unity and potential world. Thus, Jung observes: "Undoubtedly the idea of the *unus mundus* is founded on the assumption that the multiplicity of the empirical world rests on an underlying unity, and that not two or more fundamentally different worlds exist side by side or are mingled with each other. Rather, everything divided and different belongs to one and the same world, which is not the world of sense but a postulate ... That even the psychic world, which is so extraordinarily different from the physical world, does not have its roots outside the one cosmos."[17] The creative background of the manifest world is the cosmic Self, the *unus mundus,* which has an open window onto the unity of eternity.

Again, following Dorn, Jung alludes to the fact that there are three levels of transformation, beginning with the *unio mentalis,* where the body and its appetites are overcome and the intellect undergoes a psychological transformation and gains mental comprehension of the meaning of the individuation process, the individual becoming "the mental disciple of wisdom."[18] During the second phase of the individuation process there is an embodiment of insights into the daily conduct of life by way of a conscious reunification of the *unio mentalis* with the body and bodily desires. In terms of Sri Aurobindo's yoga, the first two stages of the consciously lived individuation process seem to relate to the psychic transformation, first of the intellect, then of the vital or life

17   1974c, p. 538.
18   *Ibid.*, p. 465.

area as well as the physical body, which allows spiritual insights to be lived in life.

The third and highest level of transformation of being and the goal of the alchemical quest, according to Jung's psychology of the individuation process, is the union of the whole person, soul, spirit and body, with the *unus mundus*. This involves an identity or relationship of the individual *Atman* (Self), the *Jivatman,* with the universal *Atman* (Self), and "of the individual *tao* with the universal *tao,* " for a universalization process and definition of meaning beyond the individual.[19] *Tao* can be translated as "meaning" and "the Way of integrity," or simply "the Way" and "wholeness."[20] Thus, Jung writes that "to realize *Tao*— would be the true task ... we should translate this meaning into life."[21] Translating the Tao accordingly is similar to the way Jung refers to the Self as "totality of the whole psyche" and "Life's goal."[22] In reference to the universal Self and cosmic Tao, Jung writes: "What is meant by the Self is not only in me but in all beings, like ... the *Tao*. It is psychic totality."[23] Inasmuch as union with the *unus mundus* involves the identity of the individual Tao with the cosmic Tao, it refers to the individual living in complete harmony with the archetypal principles that govern and give meaning to life; it refers to living in synchronicity.

The *Atman* refers to "the timeless, spaceless One that supports the Many."[24] This understanding of the *Atman* is similar to Jung's definition of the Self as "the central archetype" and "the center ... of the whole psyche."[25] The *Atman* is universal and transcendent and individualizes itself as the *Jivatman*. Inasmuch as union with the *unus mundus* involves identity of the individual *Atman* or *Jivatman* with the uni-

---

19   *Ibid.*, p. 535.
20   David Rosen, 1996, pp. 9, 23,155.
21   *Ibid.,* p. 154
22   *Ibid.*, p. 23.
23   *Ibid.*, p. 122.
24   Sri Aurobindo, 1978, p. 6.
25   David Rosen, 1996, p. 122.

versal *Atman*, there is realization of underlying unity of the potential timeless-spaceless world of the first day of creation. With Jung, there is no formal reference of his attaining the transcendent *Atman*, which Sri Aurobindo calls for in his supramental yoga. Union with the *unus mundus*, however, reflects a high level of spiritual transformation and, in addition to the differentiated realization of intuition, the intellect and the vital or life area proper as quaternary functions of the fourfold Self, it includes the tendency to spiritualize matter and concretize the spirit in the formation of a spiritualized or glorified body, which requires integration of the physical body as a specific quaternary differentiation of the fourfold Self. This line of thought opens up the difficult question of how Jung's *unus mundus* compares with Sri Aurobindo's Supermind and Overmind, the subject of the next chapter.

CHAPTER 18

Sri Aurobindo's Supermind and Overmind, and Jung's *Unus Mundus*

Sri Aurobindo writes that "there is only one way, one path" and that involves, first, an inner movement and psychic transformation.[1] Of course, this should not be taken too literally as, for some individuals, the path can begin with spiritual experiences or there can be, from the outset, both a psychic and a spiritual opening. Still the "one way" of Sri Aurobindo and the Mother's path must include the psychic transformation prior to embarking on the supramental craft itself. After the psychic transformation, there is the spiritual transformation, which involves the whole being ascending upwards, rising above the intellect through the Higher Mind and then the Illumined Mind, to the Intuitive Mind and, finally, attaining Overmind and a global consciousness. In order to reach the Overmind, there is a need for a wide integration of the archetypal psyche, otherwise articulated as realization of the cosmic mind. There is, in other words, a distinct parallel between Sri Aurobindo's overmind plane and Jung's *unus mundus,* the Mind of God that contains the world of the archetypes.

Sri Aurobindo observes that in order to attain the overmind plane, "high and intense individual opening upwards is not sufficient" as there must be, in addition, the need for a "vast horizontal expansion of consciousness into some totality of the spirit."[2] Here it is significant that paths other than those of Sri Aurobindo and Jung, including

---

1   Sri Aurobindo, 1970e, p. 251.
2   1970d, p. 950.

Advaita Vedanta, do not specifically concern themselves with this horizontal expansion of consciousness. When Jung was in India in 1938, he realized this to be the case, especially in his discussion with a monk of the Ramakrishna Advaitan order, Swami Pavitrannanda, who was astonished to learn from Jung that the unconscious could be represented by concrete symbols and was not just a metaphysical abstraction.[3] The foundation of the overmind plane, as Sri Aurobindo describes it, is "the Supreme Self, one with the universe in extension and yet a cosmic centre and circumference of the specialized action of the Infinite."[4] This statement is reminiscent of one of Jung's favorite ways of describing God, quoting Bonaventure, as "an intelligible sphere whose centre is everywhere and whose circumference is nowhere," suggesting that Jung is relating to the same thing as Sri Aurobindo.[5] What the latter observes here, therefore, supports the argument that Jung's path culminates in a vast spiritual transformation of being fully in harmony with the path of Sri Aurobindo. Sri Aurobindo writes: "The overmind change is the final consummating movement of the dynamic spiritual transformation; it is the highest possible status-dynamism of the Spirit in the spiritual-mind plane."[6] There is, however, one further stage in Sri Aurobindo's Integral Yoga that is not apparent in Jung's path, and that is the supramental conversion and integral consciousness beyond the Ignorance, which culminates with the Overmind.

According to his recorded experiences and some of his comments, Jung personally came to a realization of the Oneness of the cosmic Self and defined the transformation of being, at least to a point, in terms similar to the principle goal of psychic and spiritual transformation of Sri Aurobindo's Integral Yoga; but he never put it forth as a goal of the individuation process per se for others. Yet, Jung's revelatory

3   Sulagna Sengupta, 2013, p. 162.
4   *Ibid.*, p. 952.
5   1974c, p. 47.
6   Sri Aurobindo, 1970d, p. 952.

visions are remarkable and worthwhile pondering in relationship to Sri Aurobindo's nomenclature.[7] His visions, which I amplify further below, consist of multiple images of the *mysterium coniunctionis,* a highly mystical attainment, from three different traditions, Greek, Jewish and Christian.

Jung's visions also include a deep relationship with the Hindu tradition. Thus, he reports finding himself 1000 miles above the Earth, with Sri Lanka below his feet. He turned toward the south and the Indian Ocean as a gigantic pneumatic dark rock temple appeared to his view. He realized, on entering, he would have received answers to all his questions about the meaning of his life and assumptions. He also saw a Hindu wearing a white gown sitting in lotus style, seated at the right side of the entrance to the temple rock. He was expecting Jung, who understood that by entering the black rock and its inner temple he would attain absolute knowledge. He would know the truth about his life and the cultural horizons of his life, which sounds like being connected to the upper limits of the Overmind or, possibly, the Supermind. Jung's realization suggests he could well have been at the door of the Supermind itself, described by Sri Aurobindo as "Truth-Consciousness."[8] In fact, there is a superordinate wholeness to these visionary images that supports the hypothesis of overmind experience, and possibly some influences of the Supermind.

Jung conceives of the *unus mundus* as the cosmic Self and unitary matrix consisting of multiple archetypal images and absolute knowledge, and authentic experiences of synchronicity, or meaningful coincidences of inner and outer events, as acausal without causal precedents. Jung defines synchronistic events as "a particular instance of general acausal orderedness," where a reflective observer is able to recognize their meaning.[9] Synchronicity, he believes, involves sporadic

---

7   1983, p. 289–98 passim.
8   1970c, p. 132.
9   As reported in von Franz, 1992a, p. 271.

acts of creation in time of a continuous creation of an eternally existing pattern. Such acts of creation involve an irruption of the *unus mundus,* which transcends both psyche and matter, through the archetype into the continuous flow of time or space-time.

These acts are experienced as meaningful in that one is connected through them to transcendental universal meaning, while participating in "absolute knowledge" that touches both the heart and the mind of the whole person.[10] In relation to its relatively focused light of conscious-ness, Jung refers to a universal mind with "absolute knowledge," as "luminosity" and a "cloud of cognition" that has access to a vast field of information. In relationship to everyday consciousness, its meaning speaks in a soft voice and, generally, is not so evident unless one is particularly observant and reflective.[11] The sense of orderedness, the existence of "absolute knowledge," the creative act of a pattern that exists from all eternity, and the relationship to universal meaning, as well as the transcendence of both psyche and matter, and the unitary yet multiple nature of the *unus mundus,* all seem to harmonize it with the Overmind, if not the Supermind, with synchronicity being the experi-ence of it in the throes of everyday life.

Marie-Louise von Franz explains the *unus mundus* by referring to two levels of existence underlying the wisdom found in the *I Ching:* "the mandala of the 'Order of Earlier Heaven,' which is a timeless unity, and the mandala-wheel of the 'Inner-worldly Order of Later Heaven,' which brings forth cyclic time."[12] Although the two mandalas are not conceived as interacting with each other, they illustrate the timeless unity of the *unus mundus* and "its intrusions into time in synchronistic occurrences."[13] As Jung observes: "Undoubtedly the idea of the *unus mundus rests* ... on the assumption that the multiplicity of the empirical

---

10   von Franz, 1992b, pp. 256, 257.
11   *Ibid.*, pp. 253, 254.
12   1975, p. 249.
13   *Ibid.*

world rests on an underlying unity" and that "everything divided and different belong to one and the same world, which is not the world of sense."[14]

In a way that is reminiscent of the two explanatory mandalas of the *I Ching*, the Mother observes that "One might say that ... the 'Supreme' and the 'creation' .... In the Supreme, it is a unity ... in creation, it is ... the projection of all that makes up this unity by dividing the opposites ... by separating them."[15] Like Jung regarding the *unus mundus*, she notes that "the whole of it altogether mediated by the Supermind is a perfect unity immutable and ... indissoluble," where "creation means separation of all that constitutes this unity."[16] Regarding the supramental Truth behind all things, the Mother notes that without it, "the world could never have been organized, even as it is organized now."[17] As if in agreement with Jung, she notes, "In fact, your difficulty in perceiving the Supermind or the Truth-Consciousness behind things indicates the *exact* measure of your personal ignorance and unconsciousness .... For one who has gone beyond this state of unconsciousness," she insists, "it is not difficult to find the Supermind; it is very perceptible."[18] Conscious experiences of synchronicity clearly open the door to that perception.

How far Jung went in terms of the overmind transformation, or whether he attained that level of being at all, is not evident. Yet, in his autobiography, Jung writes that what he had written in his alchemical treatise about the *mysterium coniunctionis* and *unus mundus*, he later feelingly experienced in an ecstatic vision that he observed with completely objective cognition and a feeling of being "interwoven into an indescribable whole."[19] This led to his unconditional accep-

---

14   As reported in von Franz, *Ibid.*
15   2004c, p. 80.
16   *Ibid.*
17   *Ibid.*, p. 29.
18   *Ibid.*
19   Jung, 1983, p. 296.

tance of things as they are and, rather than continuing to assert his own opinions, he surrendered to the "current of [his] thoughts," which resulted in the writing of most of his principal works, post-1944.[20] Given Jung's spiritual attainment and the archetypal nature of the subject matter, especially of the Self, in his later writing, it is fair to say that the current of his thoughts were not personal but archetypal and universal; that is, they came from the cosmic mind. He stated that he no longer wrote to please others but according to the truth as it was revealed to him. This suggests he was surrendered to Sophia, the Mind of God—in Hindu terms, the Parashakti, the unitary wisdom and knowledge of the unconscious.

As further amplification on the state of consciousness he attained, the concluding sentence of his *Answer to Job* reads: "Even the enlightened person remains what he is, and is never more than his own limited ego [*purusha*] before the One who dwells within him, whose form has no knowable boundaries, who encompasses him on all sides, fathomless as the abysms of the earth and vast as the sky," which parallels what Sri Aurobindo says regarding the overmental realization.[21] The latter observes that "thought, for the most part, ... manifests from above or comes in upon the cosmic mind waves ... the source of the revelation is not one's separate self but in universal knowledge; the feelings, emotions, sensations are similarly felt as waves from the same cosmic immensity."[22] Jung's experiences and observations, and Sri Aurobindo's remarks on overmental realizations are remarkably similar, especially if one allows for considerable plasticity and multiple possibilities of experience in overmind consciousness, as Sri Aurobindo contends is the case.

As for Sri Aurobindo, for Jung there is a unitary cosmic reality that contains all the archetypal patterns, a *unus mundus* that creates

20   *Ibid.*, p. 297.
21   Jung, 2002, p. 108.
22   Sri Aurobindo, 1970d, p. 950.

an ordered world at all levels of being. With Sri Aurobindo, the central creative source of life is the Supermind, which exists on its own
plane and, through involution, is also involved occultly in the material Inconscient, from where it engages in an evolutionary ascent. Jung
never accounts for an involutionary process per se, although, in this
context, it is relevant that he follows the alchemists in their emphasis
on the multiple *scintillae* or *lumen naturae,* the light of nature, which
he understands to be archetypal points of intelligence, in contrast to
revelation of the Holy Spirit from above. "The *scintilla* or soul-spark,"
writes Jung, "is the innermost divine essence of man" and can "just as
well express a God-image, namely the image of God unfolding in the
world, in nature and in man." [23]

The idea of the *scintillae* finds its origin in "the seven eyes of the
Lord," which in turn refers to the seven planetary gods that alchemists
believed could be found in an underground cave.[24] The light of nature
is related to the immanent Divine which can be found in the darkness
of all quarters of the natural world as well as within the human being.
The *lumen nature* can be discovered by penetrating the darkness of the
unconscious, which is a largely autonomous psychic system that is not
only instinctual, but transcends consciousness with archetypal symbols which can be assimilated to the conscious process. As Jung writes,
the unconscious "is therefore quite as much a 'supra-consciousness' as
instinctual."[25] The *lumen naturae* or light of nature, therefore, can be
visualized as extending from the physical and instinctual to the spiritually transcendent psyche.

Inasmuch as the light of nature can be found in the darkness of the
physical and instinctual being with an image of the hidden God, there
is some relationship to the involved Supermind or Truth-Mind of Sri
Aurobindo's cosmology. In discussing the depths of the soul, Jung, in

---

23   1975e, p. 389.
24   *Ibid.*, p. 140 n.
25   1970a-3, p. 185.

fact, refers to the alchemical notion that "the whole machinery of the world is driven by the infernal fire of Hell."[26] Jung observes that this is "nothing other than the *Deus Absconditus* (hidden God) also known as Mercurius," reflecting that the "highest and lowest both come from the depths of the soul."[27] Jung regards this alchemical image as a "mandala" and "the projection of the archetypal pattern of order," representing totality.[28] As Truth-Mind, the Supermind is the archetype of order par excellence, reconciling and transcending the opposites of the lowest and highest. For Sri Aurobindo, the Supermind is both integral knowledge and effective power and, based on unity that has taken up the multiplicity, it is the creative source of the becoming.

Jung's *unus mundus* is, for him, the creative source of the becoming and as is the case with the Supermind, where the stress is on unity, synchronistic experiences are always based on non-dual reality, the unitary world. Yet, given the emphasis on experiences in life, even if eternal life, rather than the *unus mundus* per se, his description seems to conform to what Sri Aurobindo refers to as the Overmind, which is still an aspect of the Mind or psyche, though at its highest level. A key difference between the two superconscient planes of being is that the Supermind requires total abolition of the ego in its surrender to the transcendent *That*, which is eventually individualized; the Overmind is contained within the cosmos, and although the soul is at one with the transcendent *That*, ego surrender, while being extensive, is not as complete.

The Gnostic Pleroma, according to Jung, is a metaphysical state of plenitude, where all psychic potentials intermingle in a condition of mutual contamination, preexistent to the opposites and form. It is the primal condition of the archetypal unconscious out of which creation emerges. In a reported conversation with Nora Mindell, Marie-Louise

---

26   1975a, p. 135.
27   *Ibid.*
28   *Ibid.*

von Franz differentiated the Gnostic Pleroma from the *unus mundus*, regarding the former as the original source of the creation, and "more complete, mysterious and irrational" than the *unus mundus*, yet similar.[29] For both Jung and von Franz, comparatively, the Pleroma is a more dynamic and creative fullness, "the Mother of the world."[30] In contrast to the Pleroma itself, von Franz envisions the *unus mundus* as more "Neoplatonic and rational," although, like the Pleroma, containing the seeds of creation.[31] The differentiation of the *unus mundus* from the Pleroma, yet their clear inter-relatedness, begs for a comparison of the former with the Supermind and the Overmind. Yet, given the *unus mundus'* rational limits and apparent openness, if not potential for considerable surrender to the Neoplatonic One, there is support for my contention that the *unus mundus* could be similar to the Overmind in Sri Aurobiondo's definition, but not the Supermind, which involves complete surrender to *That*.

As I discuss above, like the Pleroma, *Sachidananda* is an egoless state, to where the center can be shifted upwards to be established in God, and from where advanced beings can lean down as instruments of God's will in action. Such a state of being can exist on different levels of spiritual reality, but always involving "a settled existence in the one and infinite and identified with it," which Sri Aurobindo equates to samadhishta of the *Bhagavad Gita* as a self-gathered waking and "divine Samadhi."[32] On the overmind plane, according to him, the *Jivanmukti* lives in oneness with the Transcendent, a formless state of non-duality, where there is no sense of ego bondage but the work is done by "the cosmic Force," which puts on its own limitations to the work.[33] On the supramental plane, he observes, both work and the spiritual realization are, "as it were, one," whereas, otherwise, at its most perfect, the

29   2006, p. 397
30   As reported in Mindell, *Ibid.*
31   *Ibid.*
32   1971d, pp. 307, 308.
33   Sri Aurobindo, 1970a, p. 683.

spiritual condition remains through the work.[34] The evidence suggests that Jung may have experienced the Overmind, but not the Supermind. Having made such an assertion, it is important to note here that Sri Aurobindo's requirement that, on the overmind plane, the liberated soul lives in oneness with the Transcendent *That* was apparently not fulfilled by Jung, despite the probability of him having had experiences of *nirvana*.

In Jung's case during his 1944 vision, he describes his experience as being painfully stripped of "the whole phantasmagoria of earthly existence" but that "something remained."[35] He reports: "I consisted of my own history, and I felt with great certainty: this is what I am .... I existed in an objective form; I was what I had been and lived."[36] He goes on to say that "I had the feeling I was a historical fragment" without awareness of the preceding and succeeding texts.[37] Jung also recounts being in a timeless state, where "present, past and future are one," and the happenings of time coalesced "into a concrete whole."[38] At another timeless moment, he reports feeling as if "safe in the womb of the universe in a tremendous void, but filled with the highest possible feeling of happiness."[39]

While contemplating his status with all the unanswered questions about his life, a being in the form of his doctor floated up to him from the direction of Europe as a delegate from the earth. He informed Jung that he must return, which is, metaphorically, what he did. Three weeks later he made a decision to live, and subsequently he produced his most important books. Jung's 1944 and post-1944 surrender to the Godhead is exceptional, resulting in differentiated psycho-spiritual knowledge of the individual, the culture, the spiritual psyche and the becoming, as

34   *Ibid.*
35   1983, pp. 290, 291.
36   *Ibid.*, p. 291.
37   *Ibid.*
38   *Ibid.*, p. 296.
39   *Ibid.*, p. 293.

"infinitely long duration [Aion]" that is acting as a catalyst and helper for the individuation of humankind.

The Mother encourages her disciples to "develop your interior individuality, and you will be able to enter these *same* regions in full consciousness, and have the joy of communion with the highest of these regions, without losing all one's consciousness and returning with a zero instead of an experience."[40] Jung's visionary experiences need to be understood in this light. From relatively early on, Jung, in fact, was very aware of the value of experiencing the primal void and returning with renewed consciousness, as is evident in his discussion of the "breakthrough" experience of the Godhead and non-dual Reality of the German mystic, Meister Eckhart.[41] The question is whether or not the purified ego in Jung's case, which in his thought is similar to the *purusha*, involves the possibility of the psychic being or *caitya purusha*, the incarnated soul-personality, extending itself to the point of bridging non-dual Reality—or at least a high region of the psyche or Mind—with the waking state. The visionary experiences described above, and the fact that, subsequently, Jung was able to write his most important works, suggest that to be the case.

In Jung's visions, at one timeless moment, he realized an ecstatic state of pure or primal being carried in a tremendous void as in a universal womb; and there was, at another moment, a sense of underlying identity with the mystic marriage that can be translated as the Being and Consciousness-Force or Creative Power of the divine. The Mother regards this kind of experience, the duality Ishawara-Shakti, as *"the Divine in his Being and the Divine in his Force of cosmic realisation."*[42] In fact Jung's experience of the *mysterium coniunctionis* was differentiated threefold, as the Kabbalistic marriage of Malchuth with Tiffereth,

40   1978b, p. 314.
41   As reported in Dourley, 1992, pp. 114–135 passim.
42   2004c, p. 40.

the Christian "Marriage of the Lamb" and the consummation of marriage of All-Father Zeus with Hera as recorded in the *Iliad*.[43]

These visions deserve elaborate amplification and reflection. For now, briefly considered, I propose the following. The Kabbalistic marriage refers to the union of the male Tifferth, which, like the psychic being, brings balance, beauty and love, and relationship to all aspects of the Tree of Life, including the purely impersonal Godhead as the male principle; with Malchuth, the physical aspect, giving the realization of the Kingdom of God on earth, while revealing the hidden God, the feminine Shekinbah or Wisdom. The "Marriage of the Lamb" can be understood to refer to the marriage of the individual in surrender to a God and the deeper spiritual needs of the community of people. The marriage of Zeus and Hera refers mainly to the marriage of masculine and feminine divine opposites in the area of the vital or life itself, for example, regarding power, ambition and sexual energy; in other words, it reflects the spiritualization of life itself. All in all, this differentiated vision refers to the psychic and spiritual transformation of being and personal surrender in all areas of life, realized on Earth and involving suffering others in the community. Jung experienced this high level of psychic reality consciously, indicating an extended ladder of being and that he consciously lived out the vision's significance in his own life, as a true helper of humanity leading it toward the realization of a new world.

The fact that Jung's primal being remains distinct while being carried in a great void seems to be something like consciously existing and surrendered at the edge of the universe, on the verge of entering non-dual Reality. His conscious realization of these exalted states is in perfect harmony with the Mother's recommendations to her disciples. Indeed, the fact that Jung had such lofty conscious experiences leads me to believe that it is likely he experienced non-dual Reality in one

---

43   1983, p. 294.

way or another, although he never wrote about it formally. His principal interest was in building an extended ladder of being, and that could be a good reason why he spoke so consistently against having such a goal. Still, there is no explicit evidence of his aspiring toward or experiencing the egoless state of the liberated soul in a self-gathered state of samadhi trance, where the ego has been shifted upwards in oneness with the Transcendent, and established in God rather than nature. This puts into question whether Jung actually attained the overmind plane in his 1944 experience, or a lesser plane of being.

The Mother's[44] description of having an individual conscious relationship with the Transcendent *That* does, in fact, have some parallel with Jung's experiences, especially considering that she came to believe the meaning of creation was to unify the distinct "individual consciousness" with "consciousness of the whole."[45] Yet there are differences. The Mother describes the individual consciousness of the experience as consisting of "a plenary consciousness total and simultaneous beyond Time and Space, a global perception, with 'no Time' ... and no 'Space.' One experiences eternity and the universe," she observed, as "pre-existent, but not manifested."[46]

Although this is reminiscent of the mystic marriage in Jung's vision, where the seeds of creation are contained in a state of gestation, the Mother's emphasis on no "Time" and no "Space" was not apparent in Jung's case. He reports, rather, experiencing "the ecstasy of a nontemporal state in which present, past and future are one."[47] Regarding this experience, the Mother is reported as saying that "only right at the top of the ladder, when one reaches what could be called the centre of the universe, the centre and origin of the universe, everything is instantaneous. The past, present and future are all contained in a total and si-

---

44   2004c, p. 38.
45   *Ibid.*, p. 52.
46   *Ibid.*
47   Jung, 1983, pp. 295, 296.

multaneous consciousness, that is, what has always been and what will be are as though united in a single instant, a single beat of the universe, and it is only there that one goes out of Time and Space."[48] Given this background, one could say that Jung built a ladder of being right up to the center of the universe, a state of consciousness just prior to entering the realm of *That* and non-dual Reality, identification with which Sri Aurobindo regards as the realization of "true freedom."[49]

With regard to the experience of eternity in relationship to space and time, both the Mother and Jung wrote of movement that translates into psychological and physical phenomena in the manifest world through individual consciousness. In reference to his experience, Jung put it that there was "*eternal* movement, (not movement in time)" and he noted that the psyche's involvement in space and time may be the result of the brain acting as a "transformer station" in which it draws the infinite intensity of the psyche proper into the manifestation through "perceptible frequencies" or "extensions."[50] Even more explicitly than with Jung, the source of movement according to the Mother is identified as Consciousness, which, in a state of Immortality, "is like staggeringly rapid waves, so rapid that they seem immobile. It is like that," she said, "—nothing moves (apparently) in a tremendous Movement."[51] As with Jung, movement in thought, feelings, and the physical are brought into the manifestation through individual consciousness.

The evidence as discussed above seems to point to Jung having built a bridge to the center of the universe in these experiences, although he did not leave the universe in order to merge with *That* and attain the status of a liberated soul. The testimony of Jung's spiritual achievements according to his final dream-vision, which he was able to have recorded just prior to his passing away, do not suggest otherwise.

---

48   2004c, p. 45.
49   As reported in the Mother, 2004c, p. 38.
50   As reported in Adler, 1975, p. 358.
51   2004c, p. 30.

I discuss the dream and its significance below. In the meantime, I believe it is fair to say that whether or not Jung attained the level of *Jivanmukti,* or liberated soul, and identification with *That,* there can be little doubt that his life is exemplary in his having been open to and having followed, in a superlative fashion, the Will of God. In fact, according to his deathbed confessions, as discussed above, he did attain the status of nirvana, although not that of a liberated soul according to Sri Aurobindo's definition.

Sri Aurobindo's Visionary Experiences as Recorded in *Savitri:* Comparisons with Jung

Sri Aurobindo indicates that the surrender required to attain the Supermind is more complete than at the level of the Overmind; indeed it is total, resulting in bringing down Truth to Earth. In Sri Aurobindo's *Savitri,* in his one-pointed quest for the Unknowable, King Aswapathy experiences *That* beyond the world of forms, where:

> All he had been and all towards which he grew
> Must now be left behind or else transform
> Into a self of That which has no name.
> ...
> The symbol modes of being helped no more.
> ...
> Transcending every perishable support
> And joining at last its mighty origin
> The separate self must melt or be reborn
> Into a truth beyond the mind's appeal.
> ...
> Nothing remains the cosmic mind conceives.
> ...
> Only a formless form of self remained.
> ...
> The undying Truth appeared, the enduring power
> Of all that here is made and then destroyed
> The Mother of all godheads and all strengths
> Who mediatrix, binds earth to the Supreme.
> ...

Once seen, his heart acknowledged only her.

...

This was a seed cast in endless Time.
A Word is spoken or a light is shown,

...

Her light, her bliss he asked for earth and men.

...

In the mind's silence the Transcendent acts
And the hushed heart hears the unuttered Word.
A vast surrender was his only strength.
A Power that lives upon the heights must act,

...

Only he yearned to call her ever down
Her healing touch of love and truth and joy
Into the darkness of the suffering world.
His soul was freed and given to her alone.[52]

Surrendering to *That* beyond form and the cosmic mind does not result in annihilation of the living soul, but the appearance of Truth, the Mother of All, who makes manifest the Supreme Will. Aswapathy now surrenders to the Mother, the creative source of life, yearning to bringing her down on Earth along with the seed of new creation and the Word for the healing of a suffering world.

Jung's level of surrender, although apparently not as total, advances the path of conscious individuation to clearly include full spiritual transformation as an accessible phenomenon in the forthcoming Age of the Holy Spirit. The path is new, more thorough and comprehensive than in the past and includes opening, through the *unus mundus* and synchronicity, to new acts of creation in time. Jung's early initiatory experience of the god of unending Time, Aion—recorded in *The Red Book*, and one of his later books, where he works through some four thousand years of Western history, including the Christian aeon, culminating in a highly differentiated description of the Self consisting of fourfold quaternities—reflects detachment from the power of becoming

---

52   1970a*, pp. 307–316.

in Time. As I indicate above, it also implies that Jung was capable of consciously entering the new age, the Age of the Holy Spirit, which he discusses in correspondence with the Dominican, Victor White; although he notes that "this state is not quite understandable yet. It is a mere anticipation."[53] This is some nine years after his 1944 visions, which demonstrates extreme surrender of being on Jung's part.

In the letter he writes, "You look forward beyond the Christian aeon to the Oneness of the Holy Spirit … the pneumatic state the creator attains through the phase of incarnation. He is the experience of every individual that has undergone the complete abolition of his ego through the absolute opposition expressed by the symbol Christ versus Satan."[54] Jung fully recognizes the need to reconcile the most extreme opposites of good and evil, and for total surrender of the ego. He goes on to write: "The state of the Holy Spirit means a restitution of the original oneness of the unconscious on the level of consciousness."[55] Jung foresaw the coming supramental manifestation as conscious oneness, but there is little evidence that he had access to the Word or the power of planting the seed for a new creation as did Sri Aurobindo and the Mother, as expressed above in *Savitri.*

The level of surrender Sri Aurobindo indicates is necessary for his supramental yoga leads to full embodiment of the Supreme Will and direct inner involvement in the new divine creation in time. God's "most evident Power of becoming and the essence of the whole universal movement," writes Sri Aurobindo, is "imperishable, beginningless, unending Time." The "seed cast in endless Time" and the spoken "Word," the Logos, and "light" portend a new creation and transformed "Power of becoming in Time."[56] Jung's relatively early identification and then detachment from Aion, the god of "endless time," described earlier in

---

53   As reported in Lammers and Cunningham, 2008, p. 220.
54   *Ibid.*
55   *Ibid.*
56   1970a*, 315.

this document, shows striking sympathy with Sri Aurobindo and the Mother's work, even if his level of surrender is not as total.

At this juncture, it might help to put Jung's case in perspective by describing Aswapthy's journey just prior to his surrender to *That* and bringing in the seed of new creation and the Word, while yearning for the incarnation of the Mother and her healing touch. During his inner travels he eventually arrives at and explores the world soul, the *anima mundi*, where his conscious soul arrives at "the source of all things human and divine."[57] Reminiscent of Jung's[58] 1944 visionary experience, where he reports being "thronged around with images of all creation," Sri Aurobindo writes:

> There he beheld in their mighty Union's pose
> The figure of the deathless Two-in-One,
> A single being in two bodies clasped,
> A diarchy of two united souls,
> Sealed absorbed in deep creative joy;
> Their trance of bliss sustained the mobile world.[59]

Then, apparently, going deeper and/or higher than Jung, Sri Aurobindo recounts:

> Behind them in a morning dusk One stood
> Who brought them forth from the Unknowable,
> …
> She guards the austere approach to the Alone.
> …
> Above them all she stands supporting all,
> The sole omnipotent Goddess ever-veiled
> of whom the world is the inscrutable mask;
> …

---

57   Sri Aurobindo, *ibid.*, p. 295.
58   1983, p. 294.
59   *Ibid.*

And all creation is her endless act.[60]

...

Then in a sovereign answer to his heart

...

One arm half-parted the eternal veil.

...

He saw the mystic outline of a face.

...

He cast rent from the stillness of his soul
A cry of adoration and desire
And the surrender of his boundless mind
And the self-giving of his silent heart.
He fell down at her feet unconscious, prone.[61]

Both the receptive and active engagement of Aswapathy in the process of surrender to the Goddess is noteworthy.

In Jung's case he describes the feeling that everything he aspired to or wished for "fell away or was stripped from me—an extremely painful process" until he existed "in an objective form," without desire.[62] This objectivity, he believes, is "part of a completed individuation."[63] "Objective cognition" lies behind "the attraction of the emotional relationship, with its archetypal foundation that draws one into worldly pursuits;" it "is the central secret," he observes, as only detachment makes the real *coniunctio* possible.[64] Jung goes on to write about the feeling that "present, past and future are one," saying, "One is interwoven into an indescribable whole and yet observes it with complete objectivity."[65] Although Jung's experiences are remarkable, Aswapathy, really Sri Aurobindo, seems to have arrived here at a higher level of conscious realization and surrender than did Jung during his visions.

---

60   *Ibid.*
61   *Ibid.*, pp. 295, 296.
62   1983, p. 290, 291.
63   *Ibid.*, p. 296.
64   *Ibid.*, p. 297.
65   *Ibid.*, p. 296.

He surrenders to the One, the divine world-creatrix that is poised to guide him on to the Unknowable.

In actual fact, according to evidence from Appendix C in *The Red Book*, Jung's soul, depicted in image 155, similar to Sri Aurobindo's description, with a face partly veiled, speaks with the voice of Sophia, the Parashakti, and admonishes Jung as follows: "*You should worship only one God.*"[66] The other gods are unimportant. "*Abraxas is to be feared.* Therefore it was a deliverance when he separated himself from me."[67] Here Jung is referring to the Gnostic myth, where Sophia separates herself from the demiurge. He, too, is encouraged to detach from the spectacle of life and yet remain in the middle of life, suspended by the opposites in sacrifice to the one God. Jung's guide henceforth becomes the "*one* God, the wonderfully beautiful and kind, the solitary, starlike, unmoving ... beyond death and beyond what is subject to change."[68] This one God, described as a solitary star, which Jung is ultimately destined to become, is his life's guide. Jung's path, in this regard, seems similar to that of Sri Aurobindo's, although his vision does not depict him meeting Sophia at the edge of all the potentially knowable and, later, for departure to the Unknowable, as is the case of Aswapathy in Sri Aurobindo's *Savitri*.

Aswapathy continues his travels into the "Kingdoms of the Greater Knowledge," where he eventually arrives at the "top of all that can be known," and his "sight surpassed creation's head and base."[69] Finally he comes to a place where:

> An all embracing knowledge seized his heart:
> Thoughts rose in him no earthly mind can hold,
> Mights played that never coursed through mortal nerves:
> He scanned the secrets of the Overmind.

---

66   2009, p. 371.
67   *Ibid.*
68   *Ibid.*
69   Sri Aurobindo, 1970a*, p. 300.

He bore the rapture of the Oversoul.
Attuned to the supernal harmonies,
He linked creation to the Eternal's sphere,
His finite parts approached their absolutes,
His actions framed the movements of the Gods,
His will took up the reins of cosmic Force.[70]

It is as if, through Aswapathy, Sri Aurobindo is travelling a considerable distance beyond where Jung left off in his remarkable 1944 visions, to arrive at greater knowledge of creation, which he is able to
link to eternity. He is led to the heights of the Overmind, which exist
at the extreme summit of the psyche or mind, presumably with the
clarity of the Mind of Light, which he wrote about in late life. He has
clear understanding of the cosmic nature of the Overmind, unveiling
its secrets while being in tune with its divine harmonies, his cosmic
soul enraptured as he is open and receptive to extraordinary truths and
power. As he is consciously identified with the cosmic Self, he is not
just receptive to sublime thoughts with the power of their effective realization, he dynamically and consciously works with these universal
archetypal energies in a fashion that is, apparently, typical of the upper
reaches of the Overmind.

Jung's concluding sentence in *Answer to Job*, "Even the enlightened person remains what he is, and is never more than his own limited
ego [*purusha*] before the One who dwells within him ... who encompasses him on all sides," seems similar to what Sri Aurobindo writes
regarding the overmental realization. Yet, in comparison to what Sri
Aurobindo hints at regarding the nature of the heights of the overmind
plane, however beautiful and meaningful Jung's statement, it describes
a lesser status of being, even if it is still the Overmind.[71] Although in
the *coniunctio* visions, Jung did have an underlying identify with the
cosmic Self as depicted in the images of the *mysterium coniunctionis*,

70   *Ibid.*, p. 302.
71   Jung, 2002, p. 108.

in this particular statement he is not identified with the cosmic Self as Sri Aurobindo is in Ashwapthy's experience, but with the individual *purusha*.

Now let us return to Aswapathy in Sri Aurobindo's *Savitri*, book three: "The Book of the Divine Mother, Canto One: The Pursuit of the Unknowable" and the realization of *That*.[72] Unlike many spiritual paths, the journey of the soul's self-discovery does not end with this realization and spiritual freedom. In the following Canto Two, "The Adoration of the Divine Mother," the statement is made: "O soul, it is too early to rejoice!" Then, the question is posed: "But where hast thou thrown self's mission and self's power?"[73] It soon becomes clear that "the Lover's everlasting Yes" to the manifestation is essential to fulfilling the soul's vocation. Thus:

> A huge extinction is not God's last word,
> …
> The meaning of this great mysterious world.
> In absolute silence sleeps an absolute Power.
> …
> It can make the world a vessel of Spirit's force,
> It can fashion in clay God's perfect shape.
> …
> Here to fulfill himself was God's desire.[74]

In this canto, the reader is presented with the uniqueness of Sri Aurobindo's Integral Yoga, which distinguishes it from all other spiritual paths including Jung's path. At the same time there are elements indicated here that can be found with Jung as well, even if not so differentiated. I will attempt to isolate other lines that discern the ground of Sri Aurobindo's spiritual genius and its eventual outcome.[75]

---

72   1970a*, pp. 305–309.
73   *Ibid.*, p. 310.
74   *Ibid.*, pp. 311–312.
75   *Ibid.*, pp. 312, 313.

Even while he stood on being's naked edge
And all the passion and seeking of his soul
Faced their extinction in some featureless Vast,
The presence he yearned for suddenly drew close,
Across the silence of the ultimate Calm,
...
A body of wonder and translucency
...
Had come enlarged out of eternity,
Someone came infinite and absolute.
A being of wisdom, power and delight,
...
Imaged itself in a surprising beam
And built a golden passage to his heart
Touching through him all longing sentient things.
...
A Nature throbbing with a Heart divine
Was felt in the unconscious universe;
...
Eudaemonised the sorrow of the world,
Made happy the weight of long unending Time,
The secret caught of God's felicity.

The key to this unique path is that the Divine Mother, the Heart divine, as wisdom, power and delight, has descended from the Transcendence' core, and built a golden bridge to Aswapthy's heart. In the process, through him, she touches all sentient beings. Of immense importance for the new creation,

> The hidden Word was found, the long sought clue,
> Revealed was the meaning of our spirit's birth.[76]

Sri Aurobindo received the Word from the Divine Mother and, along with it, the high meaning of his birth. Here it may be pertinent to recall that, during his 1944 visions, Jung found himself some thousand miles in space, and he knew that when he entered an illuminated room in a

---

76   *Ibid.*, p. 313.

black pneumatic stone, the size of his house or bigger, he would "meet all those people to whom I belonged in reality. There I would at last understand—this too was a certainty—what historical nexus I or my life fitted into ....I would receive an answer to all these questions as soon as I entered the rock temple."[77] He knew he was to enter the temple and that he "would reach full knowledge."[78] While he was reflecting on these matters, he was called back to Earth under protest against his imminent departure. In fact, after his cure from his heart ailment, he wrote several of his most important books.

Although Jung didn't personally receive the Word directly from the source, he went on to write significant books that open up to the coming new age of the Holy Spirit, which he foresaw. *The Red Book*, which Jung worked on between 1913 and 1928, begins with a section in the *Liber Primus* entitled "The Way of What is to Come," in reference to the future and the coming Age of Aquarius, along with the constellation of a new God-image.[79] The book mainly consists of a transcription of his experiences during 1913–1916 in elegantly transposed calligraphy and with beautiful paintings elaborately worked on between 1917 and 1928. In 1917 he added the *Septem Sermones ad Mortuos* (*Seven Sermons to the Dead*), a summary Gnostic statement. The book, which according to Lance Owens he "composed" in 1915, is the product of his active engagement with the unconscious and was the seed of all his later writings.[80] If nothing else, it reflects stages of growth in the individuation process, if one takes into account the individual nature of the adventure.

Jung observes: "It all began then; the later details are only supplements and clarifications of the material that burst forth from the unconscious, and at first swamped me. It was the *prima materia* of a lifetime's

77   1983, p. 292.
78   Jung as recorded in Adler, 1973, p. 358.
79   2009, pp. 229–232 passim.
80   2013, p. 30.

work."[81] Here, in a way, is the natural Jung, without the sophisticated language he later developed to support his scientific method and depth psychology. Here he speaks in the language of the image and the symbol, which can be seen as superior to the analytical intellect and closer to the truth. In "The Way of What is to Come," Jung writes:

> My speech is imperfect. Not because I want to shine with words, but out of the impossibility of finding these words. I speak in images. With nothing else can I express the words from the depths.[82]

Jung, in fact, expresses himself in *The Red Book* through mythopoeic speech, using metaphor, the language of poetry, ritual and incantation and painted imagery as well as the ornate script of calligraphy. Not only the analytical intellect but the discursive intellect was not adequate. Only the imagistic and symbolic language of the primordial mind was sufficient to the task.

Jung refers to his relationship to the archetypal symbol that expresses itself through him to others, mirroring Aswapathy's status when the Mother touched "through him all longing sentient things." In *The Red Book*, Jung writes: "Insofar as it takes place in me, and I am a part of the world, it also takes place, through me in the world, and no one can hinder it."[83] Jung did not receive the fullness of the Word as the creative Truth like Sri Aurobindo; rather, according to the former's logic, the symbol, which works through him, is the divine Word. Again, in *The Red Book*, he writes: In fact, in his active imagination, his soul informs him that he has broken the compulsion of the law of fate, saying, "You possess the word that should not be allowed to remain concealed."[84] Earlier Jung notes; "The symbol is the word that goes out of the mouth,

81   1983, p. 199.
82   2009, p. 230.
83   Jung, 2009, p. 250.
84   *Ibid.*, p. 346.

that one does not simply speak, but that rises out of the depths of the self as a word of power and great need and places itself unexpectedly on the tongue."[85]

The mother for Jung is the source of all individual, cosmic and physical phenomena as well as spiritual and psychological transformation. Given his understanding of the psyche as infinite intensity and *ousia* (or substance, essence, as discussed below), the mother for him is also, arguably, Transcendent and formless as well. Regarding the physical mother, he refers to a stone as "mother stone," avowing, "I love you."[86] He also writes about the "mother, my soul," who gives birth to a child, emphasizing the individual aspect of the mother.[87] Regarding the cosmic and spiritual mother, he notes: "The image of the Mother of God with child that I foresee indicates to me the mystery of the transformation."[88] A vision of the mother of God is a numinous experience that turns "desire away from the flesh toward the humble veneration of the spirit."[89] Regarding the transformative spiritual Mother, he once refers to the "virginal or maternal quality of the prima materia, which exists without a man and yet is the 'matter of all things'"; "Above all," Jung writes, "the prima materia is the mother of the lapis, the *filius philosophorum*."[90] There are many more references to the mother in all her plenitude, as individual, cosmic and Transcendent, while embracing both darkness and light, as well as to symbolic aspects of the mother such as a body of water, like a well, river, lake and ocean, and in the form of dove, worm and serpent, as Dourley points out.[91]

As with Sri Aurobindo, as described in *Savitri*, where the Mother is both the power of Silence and the Word, the Mother, for Jung, is

85   *Ibid.*, p. 311.
86   Jung, 2009, p. 271.
87   *Ibid.*, p 244.
88   *Ibid.*, p. 280.
89   *Ibid.*, p. 367.
90   1974c, p. 18.
91   2010 passim.

ultimately established in the Gnostic formless silence, the source of the Word and beyond both the cosmic and individual psyches.[92] In *Mysterium Coniunctionis,* Jung quotes what he refers to as a "remarkable" text on Gnostic metaphysics from the third-century Christian theologian, Hippolytus, which includes the following: "There are two offshoots from all the Aeons, having neither beginning nor end, from one root, and this root is a certain power, an invisible and incomprehensible Silence."[93] *Prayers and Meditations,* written by Sri Aurobindo's spiritual colleague, the Mother when she was a young woman, is a wonderful testimony to Silence.[94] Notwithstanding her natural affinity with Silence, however, she ardently aspires to a state beyond Being, beyond the "Silence that is united with That," indicative of the intensive measure of Sri Aurobindo and the Mother's yoga.[95]

In the Vedas, India's original scriptures, the progenitor and creator god is Prajapati, a title meaning "Lord of the creatures."[96] According to these scriptures, although both *Manas* or Mind and *Vāc* or Speech are yoked for the sacrifice, Prajapati chose "undefined" Mind, which contains Silence along with "undefined" substance of being, as supreme. Roberto Calasso, who writes creatively about both Indian and Western mythology, makes the highly meaningful observation that in contrast to India, in ancient Greece, despite Noûs being recognized as an independent power of intelligence, Speech (Logos) is supreme, not the Mind.[97] He argues that in the West, both Jerusalem (Judeo-Christianity) and Athens (Greece) colluded on the supremacy of Logos and its connection to speech.[98] Relevant to this discussion is the fact that Jung's path, with its relationship to Gnosticism and the formless Silence, as

---

92   John Dourley, *ibid.*, p. 125.
93   1974c, p. 136.
94   1979, 2003 passim.
95   *Ibid.,* p. 249
96   Roberto Calasso, 2014, p. 67
97   *Ibid.,* p. 110
98   *Ibid.,* p. 111

well as the primary importance of the archetypal psyche as an expression of Logos, goes beyond the Greek/Jerusalem formulation, while forging a direct link to India and the East that finds its most significant root-source in the Vedas of India, where both *Manas* (Mind) and *Vāc* (Speech) are united for the sacrificial offering.

There are also several references to solitude, stillness and silence in *The Red Book*, as well as to the importance of symbol creation and personality transformation. "The solitary loves deep stillness; it is a mother to him."[99] Jung describes a meditative process he later calls active imagination: "The training consists first in systematic exercises for eliminating critical attention thus producing a vacuum in consciousness."[100] There is, in other words, a need to empty the mind of discursive thoughts and to allow for the imaginal psyche and the play of symbol formation. One is enjoined to "be silent and listen," which opens one up to the archetypal psyche.[101]

Jung, in fact, observes that the creation of symbols is the most important function of the unconscious, as, through the symbol, there is personality transformation, which can affect others. In fact, Jung comes to understand that he has the key that opens the future, which "takes place through his transformation."[102] He reasons that "the binding and loosing takes place in me. But insofar as it takes place in me, and I am part of the world, it also takes place through me in the world, and no one can hinder it."[103] The transformation, it need be noted, does not happen according to Jung's conscious will, but due to the radiating effect of his having submitted to the Self.

At one point, his soul actually says to him that "the new religion and its proclamation is your calling."[104] As a matter of fact, in *The Red*

---

99   Jung, 2009, p. 269.
100   *Ibid.*, p. 209.
101   *Ibid.*, p. 298.
102   *Ibid.*, p. 250.
103   *Ibid.*
104   *Ibid.*, p. 211.

Book, Jung does identify with Christ as well as this vocation. He writes, "Go there, drink the blood and eat the flesh of him who was mocked and tormented for the sake of our sins, so that you totally become his nature, deny his being apart from you: you should be he himself, not Christians but Christ, otherwise you will be of no use to the coming God."[105] By becoming Christ, one does not mimic Christ, but suffers one's own unique life, with its peculiar unfolding conspiracy of circumstances, while carrying one's own cross of opposites.

It is noteworthy that in 1939, at the age of sixty-four, Jung was moved by a vision of a greenish-gold figure of Christ on the Cross at the foot of his bed. He defines the green-gold in alchemical terms as the ingestion of the living spirit in humans and matter. This symbolic portrayal of Christ is much more complete than images of Christ in traditional Christianity, which Jung regards as narrowly one-sided in its exclusion of the shadow, sexuality and the body. Jung's experience, which I amplify more fully below, points to identity with the immanent divinity in a relationship of unity with the transcendent One that embraces all life including matter.

Although Jung never denies the experience of identity with Christ, he eventually repudiates any identification with his subjective experiences, and never claims any prophetic or other role than being a psychiatrist and an empirical scientist. Thus, he writes: "Though I am sure of my subjective experience, I must guard against identifying with my subjective experience. I consider all such identifications as serious psychological mistakes.[106] Had Jung taken a different position he could very well have instituted a new religion. His view on religion is identical to that of Sri Aurobindo, who writes: "I may say it is far from my purpose to propagate any religion new or old for humanity in the future. A way to be opened that is still blocked, not a religion to be founded, is

---

105   2009, p. 234.
106   Jung as recorded in Adler, 1975, p. 376.

my conception of the matter."[107] The path for the truly modern person today is primarily one of individual openness to the down-pouring of the spirit, transformation and individuation, and not the establishment of a new religion.

Although Jung never assumes the mantle of someone spearheading a new religion, his work does open up the way to the future as a kind of religion in *status nascendi*. In fact, Jung is clear about the fact that he had discovered the origins of religion, and he writes: "It is a telling fact that two theological reviewers of my book, *Psychology and Religion*— one of them Catholic, the other Protestant—assiduously overlooked my demonstration of the psychic origin of religious phenomena.[108] For that matter, as Dourley points out, he found the origins of other disciplines such as philosophy, theology and science, and the basis of the secular order in the archetypal psyche as well.[109]

Regarding Christianity, Jung writes:

> If I have ventured to submit old dogmas, now grown stale, to psychological scrutiny, I have certainly not done so in the priggish conceit that I knew better than others, but in the sincere conviction that a dogma which has been such a bone of contention for so many centuries cannot possibly be an empty fantasy. I felt that it was too much in line with the *consensus omnium*, with the archetype, for that .... A knowledge of the universal archetypal background was, in itself, sufficient to give me the courage to treat "that which is believed always, everywhere, by everybody" as a *psychological fact* which extends far beyond the confines of Christianity, and to approach it as an object of scientific study.[110]

Here, Jung indicates how he reconciles science with religion through recognition of the archetypal nature of the psyche. He was fully con-

---

107   2011, p. 696.
108   1977, p. 9.
109   2014, p. 25–33 passim.
110   1975c-1, 199, 200.

vinced that religious dogma and symbols, specifically Christian in the case of the Western mind, were rooted in the psyche. He writes:

> Christian civilization has proved hollow to a terrifying degree: it is all veneer, but the inner man has remained untouched and therefore unchanged ....
>
> Christianity must indeed begin again from the very beginning if it is to meet its high educative task. So long as religion is only faith and outward form, and the religious function is not experienced in our own souls, nothing of any importance has happened. It has yet to be understood that the *mysterium magnum* is not only an actuality but is first and foremost rooted in the human psyche. The man who does not know this from his own experience may be a most learned theologian, but he has no idea of religion and still less of education.[111]

Jung is not speaking to people for whom religious dogma and symbols are contained by the religion, but to those for whom that is no longer the case. If he reinterprets Christian dogma and symbols, it is because, in this way, he reaches the depth of the modern (Western) mind in a fashion that is accessible today. This observation is based on the fact that dogma and symbols embody the same underlying patterns as the newly interpreted truths.

Regarding the Divine Mother, Sri Aurobindo writes these stirring words, which defines her magnificence:

> The Formless and the Formed were joined in her.
> ...
> Alone her hands can change Time's dragon base.
> ...
> She is the golden bridge, the wonderful fire.
> The luminous heart of the Unknown is she,
> A power of Silence in the depths of God;
> She is the Force, the inevitable Word
> The magnet of our difficult ascent,

---

111   Jung, 1977, p. 12.

...
Once seen, his heart acknowledged only her;
His base was gathered into one pointing spire.
Thus was a seed cast into endless Time.[112]

The seed of new creation leads to Canto Three, "The House of the Spirit and the New Creation," where "a new and marvellous creation rose";[113] otherwise it is stated that, along with great resistance, "a new creation from the old shall rise."[114] Then, in Canto Four, the reader finally comes to "The Vision and the Boon," where the aspirant, Aswapathy, is advised as follows:

Only one boon, to greaten thy spirit, demand,
Only one joy, to raise thy kind, desire,
Above blind fate and the antagonist powers
Moveless there stands a high unchanging Will;
To its omnipotence leave thy work's result.
All things shall change in God's transfiguring hour.[115]

Despite resistance and feelings of despair, a new world is born with the premonition that all things shall change, for which there are already signs in all aspects of life, from architecture that has become extraordinarily plastic and open to a variety of beautiful forms, hitherto impossible, to advances in sports through improved training and athleticism, to medicine, science and technology everywhere, as well as in political and human rights breakthroughs, often after elevated, seemingly insoluble conflicts, and so on. It seems as if there are two worlds existing side by side, the old one and the emerging new world. Finally Sri Aurobindo gives a beautiful poetic vision of the future in the following lines:

112   1970a*, pp. 314, 315.
113   *Ibid.*, p. 323.
114   *Ibid.*, p. 330.
115   *Ibid.*, p. 341.

> The unfolding Image showed the things to come,
> A giant dance of Shiva tore the past,
> ...
> I saw the Omnipotent's flaming pioneers
> ...
> Out of the paths of the morning star they came
> Into the little room of mortal life.
> I saw them cross the twilight of an age,
> The sun-eyed children of a glorious dawn,
> The great creators with wide brows of calm,
> ...
> The architects of immortality.[116]

The Mother's play with numbers, described above, when understood esoterically, indicates the reality of the new creation as an act from the Divine Mother as Sophia or Parashakti herself in Time. Sri Aurobindo's poem *Savitri* is a symbolic creation myth for our times, which not only envisions the unfolding future, but outlines the complex path of his yoga of triple transformation.

According to Sri Aurobindo, the Overmind consists of global knowledge, while the Supermind's knowledge is integral. The global knowledge of the Overmind, according to him, still needs to work out each line of evolutionary development to its end; whereas, with the Supermind, this is not necessary, as it is based on integral Knowledge and the Power and descent of Truth. Jung's later writings no doubt came under the influence of the Overmind or other lesser mental planes and not the Supermind per se. However, despite what Sri Aurobindo writes about the Overmind here—that is, about the need to work out the evolutionary line of development of any particular subject to its end—Jung's approach to psychology is, in fact, not boxed into a rigid line of thought; having opened many doors relating to different developmental potentials, his approach is rendered extraordinarily catholic

---

116   *Ibid.*, pp. 343, 344.

and encourages openness to truth. This could be explained by the fact that, especially post-1944, Jung was a quaternary thinker, which I argue below, is open to Supramental intuitions.

The Overmind influence may, nonetheless, be reflected in that Jung's main effort was spent in coming to terms with Western evolutionary development and cultural history, especially Christianity, needing also the compensatory influences from Western Gnosticism and alchemy. With Jung, the Christian emphasis is predominant since he understands Christ to be, outside of the Buddha, the most differentiated symbol of the Self and still "the living myth of our culture."[117] In a seminar lecture held in 1940, he also observes that "Christ is really the example of how a human life should be lived," referring to his "absolute humility and obedience."[118] By this statement Jung does not mean external imitation of Christ's life, but living one's own life as intensely as did Christ; thus an imitation of the archetype of the Self.

However, it is evident that Jung's more profound answer to the dilemma of the Western psyche and its impoverished religious and philosophic condition was to build a bridge from the past to the present and on into the future, finding psychological meaning for Christian dogma and symbols, by way of Gnosticism and its historical development in alchemy and the Kabbala. His relationships with alchemy and Gnosticism, seeing them through the lens of depth psychology, were particularly important. In *Memories, Dreams, Reflections*, Jung writes:

> When I began to understand alchemy I realized that it represented an historical link with Gnosticism, and that a continuity therefore existed between past and present .... Alchemy formed the bridge between, on the one hand into the past, to Gnosticism, and on the other into the future, to the modern psychology of the unconscious .... The possibility of a comparison with alchemy,

---

117   1976a, p. 36.
118   C.G. Jung, 1959, p. 257.

and the uninterrupted intellectual chain back to Gnosticism, gave substance to my psychology.[119]

This development, in fact, draws Jung much closer to India and the East, which has a long tradition of a Yoga of Knowledge [Gnosis], Tantra and alchemy.

Still, with Jung, there is reference to the example of Christ's life, and it seems to me that it is valid for the West in general, but it is less relevant for other cultural spheres. In India, Krishna's teachings of liberation to Arjuna in the *Gita* may be a more evident choice; and there are other paths in that spiritually multivalent and open culture. Although the real issue is imitation of the Self and following its lead, one cannot avoid acknowledging the fact that the Advaitan path of the *Gita* leads to spiritual liberation and attaining identity with *That* or non-dual Reality; whereas the Christian path primarily involves suffering the opposites, leading to the embodiment of Love, even though there is also a Christian path of mystical liberation. I use the example of Krishna and Advaita since Sri Aurobindo emphasizes the relevance of the *Gita* and the need to attain *That* in his Integral Yoga. Jung is well aware of the difference in mentality between the East and West when he observes that Westerners go from "the outer into the inner world," whereas the "Eastern experience descends from the unity of the divine spirit, so to speak, and sets the wheel of truth in motion."[120] The difference in emphasis therefore may simply be a question of cultural predisposition, where integrity demands that one sincerely and honestly work through one's historical heritage and not blindly adopt foreign beliefs and values. Even in the Christian sphere of influence, which includes India, there are vast cultural differences that need to be accounted for in defining one's inner path.

I write the above notwithstanding the fact that Jung reflects on a

---

119   1983, p. 201.
120   *Ibid.*, p. 252.

much longer and broader history of *homo sapiens* than the Christian aeon and its sphere of influence; and he recognizes other incarnations of the Self besides Christ, as I indicate above. In her reflections on Jung's book *Aion,* Marie-Louise von Franz observes that there is "an evolving creation and evolving God-image" that is "developing towards new forms of consciousness."[121] In writing the book, where he discusses the Christian aeon, Jung was actually more interested in bringing historical material to bear in order to differentiate the nature of the Self, than in Christianity per se. He was also powerfully influenced by the East and fully recognized the West's need for its spiritual values, but felt that Westerners have to individuate out of their own cultural history and not blindly jettison it for an Eastern path, a point of view to which I generally concur.

Here, however, it is noteworthy that Sri Aurobindo was educated in England from the age of 7 to 21 and attended Cambridge, after which he returned to India; and the Mother was French, born into a Jewish family with Turkish and Egyptian roots. The Mother lived in Pondicherry, India permanently since April of 1920 and declared on August 15, 1954 that India was her home in soul and spirit, while complementing her French origins. She was subsequently granted Indian citizenship without losing her French birthright. Individually and together they represent a full integration of the East and West as well as embodying the divine masculine and feminine principles. This superior level of cultural and spiritual integration is, in fact, evident in their teachings, and their Integral Yoga is relevant to Westerners as well as Indians.

The Mother and the Transformation of the Cells and Jung's Glorified Body

There are two important interrelated aspects of Sri Aurobindo and the Mother's Integral Yoga, one being the effect on world culture, the other

121   2004, p. 135.

being the transformative effect on the individual. The Mother went so far as to experience a supramental transformation of the cells, which means Truth entered the cells of her body. She recounts how "the supramental light entered my body directly ... through the feet."[122] She later refers to "that luminous power ... so compact ... it gives the impression of being much heavier than matter."[123] She describes the experience of supramentalizing the cells, first involving "a wave of disorganization, and then something stops: first a feeling of joy, then a light, then harmony—and the disorder is gone. And immediately a feeling of living in eternity, for eternity, comes into the cells."[124] As the Mother says, these experiences are for the Earth and not her body per se. They refer to the potential for the realization of the transformative power of Truth at all levels of becoming, including the physical body and the creation of a new species.

Jung writes of a glorified body and the tendency to concretize the spirit, showing some relationship to this dynamic. In his discourse in *Aion*, Jung does reflect on the interactive influence between psyche and matter and the fact that the *Lapis Quaternio* depicts a descent of the archetypal idea of wholeness and unity through organic matter, then inorganic matter to pure energy. In a private letter from Marie-Louise von Franz, dated January 20, 1997, in reply to my letter on the question of the descent of a spiritual force through the crown chakra, she replied as follows: "There is such an experience of the spirit entering the top chakra into the body, a descent into Muladhara and—according to Jung into chakras below Muladhara. One could call it a movement of the Holy Ghost toward incarnation. It is an individual event like all features of the individuation process." It is noteworthy that von Franz refers to the descent through the crown chakra as an individual event, as if to say, it does not describe a process open or even necessary to

---

122   As recorded in Satprem, 1982, p. 163.
123   *Ibid.*, p. 193.
124   *Ibid.*, p. 191.

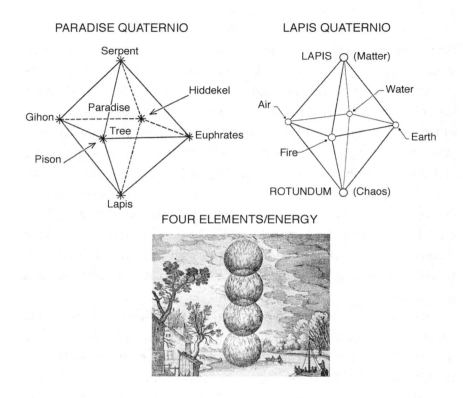

PARADISE QUATERNIO

Serpent

Hiddekel

Paradise

Gihon

Tree

Euphrates

Pison

Lapis

LAPIS QUATERNIO

LAPIS (Matter)

Water

Air

Earth

Fire

ROTUNDUM (Chaos)

FOUR ELEMENTS/ENERGY

everybody in the uniqueness of their individuation process. In my letter, I also asked her why Jung never wrote about it explicitly. She wrote in reply: "Jung probably didn't speak of it in order to avoid that people turn it into nonsense, as they already do with what he said."

Given the above observations by Marie-Louise von Franz, it is obvious that Jung's equation is experiential and not just based on a speculative process. Clear evidence for this observation can be seen in two remarkable images from *The Red Book*, shown on these pages, Image 125 and Image 155. Image 125 is an extraordinary picture of the descent of the Holy Spirit as a self-contained mass of golden light into a human receptacle. Image 155 is an image of Jung's soul as Sophia, who is centered in the cosmic Self. She is understood to be a figure that opposes the spectacle of the demiurge and is found in every tissue of the web of life, while pervading the cosmos with Consciousness and Force.

MARIE-LOUISE VON FRANZ'S LETTER
ON THE DESCENT OF THE HOLY GHOST

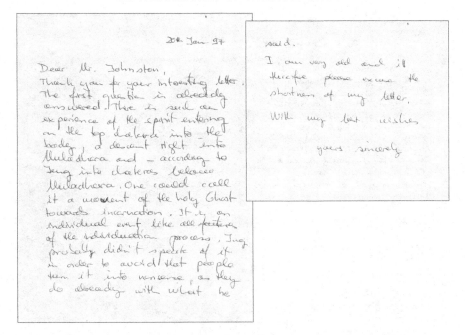

It is also well to keep in mind von Franz's concern that Jung was careful not to write about things that people would readily misconstrue. It is quite conceivable that he didn't write about non-dual experiences of *That* or *nirvana* in his formal writings for this very reason, although it turns out he spoke privately about non-dual experiences of *nirvana* on his deathbed, as already discussed. As it was, he was often accused of being a mystic and not a scientist, as well as of reducing God to a psychological phenomenon.

According to Murray Stein, the body begins to change when the archetypal principal of wholeness and unity enters the *Paradise Quaternio* based on the Serpent–*Lapis* polarity.[125] Since life at the level

---

125   1998.

IMAGE 125: DESCENT OF THE HOLY SPIRIT INTO A HUMAN RECEPTACLE

of organic matter is organized around the carbon molecule, the molecules themselves are rearranged by the descending archetypal blueprint
of wholeness and unity. Stein interprets the nadir of the *Lapis Quaternio*

IMAGE 155: SAPIENTIA (SOPHIA) CENTERED IN THE COSMIC SELF
AND ITS EFFERVESCENT DESCENT

in Jung's symbolic diagram, the level of the Rotundum, as referring to "the idea of energy," which passes through the atomic and subatomic levels of the material body.[126] "Here," observes Stein, "lies the origin of the crystallization of energy into matter"; and, at this level, he believes, the descending organizing principle of wholeness and unity transforms energy itself.[127] Stein's reflections on the *Paradise* and *Lapis* quaternities are astute, especially in light of Jung's remarks on spirit, matter and

---

126   *Ibid.*, p. 166.
127   *Ibid.*, p. 196.

a glorified body. Jung's equation is extraordinary, although it seems to be based on spiritual and not supramental phenomena, despite Stein's highly interesting remarks.

There is no evidence for Jung's formula of the Self being made with reference to experiences like those reported by the Mother; nor is there any reference to the evolution of a new species per se in *Aion* or in other works by Jung. In fact there is evidence to suggest that, in Jung's case, there remained some clouds of unconsciousness, which could be attributed to the Inconscient, despite a fully individuated life devoted to increasing consciousness. He writes in his autobiography: "When Lao-tzu says: 'All are clear, I alone am clouded,' he is saying what I now feel in advanced old age. Lao-tzu is the example of a man with superior insight who has experienced worth and worthlessness, and who at the end of his life desires to return into his own being, into the eternal unknowable meaning."[128]

Jung's experiences and knowledge are remarkable and reflect a fully individuated and spiritualized life. His psychological and spiritual development continued until the end of his life, while he worked productively "to the last weeks of his life in June 1961."[129] Indeed, his path seems to point in the same direction as the Integral Yoga of Sri Aurobindo and the Mother. Consistent with their differentiation of the nature of supramental yoga, however, Sri Aurobindo and the Mother's realizations go well beyond those recorded by Jung. As indicated above, for instance, the Mother worked toward the supramentalization of the cells and forming a bridge between a realized supramentalized subtle body and the external body until the very end of her physical life. The discussion above on Jung's psychological attitude to the mother, and the actual phenomenon and experiences of the Mother, calls for some elaboration on Jung's relationship to the Mother Goddess, which is the subject of the following chapter.

---

128   C.G. Jung, 1983, p. 359.
129   Anthony Stevens, 1990, p. 227.

CHAPTER 19

Jung and the Mother Goddess

The Divine Mother, the omnipotent Mother Goddess, is front and center in the Integral Yoga of Sri Aurobindo and the Mother. In Jung's case, the relationship with the mother, whom he often refers to as the Great Mother or the Goddess, is neither as direct nor as personal as with Sri Aurobindo; but a clear case can be made (as Dourley does) that in the deeper sense of the word, Jung's life and psychology is dedicated to the Divine Mother. Jung once writes, for instance, that "the unconscious is the mother of consciousness," using reference to "the mother" in order to define the matrix and womb of all consciousness.[1]

During his engagement with the unconscious of *The Red Book* period, Jung realized that there were "things in the images" that emerged from his unconscious that "concerned not only myself but many others also."[2] "It was then," he writes, "that I ceased to belong to myself alone, ceased to have the right to do so."[3] "From then on, my life belongs to the generality."[4] Believing his life belongs to the generality means that his work has universal validity and many others can benefit from his experiences and psychological, spiritual and cultural discoveries. In fact, after being intensely immersed in the images and inner dialogues of *The Red Book* period in his "confrontation with the unconscious," Jung felt the need to engage the world with

---

1 1975c, p. 96.
2 1983, p. 182.
3 *Ibid.*
4 *Ibid.*

his insights and methodology.[5] According to Sonu Shamdasani in his introduction to *The Red Book,* Jung later notes that "when he reached this central point, or *Tao,* his confrontation with the world commenced and he began to give many lectures."[6]

In his experiences recorded in *The Red Book,* Jung thought of himself as having undergone the original experience and, yet, to validate his discoveries, he felt the need to "plant the results of my experience on the soil of reality; otherwise they would have remained subjective assumptions without validity."[7] "It was then," he writes, "that I dedicated myself to service of the psyche," the mother of conscious life, "the mother of all our attempts to understand Nature."[8][9] Jung refers to the need to turn back to "the mother of humanity, to the psyche, which was before consciousness existed, and in this way they make contact with the source and regain something of that mysterious and irresistible power from being part of the whole."[10] Planting the results on the soil of reality turns out to mean, on the one hand, contending with scientific and phenomenological validity and, on the other, building a bridge to the past and forward into the future.

In order to do this, Jung distinguishes the spirit of the times and the spirit of the Depths, which speaks in images and symbols, and which alone brings psychic renewal and "a new spring of life."[11] Not only was he challenged to descend to the visionary psyche, he was charged with the task of discovering a unifying symbol, which began to emerge in 1917 and 1918 as mandalas in the shape of a cross and circle, and, in 1919, he painted an image for *The Red Book* of what he refers to

---

5   2009, p. 219.
6   2009, p. 219.
7   1983, p. 192.
8   Jung, 1975, as reported in Adler, p. 567.
9   *Ibid.*
10   1974a, p. 178.
11   2009, p. 210.

as "the Philosopher's stone."[12] The alchemical philosopher's stone, or *lapis,* is the *"filius macrocosmi,* "Son of the Great World," as opposed to the *filius microcosmi,* the "son of man."[13] The stone is, according to different early legends, "the birthplace of the gods," in other words, the multiplicity of the archetypal psyche.[14] As stone, there is also emphasis on the physical world, and "the *deus absconditus,* the god hidden in matter."[15] Particularly relevant to Jung's image is its relationship to "the incorruptible body, the invisible, spiritual stone, or *lapis aethereus.*"[16]

Thus, concerning the image he painted of the philosopher's stone, Jung writes: "This stone, set so beautifully, is certainly the *Lapis Philosophorum.* It is harder than diamond. But it expands into space through four distinct qualities, namely breadth, height, depth and time. It is hence invisible and you can pass through it without noticing it. The four streams of Aquarius flow from the stone ... it is the monad that counterveils the Pleroma."[17] According to these comments Jung had attained consciousness of a solid unifying center of being that not only links him to the past through alchemy and perforce, Gnosticism, but to the new Age of Aquarius. Countervailing the Pleroma means effective differentiation and individuation as opposed to being swayed by the spirit of the time and the paradoxes of life, in other words, unconsciousness. Having attained Tao, Jung was ready to engage the world with his discoveries.

To put these reflections in their proper perspective, it is interesting what Jung had to say about psyche later in his life. In *Mysterium Coniunctionis* he writes that "The psychic is a phenomenal world in itself, which can be reduced neither to the brain nor to metaphysics."[18]

---

12   Jung, 2009, p. 305, n. 229.
13   Jung, 1970 a-1, p. 96.
14   *Ibid.,* p. 97.
15   *Ibid.,* p. 104.
16   *Ibid.*
17   *Ibid.*
18   Jung, 1974c, p. 468.

Thus, according to Jung, the psyche is an objective reality that cannot be explained by biochemistry or metaphysical statements of any kind. As far as reducing the psyche to the brain and biochemistry is concerned, Jung was always concerned about the tendencies of the science of psychology to do just this. Even today, neuropsychology has explanatory power that advocates see as sufficient to identify the psyche as a product of the brain, or at least to put primary emphasis on the brain.

Jung, in fact, lays claim to being an empiricist, and considers his psychology to be based on scientific premises and practices. However, inasmuch as science, as it is currently practiced, depends on external sense data and seeks repeatability, there is a huge difference between its methodology and Jung's. Jung's approach to empirical psychology depends on intense scrutiny and consideration of inner experiences and synchronicities by all the functions of consciousness, along with extraversion and introversion, not just extraverted thinking and sensation like Newtonian science. This approach is unlike normal contemporary science, where observation is external and statistics determine the experimental results, while synchronicities are considered irrelevant. Regarding the scientific need for repeatability, given the unique nature of the individual psyche and its journey, both in terms of the competency of the ego and its relationship to the Self, as well as the constellation of the unconscious, it is not possible to incorporate repeatability in Jung's science. Given the universal nature of archetypes, the contents of the psyche, there are, nonetheless, similar dynamics at play in every case of psychic unfolding and individuation that can be systematically recorded.

Jung's views on a science of psychology are, in fact, very similar to those of Sri Aurobindo, who defines a complete psychological science "as being a "compound of science with a metaphysical knowledge" and "as the science of consciousness and its states and operations in

THE PHILOSOPHER'S STONE

nature."[19] Jung's empirical approach to psychology fulfills the scientific dictum, notably with regard to consciousness and its operations in nature, especially amplified through alchemical states and operations. Jung's approach to psychology, in addition, fulfills Sri Aurobindo's requirement for empirical and intuitive knowledge of the psyche and its relationship to the spirit and its transformative exigencies.[20] As I demonstrate above, Jung was naturally drawn to alchemy since he was a schoolboy and began to take it seriously after he completed *The Red*

---

19   1978, p. 124.
20   *Ibid.*, p. 156.

Book in 1928. On receiving a copy of a Chinese alchemical treatise, *The Secret of the Golden Flower*, from Richard Wilhelm, he realized that the material in *The Red Book* had a decided affinity with alchemy. Although alchemy was a search for knowledge and wisdom and compensatory to Christianity in the West, it is also the mother of science in that its laboratory techniques, apparatus and methodology developed into a paradigm for scientific chemistry. Jung rekindled this tradition in its contemporary manifestation as the science of depth psychology, bringing together science, spirituality and religion.

Regarding metaphysics, Jung states: "Nor is the possibility of a metaphysical background denied"; psychology cannot take a position "either for or against the objective validity of any metaphysical view."[21] Yet he, himself, makes metaphysical assertions about the psyche as can be seen below. I take any ambiguity here to imply that Jung was concerned about the rigid application of Christian or other religious dogma or doctrines to criticize or override the empirical discoveries of the psyche, rendering it inconsequential. In fact, his metaphysical observations are always based on empirical evidence, both his own and those of his patients or colleagues.

In a letter dated December 31, 1949, to the Dominican Father Victor White, Jung writes, "I firmly believe that psyche is an *ousia*, the source of good and evil as 'the equivalent moities of a logical judgment.'"[22] *Ousia* is an ancient Greek word meaning essence, or substance, often used to refer to Being or God; in Jung's case, evidently it refers to the psyche as the Mother Goddess, the permanent substrate and matrix of life. In another letter, dated February 29, 1952, Jung writes to an English psychiatrist interested in psychical research, John Raymond Smythies, about the psyche in a highly intriguing manner that seems to me to amplify his description of it as an *ousia*. He proposes giving up "time-space categories altogether when we are dealing with

---

21   Jung, 1974c, p. 468.
22   As recorded in Adler, 1973, p. 540.

psychic existence."[23] He suggests that the archetypes are eternal and that "psyche should be understood as *unextended intensity* and not as a body moving in time."[24] He goes on to write: "One might assume the psyche gradually rising from minute extensity to infinite intensity, transcending the velocity of light and thus irrealizing the body."[25] He explains minute extensity of the psyche by the brain functioning as "a transformer station, in which the relatively infinite tension or intensity of the psyche proper is transformed into perceptible frequencies or 'extensions.'"[26] As the mother of all consciousness and the womb of psychic life, these speculations suggest that the psyche proper resides in the formless maternal essence beyond form.

From a material perspective, in Jung's cosmology, the psyche and psychic consciousness is a product of the rhizome. In 1950 he writes:

> The psyche is not of today: its ancestry goes back many millions of years. Individual consciousness is only the flower and the fruit of a season, sprung from the perennial rhizome beneath the earth, and it would find itself in better accord with the truth if it took the existence of the rhizome into its calculations. For the root matter is the mother of all things.[27]

In this description, the mother of the psyche is the collective unconscious down to the level of the rhizome beneath the earth; which could explain his intense desire to discover the reality of the myth of his life, which he regards as "the task of tasks."[28] He writes: "I just had to know what unconscious or preconscious myth was forming me, from the rhizome I sprang."[29] Although Jung writes for humanity, he was person-

---

23   Jung as reported in Adler, 1975, p. 45.
24   *Ibid.*
25   *Ibid.*
26   *Ibid.*
27   Jung, 1974a, p. xxv.
28   *Ibid.*
29   *Ibid.*

ally engaged with coming to terms with the collective unconscious and the objective psyche, in a relationship which he felt ethically obliged to assimilate to consciousness.

Jung's psychology goes well beyond the ego and personal unconscious. He was fully devoted and in service to the mother (the mother of all consciousness), through a phenomenological and scientific relationship with the objective reality of the psyche. The fact that Jung had the feeling that all his writings were "tasks imposed from within" and that he was "impelled to say what no one wants to hear", combined with the growing reception for his ideas in the general population, is testimony to his having served the Divine Mother and the future and not the general consensus of society or any collective.[30]

Attributing the Word, the Logos, to the Divine Mother emphasizes not only the value of divine reason and discernment, but also the quality of Eros and relatedness, through wisdom, power and delight. In *Savitri*, the Goddess from the Transcendence's core builds a bridge to the heart of the protagonist, Aswapathy, while embracing the cosmic and individual dimensions of being. Throughout his work, Jung makes ample reference to the Logos principle and its perversion in the West and the contemporary world. In *The Red Book,* Jung engages in an interesting imaginal conversation with the anchorite, Ammonius, who has intriguing views on the Logos as presented in "the Gospel according to Saint John," where the prologue begins as follows:

> In the beginning was the Word;
> The Word was with God
> And the Word was God.
> …
> All that came to be had life in him
> And that life was the light of men,
> A light that shines in the dark,
> A light that darkness could not overpower.

---

30   *Ibid.*, p. 222.

> The Word was the true light
> …
> The Word was made flesh,
> he lived among us
> and we saw his glory,
> the glory that is his as the only Son of the Father,
> full of grace and truth. (*John* 1: 23)

The masculine, patriarchal quality of the Christian Logos is clearly depicted, although feminine values are evident in the emphasis on life that was the light of men. Ammonius argues that the Word, as the true light of consciousness, and life, belong together, mirroring the Word of Sri Aurobindo in *Savitri*, which is embodied by the Divine Mother as the supramental Parashakti, Consciousness-Force. It is relevant that Consciousness-Force is directly linked to the manifestation, especially by way of consciousness and the vital, of the play of life, relating life to the Word.

In *The Red Book*, Ammonius observes that in Christianity, originally, the Logos coexisted as light and life; although with time, wordiness, and words as dead concepts, divorced from the source, were used to repress life. In the same category one could add ideologies, repressive dogma and doctrine, and the use of reason for the sake of power and manipulation, rather than for sacred contemplation. The need for life and the light of consciousness to coexist and not be in opposition is a constant theme in Jung's work. Jung writes; "This life is the way, the long sought after way to the unfathomable which we call divine."[31] Later on he observes, "Life is a touchstone for truth of the spirit. Spirit that drags a man away from life, seeking fulfillment only in itself, is a false spirit …. Spirit gives meaning to his life, and the possibility of its greatest development. But life is essential to spirit, since its truth is

---

31   Jung, 2009, p. 232.

nothing if it cannot live."[32] These pearls of wisdom from Jung point the way to a spirituality that does not repress life but enhances it.

Although the individuation process demands a renewal of this contract with the Logos, Jung warns that the word "has a perilous shadow side" and "that through universal education, the original connection of the word with the divine source has become lost."[33] Thus "the distinguishing mark of the Christian epoch, its highest achievement has become the congenital vice of our age: *the supremacy of the word*, the Logos, which stands for the central figure of our Christian faith."[34] What this amounts to is a predominance of the intellect, the identification of intellectual reason with truth, and the repression of the color and music of life. Like Sri Aurobindo, Jung wants life to be liberated as a source of power and pleasure, and to undergo a transformation process according to its higher destiny. Service and surrender to the Divine Mother is central to Sri Aurobindo's path of Integral Yoga, while service to the psyche and surrender to the mother in her multiple guises, as required by the Self, for Jung, are central to Jung's way of integral individuation.

On November 1, 1950, Pope Pius XII declared as dogma the doctrine that the body of the Blessed Virgin Mary assumed to Heaven along with her soul. Both Jung[35] and Sri Aurobindo regard the Assumption of the Virgin Mary as representing the divinization of matter.[36] Jung believes that Mary's assumption, along with her designation as *theotokos* or mother of God, paved the way for her recognition as a goddess, worthy of "worship and devotion ... to which she is entitled," and not just veneration, her official status in the Church.[37] Jung saw this event, now Church dogma, as the return of Sophia, as understood in earlier

---

32   Jung,1975, p. 337.
33   *Ibid.*
34   *Ibid.*
35   1983.
36   The Mother, 1978b, p. 308.
37   Jung, 1975c-1, p. 171, n. 1.

elaborations of her in Gnostic myths, and later mostly forgotten. In *Answer to Job* he writes, "Mary as the bride is united with the son in the heavenly bridal chamber, and as Sophia, with the Godhead."[38] Indicative of his personal devotion to Sophia, Jung also writes: "We also need the Wisdom Job was seeking," which during his time was hidden.[39] "That higher and complete man," he writes, is begotten by the "unknown father and born from Wisdom."[40] He is the *puer aeternus*, "the boy born from the mature man" who "represents our totality, which transcends consciousness."[41] Devotion to Sophia brings to birth the complete person of the future. The Islamist scholar and theologian Henri Corbin believes that, based on Jung's treatment of Sophia in *Answer to Job*, and his ideas on her assimilation to the Christian Trinity, Jung will eventually be seen as the "prophet of the eternal Sophia."[42]

Jung also emphasizes Mary's important position in the quaternity, as matter represents the "*concreteness* of God's thoughts and is, therefore, the very thing that makes individuation possible."[43] The devil, like matter, is a source of resistance, and he is, consequently, conceived as the soul of matter, without which the autonomy of individual existence, writes Jung, "would be simply unthinkable."[44] The inclusion of matter in the heavenly realm, therefore, assumes the inclusion of evil, which Jung believes is an essential aspect of the drama of redemption. Nonetheless, the popular image of Mary does not seem to include qualities of the natural world and reconciliation of the opposites as in earlier Mother Goddess traditions. Like Christ, Mary is generally depicted as all light and all virtuous.

It is therefore of singular interest that near the end of her life,

---

38   Jung, 1975g, p. 458.
39   *Ibid.*, p. 457.
40   *Ibid.*
41   *Ibid.*
42   Jaffé, 1989, p. 94.
43   Jung, 1975c-1, p. 171.
44   *Ibid.*, p. 172.

AUTHOR'S IMAGE OF LIFE AND LIGHT (LOGOS WITH LIFE)

The author's painting of this image has a cadmium red border sur-
rounding a salmon-pink interior along with yellow for both LIFE and
LIGHT.

Mary-Louise von Franz recounts two dreams involving Jung that concern the marriage of the Black Virgin on Earth.[45] In one dream, she
and Jung were preparing food in the kitchen of the monastery in the

---

45   As recorded in Rafael Monzo, 2006, pp. 413–420 passim.

sanctuary of the Black Madonna, at the Benedictine Monastery in Einsiedeln.[46] In the other dream,

> *she was working in the laundry at the monastery at Einsiedeln.*
> *She was told that Jung would return from the heavens for the*
> *wedding of the Black Virgin. And that she would belong to the*
> *one hundred elect that would participate in the festivities.*[47]

These dreams seem to concern Jung himself and not projections of Jung, as well as von Franz. According to the latter's reported reflections, the unconscious is preparing a union of above and below, between spirit and matter. It is not a question here of realizations taking place above in the heavens, but on Earth itself, which include the feeling and physical realms of being. It seems that the lives and works of Jung and Marie-Louise von Franz are important for the realization of this eventuality, as they are preparing spiritual nourishment for aspiring seekers of the spirit of the Black Madonna. In this regard, one of von Franz's last public lectures was entitled "Jung's Rehabilitation of the Feeling Function in Our Contemporary Civilizations," emphasizing the importance they both put on Eros, relatedness, and the feeling function, feminine dimensions of being.[48] They are also providing the service of cleansing attitudes and values for more truthful lives, which include living with conscious feeling and Eros values and their spiritualization. The rehabilitation of love is of the utmost importance everywhere in the contemporary, one-sided materialistically governed world.

The legends of the Black Madonna and Mary Magdalene, who according to Gnostic tradition was the spouse of Christ, are interwoven. In some depictions of the latter she is black or dressed in black, or has a black face, suggesting obscurity and relegation to the unconscious, exiled from consciousness. Amongst some Gnostic designations of Mary

46   *Ibid.*, p. 418.
47   *Ibid.*, p. 420.
48   *Ibid.*, p. 420.

Magdalene, she is Sophia lost in matter, while in other portrayals, she wears green as a symbol of fertility and nature. According to Margaret Starbird, her most significant color is red, denoting values of Eros and relatedness and "the flesh and blood of the human condition" that demands making inner experiences real.[49]

Starbird observes that the name *Magdalene* has, at its root, *mag*, meaning "great lady" or "great mother"; she sees her as the "pre-eminent woman in the Christian gospels" and the incarnation of "the archetype of the goddess of love, fertility, compassion and wisdom."[50] The figure of Mary Magdelene teaches compassion and the ability to listen with sympathy and empathy, relationship to the Earth and kinship with all nature, corresponding with Jung's and von Franz's efforts to rehabilitate Eros and the feeling function. One can say she represents the individual and personal aspect of the Goddess, a Persephone figure, where the heavenly Mary is a figure like Demeter. Whereas the Virgin Mary, as Goddess, comes in various archetypal templates, most pointedly as Wisdom, Strength, Relatedness and Service with execution in detail, the Black Madonna/Mary Magdalene figure represents the Goddess as a divine individual consciously realizing these different archetypal patterns in the world.

In addition to von Franz's dream, legitimate scholarship around Mary Magdalene is growing substantially, and popular interest in the book and movie *The Da Vinci Code*, by Dan Brown, point to the return of the great Goddess. In support of this observation, von Franz herself observes that she has witnessed numerous dreams of the Black Madonna of Einsiedeln by both Protestants and Catholics alike. By all accounts, then, the unconscious seems to be preparing the way for conscious acceptance and integration of the message brought by the black virgin goddess. Von Franz was overjoyed by the fact that the wedding

49   2005, p. 146.
50   *Ibid.*, p. 147.

in her dream was taking place in the Christian context, which she had hitherto felt was impossible.

The suggestion is that the Christian world is going through a profound transformation that will eventually lead to embracing the Black Madonna and, more fully, the legendary stories about Mary Magdalene, who, according to some Gnostic traditions, was wedded to Jesus. In his intriguing book, *The Magdalene Legacy,* Laurence Gardner explores the Jewish tradition of the sacred marriage, showing that such an eventually has legitimate Hebrew roots. Further amplification on her relevance can be found by contemplating several artistic depictions of Mary Magdelene that indicate that, sometime after the sacrifice of Jesus, she, along with a few fellow travellers, voyaged by boat to Marseilles in southern France, where many relics and images of her continue to exist.

Von Franz's revelations suggest that Jung's path and the Christian world is now open to a sacred quaternity: with two goddesses, one heavenly and cosmic, the other, earthly and dark, both Sophia figures; and two male representatives of the Logos principle, Christ in the heavenly bridal chamber, and a figure, undoubtedly Jesus, below on Earth. This is a direct fulfillment of Jung's *unus mundus* upon the Earth. Indeed, my view on her two dreams is that it is a profound reflection of a highly significant event involving Sri Aurobindo and the Mother's Yoga, concerning the descent of the Supermind onto the Earth on February 29, 1956.[51]

The Mother describes the supramental manifestation during a collective meditation as follows:

> This evening the Divine Presence, concrete and material, was there present amongst you. I had a form of living gold, bigger than the universe, and I was facing a huge massive golden door, I knew and willed, in a single movement of consciousness, that

51   2004e, p. 94.

"the time has come," and lifting with both hands a mighty gold-
en hammer I struck one blow, one single blow on the door and
the door was shattered to pieces. Then the supramental Light
and Force and Consciousness rushed down upon earth in an uninterrupted flow.[52]

Here the Mother describes herself as a monumental Sophia figure,
as only she, as the supramental Shakti, could have the consciousness
of Truth and strength to act so decisively. The manifestation of the
Supermind or Truth upon the Earth is one of the most significant events
in the history of the world, portending its profound transformation. By
way of explication of the meaning of the supramental manifestation,
the Mother writes: "Tellingly, the future expectation had become the
present realization."[53]

As if to add further explanations she also writes:

1956
29 February–29 March
Lord, Thou hast willed, and I execute:
A new light breaks upon the earth,
A new world is born.
The things that were promised are fulfilled.[54]

The expectation she refers to is the ubiquitous aspiration to bring heav-
en down to Earth, for instance, as depicted in the Christian Book of
Revelation. That is the new world, to be fully realized during the Age
of Aquarius. At the same time, the Mother had the following declaration published, under the date 24 April 1956:

"The manifestation of the Supramental upon earth is no more a
promise but a living fact, a reality. It is at work here, and one day
will come when the most blind, the most unconscious, even the

---

52   *Ibid.*
53   *Ibid.*
54   *Ibid.*, p. 95.

most unwilling shall be obliged to recognize it." Henceforth in
the Ashram 29 February was called the Golden Day.[55]

In 1960, the Mother changed the name of the day that commemo-
rates the supramental manifestation from the Golden Day to "the day
of the Lord," presumably to represent its full significance.[56] The Mother
also declares: "In 1967 the Supermind will enter the phase of realizing power."[57] By realizing power, she means "acting decisively on the
mind of men and the course of events."[58] Truth is acting in the world
and stirring up events, for the sake of bringing in a new world. Even
when there are catastrophes and very disrupting events, out of the tension, new more authentic possibilities often emerge. It is as if the collective shadow needs to be part of the transforming experience and is
fully embraced by the supramental consciousness. In terms of individual psychology and personality transformation, integrating shadow
and the dark aspects of the feminine, including the Black Madonna,
are essential. Sincerity acts like a transformative magnet bringing in
new prevailing conditions for the individual concerned. The Mother
put emphasis on humility in light of one's insignificance in front of the
enormity of the change taking place.

---

55   *Ibid.*, p. 96.
56   *Ibid.*, p. 99.
57   *Ibid.*, p. 99.
58   *Ibid.*, p. 104.

CHAPTER 20

Jung in Sri Aurobindo's Classification
of the Mind and Supermind

However tentative, I would now like to briefly attempt to identify where Jung might fit into Sri Aurobindo's classification system of the Mind, which includes the Higher Mind, the Illumined Mind, the Intuitive Mind and the Overmind in ascending categories of the psyche, which eventually culminates beyond the Mind with the Supermind. Already as a young man of 22 and 23, in his Zofingia lectures put on by his fraternity, Jung had begun to intelligently examine issues that would preoccupy him throughout his life, and about which he bemoans that none of his schoolmates could understand him. His uncommon interest in the problem of opposites began at that time and continued until his opus *Mysterium Coniunctionis* and other late works.

In these early lectures, he critically refers to the thought of Schopenhauer, Kant, von Hartman, Nietzsche, Albrecht Ritschl (a Lutheran theologian), and others, as well as the science of his day. He already holds that "all is One," that the soul "extends far beyond our consciousness," and that it "is intelligent (purposeful in its acts) and independent of space-time," positions that remained with him all his life.[1] This fundamental viewpoint also implies an unconscious psyche, which later became pivotal to his understanding of psychology. In his critical discussion on Christianity, he notes that he cannot return to the Christianity of the Middle Ages, when it was a vibrant

---

1   Jung, 1983a, pp. xviii, 77.

force, and undo the civilizing advances vis à vis the study of nature made since then.

Jung begins by adopting the position of the modern man who can no longer believe on the basis of blind faith but depends on reason in its place. The acknowledged loss of a spiritual rudder led him to realize in 1912, when he was thirty-seven, the need to find his own myth with the aid of a meditative process he calls active imagination. He eventually came to believe that it amounted to dreaming Christianity forward and integrating the shadow and the feminine principle as nature into the Godhead. As a student, Jung didn't have all the final answers to the psychology of life, let alone life experience with which to ground his thinking in reality. Yet, according to Sri Aurobindo's definition, where the Higher Mind is ruled by clarity of reason and a unitary, yet multi-dimensional dynamism of knowledge, one can discern clear signs of a philosophic or Higher Mind with intuitive undertones, however rudimentary in its sophistication, already at work.

In 1909, Jung had the following revelatory dream, here simplified and paraphrased:

> I find myself in the upper storey of a 2-storey house, appointed with rococo style furnishing and fine paintings on the wall. I then explore the complete house. The ground floor dated from the fifteenth or sixteenth century, with mediaeval furnishings and a red brick floor. The cellar, with brick and ordinary stone blocks, dated from Roman times. Below the cellar was a low cave cut in a rock. There was old broken pottery of a primitive culture and two half disintegrating skulls.[2]

This dream is a symbolic rendition of the collective unconscious as well as alluding to phylogeny and the evolution of the species. The meaning of the dream found expression in Jung's writing about the archetypes of the collective unconscious, beginning with *Symbols of*

---

2   1983.

Transformation written two years later in 1911, when he was thirty-six years old and entering the second half of life. The book, which was published in 1912, led to his break from Freud.

This was the beginning of the intense period Jung refers to as "Auseinandersetzung mit der Unbewustsein," which has been translated in *Memories, Dreams, Reflections* as "Confrontation with the Unconscious." The German significance of the expression, however, is less a confrontation than "Sitting together in Dialogue with the Unconscious." This understanding more clearly characterizes the dynamic meditative approach of active imagination, which involves a dialogue between the ego and the collective unconscious. Still, when he first experienced archetypes from the collective unconscious, he became disorientated, as events and knowledge inundated him like a landslide. He writes "the material ... burst forth from the unconscious, and at first swamped me."[3] The knowledge gained freed him from the restrictive reductionism of Freudian psychology and its disinterest in the teleological directedness of the psyche.

With completion of *Symbols of Transformation,* Jung recognized the value of living with a myth and having a symbolic relationship to the archetypal psyche. Living without a myth or outside it, as does the modern person, he now understood, has detrimental psychological effects that uproot one from the past and ancestral life and, therefore, from an in-depth relationship with contemporary society. *Symbols of Transformation* is a book pertaining to the nature of the collective unconscious and the hero's quest for psychological freedom. It represents a definite advance in psychological knowledge in the West that continues to be relevant. From the point of view of this discussion, with this book, which imposed itself with urgency, Jung made a definite breakthrough in thought-power that seems to place him in the category of working with an Illumined Mind, which in Sri Aurobindo's conception

---

3   *Ibid.*, p. 199.

is the revelatory, visionary and creative mind of the seer, accompanied with enthusiasm and power.

Jung's description of the nature of the symbol in a letter dated January 10, 1929, to Kurt Plachte, a Protestant theologian and minister, unquestionably refers to *The Red Book* experiences, and fully supports my contention that Jung was writing with an Illumined Mind during the period he compiled it and wrote *Symbols of Transformation*. The symbol, he says, is "the sensuously perceptible expression of an inner experience" and is "the highest form of intellectual expression."[4] This statement surely mirrors Sri Aurobindo's understanding of the Illumined Mind. Then, as if to explain the enthusiasm and power the latter says accompanies the Illumined Mind, using Gnostic references, Jung writes:

> For my private use I call the sphere of paradoxical existence, i.e., the instinctive unconscious, the Pleroma .... The reflection and formation of the Pleroma in individual consciousness produce an image of it (of like nature in a certain sense), and that is the symbol. In it all paradoxes are abolished. In the Pleroma, Above and Below lie together in a strange way and produce nothing, but when it is disturbed by the mistakes and needs of the individual a waterfall arises between Above and Below, a dynamic something that is the symbol. Like the Pleroma, the symbol is greater than man. It overpowers him, shapes him, as though he had opened a sluice that pours a mighty stream over him and sweeps him away.[5]

The fact that Jung was later able to reflect on his experiences, to understand and metaphysically articulate them, suggests that he had, by then, risen above the initial symbolic expressions. His extensive revision, written thirty-seven years later in 1948/49, where he was able to provide connecting links to different fragments of the book without

---

4   Jung, as reported in Adler, 1973, p. 61.
5   *Ibid.*

undoing its main edifice, undoubtedly reflects the fact that his psyche had advanced to another level of wholeness altogether in comparison to when he wrote the earlier edition.

IMAGE OF JUNG'S PAINTING OF PHILEMON WITH BULL'S HORNS AND FOUR KEYS

Sometime between 1913 and 1914 Jung had a dream of a being he called Philemon, with whom he began to engage in a continuous inner dialogue. At times he seemed quite real to Jung and he would walk up and down the garden with him in intense discussion. Psychologically, Jung regards him as a kind of guru with superior insight, which, given his recitation of the *Septem Sermones ad Mortuos* to Jung as recorded in *The Red Book*, means superior spiritual knowledge or gnosis. This knowledge includes the nothingness of the infinite and eternal Pleroma itself, as well as the individuation process and individual differentiation, possible thanks to the presence of the infinite and eternal Pleroma in the psyche. In fact, Jung writes that he later fully integrated Philemon into consciousness. Here is the dream:

> *There was a blue sky, like the sea, covered not by clouds but by flat brown clods of earth. It looked as if the clods were breaking apart and the blue water of the sea was becoming visible between them. But the water was the blue sky. Suddenly there appeared from the right a winged being sailing across the sky. I saw that it was an old man with the horns of a bull. He held a bunch of four keys, one of which he clutched as if he were about to open a lock. He had the wings of a kingfisher with its characteristic colors.[6]*

The first book that comes under the influence of this material, actually written during the time he was so intensely engaged with the unconscious, is *Psychological Types,* a masterpiece replete with a plethora of complex material along with grounding in clinical reality. It is glued together in an intuitive synthesis and supports my conviction that, by now, Jung was writing with direct influences from the Intuitive Mind according to Sri Aurobindo's description.

Jung wrote *Psychological Types* between 1913 and 1917/1918, a highly researched description of different conscious personality structures that determine judgment and relationships with people and objects. To validate his thinking, Jung drew on a vast amount of material, some with considerable spiritual depth, including the Vedas and Upanishads of India, and Western classical and medieval thought, along with the philosophy/psychology of Nietzsche, Schiller and William James, and

---

6   *Ibid.*, pp. 182, 183.

the poetry of Spitteler and Goethe for biographical width and pathology. Most importantly, the book is based on many years of observations and impressions of a practicing psychotherapist, and is, therefore, grounded in the reality of life. This and subsequent books, until his experience of the *mysterium coniunctionis* in 1944, are the end result of his seed experiences and knowledge gained during his having it out with the unconscious and the creation of *The Red Book*, which was published in 2009.

Thus, in his autobiography, Jung writes:

> The years when I was pursuing my inner images were the most important in my life—in them everything essential was decided. It all began then; the later details are only supplements and clarifications of the material that burst forth from the unconscious, and at first swamped me. It was the *prima materia* for a lifetime's work.[7]

These seed experiences apparently influenced Jung and his work throughout his life. After his experience of the *mysterium coniunctionis*, however, there was further movement towards a complete surrender to the Self.

Jung's description of Philemon and his experiences that he elaborated over a lifetime seem to suggest that the latter is a superior Being with penetrating insight, reminiscent of the Intuitive Mind, which Sri Aurobindo describes as having some relationship to the Overmind. In fact, at the end of *The Red Book,* Philemon reveals himself to be Simon Magus—if not the father, one of the primal founders, of Gnosticism.[8] According to reports, at times he presented himself as the transcendent God of Gnostic cosmology, and, at other times he claimed to be the redeemer.[9] Above the picture of Philemon in *The Red Book,* Jung writes

---

7   *Ibid.*, p. 199.
8   Jung, 2009, p. 359.
9   E.M. Butler, 1979, pp. 73–83 passim.

in Greek: "Father of the Prophets, Beloved Philemon."[10] He painted Philemon again in his tower on a bedroom wall, with the following inscription placed above it: "Philemon, the Prophets' Primal Father."[11] According to Cary Baynes, Jung privately refers to Philemon as 'the master' "…who inspired Buddha, Mani, Christ, Mahomet – all those who may be said to have communed with God."[12] Jung clearly has an intensely loving relationship with Philemon, whom he believes has access to the Word of God, if he doesn't actually embody it.

The four keys held by Philemon could well refer to different ways of elaborating the structure and dynamics of the Self, where the symbol of the Self or Truth is based on the number four, as I show through amplification below. The fundamental meaning of the four keys is surely the fourfold power of Truth as described by Sri Aurobindo in relationship to the Intuitive Mind. His description of intuition as being close to knowledge by identity, and having the fourfold power of "truth-seeing," "truth-hearing," "truth-touch" (or understanding the significance of things), and "truth-discrimination," strike me as being descriptive of Jung post-Philemon, and evocative of the potency of Jung's written work and seminars after this intense period of coming to terms with the unconscious.[13] Jung observes that, in addition to a kind of earth demon, the *ka*, which emerged from below, he "integrated" Philemon to consciousness, suggesting that he writes with the same superior insight and meaning he attributed to Philemon as well as being fully grounded in creative nature.[14] His later writings are all elaborations of the intuitive insights he gained during this period of time and of having assimilated Philemon and the *ka* to consciousness. According to Sri Aurobindo's description, it seems evident to me that Jung then writes under the

---

10   As reported by Lance Owen, 2013, p. 24.
11   *Ibid.*
12   As recorded in Jung, 2009, p. 213.
13   Sri Aurobindo, 1970d, p. 949.
14   1983, p. 185.

influence of the Intuitive Mind, as I will elaborate further below in my discussion on Jung's late differentiation of the Self.

Beside the picture of Philemon on page 154 of *The Red Book*, Jung writes the following verse in English from the *Bhagavad Gita*:

> Whenever there is a decline of the laws and an increase of iniquity / Then I put forth myself for the rescue of the pious and the destruction of the evil doers. / For the establishment of the law I am born in every age.[15]

The reference in the verse is to Lord Krishna as an avatar of Vishnu, who, according to Hindu belief, incarnates from time to time, according to need, in order to raise the level of human consciousness to a higher level and, today, to bring in a new world. I take Jung's use and placing of the quote to signify the importance of the times for an evolutionary increase in consciousness and that the prophetic messenger for him is Philemon, who came to impart to Jung the path and the goal.

Facing the image of the painting of Philemon on page 154 is, on page 155, an image of a painting of Jung's soul as Sophia or Wisdom.[16] According to the ancient story, Philemon has a female companion, Baucis, and, in Gnostic belief, Simon Magus has a companion, Helen, who is, in fact, the fallen Sophia. In Jung's *The Red Book,* he first meets the prophet Elijah with his daughter and companion, the blind Salome, whom he identifies as his Wisdom, meaning Sophia. Like the Gnostic Sophia, she is spiritually blind and needs a guide in Elijah. Elijah was an Old Testament prophet, whom Jung describes as being both an historical figure and an embodiment of the "living archetype who represented the collective unconscious and the self" with the capacity to bring to consciousness new contents for collective assimilation.[17] Salome was the step-daughter of King Herod and pleased him by dancing for him.

---

15   Jung, 2009, p. 154.
16   *Ibid.*, pp. 154, 155.
17   2003, p. 245, n. 157.

As recompense, the king offered her whatever she wished for, which turned out to be the head of John the Baptist.[18]

In Jung's active imagination, Elijah claims Salome loved the prophet John and that Jung will know her by her love. Salome tells Jung that she loves him and he will love her, which, in the garden, he ultimately admits. Salome eventually gains her sight, following Jung's deification experience, where he is encircled by a serpent, with his face taking on the features of a lion or tiger.[19] Salome says to Jung that he is Christ, as his outstretched arms take on the image of crucifixion.

Then, Salome's eyes open and she sees light. Elijah is subsequently transformed into a pillar of white light and she kneels down in devotion to the light. No longer blind, Salome assumes the authentic role of Sophia, now redeemed, no longer in need of Elijah. She is eventually replaced by Jung's soul and mother, a feminine force, as Sophia; and Elijah is superseded by Philemon, who teaches Jung how to relate to his soul and how to respond to the dead. In the Scrutinies section of *The Red Book*, there is eventually a conversation between Philemon and Christ as a shade, where Philemon declares that Christ also has a serpent nature, where "lamentation and abomination" are the worm's gift.[20] In reply to Philemon's request to Christ regarding what he will give in return, the latter says: "I bring you the beauty of suffering. That is what is needed for whoever hosts the worm."[21]

Although Jung only identifies with Christ fleetingly, it is evident from Jung's deification experience and a sympathetic reading of his life that he, too hosted the worm, and suffered from the burden of his epochal task. Together, for Jung, Philemon, beloved father of the prophets, and the soul, as Sophia, represent Logos and Eros. According to Owens, in 1924, Jung inscribed above her image, on page 155, "*Dei*

---

18   *Ibid.*, n. 158.
19   *Ibid.*, p. 252, n. 211.
20   *Ibid.*, p. 359.
21   *Ibid.*

sapientia in mysteria," meaning "The Wisdom of God in mystery."[22] Jung's integration of both Philemon and his soul, as Sophia, as well as his ability to suffer gracefully, go a long way to explain the power and wisdom found in his psychology, its relevance to the times and its harmony with the Integral Yoga of Sri Aurobindo and the Mother.

JUNG'S GENERAL FORMULA OF THE SELF
WITH DIFFERENTIATION OF THE FOUR ELEMENTS

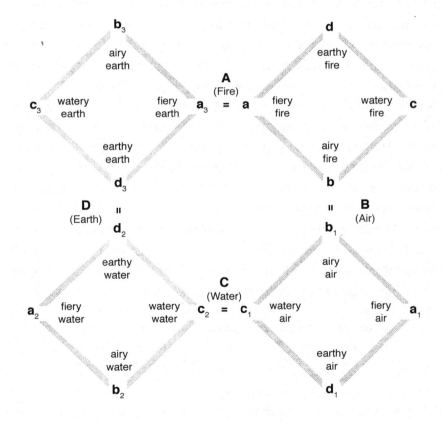

Jung's Late Differentiation of the Self

Jung, in fact, derives a general abstract formula for the structure and dynamics of the Self found in *Aion* based on fourfold quaternities, which reflects the differentiation of truth in a way that is similar to Sri Aurobindo's discernment. The latter refers to forms of matter as consisting of combinations of the five elements, ether, air, fire, water and earth.[23] Fire is related to seeing, air to touch, water to taste and earth to smell. According to this classification, Jung's formula consists of truth-seeing (fire), truth-touch (air), truth-feeling or understanding the value and significance of things (water), and truth-discrimination (earth). Although, according to Jung's formula, there is no ether, which is related to vibrations and sound, in the original formulas of the four-fold quaternities, it is accounted for elsewhere in his work as early as *The Red Book*, notably by image 151 of the *lapis aethereus,* illustrated above. He refers to the image as representing the incorruptible and invisible spiritual stone from which flow the four rivers of the Age of Aquarius. Consisting of aether, it is invisible, although it permeates life in all dimensions of space-time.

In his challenging essay, *Flying Saucers: A Modern Myth*, written in 1958, some nine years after *Aion*, Jung discusses the significance of the quintessence, also referred to as aether and represented by the quincunx, the centered 5, as is depicted on a playing die. He writes:

> The fourth antitheses, *unity and quaternity*, appears united in the quincunx ... the four forming ... a frame for the one, accentuated as the centre. In the history of symbols, quaternity is the unfolding of unity .... So long as a thing is in the unconscious it has no recognizable qualities and is consequently merged with the universal unknown, with the unconscious All or Nothing, with what the Gnostics called a "non-existent all-being." But as soon as the unconscious content enters the field of consciousness it has already split into the "four," that is to say

23   Sri Aurobindo, 1970d, p. 81.

it can become an object of experience only by virtue of the four
basic functions of consciousness. It is *perceived* as something
that exists (sensation); it is *recognized* as this and *distinguished*
from that (thinking); it is *evaluated* as pleasant or unpleasant,
etc. (feeling); and, finally, intuition tells us where it came from
and where is it going. This cannot be perceived by the senses or
thought by the intellect. Consequently the object's extension in
time and what happens to it is the proper concern of the intuition
… through the act of becoming conscious the four basic aspects
of a whole judgment are rendered visible.[24]

The quintessence, also described as aether, is the most subtle unity
of four qualities, and corresponds to the centered four, the quincunx,
with emphasis on the central point of unity. The four aspects of the Self
are here described as the four functions of consciousness; when all four
are functioning consciously, wholeness in judgment is brought to bear.
This not only involves observers acting in their wholeness within the
parameters of their understanding, but also within the context of finite
reality. It does not include the (still unconscious) realm of infinite possibilities, as, when a thing is still submerged in the unconscious, there
are no discernible qualities. The limits of finite reality are set by one's
wholeness, the Self, and have nothing to do with the demands of complexes and desires of any kind. Of considerable significance is the fact
that realizations involve not only the ego but the individual's wholeness, which by definition includes the four functions of consciousness
as well as a relationship to the archetypes of the "objective psyche,"
the Circumconscient in Sri Aurobindo's terms, both of which have the
characteristic of "participating in the surroundings and the actual moment in time."[25] This understanding of the role of aether as the uniting center and wholeness in judgment regarding experiences in finite

24   Jung, 1970f, pp. 407, 408.
25   Marie-Louise von Franz, 1974, p. 122.

reality is easily adaptable to Jung's formula for the fourfold quaternities as described in *Aion*.

Intuition and the Lapis Philosophorum

In 1945 Jung wrote a long monograph entitled *The Psychology of the
Transference*, where he discusses the problem of transference in human
relationships and its relevance to the individuation process, commenting on a series of alchemical pictures from the alchemical *Rosarium
Philosophorum*. Regarding the individuation process he indicates the
need to go through three stages of development, which includes inte-
grations of the heart and feeling values in addition to intellectual understanding and assimilation of the sensation function. Realization through
feeling, he indicates, is not the final stage for complete individuation,
but a fourth stage involving intuition is required as "anticipation of the
lapis" or philosopher's stone and psychological wholeness.[26] In these
remarks, Jung is not referring to personal functional typology of a contemporary individual, let alone his own typology, but to the work of
alchemists of the Middle Ages.

Here, Jung goes beyond his usual definition of intuition as referring to insights into possibilities from the unconscious, but writes of
the "imaginative activity of the fourth function—of intuition" that connects to possible realities.[27] He refers to the "*lapis* as a stone that is no
stone," taken from Greek alchemy, which is a reflection of the spiritual
quality of the *lapis*.[28] Its paradoxical nature is reflected in the fact that
"Intuition gives outlook and insight; it revels in the garden of magical
possibilities as if they were real."[29] Jung then states that "nothing is
more charged with intuitions than the *lapis philosophorum*," the ex-

---

26   C.G. Jung, 1970d, p. 281.
27   *Ibid.*
28   *Ibid.*
29   *Ibid.*

perience of which rounds off "into an experience of the totality of the individual."[30]

Jung is describing highly differentiated intuition, which, inasmuch as it includes the play of possibilities as if they were real, takes intuition beyond itself to embrace the subtle physical realm of being, where possibilities are made real. In fact, in this essay, Jung relates the alchemical goal of the highly prized *lapis* as involving the production of a subtle body that can be conceived as the *corpus glorificationis*, which requires the spiritualization of matter and concretization of spirit. The alchemist Gerhard Dorn, whom I refer to above, believed that if God could immortalize the body, so, by psychological work, could the alchemist during his lifetime "if he could get in contact with God's creative spirit."[31] According to Jung's description of the *lapis philosophorum*, this appears to be the case here. In Sri Aurobindo's nomenclature, Jung seems to be defining something like the Overmind, which, according to the latter, is grounded on the truth of the play of possibilities and the individualization of the archetypes, where, at its highest, human totality, the individual Self can merge in identity with the cosmic Self. At any rate, Jung appears to be describing, if not the Overmind, what he refers to as the *unus mundus,* where spirit and matter comingle.

Jung's notion of wholeness and completed individuation involving a deep relationship to the cosmic Self can be seen in a vision Jung had in 1939 as well as in his 1944 *mysterium coniunctionis* vision. Jung writes that he was "profoundly shaken" by the image of a "not quite life-size" "figure of Christ on the Cross" ... "bathed in light on the Cross at the foot of my bed."[32] In his vision, Christ's body consisted of "greenish gold," which alchemists regarded as the living

---

30   *Ibid.*
31   Marie-Louise von Franz, 1979, p. 104.
32   1983, p. 210.

spirit poured into man, as well as inorganic matter.[33] The greenish-gold Christ on the Cross brings together the Christ figure in his incarnation as Love with the alchemical *aurum non vulgi* (the not-common gold), the philosophical gold, along with *viriditas*, the blessed greenness of alchemy. The legendary words spoken by Christ on the Cross, "I and my Father are one," indicate differentiated unity between Christ and the Transcendent, the One. This implies that, in Jung's vision, the same unity is being portrayed. The green-gold, writes Jung, "is an expression of the life-spirit, the *anima mundi,* or *filius macrocosmi*, the *Anthropos* who animates the whole cosmos," and is "a union of spiritually alive and physically dead matter."[34] In other words, the vision is a refined feeling experience of the Self as *unus mundus,* with spiritual properties that range throughout the cosmos and incarnate in inorganic matter as well as in the individual. This experience is later amplified in a series of visions in 1944 of the *mysterium coniunctionis,* which, Jung relates, "at bottom was I myself" and which portrays a symbolic identification of the individual Self with the cosmic Self in a feeling experience of the *unus mundus.*[35]

Involution from Above and Evolution from Below

As indicated above in the section on the involution and evolution of Consciousness, the Mother contends that there are involutionary beings that incarnate by uniting with an evolved soul. Both the Mother and Sri Aurobindo have commented on this phenomenon. According to them, integration results in expanded capacities according to the nature of the incarnated being that is potentially used to further the evolutionary process. These comments are highly interesting in light of Jung's relationship with Philemon. Assimilation and consolidation

---

33   *Ibid.*, p. 211.
34   *Ibid.*, p. 211.
35   *Ibid.*, p. 294.

of Philemon in his consciousness indicate that Jung himself became conscious of holding the four keys of Truth along with superior insight, which is evident in his writings and seminars, as well as in his relationship with some of his analysands.

In fact, as time goes on, it is becoming increasingly clear how far Jung and his psychological model are in advance of his time. Brain research and neuro-psychology, for instance, are now making discoveries that support Jung's psychological model, as I indicate above in the section on Daniel Siegel. There is also growing testimony from individuals worldwide on how Jung's map of the soul is serving their individuation process and the evolution of consciousness. In fact, the importance of individuation or, in the language of Sri Aurobindo and the Mother, individualization, that is the process of individual differentiation, is attested to by both Sri Aurobindo and Jung, each of whom, recognize that individuals, not collectivities, are the driving force for creative change in the community.

According to Sri Aurobindo and the Mother, an important aspect of the evolution of consciousness regards a descent of consciousness from above, through beings with a higher consciousness. In their case it is a descent of the avataric consciousness for our time; for Sri Aurobindo, it is the incarnation of Avatar or the Supreme Himself, while in the Mother's case, it is the Divine Mother, the Parashakti or Sophia Herself. Together, they are the differentiated embodiment of the *Anthropos*. In Jung's case, it is the superior being he refers to as Philemon.

But the descent from above and involution is not enough. There is another significant aspect required for the evolution of consciousness to take place. There is also the important ingredient of an evolutionary dynamis from below that works in tandem with the descending spirit. Sri Aurobindo observes "it is quite conceivable that such an evolution from below and such a descent from above co-operated in the appearance of humanity in earth nature."[36] If it happened for the evolution of human beings, there is no reason to assume that it wouldn't happen again, even in our times, which is Sri Aurobindo's and the Mother's contention.

When Jung was between three and four years old, he dreamt of an underground ritual phallus about twelve to fifteen feet high and up to two feet thick, standing upright on a golden throne. On top of its rounded head was an upward gazing eye. Above the head was a bright aura, the room's source of light. Jung refers to it as "a subterranean God" not to be named. Jung interprets the dream as being a "kind of burial in the earth" and an initiation into "the secrets of the earth" and "the realm of darkness," from which, he writes, he emerged many years later.[37] In less mysterious terms, the kingly phallus seated on a royal throne, with a natural vertical gaze of aspiration related to an aura of light, seems to be something like or related to the self-contained physical *purusha* that brings the light of consciousness to the physical Subconscient, using Sri Aurobindo's nomenclature. In the dream, Jung wasn't sure if his mother warned him to be aware that "*That* is the man-eater" or, "that is the *man-eater*," suggesting that the king-phallus is the *purusha-Self* as sacrificer and *man (Jung), the eaten one*, is the sacrificed.[38] This is a variation of the sacred theme that the priest of the sacrifice or quest hero is both sacrificer and sacrificed and is suggestive of the dynamics of Jung's actual subsequent life.

In Jung's tenth year, he allayed his feelings of personal disharmony and insecurity by carving a two-inch long manikin, which he cut off from the end of a ruler. He gave it a coat made out of wool; having carved it with a top hat and shiny boots and colored it with black ink. He kept the manikin in a metal pencil case and hid it in the forbidden attic with rotten flooring, and he would access it in time of need. It was his secret. He also included an oblong blackish stone that he painted

---

36   1970d, p. 840.
37   1983, p. 15.
38   C.G. Jung, 1983, p. 12

JUNG'S BOLLINGEN STONE WITH TELESPHOROS IN THE CENTER

to emphasize that it consisted of two halves. Although it was the mani-kin's stone, Jung puts emphasis on the fact that: "It was *his* stone."[39] Each time Jung would visit the manikin, he would give it a scroll with a message on it in a solemn ceremony. In this way, the manikin ac-cumulated a library, most likely consisting of observations that were pleasing to the ten-year-old Jung.

Later Jung believed that the manikin was the first, albeit unconscious

39   1983, p. 21.

attempt to give expression to his dream of the phallic god. In his autobiography he identifies it as "god of the ancient world, a "Telesphoros"
like one finds on monuments of Aesclepios, "who reads to him from a
scroll," therefore, reminiscent of the library of scrolls Jung placed in
the manikin's pencil case abode.[40] The manikin, observes Jung, was
ultimately "a *kabir,* " a chthonic deity that presides over the sacred fire.
In 1950, when Jung was seventy-five, he made a monument out of a cu-
bic-shaped stone to represent the meaning of his retreat in Bollingen. In
the center of the stone, a figure of Telesphoros of Asclepios, the ancient
Greek god of healing, predating Hippocrates by some three thousand
years, emerged, as depicted in ancient statues, wearing a hooded cloak
and carrying a lantern. Jung indicates that "he is a pointer of the way,"
with the following incandescent words he inscribed on the monument
dedicated to the deity of creative life:

> Time is a child—playing like a child—playing a board game—
> the kingdom of the child. This is Telesphoros, who roams
> through the dark regions of this cosmos and glows like a star
> out of the depths. He points the way to the gates of the sun and
> to the land of dreams.[41]

The first sentence is from Heraclitus, about which Sri Aurobindo
writes: "the Kingdom of the child touches, almost reaches the heart
of the secret. For, this kingdom is evidently spiritual … the mastery to
which the perfect man arrives; the perfect man is a divine child!"[42] The
heart of the secret of life is "spiritual beauty and spiritual delight."[43] It
is "divine knowledge" and "the joyous play of the divine Will," while
being "lost in spontaneity of the divine ananda."[44] Jung was evidently

---

40   *Ibid.,* p. 23.
41   *Ibid.,* p. 227.
42   1971b, p. 371.
43   *Ibid.,* p. 370.
44   *Ibid.,* p. 371.

associated with the guiding instinct of the divine child from early on in his life.

In addition to the descent of a being with superior consciousness in Philemon, along with his soul as Sophia, which Jung assimilated to consciousness, he integrated chthonic qualities that allowed him to dynamically live out the meaning involved in the descent of higher consciousness for the sake of evolution. It is significant that, according to Jung's recollections, the god Telesphoros, who was associated with the ancient Greek healing god, Asclepios, also accompanied Jung throughout his life. He, presumably, continuously pointed the way for him as the most important contemporary healer of the Western psyche.

There are other indications of spiritual power and creative force that emerge from below that give more evidence of the nature of the unfolding evolutionary dynamis in Jung's psyche. To begin with, during his confrontation with the unconscious, in addition to Philemon, there is another key figure that Jung eventually integrates to consciousness. He is the *ka*, which emerges "from below, out of the earth as if out of a deep shaft."[45] Jung equates the *ka* to an earth or metal demon and writes that, although Philemon refers to "the spiritual aspect or meaning," the *ka* is "a spirit of nature" which, on the one hand, makes everything real and, on the other, obscures or replaces spiritual meaning with "beauty."[46] Jung observes that the *ka* is saying "I am he who buries the gods in gold and gems."[47] This seems to imply that, while the importance of Philemon lies in meaning, the importance of the *ka* lies in its insistence on the evolution of spiritual dynamis—and its incarnation through beauty. There is a need to integrate these two opposite tendencies in a synthesis, which, given Jung's artistic sensibility as indicated in *The Red Book,* along with his superior insights, was the case for Jung himself. Emphasis on beauty and the aesthetic mind, however,

---

45   C.G. Jung, 1983, p. 185.
46   *Ibid.*
47   *Ibid.*

JUNG'S DEPICTION OF BRAHMANASPATI IN THE RED BOOK

can bury the gods, suggesting that they can also prevent one from experiencing their raw truth and energy. Aestheticism, the cult of beauty, can divert attention away from engaging the chthonic gods, which have been collectively repressed since the institutionalization of Christianity in Europe. The opposites, in fact, include not only beauty but ugliness, both of which belong to manifest reality. The deeper opposites requiring synthesis today are spiritual meaning and the energism of the dynamic pole of the chthonic psyche.

In *The Red Book,* which Jung was immersed in between 1912 and 1920, there are stunning pictures of two of his paintings, one of *Brahmanaspati* from the *Rig Veda,* and another of *Agni,* the sacred fire from the *Çatapatha brâhmanam 2, 2, 4.* Jung depicts *Brahmanaspati* as something like the ancient Egyptian *Agathodaimon* serpent, surrounded by fire, powerfully emerging from the dark depth of the unconscious and giving birth out of its mouth to what appears to be something like the living Tree of Life and Knowledge surrounded by a blue sky. Sri Aurobindo refers to *Brahmanapasti* as uniting the qualities of *Brihaspati* as *"Purusha"* and "Bull of the Herds," master of the supreme "Word of Knowledge," "the Soul that emerges out of the Subconscient in Man and rises towards the Superconscient, and the word of creative Power welling upward out of the Soul."[48] In *Symbols of Transformation,* Jung refers specifically to *Brahmanaspati* as a "preworldly" creative "prayer-word."[49] In *Psychological Types,* he writes that "Brahman is a combination of prayer and primordial creative power," and that the concept coincides with "a dynamic or creative principle which I have termed libido."[50]

Overall then, the feeling of the painted image itself and these amplifications indicate consciousness of emerging creative Soul-power that gives birth to the Word of Knowledge. It is Soul-power in evolutionary

---

48   1971c, pp. 311, 307, 306.
49   1974a, p. 359.
50   C.G. Jung, 1974b, pp. 203, 201.

JUNG'S PAINTING OF PHILEMON DEPICTED IN THE RED BOOK

becoming and the creative word that rises toward the Transcendent. In Sri Aurobindo's commentary on *Rig Veda IV.50*, he observes that, ideally, humans are led by this soul-force as well as realizing themselves as *Indra*, Lord of the Mind, figured as the Bull, "the sole lord of the cows" and "Master of Mental Force."[51]

These commentaries by Sri Aurobindo are interesting in light of Jung having realized himself as Philemon, a being with kingfisher wings and bull's horns, as is evident in the image of Philemon in a

---

51   1971c, pp. 149, 515.

painting by Jung shown on these pages, with definite affinities to *Indra*, even if an emanation, justifying Jung's qualifying him as "the master." The kingfisher of the *halcyon* genus, according to Greek mythology, has the power to calm the seas and wind during the winter solstice, suggesting an apt symbol for a calm mind and for mastery over the mind. In addition, Philemon is not only a bull-figure like *Indra*, similar to the latter, he is associated with the number four or Truth. Philemon is described by Jung as having four keys, with which he can discern different aspects of Truth, while *Indra* has the ability to exceed the mind and dwell in Truth itself. Thus, "when *Indra* exceeded Mind and entered *Mahas*, yet maintained the lower firmaments," then, a hymn to Indra (verse 4 of *Rig Veda X.54*) states: "Four, verily, are thy untameable mightiness when thou dwellest in the Vastness.[52] The path to perfection as completeness of being requires assimilation of both *Brihaspati* as soul-force and *Indra* as mental-force. Sri Aurobindo writes: "Indra and Brihaspati are thus the two divine powers whose fullness in us and conscious possession of the Truth are the conditions of our perfection."[53] Evidently, with his relationship to *Brahmanaspati* and realization of Philemon, Jung and his model of psychology have undeniable affinities to Sri Aurobindo and the Mother's path of Integral Yoga, in full harmony with contemporary evolutionary exigencies.

On December 13, 1913, at the beginning of Jung's confrontation with the unconscious, he had the following dream depicting the necessary sacrifice of conscious attitudes and ideals, which eventually led to his study of alchemy and relationship with the maternal depth of being:

> *I was with an unknown, brown-skinned man, a savage, in a lonely, rocky mountain landscape. It was before dawn; the eastern sky was already bright, and the stars fading. Then I heard Siegfried's horn sounding over the mountains and I knew we had to kill him. We were armed with rifles*

52   Sri Aurobindo, 1971c, p. 515.
53   *Ibid.*, p. 313.

and lay in wait for him on a narrow path over the rocks.

Then Siegfried appeared high up on a crest of the mountain, in the first ray of the rising sun. On a chariot made from the bones of the dead he drove at a furious speed down the precipitous slope. When he turned the corner, we shot at him, and he plunged down, struck dead.

Filled with disgust and remorse for having destroyed something so great and beautiful, I turned to flee impelled by the fear that murder may be discovered. But a tremendous downpour of rain began, and I knew it would wipe out all traces of the dead. I had escaped the danger of discovery; life would go on, but an unbearable feeling of guilt remained.[54]

Jung interprets Siegfried, the hero of Nordic mythology, as representing the Germans' imposition of their will, and the idea that where there's a will there's a way. Jung, who was a multifaceted man with a Nordic accent, was an exemplary embodiment of masculine values with a comprehensive and competent ego that allowed him to fulfill himself in a way that went well beyond the norm for his time. He was at the top of his profession as a psychologist, he had been in an international leadership capacity for psychoanalysis, he had successfully published books on psychiatry and psychology, he had artistic talent, he had participated in designing his own beautiful and well-appointed house in Küsnacht and he had a healthy growing family. The dream indicates that, for Jung, the attitude that bestowed on him a certain life-mastery and success was no longer suitable. The unconscious brought compensatory values to consciousness, forcing Jung to sacrifice his heroic idealism and to prostrate himself before a higher Will.

In the second selected image depicted by Jung in *The Red Book*, with reference to the *Çatapatha brâhmanam 2, 2, 4*, a figure clad in green is prostrate in front of a stream of fire pouring out from a blood-red ground/floor, with red squares and black designs as squares. On the background wall is a boat with an illuminated eye on its prow, a mast

54   Jung, 1983, p. 180.

PROSTRATION TO THE SACRIFICIAL FIRE
DEPICTED BY JUNG IN THE RED BOOK: IMAGE 64

and greenish sail, a gold disc representing the sun, and a black figure at the stern steering the ship. It is sailing on dark water with a greenish hue. The fire is the sacrificial fire, *Agni*, of which Jung writes in *Symbols of Transformation*, "Agni is the sacrificial flame, the sacrificer and the sacrificed."[55]

Regarding the sacrifice, in *Psychological Types*, Jung observes that it "always means the renunciation of a valuable part of oneself," and through it the sacrificer escapes being devoured; there is instead "equilibration and union."[56] According to Sri Aurobindo *Agni* is the priest and "leader of the sacrifice," "the flame on the altar and the priest of the oblation."[57] He is the "divine Will," "divine strength of impulsion," and flame-Power of the journey and without him there is no sacrifice.[58] The priest in Jung's image prostrates before *Agni* as a sacrifice to the divine Will to be impelled on the right path to wholeness.

The symbolism in Jung's image includes differentiated Eros and relatedness to the deeper unconscious in the red and black floor/ground as well as potential for new life values and hope in the green, the color of the water, along with the unconscious in the use of grey and black. The image painted by Jung depicts the necessary instinctual sacrifice of the ego to a superior Will in order to undertake the night-sea journey, the descent of the sun of consciousness into Jung's collective unconscious or Sri Aurobindo's psychic being into the subliminal and Circumconscient, and the Subconscient and Inconscient as portrayed in the background, for the sake of rebirth and renewal into a truer and more complete life. The evolutionary movement of consciousness comes from below in aspiration toward the assimilation of archetypal values including those of the Self.

On November 2, 1960, some six months prior to his death, Jung

---

55   1974a, p. 167.
56   1974b, p. 204.
57   1971c, p. 359.
58   *Ibid.*, p. 378.

wrote a letter to an acquaintance, artist Peter Birkhäuser, about how his painting of a black *puer aeternus* figure, the spirit of renewal, riding a white horse-boar monster, affected him. Exactly how he was affected is indicated in the dream recounted by Jung and transcribed and amplified in Chapter 1. In brief, Jung and a 50,000-year-old chieftain experienced a perilous struggle to capture, kill and carry a gigantic primordial boar back to the tribe for consumption. Although I discuss the dream earlier in relationship to Jung's intimate relationship to nature, here I consider how this late dream refers to Jung's relationship with the primal psyche, the spirit of renewal and creative evolution from below.

In Jung's free variations on the dream, he refers to the Vishnu creation myth as well as the Hindu belief that Vishnu will come as a white horse at the end of this cosmic age and "create a new world."[59] Jung further notes that the horse refers to Pegasus, who "ushers in the Aquarian Age."[60] He also amplifies the dream by a Kabbalistic redemption theme as a parallel to the Hindu myth, where, at the end of time, Yahweh will allegedly destroy the Leviathan and "serve it up as a meal for the righteous."[61]

According to Jewish tradition the flesh of the Leviathan and Behemoth will be prepared and eaten by the righteous at the messianic banquet at the end of time. Jung understands the Behemoth to be the rejected side of God that, in Christianity, has been assigned to the devil's playground. The same can be said about the Leviathan. Yet, in *Job* 40:19, in reference to the Behemoth, one reads that "He is the masterpiece of all God's work," which suggests to Eva Wertenschlagg-Birkhäuser that he represents "divine creative power" and generative "life force."[62]

Edinger, however, warns that the Behemoth is the "as yet

---

59   As reported in Gerhard Adler, ed., 1975, p. 607.
60   *Ibid.*
61   *Ibid.*
62   2009, p. 88.

untransformed God, not yet humanized by the incarnation of Christ."[63] The Leviathan and the Behemoth represent the primordial psyche, the powerful autonomous effects and energy that emerge from the collective unconscious. The upshot of these dynamics is that these two monsters represent the primal life force, which can just as well bring creative renewal as, without proper discernment, overwhelming mindless destruction.

Wertenschlagg-Birkhäuser rightfully argues that Jung's dream shows how important his work is for the creative renewal of culture today.[64] As the dream indicates, with the images of the primitive chieftain, the 50,000-year-old Great Man, and the slaughtered gigantic boar, and the recognition of them being primal, archetypal and instinctual representations of wisdom and the creative life force, respectively, Jung brought to consciousness discernment of the primordial psyche. He and the chieftain prepared a meal of the primeval boar for popular (tribal) consumption, psychologically meaning Jung prepared the ground for individuals to assimilate to consciousness this perilous aspect of the psyche, which is both creative and destructive, without being overwhelmed by it. This late dream and its amplifications indicate the depth of Jung's creative assimilation of the evolutionary dynamis from below into his consciousness and life, and represent the vital contribution he makes to society and culture toward the evolution of consciousness at the primordial and instinctual level of being. Jung's conscious relationship with this primordial dynamism gives von Franz the license to write: "I couldn't regard Kant's writings, for instance, as being a result of chthonic bull power, but Jung's work might well be, because it challenges the basis of everything."[65]

In Jung's case, there was a descent of a superior consciousness in Philemon, who, incidentally, has bull's horns, which corresponds to

---

63   1984, p. 111.
64   2009, p. 88.
65   As reported in Wertenschlagg-Birkhäuser, 2009, p. 108.

the evolutionary requirements today for expanding consciousness, according to Sri Aurobindo's reasoning. Jung integrated Philemon into consciousness along with Sophia. He also assimilated a dynamis from below that impelled him along a path of wholeness and powerful creativity, again in harmony with the evolutionary needs and the meaning intrinsic to the descent of consciousness from above. Although there is no formal evidence that Jung ever realized identity with non-dual Reality of the transcendent *That*, or attained the level of Supermind or Truth-Mind, as did Sri Aurobindo and the Mother, his approach to psychology is, otherwise, in full harmony with their teachings.

Jung's Final Dream-Vision

Jung, in fact, attained a level of individuated spiritual oneness through ego surrender and spiritual transformation that includes his individual form continuing to exist at the level of the rhizome, below the roots of a quadrangle of world trees. In other words, he became spiritually individuated down to the elemental vegetative level of being that symbolizes eternal life. While individual life forms come and go, the rhizome endures. Here is Jung's last recorded dream-vision, which relates to these comments:

> Jung saw a great round stone in a high place, a barren square, and on it were engraved the words: "And this shall be a sign unto you of Wholeness and Oneness." Then he saw many vessels to the right in an open square and a quadrangle of trees whose roots reached around the earth and enveloped him and amongst the roots golden threads were glittering.[66]

At that time, Jung is reported to have said: "Now I know the truth but there is a small piece not filled in and when I know that I shall be

---

66   As recorded in Marie-Louise von Franz, 1975, p. 287.

dead."[67] Jung's most important disciple, Marie-Louise von Franz, amplifies the dream's significance by referring to the Tao, where with the
attainment of "the meaning of the world and eternal life ... the Chinese
say: 'Long life flowers with the essence of the stone and the brightness
of gold.'"[68]

The existence of a great round stone in a *barren square*, the *open
square* of vessels and the *quadrangle* of trees also suggest a direct influence from the Overmind with delegated supramental gnosis, given
that the square and number four symbolizes the Supermind. The roots
of the trees with glittering golden threads enveloping Jung and surrounding the Earth indicate spiritual transformation of the Inconscient,
the roots of life and the material world. Given Jung's emphasis on the
reconciliation of all opposites, reference can also be made to the fulfillment of the goal for knowledge of the Upanishads and the attainment
of knowledge of *Vidya* and *Avidya*, the Eternal and the Ignorance. The
Mother's stated objective for her disciples of a "global ... consciousness at the same time individual and total" couldn't be more fully symbolized than in this dream-vision, where the round stone is a sign of
Jung's Wholeness and Oneness, suggesting unity with the immanent
deity and a differentiated relationship with the transcendent One.[69]

At the end of his life, Jung stopped using the *I Ching*, the Chinese
book of wisdom, which integrates the microcosm with the macrocosm,
the individual with the universal. This book, otherwise known as the
Book of Changes, can be understood as the embodiment of Tao that
purports to show the way for individuals to live individually in accord
with archetypal cosmic principles. Jung told Marie-Louise von Franz,
a highly trustworthy source, that the reason he no longer needed to use

67   As recorded in Dunne, 2012, p. 245.
68   1975, p. 287.
69   2004c, p. 52.

it was that "he already 'knew' in advance what the answer would be," indicating a superior degree of knowledge by identity.[70]

Von Franz herself had two remarkable dreams that indicate a superior level of personality integration as well. In one dream she was pleased to see placed in front of her an eight volume work on Arabic alchemy that she had authored.[71] Contemporary depth psychology recognizes alchemy as an important precursor, which is replete with symbolic material that helps elucidate the individuation process, while acknowledging that Arabic alchemy emphasizes Eros more than the European variety. In fact, von Franz spent much time during the last ten years of her life studying the works of an important Arabic alchemist, Ibn Umail. The dream seems to indicate that she had undergone a major transformation of being and gave expression to differentiated Eros and the Self as reflected in the number 8, which, qualitatively, means wholeness and the infinite.

In a second dream, she sees an old city with a new building with seventeen regular sides. It had formerly been believed to be impossible to construct such a form.[72] The belief that it was impossible suggests the fact that it could only be built by the Self or God in collaboration with the human instrument, and not by normal human means. The number seventeen is a highly sacred number in many traditions. There is biblical reference to the holiness of this number, which was later amplified by the Shiite tradition of Islam as referring to the presence of Allah in matter. The Arabic alchemist, Jabir Ibn Hayyan, wrote that the total earthly manifestation of "becoming and perishing"[73] does not go beyond the measure of seventeen. Similarly, in the Vedas of India, the Progenitor and Creator God is composed of seventeen parts.[74] The Mother's symbol is a mandala with 17 aspects, a unifying center, four inner pet-

70   1992, p. 259.
71   As reported by Rafael Monzo, 2006, pp. 247, 248.
72   As reported by Gothilf Isler, 2006, p. 63
73   As reported in Theodor Abt, 2005, p. 165.
74   Roberto Calasso, 2010, p. 232.

als, representing four aspects of the Mother, (Maheshwari) Wisdom, (Mahakali) Power, (Mahalakshmi) Harmony and (Mahasaraswati) Service, and twelve outer petals, representing highly differentiated qualities of manifest being.

Thus, seventeen symbolizes the union of psyche and matter and, for the individual, completed individuation and unified being. Seventeen is comprised of 4 x 4 = 16 plus 1 as the unifying center, suggesting that four aspects of the Self, wisdom, power, harmonious relatedness and devoted service, are differentiated by each of the four functions of consciousness. In the context of this dream, seventeen refers to a conscious relationship with the *unus mundus* and the New World, now, through von Franz, manifest on Earth amidst the old world. Unified being includes the (subtle physical) body organized around the Self, as reflected in a dream von Franz reported a few weeks prior to her passing away, where her body was completely healed.[75] In fact, she suffered from Parkinson's disease for the last 13 plus years of her life.

As indicated above, Sri Aurobindo differentiates several planes of being ascending from the Mind through the Higher Mind, to the Illumined Mind, and then the Intuitive Mind, where he defines intuition as "a power of consciousness nearer and more intimate to the original knowledge by identity," where original knowledge resides in the Supermind.[76] The next level up from the Intuitive Mind is the Overmind, which comes closer to the Supermind in terms of knowledge by identity. The evidence of Jung's inner life points to the fact that, in his case, the *unus mundus* and possibly some Overmind experience is far more than a conceptual reality positioned above in the heavens; it is fully embodied below down to the level of the rhizome.

75   Anne Maguire, 2006, p. 72
76   1970d, p. 946.

CHAPTER 21

The Mother, Jung and
Internalizing the Gods

The Mother is reported to have said that "the age of the gods, and consequently the age of religions," was a product of the Overmind.[1] She
goes on to say: "And now, all these old things seem so old, so out-of-
date, so arbitrary—such a travesty of the real truth. In the supramental
creation, there will no longer be any religions."[2] This should not be
mistaken to be the realization of the unity of religions, which some
people aspire toward today, because this "still belongs *completely* to
the Overmind world"; they cannot grasp the nature of the supramental creation, which they are really seeking.[3] "To grasp it a reversal is
needed" as "in the supramental creation there will *no longer be any
religions.*"[4] Rather, observes the Mother, "the whole life will be an
expression, a flowering into forms of divine Unity manifesting in the
world. And there will no longer be what men call gods."[5] She sees
this Unity as belonging to the future, observing that it is a future that
has already begun, while acknowledging that integral realization will
take time. Presumably it does not require supramental or even a full
spiritual transformation to begin to live in the new world; but with a
simple reversal in understanding that religion no longer has a place in
the organization of life, one can aspire to live the new reality.

---

1   2004b, p. 150.
2   *Ibid.*
3   *Ibid.*
4   *Ibid.*, p. 151.
5   *Ibid.*

There is a need to leave the world of religions and their gods in order to participate in bringing in the new world. This is not simply a question of leaving one's birth religion for another institution and belief system, but of relating to the Self within, and allowing for its creative unfolding. In psychological terms, it is a question of individuation; of withdrawing projections from specific cultures, civilizations and religions, along with their politicians and officiating priests, heroes, saints and realized beings, and various gods, goddesses and devils, as well as normal human beings; and internalizing their qualities in the individual human psyche. Jung's path, especially as delineated later in his life, opens one up to this new reality. I see him as being at the forefront of this endeavor, which is the deeper significance of his legacy.

The challenge of individuation is the continual withdrawal of projections by way of studying synchronicities, dreams, spontaneous fantasies and visions of numinous archetypal images. This eventually encourages the internalization of sacred energy and locates the Self within, involving the union of opposites and psychic integration, while experientially recollecting the gods from outside the psyche. Jung writes: "The self then functions as a union of opposites and thus constitutes the most immediate experience of the Divine it is possible to imagine."[6] The new world that is already born is a world where the external gods and religions no longer exist. Individuals who consciously participate in this unfolding new world are the actual locus of divinity, with lives that are eventually bound to the Self, while giving expression to forms within the limits of creative freedom.

It is easy to mistake this realization by drawing a parallel between Jung's notions of the Self and the Advaitan Self, where, according to Ramana Maharshi, God is discovered through Self-inquiry and deepening one's relationship to the Heart, the seat of Consciousness and the "very core of one's being."[7] Although both Jung and Advaita may

---

6   Jung 1969c, p. 261.
7   1988, p. 91.

locate God within, what is missing in Advaita is any relationship whatsoever with the creative source of life, Jung's *unus mundus* or Sri
Aurobindo's Supermind, each of which links the world of unity with
the multiplicity. Whatever way one cuts the cake, Advaita conceives of
the world as "dependent, unself-conscious (and) ever-changing" and
therefore "unreal."[8] According to Ramana, "Reality is *sat-chit,* Being-
Consciousness and never merely the one to the exclusion of the other."[9]
In this formulation, there is only Being and Consciousness; there is
no recognition of the *Shakti,* the Divine feminine, and the formulation *Chit-Shakti,* Consciousness and Force, as the creative source of the
manifestation. An unreal world is not a creative world in intelligent unfolding process. A real world permeated with Consciousness-Force is
unfolding intelligently. In psychological terms, this means that, whatever the nature and extent of transformation there is in Advaita, in-
depth personality transformation as understood by Sri Aurobindo and
the Mother, or by Jung, is not a concern.

Jung defines the creative state of being as related to the cosmic
Self, the *unus mundus,* with its psychological and artistic equivalent
being mandalas, and the experience of synchronicity, where time and
non-dual Reality intersect. In harmony with the Mother's observations
about the new supramental creation, no more religions and the dis-
appearance of the gods, Jung writes: "Everything of a divine or de-
monic character outside us must return to the psyche, to the inside of
the unknown man, whence it apparently originated."[10] Given the state
of world affairs and human evolution and, otherwise, the lack of evidence, he also disagrees forthrightly about assigning consciousness to
a world creator. "The naïve assumption that the creator of the world
is a conscious being," Jung argues, "must be regarded as a disastrous
prejudice which later gave rise to the most incredible dislocations of

---

8   *Ibid.,* p. 90.
9   *Ibid.*
10   1975c, p. 85.

logic."[11] In Sri Aurobindo's terms, Jung is referring to experiences of the overmental creation, which is the one we all know and which is in the process of being left behind.

One might add here that, in the new supramental creation, one could eventually come to a different perspective on the creator, seeing it embodied in the Avatar and Divine Mother, though still allowing that the gods need recalling in order to live within. According to Jung, images of the numinous lay within the psyche, making it essential today to work on withdrawing projections from all external objects and situations in order to realize the true creative source of life. Participating in the new creation begins, in Jung's terms, with "individuation ... with the individual conscious of his isolation, cutting a path through hitherto untrodden territory."[12] One distant goal of the individuation process is realization of the cosmic Self, uniting the individual Tao with the cosmic Tao and the individual *Atman (Jivatman)* with the universal *Atman* as discussed above. In reference to the cosmic Self, according to Jung, the individual Self is the Self of all, existing not only in the individual, but *"in all beings ... forming a psychic totality,"* a statement which dispels any criticism of Jung's path being self-centered and solipsistic.[13]

Jung refers to the work of the alchemist, Gerhard Dorn, in order to describe his three-step transformation process of individuation. The first stage beyond the natural man and the *unio naturalis* is the *unio mentalis*, which requires psychological separation from the body; after which one proceeds to stage two, which is a return to the body, now relating to it with the *unio mentalis;* and, finally, in stage three, realization of the *unus mundus*. These stages, in fact, do not necessarily work in strict sequential development, but often with overlaying patterns of experience.

The first stage of the threefold process of transformation is the *unio*

11   1975g, p. 383, fn 13.
12   1975b, p. 59.
13   As reported in David Rosen, 1996, p. 122

mentalis, which involves overcoming the body by way of the union of spirit and the psyche or soul, separate from the body. Symbolism of decapitation depicts this stage, about which Jung writes:

> Beheading is significant symbolically as the separation of "understanding" from the "great suffering and grief" which nature inflicts on the soul. It is an emancipation of the "cogitatio" which is situated in the head, a freeing of the soul from the "trammels of nature." Its purpose is to bring about, as in Dorn, a *unio mentalis,* "in the overcoming of the body."[14]

A mental and spiritual counter-position with rational insight is established, where projections are dissolved that tie the individual to the objects of the world, along with concomitant bodily desires, emotional affects and passions. By way of withdrawing projections, one becomes conscious of aspects of the shadow, including some of the collective shadow. In Sri Aurobindo's yoga, this refers to transformation of the mental being through increased understanding, as well as some transformation of the vital or life being and, as will be shown, attaining self-knowledge through contact with the psychic being. It can also involve forming a conscious relationship with the individual *Atman,* the *Jivatman,* which has the merit of accessing a field of spiritual energy and peace above the head, aiding immeasurably in rising above storms of desire and emotional affects.

In fact, according to Jung, the *unio mentalis* brings about not ego-knowledge, but true self-knowledge, in the deeper sense of the word, thanks to the release of a product that alchemists called the *caelum,* which, like the psychic being, is the inner truth and unity of being. Jung makes the interesting observation that "Christianity was a *unio mentalis* in the overcoming of the body," where there is a relationship established between the *unio mentalis* and the body and bodily passions. This perspective helps to explain the virtue of Christianity as well as

---

14   1975, p. 513.

its limitations. Although a relationship is established between the ego and the body along with its passions, Christianity does not carry the individual onwards to the second stage of transformation.

The alchemists, who projected their psyche into chemical solutions and procedures, produced a purified product they referred to as the *caelum*, which was the blue color of air that floated to the top of the chemical solution. This was the result of distilling the "philosophic wine" through the "repeated sublimation of the soul and spirit from the body."[15] According to Dorn, the *caelum* was the secret "truth," the "sum of virtue," the "treasure," although the cheapest thing, for the wise, of great value and worthy of love.[16] It was a blue tincture, "the heavenly substance in the body," the "truth."[17]

In psychological terms, Jung regards the alchemical procedures and beliefs as a kind of active imagination and representation of the individuation process, although in projection. The task today is not to leave the representations of the individuation process in projections but to withdraw projections and assimilate them to consciousness. This involves connecting to the *caelum*, the subjective truth. There were several alchemical operations where the *caelum* was mixed with various ingredients that were psychologically indicative of its nature. These ingredients included honey, magic herbs and "rosemary flowers," alluding to qualities of sweetness, signifying the joy of life and joy of the senses, personality transformation "from below upwards," and the binding power of love.[18]

Jung adds the plant *mercurialis* to the ingredients, bringing in the attraction of sexuality and passion. He compares *mercurialis* with *moly*, the ingredient that the seductress Circe uses in *The Odyssey* to transfigure Odysseus' companions into pigs, and with which she later

---

15   *Ibid.*, p. 486.
16   *Ibid.*, p. 487.
17   *Ibid.*, p. 489.
18   *Ibid.*, pp. 490, 492.

tries to seduce the hero likewise. The pig is an apt symbolic representation of what Sri Aurobindo refers to as the "the vital-physical," with its "small desires and greeds," pleasure seeking, and so on; along with the nervous being, which governs "the reactions of the nerves and the body consciousness and reflex emotions and sensations," which "in its lowest part (vital-material) … is the agent of pain, physical illness, etc."[19] He, in fact, highly differentiates between different levels of the mental, vital and physical natures, in a way that is more explicit than with Jung.

Yet, from the outset Jung defines the psyche as based on a unitary reality "situated between the 'infrared' pole of material bodily reactions (somatic processes) at the one end, and the 'ultraviolet' pole of the archetype at the other."[20] Thanks to his experiences and interest in synchronicity, he takes his original definition further, recognizing the transcendental, therefore irrepresentational, unity behind spirit and matter. Indeed, he has no objection to regarding psyche as a "quality of matter" or matter as a "concrete aspect of the psyche," as long as "psyche" is defined as "the collective unconscious."[21] By defining psyche accordingly, he is not necessarily suggesting that it involves the unknown psychoid aspect of spirit and matter, which he defines as being inaccessible to consciousness. There is some ambiguity here, however, since Jung writes that, at its lowest level, the psyche is simply nature, "which includes *everything,* thus also the unknown, *inclusive of matter.*"[22] The polarity of spirit-matter is a dualistic expression of the *unus mundus* and potentially accessible through psychic experiences.

Jung came to believe that the natural number is a key to the mystery of the unity of existence, the *unus mundus,* given that it relates precisely to both matter and spirit. He writes: "Synchronicity, though in practice a relatively rare phenomenon, is an all-pervading factor or principle

---

19   1970e, p. 344.
20   As recorded in Marie-Louise von Franz, 1974, p. 4.
21   *Ibid.,* p. 8.
22   *Ibid.,* pp. 7, 8.

in the universe, i.e., in the *unus mundus*, where there is no incommensurability between so-called matter and so-called psyche .... In this connection I always come upon the enigma of the *natural number*."[23] Von Franz[24] took up the challenge and addressed the qualitative nature of numbers in her erudite book, *Number and Time*. Experiences of synchronicity are experiences of the *unus mundus*, where non-dual Reality intersects with time, and psyche and matter are experienced as one.

Sri Aurobindo writes that the vital is made up of "desires, sensations, feelings, passions, energies of action, will of desire, reactions of the desire soul in man and of all that play of possessive and other related instincts, anger, fear, greed, lust, etc."[25] For him, the goal of the vital transformation is to attain the true vital, meaning awareness of being the vital *Purusha*, "a projection and instrument of the Divine ... the divine warrior, pure and perfect ... an instrumental force for all divine realizations."[26] Here, Sri Aurobindo seems to be writing about the need for the same level of transformation as Jung alludes to in the second stage of transformation, although he is more explicit about what the transformation entails. In any event, he takes his explanations beyond symbolic representations, while appealing directly to mental discernment. Although he also adds pertinent psychological commentaries, Jung makes ample use of the image here as elsewhere in his writing, with the decided advantage of appealing to the whole person, albeit with less differentiation.

According to Jung, there is an additional symbolic content to the *caelum*, the red lily, which is analogous to blood, the vital essence of life, thus incorporating psychic totality. Releasing the *caelum,* in other words, encourages a move toward centering the whole psyche from top to bottom, including the body and its appetites, around the Self

---

23   *Ibid.*, p. 9.
24   *Ibid.* passim.
25   1970e, p. 321
26   *Ibid.*, p. 309.

and not the ego. After a period of ascetic withdrawal and introversion during the first stage and releasing the *caelum*, the second stage of the transformation process proceeds, whereby the *caelum* operates in such a way as to establish a relationship between the *unio mentalis* and the body and its sensual desires. The body becomes reanimated by the soul and spirit—in Sri Aurobindo's language, the vital and psychic being—and the insights and truth gained in the first stage can now be lived out in the reality of everyday life. In alchemical language the first stage resembles the state of *albedo,* the whitening, an abstract condition of receptivity and insight. The second stage resembles the *rubedo*, the reddening, where the abstract state gives way to living one's wholeness, authenticity and truth in the full-blooded reality of everyday life.

The second stage produces a synthesis of personality, where the *caelum*, which has been described as being the truth hidden in the body is, in reality, the *imago dei* imprinted in man, the true quintessence and the "virtue" of the philosophic wine."[27] In this stage of transformation the psyche is subjected to the ever-present reality of the incarnated *imago dei* and subjective truth. From the discussion above, it is evident that the striking quality of the *caelum*, as incarnated *imago dei,* is that it unites all levels of being, not only the mental being but all levels of the life nature and the body itself, which functions with considerable inertia without the animating influence of the soul, psyche or the vital. In Sri Aurobindo's terms, the emphasis here is on the vital transformation through the influence of the psychic being. In a larger sense, it is what he refers to as the psychic transformation, which is the first stage of his triple transformations, namely the psychic transformation, the spiritual transformation and the supramental transformation. Ultimately, the psychic transformation involves all levels of being, as does Jung's stage two transformation.

Jung equates the *caelum* to *mercurius,* the nature of which he

27   Jung, 1974c, p. 478.

summarizes at the beginning of his last chapter in "The Spirit of Mercurius," a companion essay to his magnum opus, *Mysterium Coniunctionis*. He writes:

> The multiple aspects of Mercurius may be summarized as follows:
> 1. Mercurius consists of all conceivable opposites. He is thus quite obviously a duality, but is named a unity in spite of the fact that his innumerable inner contradictions can dramatically fly apart into an equal number of disparate and apparently independent figures.
> 2. He is both material and spiritual.
> 3. He is the process by which the lower and material is transformed into the higher and spiritual and vice versa.
> 4. He is the devil, a redeeming psychopomp, an evasive trickster, and God's reflection in physical nature.
> 5. He is also the reflection of a mystical experience of the artifex that coincides with the *opus alchemicum*.
> 6. As such, he represents on the one hand the self and on the other the individuation process and, because of the limitless number of his names, also the collective unconscious.[28]

As representation of the collective unconscious, the Self and the individuation process, *mercurius*, like the *caelum,* can be equated, at least in part, with the psychic being in Sri Aurobindo's lexicon. His embodying all opposites, including the material and spiritual, the devil,

---

28   Jung, 1970a, p. 237.

the trickster, God's reflection in physical nature as well as the mystical experience of the alchemist, is an indication of the height, depth and breadth of its influence. Sri Aurobindo identifies the individual *Atman,* the *Jivatman,* as a portion of the cosmic *Atman,* and the psychic being as the incarnation of the *Jivatman* in the individual, roughly located behind the heart and solar plexus, which delegates three different *purushas*, physical, vital and mental. The psychic being knows the truth through feeling and is the center of incarnated being, relating to all aspects of the psyche including the archetypal and spiritual, vital and physical realities. It is the incarnated aspect of the Self and the principle of individuation. Jung's emphasis on Eros and feeling indicates his reliance on knowing through feeling as well, even if he doesn't discuss it in relationship to *mercurius* or the *caelum*. Sri Aurobindo and the Mother are enthusiastic about the value of their disciples bringing the psychic being forward and letting it direct and transform their lives. For the most part, the similarity in status and function of the psychic being to the *caelum* and *mercurius*, at least in part, is very striking.

The third stage of Jung's scheme for the threefold transformation of personality is realized with what he refers to as the *unus mundus,* one world, based on the goal of the alchemical opus described by Gerhard Dorn. After the psychic transformation in Sri Aurobindo's yoga, there is the spiritual transformation. Jung's third stage can also be described as spiritual transformation, which finds fulfillment with the feeling realization of the *unus mundus*; as I suggest above, this was the case of Jung himself. In both Sri Aurobindo's and Jung's case, the whole psyche is involved in the transformation process, which is, typically, not evident with other spiritual paths, where the goal is realizing nondual Reality or nirvana, while effectively ignoring the psyche altogether or treating it as an unwelcome nuisance.

With Sri Aurobindo there is still insistence on realizing *That* and returning with one's relationship to non-dual Reality intact, in a state known as samadhishta samadhi, while engaging the world. In that way his spiritual transformation includes both the transformation of the psyche as well as the traditional insistence on realizing identity with *That*, the One without a second, which, presumably, takes the spiritual transformation process to its limits. The final level of spiritual realization for Sri Aurobindo is the upper limit of the overmind plane as I have previously discussed. With Jung, there is more ambiguity around his relationship to *That*, although he, at the very least, stands before "the nothing that is the All," even if he never did cross the threshold to attain identity with *That* or attain *nirvana*, the latter which he, in fact, seems to have done as previously discussed.

Attaining the *unus mundus* means attaining the whole person, the *unio mentalis* united with the animated body now in unity with the world, a state of continuous synchronicity and egolessness. As I indicate previously, this refers to realizing the cosmic Tao as well as the cosmic *Atman*, along with conscious experience of the *anima mundi*, the world soul, as did Jung in his 1944 visions. Although Jung reports that all his writings were imposed from within, after this series of experiences, he takes the process further and writes that "I no longer attempted to put across my own opinions but surrendered myself to the current of my thoughts."[29]

The fact that his most important works were written at this time is a testimony to the level of his realization. If Jung's life is any indication, the third level of his transformation process leads to attaining a direct experience of the *unus mundus* and being transformed accordingly. As I argue above this seems to be something like experiencing Sri Aurobindo's Overmind with supramental gnosis and the Mind of Light, along with some overmental transformation. For Sri Aurobindo there is another level of transformation beyond the spiritual, which he refers to as the supramental transformation, the transformation by the Truth-Mind, which exists beyond the mind or the psyche, in the Ignorance.

---

29   1983, p. 297.

The Supermind, the Axiom of Maria and the Four

Sri Aurobindo symbolizes the Supermind with the number four. As I demonstrate early on in this study, the fundamental structure of the Universe is based on four forces in nature. Likewise, variations of both the codes for genes, DNA, and memory substance, RNA, are grounded on a formula with a base four. Sri Aurobindo delineates four soul-types based on the original fourfold order of society, the *caturvarna*. Jung defines a personality typology based on the four functions of consciousness, and defines the Self and wholeness or completeness in terms of the number four, often referring to the integration of four functions of consciousness. There are four Christian gospels; and the fourth, the Gospel of St. John, with its more mystical orientation and introduction of the Logos principle, betrays a Greek background, while the other three are more representative of the Hebrew tradition. There are many more examples of the fundamental significance of the number four, as alluded to in Chapter 2, but this accounting should suffice for purposes of this study.

The number four resonates meaningfully at different levels of nature, suggesting it represents the basic structure of the psyche and matter, and the truth of being in nature. The question is, then, how might Jung's interest in the number four relate to Sri Aurobindo's Supermind, with its symbol also being the number four? It is helpful here to turn to the oft-repeated alchemical Axiom of Maria, which Jung often refers to approvingly, where she is recorded as saying: "Out of the One comes Two, out of Two comes Three, and from the Third comes the One as the Fourth."[30] Since, as von Franz has shown in *Number and Time*, all numbers are qualitatively based on the one-continuum or *unus mundus*, in the formula, the number three as a unity (i.e., grounded on the one-continuum) relates to the primal One and becomes the Fourth. Qualitatively, the number four is not arrived at through a progression

---

30   As reported in Marie-Louise von Franz, 1974, p. 65.

of steps leading to four, but always exists in its qualitative just-so value as do all numbers.

Jung discusses the psychological significance of this formula by examining the qualitative meaning of each of the four numbers. Regarding One, He writes:

> One, as the first numeral, is unity. But it is also *"The Unity,"* the One, All-oneness, individuality and non-duality—not a numeral but a philosophical concept, an archetype and attribute of God.[31]

Elsewhere, regarding the numbers One to Three, he writes:

> The number one claims an exceptional position, which we meet again in the natural philosophy of the Middle Ages. According to this, one is not a number at all, the first number is two. Two is the first number because, with it, separation and multiplication begin, which alone make counting possible.
>
> With the appearance of the number two, *another* appears alongside the one, a happening which is so striking that in many languages 'the other" and "the second" are expressed by the same word. Also associated with the number two is the idea of right and left, and remarkably enough, of favourable and unfavourable, good and bad. The "other" can have a "sinister" significance—or one feels it, at least, as something opposite and alien.... In other words, as soon as the number two appears, a unit is produced out of the original unity, and this unit is none other than the same unity split into two and turned into a "number." ... Thus there arises a tension of opposites between the One and the Other. But every tension of opposites culminates in a release out of which comes the "third." In the third, the tension is resolved and the lost unity is restored .... Three is an unfolding of the One to a condition where it can be known—unity become recognizable; had it not been resolved into polarity of the One and the Other, it would have remained fixed in a condition devoid of every quality.[32]

---

31   *Ibid.,* p. 39.
32   *Ibid.,* pp. 97, 98.

Thus, one is unity, and when two emerges, and the unity is split into two, a tension is created with the One that is resolved in the third, which restores unity. Qualitatively, the One unfolds through the two to the three, a condition of insight and knowledge.

Jung describes how numbers can be associated with specific functional psychological attitudes and the growth of consciousness. He writes:

> At the level of one, man still naively participates in his surroundings in a state of uncritical unconsciousness, submitting to things as they are. At the level of two, on the other hand, a dualistic world and God-image gives rise to tension, doubt, and criticism of God, life nature and oneself. The condition of three by comparison denotes insight, the rise of consciousness, and the rediscovery of unity on a higher level, in a word, *gnosis,* and knowledge .... Trinitarian thinking lacks a further dimension; it is flat, intellectual, and consequently encourages intolerant and absolute declarations. The "eternal" character and "absolute validity" of certain archetypal structures is certainly recognized, but ego-consciousness assumes the role of herald. From this standpoint one overlooks the fact that although these structures may well be timeless they become modified when they make the transition into the field of individual consciousness.[33]
>
> When one becomes aware of this phenomenon there is a transformation of consciousness and insights are no longer identified as "eternal verity." There is detachment and one becomes capable of comprehending the insight as only one of many possible revelations contained within the unknown psychic and universal background of existence. Instead of proclaiming absolute dogmas, a "quaternary" attitude of mind develops which, more modestly, seeks to describe reality in a manner that will—if it is based on archetypal concepts—be understandable to others.[34]

---

33   *Ibid.*, pp. 124, 125.
34   *Ibid.*, p. 126.

According to Jung's observations here, the step from trinitarian thinking to quaternary thinking is of considerable interest in understanding the demands for the evolution of consciousness today: "from a purely imaginary standpoint on the world to one in which the observer experiences himself as a participant on the level of a thinking and *experiencing* being."[35] In addition, quaternary thinking involves a more open, un-dogmatic and detached stance toward the many possible interpretations of the nature of reality than trinitarian thinking, which is attached to the "eternal truth" of its particular archetypal status. The trinitarian position has limits to its knowledge and insight, individual truths that always require further elaboration, reminiscent of the limits intrinsic to the Overmind, while quaternary thinking is based on supramental intuition and truth, if not Truth. Jung, in fact, was preoccupied during his entire working life with amplifying the number four in various ways and giving evidence for its psychological and spiritual importance. The qualitative problem of the three and the four was, in fact, already apparent with Plato and clearly demonstrated in his book *Timaeus,* as well as in later medieval Christianity. Both Plato and Christianity had difficulty dealing with the heaviness of material reality and the limits it imposes, as well as with evil and imperfection. Although European alchemists took up the problem throughout the Middle Ages, it is only with the contemporary discoveries of C.G. Jung that the dynamics are properly understood, even if integrating a relationship with material reality remains a daunting task.

One way of studying the problem, psychologically, is through Jung's personality typology, consisting of four functions of consciousness—thinking, feeling, sensation and intuition. In many, if not most cases today, there are only one or two conscious functions, and the problem of the three and four is not yet personally constellated. In advanced situations, in particular where there is opposition between

---

35   *Ibid.*, p. 128.

three relatively conscious functions and the unconscious inferior fourth function, the problem is relevant. The inferior function is primitive, ill-adapted, awkward and not controllable, and therefore open to shadow expressions. As it is contaminated by the archetypes of the collective unconscious, it opens to both obsessive archaic phenomena and mystical experiences.[36] In these regards, the inferior function is completely opposite in its manner of functioning than the most differentiated, superior function, which is under conscious control and civilized.

In the individuation process, when it comes time to integrate the fourth function to consciousness, there is an elevation of the inferior function along with a general lowering of the structure of consciousness altogether. Integrating the fourth function comes with painful experiences and insights on one's inferiorities, as well as personally realizing the devastating effect of other people's shadow and other complexes. The difficulty of going from three to four functions of consciousness lies not only in the fourth function's original inferiority and inadaptability, but in the sacrifice of the more differentiated functions and the fact that it carries the weight of the archetypal psyche as well. The original separation of the three functions from the fourth is the result of education and civilization, where there has been a necessary "freeing of consciousness from any excessive attachment to the 'spirit of gravity.'"[37] Although essential in early Christianity for the sake of developing clarity of consciousness and active willpower, presently the task is to return consciously to wholeness. According to the Axiom of Maria, integration of the fourth function returns the psyche through the third to the one-continuum and wholeness.

In terms of the psychological realization of consciousness, the advance from three to four refers to a change from an imaginal and conceptual relationship to life to participating in life as a thinking, feeling and experiencing being. According to von Franz, "mental processes no

---

36   *Ibid.*, p. 129.
37   *Ibid.*, p. 129.

longer revolve about intellectual theorizations, but partake of the creative adventure of 'realizations in the act of the becoming.'"[38] Thus, realizing the fourth function opens one up to experiences of synchronicity, to acts of creation in time and, with spiritual realization, eventually, to the meaning of the incarnation of Christ for the individual. Taken symbolically, Christ on the Cross strung up between the opposites can be understood as the fourth, while the Father, Son and Holy Ghost represent the Christian Trinity. In this regard, Jung writes in a letter to Elined Kotschnig dated June 30, 1956:

> The significance of man is enhanced by the incarnation. We have become participants of the divine life and we have to assume a new responsibility, viz. the continuation of divine self-realization which expresses itself in the task of individuation. Individuation does not only mean that man has become truly human as distinct from animal, but that he is to become adult, responsible for his existence, knowing that he does not only depend on God but that God also depends on man. Man's relation to God probably has to undergo a certain important change: Instead of the propitiating praise of an unpredictable kind or the child's prayer to a loving father, the responsible living and fulfilling of the divine will in us will be our form of worship and commerce with God. His goodness means grace and light and His Dark side the terrible temptation of power.
>
> Obviously God does not want us to remain little children, looking to their elders to relieve them of their mission.[39]

In 1957, Jung elaborates on this position in a reply to Rev. David Cox:

> We are cornered by the supreme power of the incarnating Will. God really wants to become man, even if it rends him asunder .... If God incarnates in the empirical man, man is confronted with the divine problem. Being and remaining man he has to

---

38   *Ibid.*, p. 131.
39   As reported in Adler, 1975, p. 316.

find an answer. It is a question of the opposites, raised at the moment when God was declared to be good only. Where then is his dark side? Christ is the model for the human answers and his symbol is the cross, the union of opposites. This will be the fate of man, and this he must understand if he is to survive at all. We are threatened with universal genocide if we cannot work out the way of salvation by a symbolic death.[40]

In Jung's path, the eventual goal of divine self-realization means full integration of the opposites and the experience of the "Oneness of the Holy Spirit," which refers to "a restitution of the original oneness of the unconscious on the level of consciousness" and the total abolishment of the ego in a conscious living relationship with the *unus mundus*.[41] The original integration of the fourth function and the initial realization of psychological wholeness eventually lead to spiritual realization of the whole person and the elevation and spiritualization of the four. For Jung and the Western world, the rejected fourth that needs human integration is the Feminine and the Devil or Antichrist, bringing completeness to the Christian Trinity. Like Christ, humans need to consciously carry their own cross of opposites. Based on the fact that the archetype is the unconscious blueprint for every human life and Christ's life was pre-eminently archetypal, Jung writes: "What happens in the life of Christ happens always and everywhere."[42] The pattern incarnated in an earlier epoch by the divine incarnation is now available to be realized by humanity at large, at least to begin with, by more evolved souls.

Sri Aurobindo refers to a dynamic fourfold soul-force consisting of *brahmin* (priest), *kshatriya* (leader), *vaishya* (trader) and *sudra* (servant), which represent dynamic personality types; to fulfill itself, each type includes qualities of the other soul-force classifications. The original rejected fourth, which particularly needs integration, would be the

---

40   Jung, 1976d, p. 735.
41   Jung, as reported in Edward F. Edinger, 1996a, p. 148.
42   1975 c, p. 89.

inferior soul-type (e.g., for the *brahmin*, it would be the *sudra*). The initial realization of the four as wholeness resembles the psychic transformation as a fulfilled fourfold soul-force, actively participating in the experiential and creative transformation of one's nature. The psychic transformation becomes the foundation for the second, spiritual transformation, which potentially spiritualizes the whole of one's nature—the mental, vital and physical as well as aspects of the Subconscient and Inconscient—to the level of the overmind plane. In Jung's language, the Inconscient and Subconscient refer to aspects of the psychoid realm of the archetypal psyche, which transcends both spirit and matter. The rejected fourth for Sri Aurobindo at the spiritual level would be the world and the physical, vital and mental beings.

The first two levels of transformation for Sri Aurobindo take place in the Mind or the psyche, meaning in the Ignorance. There is a third level of transformation through the Truth-Mind, the supramental transformation, where four is its symbolic representation, as if to say it is the full realization of the four. As I indicate above, Sri Aurobindo posits the Supermind or Truth-Mind as the link existing between the upper and lower worlds, as four in the descent of the divine trinity of *Sat Chit Ananda*, and four in the ascent of nature as mental, vital and physical. One can understand the Supermind as being an expression of *Sat Chit Ananda* as well as embracing the whole of nature, including the full mental, vital and physical beings, in addition to the Subconscient and the Inconscient. Realization of the Supermind brings greater illumination and transformation to one's nature as a whole, including the lower reaches of the Subconscient and Inconscient. Advaita, Buddhism, and other contemporary spiritual paths, skirt around or are ignorant of the Supermind, paying little heed to nature and its transformation at any level, beginning with the psychic transformation. The rejected fourth that needs integration in this case is the Supermind itself, along with nature, which is now potentially drawn up to be supramentalized.

Qualitatively, the number four represents truth at all levels of being, from the origins of the Universe to the Supermind. The Supermind seems to represent the supreme fulfillment of the number four. From a psychological and spiritual perspective, it is also a highly significant indication of wholeness, first psychological wholeness or the psychic transformation and then spiritual wholeness. Psychological wholeness means the ego is subordinate to the Self or psychic being, and it requires integration of four functions of consciousness, including, increasingly, the inferior function. Psychological wholeness is the essential foundation for the realization of spiritual wholeness, which includes subordination of the ego to the cosmic Self, the *unus mundus*. It involves, according to Jung, the realization of the Self as a fourfold quaternity, as I discuss below. Sri Aurobindo adds the Supermind as an additional stage of transformation that builds on the wholeness of the psychic and spiritual transformations; it is the fulfilled four, four in the ascent of the natural person and four in the descent from *Sat Chit Ananda*.

CHAPTER 22

Bridge to the Past, Bridge between East and West: The New World

In 1928, Jung stopped working on *The Red Book*, writing in an epilogue in 1959, that it was initiated through a book, *The Secret of the Golden Flower*, sent to him by Richard Wilhelm, the man who popularized the *I Ching* in the West. The "Golden Flower" is a Chinese alchemical text, where Jung found parallel experiences to what he had experienced and elaborated in *The Red Book* as well as in dreams he had in and before 1926. He subsequently turned to the study of Western alchemy, which, along with Gnosticism and Western mysticism, consumed the rest of his life. Jung writes that: "With the help of alchemy I could finally arrange … the overpowering force of the original experiences … into a whole."[1] In fact, in the West, Gnosticism eventually developed into alchemy, so that Jung[2] was able to write:

> But when I began to understand alchemy I realized that it represented the historical link with Gnosticism, and that a continuity therefore existed between past and present. Grounded in the natural philosophy of the Middle Ages, Alchemy formed the bridge, on the one hand into the past, to Gnosticism, and on the other into the future, to the modern psychology of the unconscious …. The possibility of a comparison with alchemy,

---

1   2009, p. 360.
2   1983, p. 201.

and the uninterrupted intellectual chain back to Gnosticism, gave substance to my psychology.[3]

According to *The Red Book*, Jung's Gnostic treatise, *Septem Sermones ad Mortuos*, was written by Philemon "in Alexandria, the city where the East toucheth the West," although, in *Memories, Dreams, Reflections*, Jung attributes the work to Basilides, an early Gnostic.[4] Reference to Alexandria and these personalities suggests that Jung's psychology forms an historical bridge from the West, through alchemy and Gnosticism and related movements, such as the Grail quest, the Kabbala and Western mysticism, to the East, including wisdom from the Upanishads and the Vedas, alchemy and Taoism. As Jung writes in *The Red Book:*

> To give birth to the ancient in a new time is creation. This is the creation of the new, and that redeems me. Salvation is the resolution of the task. The task is to give birth to the old in a new time.[5]

Jung's challenge, which he took up with great sincerity, allowed him to build a bridge between the East and the West and from the past to the present, toward the future and a New World.

In a memorial service held on May, 1930 for Richard Wilhelm, Jung attributes to the former the creation of a "bridge between East and West," giving to "the Occident the precious heritage of a culture a thousand years old."[6] In a letter to Wilhelm, dated May 25, 1929, he writes: "Fate seems to have apportioned to us the role of two piers which support the bridge between the East and West."[7] This bridge is principally built on the *Tao* or, in Jung's language, the Self as the archetype of

---

3   *Ibid.*, p. 205.
4   *Ibid.*, p. 190.
5   2009, p. 311.
6   1966, p. 53.
7   As reported in Gerhard Adler, ed., 1973.

meaning and orientation, with its important corollary, synchronicity and the qualitative nature of any given moment in time. For both Jung and the path of Tao, realizing the Self or Tao is the goal of life.

Shiuya Sara Liuh, a Jungian scholar from China with interests in the way of Tao, notes the importance of Jung and Wilhelm for maintaining this spiritual bridge between the West and China.[8] Nineteen hundred and eleven, the year of the establishment of modern China, was when Wilhelm translated *"The Secret of the Golden Flower"* into German. Ironically, the wisdom of an ancient oriental culture was transposed to the West in the same year that these same ancient teachings were repudiated in China for the sake of modernization. Now Jung, along with his integration of Chinese thought, is becoming slowly accepted by sympathetic Chinese intellectuals.

Jung describes Wilhelm's mind as being fertile and non-judgmental, of a feminine nature, which is unlike the "purely masculine" specialist's mind.[9] He writes: "a larger mind bears the stamp of the feminine; it is endowed with a receptive and fruitful womb which can reshape what is strange and can give it form."[10] Indeed, Wilhelm's ability to 'feel into the spirit of the East" he attributes to his "maternal intellect."[11] Jung, in fact, is also describing his own intuitive and fertile mind and its interpretive genius, which allows him to act as a bridge between the East and the West and the past and the future. It allows him to participate fully in Eastern ideas and their embodiment, in this context, specifically in the nature of the *Tao*, which requires a maternal mind.

The maternal nature of the *Tao* is unambiguously depicted in these thoughts of Lao-Tzu, the original master-Taoist:

> "Existence" I call the mother of individual beings
> ...

8   2012 passim.
9   1966, p. 53.
10   *Ibid.*
11   *Ibid.*

> There was something formless and perfect
> Before the universe was born.
> It is serene. Empty.
> Infinite, Eternally present.
> For lack of better name,
> I call it the Tao.[12]

The *Tao* is not only the source of the individual but also the entire universe. It is the source of the *I Ching*, which describes the interplay of opposites in time. Thus von Franz refers to the following commentary on the *I Ching* by Wang-Fu-Chih (1619–1692 CE): "the whole of existence is a continuum that is ordered in itself;" although "without manifest appearance ... its inherent dynamism manifests in images whose structures participate in that of the continuum."[13] She observes: "This idea of an irrepresentable continuum containing latent pictorial structures forms an exact parallel to Jung's concept of a *unus mundus*."[14] This statement brings further discernment to my earlier reference in Chapter 17 above on von Franz's observations on the parallel model described in the *I Ching* to the *unus mundus*. Sri Aurobindo's Supermind, with its unified field of enfolded potential, which links *Sat Chit Ananda* with the entire manifest world in time, is also conceptually similar.

I believe it is fair to say that Taoism and Chinese spiritual thought emphasizes the immanent Divine and the psychological play of opposites more than most contemporary Indian traditions or Christianity. For Baptist theologian and professor of world religions, Blake Burleson, reflections led him to contend that "Of all the world's great religious traditions, however, Taoism is the most 'at home" in this world, not the next world."[15] Jung first mentions the immanent Self by referencing the Upanishads and the writings of Meister Eckhart (1260–1328 CE),

---

12   As recorded in David Rosen, MD, 1997, p. 126.
13   1992c, p. 308.
14   *Ibid.*
15   2014, p. 182.

a Christian mystic in Psychological Types, first published in 1921. Yet, he finds further confirmation for his path in his dialogues with Richard Wilhelm, whose main achievement was translating the *I Ching* into German and giving it form that made it accessible to the Western mind. Indeed, Jung considers "the light that was kindled" in his relationship with Richard Wilhelm, was "one of the most significant events of his life."[16] Although he was already aware of the immanent Divine and the play of opposites in life, Taoism brings Jung explicit psychological and ethical insight, the significance of synchronicity and life wisdom that parallels and supports his own experiences documented in *The Red Book*. Contemporary Hindu paths, including *Advaita Vedanta*, as I argue above, could not give him this kind of knowledge. The one major exception is the way of Sri Aurobindo and the Mother, whose Integral Yoga is a path that, for the most part, runs parallel to Jung's path of the individuation process, with even greater spiritual differentiation.

As I try to show in this study, there is, in particular, a parallel to be found between Jung and the works of Sri Aurobindo and the Mother, which I use as my primary interpretive hermeneutic lens. If there is a bridge between the East and the West today, it is to be found particularly in the Integral Yoga and thought of Sri Aurobindo and the Mother. Other Hindu paths, where the psyche or world is relatively devalued, as Jung discovered in his visit to India in 1937/1938, are less relevant and do not form a true bridge for Jung's psychology to the East.[17] Jung was particularly disturbed by metaphysical assertions without any scientific evidence and the disregard of the living psyche, which he found throughout India. Sri Aurobindo's view, however, is compatible with Jung's, as indicated in the following observations: "My yoga ... is both this-worldly and other-worldly" and "Yoga is not a thing of ideas but of inner spiritual experience."[18] Unfortunately, Indian disciples of Sri

---

16   1966, p. 53.
17   Sulagna Sengupta, 2013, pp. 219–254 passim.
18   1970e, pp. 121, 161.

Aurobindo either poorly present Jung or misrepresent him, as the case of Indra Sen and Arindam Basu, respectively, attest.[19]

This realization has always disturbed me and has been a major catalyst for my desire to do comparative research of Jung, and Sri Aurobindo and the Mother that, after many years incubation, led to my writing this study. My subsequent discovery that many Jungian researchers have not fully understood the spiritual nature of Jung's opus, especially in relationship with contemporary Eastern spiritual paths and Western mysticism, further motivates me in this direction. The deeper source of my long held interest in a comparative study is the dream of Jung saying his way is similar to the path of yoga as articulated by Sri Aurobindo in *The Synthesis of Yoga* that I amplify in the Introduction.

I personally had the good fortune of having had Arindam Basu as a teacher of Sri Aurobindo's *The Life Divine* when I was living at the Ashram in Pondicherry in 1970–1973. Nevertheless, despite my heartfelt appreciation, during that time, and many years later, when I saw him in order to pay my respects and show my gratitude toward him for having been my teacher, I witnessed animosity toward Jung that I found unaccountable. From these experiences and discussions with other disciples, I have come to the conclusion that there is and has been considerable resistance to accepting Jung amongst many "leading" Indian disciples of Sri Aurobindo and the Mother that is not rational. In fact, in my response below to Basu's arguments about Jung in an essay in the Sri Aurobindo Ashram magazine, *Mother India*, and reproduced in Sengupta's book, *Jung in India*, I demonstrate, once again, the compatibility between Jung and Sri Aurobindo, with the implication that serious students of both schools can profit from studying the works of the other.

In Basu's article on Jung, he contends that there is nothing in common between what he refers to as Sri Aurobindo's metaphysical

---

19   Sulagna Sengupta, 2013, pp. 226–242 passim.

psychology and Jung's analytical psychology, even though the latter uses similar "certain key terms," because the meaning attributed to them is vastly different. One of the major differences, according to Basu, is that, for Sri Aurobindo, bringing forward the psychic being is essential for the transformation of personality, whereas Jung is oblivious to this phenomenon. As I discuss in various places above, Jung was fully aware of the workings of the psychic being and its transformative power, although he uses different terminology. Otherwise, without offering any evidence whatsoever, Basu declares that Jung has no understanding of the nature of spirit, self, or soul according to Hindu yoga philosophy, and that his rendering of *Atman* and *Purusha* is inadequate. He is also disdainful of Jung's use of the word *archetype* in reference to the soul, God and symbol, again without any reasonable explanation for his concerns. There may be some value in Basu's critique, especially concerning the *Atman* and *Purusha*—after all he has been educated by Sri Aurobindo with his spiritually refined discernment. However, in my estimation, Basu could not get past Jung's use of words, admittedly sometimes very complex, as well as his concern for unveiling Western spiritual traditions along with Eastern spirituality; and consequently, he loses sight of the genuine substance of Jung's psychology. In fact, responsibly accounting for Western traditions and bringing them to light have immense value and significance for the Western Mind. If nothing else, it takes into consideration its particular evolution and complications.

Jung rightly felt the necessity of grounding his psychology on empirical science and was wary of making any metaphysical assertions whatsoever. Living in India, with its spiritual tendencies, Sri Aurobindo attracted disciples without any obligations to satisfy external scientific demands, although his yoga, like Jung's path, does follow the tenets of phenomenologically based science as well. His obligation equivalent to Jung's empiricism, at least in part, is, rather, to respond to his disciples and critics on what differentiates his path from other spiritual paths. Needless to say, his works are full of well-differentiated articulations of metaphysical statements, while based on yogic experiences of a high order.

There are, in fact, plenty of metaphysical assumptions and statements in Jung's work as well, although his view that "metaphysics cannot be the object of science" prevents him from being overtly explicit about it.[20] Jung is more concerned about documenting an experiential relationship with the objective psyche through visions, dreams and true fantasy. In the process, Jung grounds his metaphysics on empirical experiences, as does Sri Aurobindo. For the record, I allude below to several metaphysical references in Jung's work. Most significantly, his understanding that the source of metaphysical statements is the psyche in its expression of its metaphysical reality is itself a metaphysical assertion. He writes, "It is the psyche which, by the divine creative power inherent in it, makes the metaphysical assertion ... not only is it the condition of all metaphysical reality, it *is* that reality."[21]

As a whole, Jung's archetypes are consistent with Schopenhuaer's primal Will, except that, for Jung, they are not blind as with the former's Will, but intelligent and symbolized as God-images. His notions of the *unus mundus* and synchronicity, which involves consciousness of meaningful coincidences that intersect with non-dual Reality, are new acts of creation in time. The psyche, for him, is objective, where the *imago dei* is involved and at work, a position that harmonizes with the metaphysics of the Upanishads which, along with the writings of Meister Eckhart, were Jung's initial sources for the concept of the Self. The Self in its static and dynamic fullness, as defined by Jung in *Aion* and as discussed above, in relation to the Superconscience through the *Anthropos*, and the Subconscient and Inconscient of Sri Aurobindo through the alchemical Rotundum, has significant metaphysical substance and power.

Jung writes, "It would be blasphemy to assert that God can manifest

---

20   1976, p. 708.
21   Jung, 1975 c-5, p. 512.

himself everywhere but in the human soul."[22] In psychological terms, he regards the faculty of relationship or correspondence between the soul and God as "the archetype of the God-image."[23] With reference to Jung, Anielia Jaffé writes, "God reveals himself in the psyche as an archetypal image of the godhead."[24] These are reflections on a statement by Meister Eckhart that Jung refers to often, and as early as *Psychological Types* he quotes Eckhart as follows: "The soul is not blissful because she is in God, she is blissful because God is in her."[25] This understanding of the soul in God refers to a condition of unconsciousness and projection of God outside of oneself onto external objects.

When God is born in the soul, there is a conscious relationship between the God-image and the soul and potentially greater awareness of archetypal connections in general. Dourley reflects that Jung regards it as developmentally essential for maturation of the "common" person to aspire for unity of the human and the divine.[26] As Jung observes, "The God-man seems to have descended from his throne and is dissolving himself in the common man."[27] In Sri Aurobindo's lexicon, this refers to the awakening of the psychic being, the incarnated aspect of the Self involved in all levels of life. In *Answer to Job*, Jung writes: "It was only quite recently that we realized (or rather, are beginning to realize) that God is reality itself and therefore—but not least—man. This realization is a millennial process."[28] The mature Jung considers individuation as "*the life in God*, as mandala psychology clearly shows," basing his metaphysical assertion here directly on psychological experiential

---

22   1977, p. 10.
23   *Ibid.*, p. 11.
24   1989, p. 64.
25   As reported in Jung, 1974b, p. 246.
26   2014, p. 20.
27   1975c, p. 84.
28   1975 g, p. 402.

evidence of the individual psyche that enforces the view that there is no psychological separation between the human and the divine.[29]

At eighty, in a letter to Pastor Jakob Amstutz, Jung writes: "It is unfortunately true: [the religious man] has and holds a mystery in his hands and at the same time is contained in the mystery. What can he proclaim? Himself or God? Or neither? The truth is he doesn't know who he is talking of, God or Himself."[30] For Jung, God and the Self are ultimately indistinguishable.[31] According to Jung, the source of all experiential relationships with the God-image is the psyche, where the psyche is an *ousia*, meaning divine essence or substance, a definition normally attributed to God, which contains all the antinomies, including good and evil, not just good alone, as Augustinian Christianity asserts. Another major antinomy is the immobile or static God and God as evolving. In terms of an evolving God-image, Jung writes: "The real history of the world seems to be the progressive incarnation of the Deity."[32] These are all metaphysical assertions that emphasize the oneness of the soul and God, the human and the divine.

As far as a transcendent God is concerned, Jung is personally convinced that "God is something objective that transcends the psyche."[33] Even though Jung regards the experiential God-image as archetypal, the word *archetype* refers to something imprinted, suggesting an imprinter. Thus, he can write, "That the world inside and outside ourselves rests on a transcendental background is as certain as our own existence."[34] Despite the empirical limitations Jung places on his scientific endeavor, he clearly accepts the reality of a transcendent, although ultimately unknowable God. "I don't by any means dispute the existence of a metaphysical God," he writes; "I permit myself, however,

---

29   1976d, p. 719.
30   As reported in Gerhard Adler, ed., 1975, p. 255.
31   Jaffé, 1989, p. 65.
32   *Ibid.*, p. 81.
33   Marie-Louise von Franz, 1997b, p. 374.
34   As reported in Jaffé, p. 1989, p. 4.

to put human statements under the microscope."[35] A comprehensive reading of his work shows that, over and over again, Jung does, indeed, question human assertions about the nature of God, including the contemporary Christian view of God and its historical development. He takes the point of view that statements about the nature of the deity are always anthropomorphic.

Basu acknowledges that God is both immanent and transcendent of the world and the psyche for both Sri Aurobindo and Jung. He agrees with Jung in saying that the Transcendent "cannot be affirmed in the nature of the Reality" and, in harmony with Jung, he argues that faith in such a Reality is essential for "any genuine religion and spirituality."[36] However, as I indicate above, he disputes Jung's use of the term *archetype* in relationship to God, writing dismissively that: "Even God is an archetypal symbol for Jung."[37] Basu betrays confused thinking here as, in fact, Jung is reticent about saying anything about God per se, only the God-image, which Jung defines psychologically as "a complex of ideas of an archetypal nature ... representing a certain sum of energy (libido) which appears in projection."[38] In *Memories, Dreams, Reflections*, Jung writes: "If, therefore, we speak of 'God' as an 'archetype,' we are saying nothing about His real nature but are letting it be known that 'God' already has a place in that part of our psyche which is pre-existent to consciousness and that He therefore cannot be considered an invention of consciousness."[39] Jung believes this treatment of "God" as an archetypal image brings him closer to the human soul and potential experience. The projective nature of assertions about God is what prompts Jung, as a scientist, to persistently and with great discernment question the nature of any given God-image.

For Jung, the nature of the supreme Unity is incomprehensible to

35   Jung, as reported in Gerhard Adler, ed., 1975, p. 64.
36   As reported in Sengupta, 2013, p. 315.
37   *Ibid.*, p. 314.
38   1974a, p 56.
39   1983, p. 348.

humans, who, he contends, can only know as much as their consciousness extends; a view that is compatible with that of Sri Aurobindo. So,
too, the evolutionary laws that govern the progressive incarnation of
the deity are, essentially, unknowable. Likewise, the unconscious does
not function according to conscious beliefs and attitudes, but reveals
itself through the psyche over time in unexpected ways, following the
will of the Self. The experiential realization of the Self, the God-image,
is the goal of the individuation process, and it is not attained by strain-
ing after a transcendent God or an ideal. In Jung's understanding, in
the final analysis, every life is the realization of a whole, meaning the
Self. He writes: "But every carrier is charged with an individual destiny
and destination and the realization of this alone makes sense of life."[40]
Becoming conscious of one's destiny and its realization is central to
the individuation process and a meaningful life. Again, quoting Meister
Eckhart in a letter to Rev. Morton T. Kelsey on May 3, 1958, Jung
writes: "God is not blessed in His Godhead, He must be born in man
forever."[41] God, argues Jung, has created self-reflective and conscious
man and seeks "His goal in him."[42] The supreme importance of human
consciousness, he relates, lies in the fact that "the Creator sees Himself
through the eyes of man's consciousness and this is the reason why
God had to become man."[43]

In the myth of The Seven Sermons to the Dead as printed in *The
Red Book*, Jung refers to the *Pleroma*, which is the Nothing that is the
all, nothingness that is the fullness; the Pleroma also fully permeates
the psyche "as the light of the sun everywhere pervadeth the air."[44] God
is understood to be both transcendent, and immanently pervading all
aspects of the psyche, both conscious and unconscious. As far as the
unconscious is concerned, Jung argues that it consists of the "unknown

---

40   1977, p. 222.
41   As recorded in Adler, ed., 1975, p. 436.
42   *Ibid.*
43   *Ibid.*
44   2009, p. 347.

psychic" along with the "psychoid system, of which there is no direct knowledge ... or capacity to become conscious."[45] Despite the unknowable quality of the psychoid unconscious, as I previously observe, Jung, in fact, foresees a time when one can potentially integrate so much unconsciousness that it carries one to the point of reclaiming "the original oneness of the unconscious on the level of consciousness."[46] This proposition seems to include at least some of the psychoid processes becoming conscious.

The important point, however, is that the psychic movement toward consciousness is only possible because "we are parts of the Pleroma, the Pleroma is also in us," where the Pleroma is, paradoxically, both "the eternal and the endless" and "the beginning and end of creation."[47] The all-pervasive quality of the Pleroma is reflected by the alchemical *scintillae*, which Jung refers to as "a multiple of little luminosities" or "seeds of light"; Jung quotes the alchemist Khunrath as referring to "the seed plot of a world to come."[48] The eternal in the psyche naturally inclines toward the eternal itself; that is, toward the realization of consciousness and bliss. In pragmatic terms, this means that even pathology is a perverted expression of some truth.

Associated with this line of argument on the essential reality of the human psyche is Jung's notion that reality is *"esse in anima,"* including both the mental, life and the body, inner and outer. He writes:

> *Esse* in *intellectu* lacks tangible reality, *esse* in *re* lacks mind. Idea and thing come together ... in the human psyche which holds the balance between them. What would the idea amount to if the psyche did not provide its living value? What would the thing be worth if the psyche withheld from it the determining form of its sense impression? *What indeed is reality if it is not a reality in ourselves?* Living reality is the product neither of the

---

45   1975b-4, p. 185.
46   As reported in Edward F. Edinger, 1996a, p. 148.
47   Jung, 2009, p. 347.
48   1975b-4, p. 190.

actual objective behaviour of things nor of the formulated idea
exclusively, but rather of the combination of both in the living
psychological process, through *esse in anima*.[49]

For Jung, living reality is not an intellectual enterprise of understanding, which tends to abstract from the thing and diminish its living value
and effective force. Nor is it an object or thing, concrete reality, which
lacks idea or understanding. A third mediating position of "being contained in the psyche," *esse in anima,* is required in order to relate to
what works psychologically in the human soul, rather than arguing over
the place of two universals, *res* (thing) and *intellectus* (understanding).
"The psyche," notes Jung, "creates reality every day" through "*fantasy*," establishing the psychological value of consciously accessing
true fantasy through dreams and active imagination.[50]

In Sri Aurobindo's language, reality is being contained in the
Divine through the Mother. He writes: "In all that is done in the universe, the Divine through his Shakti is behind all action, but he is veiled
by his Yoga Maya, and works through the ego of the Jiva in the lower
nature."[51] Although the language is more spiritually elevated, the essence is similar to what Jung writes from a more psychological perspective. Both Sri Aurobindo and Jung have found an intermediary
position between the intellect and the vital and physical worlds, while
relativizing the ego. In Sri Aurobindo's case it is by stressing the reality
of the Divine and his Shakti, or executive Force. He doesn't dispel with
the ego altogether, though, as he writes that a personal effort of "aspiration, rejection and surrender" is essential as long as the lower nature
is active.[52] For Jung, what is required is accessing true fantasy, which
can relegate the ego to a secondary position, requiring a surrender of
beliefs, attitudes and values. Thus, the ego is not rejected, but it enters

---

49   Jung, 1974b, pp. 51, 52.
50   *Ibid.*, p. 52.
51   1972a, p. 6.
52   *Ibid.*

into a dialogue with the unconscious with the goal of finding truth. A scrutiny of people's dreams typically indicates the need for the (dream) ego, consequently the conscious ego as well, to surrender its position for the sake of conscious integration of messages from the larger Self.

On the matter of bringing spiritual light to the individuation process, Sri Aurobindo writes as follows: "In Yoga, it is the Divine who is the Sadhaka and the Sadhana: it is his Shakti with her light, power, knowledge, consciousness, Ananda, acting upon the Adhara and, when it is opened to her, pouring into it with these Divine forces that makes the Sadhana possible."[53] Sri Aurobindo is referring to the Divine as both the disciple (Sadhaka) and the spiritual path or individuation process (Sadhana), and the need for the individual to become a vessel (Adhara) in order to receive the down-pouring of the Divine Force. Here, Sri Aurobindo brings fulfillment to Jung's understanding of the psyche being filled with an all-permeating Pleroma, infinite and eternal, while being potentially open to the transformative descent of the Divine Force from the infinite and eternal Pleroma. Although the decent is not so explicit with Jung, I believe it is present, as I argue above regarding the descent of the Holy Ghost with reference to a letter from Marie-Louise von Franz and image 125 from Jung's *The Red Book*.

Jung's scientific attitude encourages him to differentiate the nature of the libido, following which he ascertained the workings of the archetypes and their imagistic formulation through the symbol. Although he is careful not to overstep his bounds as a psychologist, he writes encouragingly about numinous experiences and the nature of the archetype as unknowable in its essence, where an image is necessary for it to be apprehended. Moreover, although he stays within his self-determined boundaries, whenever he is confronted with an unsolvable conflict of understanding or duties, he appeals to the transcendent function

---

53   *Ibid.*

for answers that take him beyond previous limits to understanding and moral responsibility.

Jung, in fact, writes compellingly about symbols and the need for a symbolic life. He writes: "Only the symbolic life can express the need of the soul—the daily need of the soul, mind you!"[54] One relevant statement regarding the symbol is that it is "the best possible description or formulation of a relatively unknown fact."[55] Likewise, the living symbol, he writes, "formulates an essential unconscious factor."[56] Yet, for Jung, "the symbol is alive only so long as it is pregnant with meaning."[57] For that eventuality, the symbol needs to be the most competent and complete expression for something anticipated but still unknown. Jung is also aware that, over time, living symbols can lose their power, and that observers and their attitude toward any given image are important in determining whether it is symbolic for them or not. The spontaneous effect of any given symbolic product on the observer is also relevant in determining its value as a symbol for the individual.

In contrast to Basu's contemptuous attitude toward Jung's treatment of the symbol, Sri Aurobindo writes about symbols in a way that does not contravene Jung's statements. For instance, Sri Aurobindo's observation that "a symbol is the form on one plane that represents a truth of another" easily translates into the symbol being a relatively unknown fact to the observer, as Jung contends.[58] In reference to what I write above regarding the relative nature of the symbol for Jung, Sri Aurobindo has a similar perspective, writing the following to a disciple: "What matters is what it means to you."[59] Without an exhaustive examination of what the two men have written on the symbol, there is,

---

54   Jung, 1976f, p. 274.
55   1974b, p. 474.
56   Jung, 1974b, p. 477.
57   *Ibid.*, p. 474.
58   as compiled by M.P. Pandit, 1966, p. 269.
59   *Ibid.*, p. 270.

as these examples show, much similarity and, when there are apparent differences, they can be easily reconciled.

Jung realizes that for contemporary people, myth, including the Christian myth, is no longer a living phenomenon, to the detriment of individuals and culture. With its account of the down-pouring of the Holy Spirit and Christ's pronouncement that his disciples will do greater works than he, the Christian myth originally allowed for evolutionary development. By and large, Christianity has not fulfilled its original mission, rather, protecting itself with adamantine dogma and doctrines, while resisting the evolutionary flow of ideas for the divine enhancement of life. The result is that, for the most part, in the contemporary world relationship to a living myth has been replaced by a void that is filled in many ways, including secularism, alcohol and drugs, excessive consumption, entertainment, video games, and trance-inducing media like the all-pervasive Internet.

New symbol formation, according to Jung, is the creative product of "the highest spiritual aspirations" and embraces both the differentiated functions of the conscious attitude as well as the primal instinctive psyche, truth from below.[60] This insight applies to Sri Aurobindo himself, who is a superior example of a creator of new symbols, especially apparent in his poetry, most notably *Savitri*. In my view, it is the most complete myth for our times and an unparalleled revelation of the present divine dispensation.

Myth is the formulation of archetypal truths that, Jung writes, "is the revelation of a divine life in man" and "speaks to us as the Word of God."[61] Jung champions the mythical human in each of us, encouraging a running dialogue and living relationship with the mythical dimension of the psyche. The individuation process, as he defines it, is a spiritual adventure that culminates in individuals finding their own unique myth, with its underlying universality. Myth according to Jung is "the

60   1974b, p. 478.
61   1983, p. 340.

natural and indispensable intermediate stage between conscious and unconscious cognition."[62] Access to the unconscious brings knowledge through the archetype, although, given its symbolic and, one could say, eternal language, it requires amplification in order to make it understandable to the individual and temporally relevant.

For Jung himself, numinous archetypal dreams and visions from childhood on laid out the ground plan for his personal myth. One significant dream he had, which differentiates his path from post-Vedic and post-Upanishad Indian yoga, took place when he was in a hospital in Calcutta.[63] It culminated with him having to swim over a channel to fetch the Holy Grail in order to bring it to a medieval castle for a celebration. He reflects that the dream was asking him to "seek for yourself and your fellows the healing vessel, the *servator mundi*, which you urgently need. For your state is perilous; you are all in imminent danger of destroying all that centuries have built up."[64] Here, it is evident that Jung's unique myth is intrinsically related to healing of the Western and contemporary soul. This realization is becoming increasingly evident, although there remains a long way to go and considerable resistance to his brand of psychology and spiritual insights.

Spiritually gifted individuals, like Jung himself, become conscious of their unique myth and the fact that it has universal relevance for the times and the evolution of culture and consciousness. Marie-Louise von Franz has written an important biography of Jung, where she doesn't attempt to systematize the development of his ideas or refer to a chronology of external dates, but, rather, "follows the basic melody of his inner myth."[65] The universal nature of the archetypal processes behind Jung's myth finds a response in the lives of many contemporary individuals, as does his method of interpretation. It speaks not only

---

62   *Ibid.*, p. 311.
63   *Ibid.*, p. 280–283 passim.
64   *Ibid.*, p. 283.
65   1975, p. 14.

to Westerners, but to people everywhere. As the embodied Avatar and Divine Mother of our time, not only was Sri Aurobindo a creator of new symbols, but his life and relationship with the Mother is fully symbolic and mythological in the sense that Jung uses the term. The poetic rhythm of their myth, as recorded in *Savitri*, is meant for humanity at large, and involves the radical transformation of consciousness and culture and the creation of the new world.

Time has passed and India is going through a major change, becoming more open to Western materialistic values, while Westerners do not find Hindu yoga and philosophy so alien and are not so naïve and awe-struck by Indian spiritual leaders (unless truly deserved) and disciples, as was the case in the 1960s and '70s. The dialogue with India that Jung desires may now be possible, especially with disciples of Sri Aurobindo and the Mother.[66] In this regard, Jung writes: "We look forward hopefully to a collaboration with the Indian mind knowing that the mystery of the psyche can be understood only when approached from opposite sides."[67] This dialogue would benefit both students of Jung and those of Sri Aurobindo and the Mother as well as those on other spiritual paths. For disciples of Jung there would be a broadened horizon in many directions, where Jung's unfinished business and metaphysical perspective would find clarification. Sri Aurobindo and the Mother's disciples could profit from Jung's honest empiricism and phenomenological approach to the unconscious, as well as his unveiling of the complexities of the Western and contemporary psyches.

In the case of Sri Aurobindo and the Mother, there is, as with Jung, an historical bridge; for them it begins with the Vedas, advancing through the Upanishads, the *Bhagavad Gita* and Tantra, up to the contemporary world, as well as, through the Mother, Western esotericism and the Kabbala. Along with the East, the West is fully included in their worldview, made possible by the fact that Sri Aurobindo was educated

---

66   Sulagna Sengupta, 2013, pp. 242–246 passim.
67   As reported in *Ibid.*, p. 242.

in England, including at Cambridge, and the Mother was French by birth. Sri Aurobindo had extensive knowledge of the literature and history of the West as well as India, as is evident in his wide-ranging writings. Especially given their in-depth knowledge of the Vedas and Upanishads, their bridge, arguably, is more inclusive and, historically, extends beyond Jung's to a more comprehensive truth. The latter explores more fully the repressed Western traditions and the value of integrating Eastern and aboriginal perspectives to the Western psyche.

I can't think of a better way to bring this chapter to a close than with a quote from a conversation Jung had with Margaret Ostrawski-Sachs late in life. Jung is recorded as saying:

> Before my illness I had often asked myself if I were permitted to publish or even to speak of my secret knowledge. I later set it all down in *Aion*. I realized it was my duty to communicate these thoughts, yet I doubted whether I was allowed to give expression to them. During my illness I received confirmation and I now knew that everything had meaning and that everything was perfect.[68]

As I show above in discussing Jung's final vision, the course his life took led him to realizing an exceptional degree of individuation, of differentiated wholeness and oneness. Everything had meaning and everything was perfect, indeed. The baton is now passed on to all those in search of the *Lapis* and Holy Grail, for their own myth and unique, although universal, path to truth for psychological and spiritual transformation and participation in the New World.

---

68   As reported in Lance S. Owen, 2013, p. 31.

CONCLUSIONS

In this study, I attempt to understand Jung and his psychology of individuation in light of the Integral Yoga of Sri Aurobindo and the Mother. From my perspective, amongst all the spiritual paths I am aware of, theirs alone has a comprehensive enough container to integrate the significance of Jung's approach to psychology without distorting it. In addition to psychic and spiritual states of being, the mental state, life itself, and the physical world are all intrinsic aspects of their Integral Yoga of transformation. Other spiritual and religious paths, in contrast, tend to bypass the psyche or significantly limit it in deference to the goal of attaining a transcendent state of non-dual Reality or nirvana or, in the case of religious Christianity, to live a moral life and attain redemption after death. Christian monasticism, on the other hand, seeks the "fullness of grace … not only in heaven," but "Here and Now"; although there is little comprehension of the living psyche and devaluation of "the image," which puts limits on the parameters of the act of grace.[1] Understanding Jung in relationship to the yoga of Sri Aurobindo and the Mother avoids the usual pitfall of comparing Jung to a spiritual or religious path and concluding superiority in spiritual understanding to the spiritual or religious path, while relegating Jung to merely dealing with the psyche and its emotional contents, and reducing God to a psychological factor.

Jung always insists on the need for increasing consciousness at all levels of being, maintaining that "man has a soul and there is a buried

---

1   A Carthusian, 2006, pp. 89, 93.

treasure in the field."[2] By "all levels of being" he is referring to the archetype as psychoid, with poles that transcend both spirit and matter while extending toward oneness, as well as the psyche and the psychic unconscious. The existence of the soul allows for finding truth, joy and life behind the perversions and pathologies of existence, and for consciousness emerging throughout the psyche. The world, in essence, is real and infused with intelligence and truth, despite the experiential "reality" of ignorance, suffering, falsehood and death. In this study, I glean evidence for the reality of the world psyche from the evolution of Jung's life and horoscope, his relationship with the natural world, the story of the intelligent unfolding of the Universe, what astrology informs us about archetypal intelligence behind life at the cosmic, individual and microcosmic levels of being, and the study of biology and the science of the brain. The data fully supports the fact that archetypal patterns of life exist at both the level of the macrocosm and the microcosm, which indicates a *unus mundus,* one world, of unity and multiplicity, which can be experienced synchronistically.

Sri Aurobindo and the Mother are equally insistent on the need for increasing consciousness rather than engaging in a one-sided ascension to non-dual Reality. Like Jung, they are also wary about attaining non-dual Reality, where consciousness dissolves into the sea of Oneness. In contrast to Jung, however, they also insist on the goal of attaining and surrendering to *That,* One without a second, although with consciousness intact. This is, apparently, possible with a developed psychic being, the individual soul-personality, which replaces the illusory ego. Thanks to the individual soul and psychic being's surrender to *That,* according to Sri Aurobindo, individuals can potentially be carried consciously to the highest plane beyond mind, which is the Supermind.

There are recorded visionary dreams that support the notion that Jung attained a high level of soul-surrender and, although there is no

---

2   As recorded in Sonu Shamdasani, 2003, p. 351.

formal evidence of him having attained *That* or the Supermind, I try
to demonstrate that he had feeling experiences of the *unus mundus* or
one world that parallel Sri Aurobindo's overmind plane, with a delegated supramental gnosis. What is significant in Jung's path is, first
of all, that he develops an intimate relationship with his anima-soul as
Sophia, or wisdom. There is, in addition, a descent of a superior being
in Philemon with four keys of truth that Jung integrated to consciousness, as well as a creative daimon from below that impels him on his
path of individuation in harmony with the descending superior insight
from above. In fact, Jung maintained a continuous relationship with
Philemon beginning with a dream sometime between 1913 and 1914
and, again, in 1948, as recounted above. This continuous relationship
with "the master" with superior insight indicates a seamless existence
that clearly suggests that Jung's life and his work are one. Arguably
this oneness began even earlier, if not at birth, perhaps at the age of
three to four, when Jung experienced the highly numinous dream of an
underground phallus.

This double action in Jung's personal psychology, from above and
from below, is what generates global knowledge and understanding;
it also renders his approach to psychology harmonious with the contemporary evolutionary need. Jung's approach is also compatible with
the Integral Yoga of Sri Aurobindo and the Mother, and to what they
refer to as psychic and spiritual transformation, though without formal
reference to submersion in *That*. If my understanding is correct, his
path ends where Sri Aurobindo and the Mother's supramental yoga
per se begins, although it may be more accurate to say that Jung's path
culminates with the supramental yoga as described by Sri Aurobindo
and the Mother.

REFERENCES

À Kempis, Thomas. 1996. *The imitation of Christ.* Translated by B. Knott. London: Fount.

Abt, Theodore. 2005. *Introduction to picture interpretation according to C.G. Jung.* Zurich: Living Human Heritage Publications.

―――. 2009. *Corpus alchemicum arabicum: Book of the explanation of the symbols by Muhammad ibn Umail: Psychological Commentary.* Zurich: Living Human Heritage Publications.

Abt, Theodore, and Hornung, Erik. 2003. *Knowledge for the afterlife: The Egyptian quest for immortality.* Zurich: Living Human Heritage Publications.

Adler, Gerhard, ed. 1973. *C.G. Jung: Letters 1: 1906–1950.* Bollingen series XCV:1. In collaboration with Aniela Jaffé. Translation from the German by R.F.C. Hull. Princeton, NJ: Princeton University Press.

―――. 1975. *C.G. Jung: Letters 2: 1951–1961.* Bollingen series XCV:2. In collaboration with Aniela Jaffé. Translation from the German by R.F.C. Hull. Princeton, NJ: Princeton University Press.

Aurobindo, Sri. 1970a*. *Savitri: A legend and symbol.* Part 1, vol. 28, Sri Aurobindo Birth Centenary Library. Popular ed. Pondicherry: Sri Aurobindo Ashram.

―――. 1970a. *Savitri: A legend and symbol.* Parts 2 and 3, vol. 29, Sri Aurobindo Birth Centenary Library. Popular ed. Pondicherry: Sri Aurobindo Ashram.

―――. 1970b. *Essays on the Gita.* Vol. 13, Sri Aurobindo Birth Centenary Library. Popular ed. Pondicherry: Sri Aurobindo Ashram.

―――. 1970b. *The life divine: Book one, part one.* Vol. 18, Sri Aurobindo Birth Centenary Library. Popular ed. Pondicherry: Sri Aurobindo Ashram.

―――. 1970c. *The life divine.* Bk. 1, vol. 18, Sri Aurobindo Birth Centenary Library. Popular ed. Pondicherry: Sri Aurobindo Ashram.

———. 1970d. *The life divine.* Bk. 2, part 2, vol. 19, Sri Aurobindo Birth Centenary Library. Popular ed. Pondicherry: Sri Aurobindo Ashram.

———. 1970e. *Letters on yoga.* Part 1, vol. 22, Sri Aurobindo Birth Centenary Library. Popular ed. Pondicherry: Sri Aurobindo Ashram.

———. 1970f. *Letters on yoga.* Part 4, vol. 24, Sri Aurobindo Birth Centenary Library. Popular ed. Pondicherry: Sri Aurobindo Ashram.

———. 1970g. *Letters on yoga: Part two.* Vol. 23, Sri Aurobindo Birth Centenary Library. Popular ed. Pondicherry: Sri Aurobindo Ashram.

———. 1971a. The human cycle. In *Social and political thought.* Vol. 15, Sri Aurobindo Birth Centenary Library. Popular ed. Pondicherry: Sri Aurobindo Ashram.

———. 1971b. Heraclitus. In *The supramental manifestation.* Vol. 16, Sri Aurobindo Birth Centenary Library. Popular ed. Pondicherry: Sri Aurobindo Ashram.

———. 1971b*. Mind of light. In *The supramental manifestation.* Vol. 16, Sri Aurobindo Birth Centenary Library. Popular ed. Pondicherry: Sri Aurobindo Ashram.

———. 1971c. *The secret of the Veda.* Vol. 10, Sri Aurobindo Birth Centenary Library. Popular ed. Pondicherry: Sri Aurobindo Ashram.

———. 1971d. *The synthesis of Yoga.* Part 2, vol. 20, Sri Aurobindo Birth Centenary Library. Popular ed. Pondicherry: Sri Aurobindo Ashram.

———. 1972a. *The Mother.* Vol. 25, Sri Aurobindo Birth Centenary Library. Popular ed. Pondicherry: Sri Aurobindo Ashram.

———. 1972b. *On himself.* Vol. 26, Sri Aurobindo Birth Centenary Library. Popular ed. Pondicherry: Sri Aurobindo Ashram.

———. 1972c. *The hour of God.* Vol. 17, Sri Aurobindo Birth Centenary Library. Popular ed. Pondicherry: Sri Aurobindo Ashram.

———. 1972d. *The Upanishads.* Vol. 12, Sri Aurobindo Birth Centenary Library. Popular ed. Pondicherry: Sri Aurobindo Ashram.

———. 1972e. *Bande Mataram.* Vol. 1, Sri Aurobindo Birth Centenary Library. Popular ed. Pondicherry: Sri Aurobindo Ashram.

————. 1972f. *Karmayoga*. Vol. 2, Sri Aurobindo Birth Centenary Library. Popular ed. Pondicherry: Sri Aurobindo Ashram.

————. 1978. *Glossary of terms in Sri Aurobindo's writings*. 1st ed. Pondicherry: Sri Aurobindo Ashram Trust.

————. 1971. *The human cycle*. Vol. 25, The Complete Works of Sri Aurobindo. Pondicherry: Sri Aurobindo Ashram.

————. 2006. *Autobiographical notes and other writings of historical interest*. Vol. 36, The Complete Works of Sri Aurobindo. Pondicherry: Sri Aurobindo Ashram Press.

————. 2011. *Letters on himself and the ashram*. Vol. 35, The Complete Works of Sri Aurobindo. Pondicherry: Sri Aurobindo Ashram Press.

Baumann-Jung, Greta. 1975. Some reflections on the horoscope of C.G. Jung. In *Spring 75*. Translated by F.J. Hopman. New York: Spring Publications.

Berlin, Isaiah. 1958. Two concepts of liberty. In Isaiah Berlin (1969) *Four essays on liberty*. Oxford: Oxford University Press.

Bourgeault, Cynthia. 2010. *The meaning of Mary Magdalene: Discovering the woman at the heart of Christianity*. Boston: Shambhala Publications, Inc.

Burleson, Blake W. 2014. *A contemporary approach to understanding world religions: C.G. Jung as phenemologist of the soul*. New Orleans, Louisiana: Spring Journal, Inc.

Butler, E.M. 1979. *The myth of the magus*. Cambridge: Cambridge University Press.

Cahill, Thomas. 1998. *The gift of the Jews; How a tribe of desert nomads changed the way everyone thinks and feels*. Hinges of History series book 2. New York: Nan A. Talese/Anchor Books: Doubleday.

————. 2013. *Heretics and heroes: How the renaissance artists and reformation priests created our world*. Hinges of History series book 6. Toronto: Random House of Canada, Ltd.

Calasso, Roberto. 2014. *Ardor*. Translated from the Italian by Richard Dixon. New York: Farrar, Strauss and Giroux.

Cantalamessa, Father Raneiro. 2011. "Father Cantalamessa on the gospel's social relevance." *Zenit* (May 28). http://www.zenit.org/article-32700=english.

Carthusian, A. 2006. *The call of silent love*. Leominster, Herefordshire: Gracewing Publishing.

Tom Cheetham (2003). *The world turned inside out: Henry Corbin and Islamic mysticism*. Woodstock, Connecticut: Spring Journal Inc.

Dourley, John P. 1992. *A strategy for a loss of faith: Jung's proposal*. Toronto: Inner City Press.

———. 2010. *On behalf of the mystical fool: Jung and the religious situation*. East Sussex: Routledge.

———. 2014. *Jung and his mystics: In the end it all comes to nothing*. New York: Routledge.

Dunne, Claire. 2012. *Wounded healer of the soul*. London: Watkins Publishing.

Dyer, Gwynne. 2015. *Don't panic: Isis, terror, and today's Middle East*. Toronto: Random House Canada.

Dyne, Sonia. 2006. *The origins of Auroville*. London: Auromira Centre.

Edinger, Edward. 1972. *Ego and archetype*. New York: Penguin Books.

———. 1984. *The creation of consciousness: Jung's myth for modern man*. Toronto: Inner City Press.

———. 1996a. *The new God-image: A study of Jung's key letters concerning the evolution of the Western God-image*. Wilmette, Illinois: Chiron Publications.

———. 1996b. *The Aion lectures: Exploring the self in C.G. Jung's "Aion."* Edited by Deborah A. Wesley. Toronto: Inner City Books.

Eggers, Dave. 2014. *The circle*. Toronto: Vantage Canada Edition.

The Jerusalem Bible. Garden City, New York: Doubleday and Company, Inc.

Farlex. 2011. *The Free dictionary*. Kypros-net, Inc.

Gandhi, Kishor. 1965. *Social philosophy of Sri Aurobindo and the New Age*. Pondicherry: Sri Aurobindo Society.

God, Sex, and the Meaning of Life Ministry. 2014. *Theology of the body.* http://www.meaningoflife.homestead.com.

Hannah, Barbara. 2011. *The animus: The spirit of inner truth in woman.* Edited by David Eldred and Emmanuel Kennedy-Xypolitas. Wilmette, Illinois: Chiron Publications.

Harper, Douglas. 2001–2010. *Online etymology dictionary.* Heartlight, Inc.

Harris, Michael. 2014, August 15. Are we connected, or are we chained? *The National Post.* Toronto.

Haule, John Ryan. 2011. *Jung in the 21ˢᵗ century: Synchronicity and science.* Vol 2. New York: Routledge.

Hitchens, Christopher. 2015, January 8. The case for mocking religions. *The National Post.* Toronto.

Isler, Gothilf. Eulogy: Given at the funeral service in Küsnacht on the 26th of February 1998. In *The fountain of the love of wisdom: An homage to Marie-Louise von Franz.* Edited by Emmanuel Kennedy-Xypolitas. Wilmette, Illinois: Chiron Publications.

Jacobi, J. and R.F.C. Hull, eds. 1974. *C.G. Jung: Psychological reflections: A new anthology of his writings.* Princeton, NJ: Princeton University Press.

Jacoby, Susan. 2008, May 15. The dumbing of America: Call me a snob, but really, we're a nation of dunces. Washingtonpost.com.

Jaffé, Aniela. 1989. *Was C.G. Jung a mystic? and other essays.* Einsiedeln: Daimon Verlag.

Jhunjhunwala, S. S., ed. 1974. *The Gita.* Auroville: Auropublications.

Jung, Andreas. 2009. Homes in the lives of Carl Gustav Jung and Emma Jung-Rauschenbach. In *The house of C.G. Jung: The history and restoration of the residence of Emma and Carl Gustav Jung-Rauschenbach.* Küsnacht: Stiftung C.G. Jung.

Jung, C.G. 1959. Notes on lectures given at the Eidgenossissche technische hochschule, Zurich by Prof. Dr. C.G. Jung. The process of individuation: 3 Eastern Texts / 4 Exercitia spiritualia of St. Ignatius of Loyola. In *Modern Psychology Vol. 3 and 4.* 2nd ed. Vol. 4. Winter Semester. November 1939–March 1940.

————. 1966. Richard Willhelm: In memoriam. In *The spirit in man, art, and literature*. Vol. 15, The Collected Works. Translated by R.F.C. Hull. London: Routledge & Kegan Paul.

————. 1970a. The spirit mercurius. In *Alchemical studies*. Vol. 13, The Collected Works. Translated by R.F.C. Hull. Princeton, NJ: Princeton University Press.

————. 1970a-1. The visions of Zosimos. In *Alchemical studies*. Vol. 13, The Collected Works. Translated by R.F.C. Hull. Princeton, NJ: Princeton University Press.

————. 1970a-2. The philosophical tree. In *Alchemical studies*. Vol. 13, The Collected Works. Translated by R.F.C. Hull. Princeton, NJ: Princeton University Press.

————. 1970a-3. Paracelsus as a spiritual phenomenon. In *Alchemical studies*. Vol. 13, The Collected Works. Translated by R.F.C. Hull. Princeton, NJ: Princeton University Press.

————. 1970b. The aims of psychotherapy. In *The practice of psychotherapy*. Vol. 16, The Collected Works. Translated by R.F.C. Hull. Princeton, NJ: Princeton University Press.

————. 1970c. Psychotherapy today. In *The practice of psychotherapy*. Vol. 16, The Collected Works. Translated by R.F.C. Hull. Princeton, NJ: Princeton University Press.

————. 1970d. The psychology of the transference. In *The practice of psychotherapy*. Vol. 16, The Collected Works. Translated by R.F.C. Hull. Princeton, NJ: Princeton University Press.

————. 1970d-1. The role of the unconscious. In *Civilization in transition*. Vol. 10, The Collected Works. Translated by R.F.C. Hull. 2nd ed. Princeton, NJ: Princeton University Press.

————. 1970e. The undiscovered self. In *Civilization in transition*. Vol. 10, The Collected Works. Translated by R.F.C. Hull. 2nd ed. Princeton, NJ: Princeton University Press.

————. 1970f. The spiritual problem of modern man. In *Civilization in transition*. Vol. 10, The Collected Works. Translated by R.F.C. Hull. 2nd ed. Princeton, NJ: Princeton University Press.

———. 1970f. Flying saucers: A modern myth. In *Civilization in transition*. Vol. 10, The Collected Works. Translated by R.F.C. Hull. 2nd ed. Princeton NJ: Princeton University Press.

———. 1974a. *Symbols of transformation*. Vol. 5. 2nd ed. Bollingen Series XX, The Collected Works. Translated by R.F.C. Hull. Princeton, NJ: Princeton University Press.

———. 1974b. *Psychological types*. Vol. 6. 2nd ed. Bollingen Series XX, The Collected Works. Translated by R.F.C. Hull. Princeton, NJ: Princeton University Press.

———. 1974c. *Mysterium coniunctionis*. Vol. 14. 2nd ed. Bollingen Series XX, The Collected Works. Translated by R.F.C. Hull. Princeton, NJ: Princeton University Press.

———. 1974d. *The development of personality*. Vol. 17, The Collected Works. Translated by R.F.C. Hull. Princeton, NJ: Princeton University Press.

———. 1975a. *Aion: Researches into the phenomenology of the self.* Vol. 9: II. 2nd ed. Bollingen Series XX, The Collected Works. Translated by R.F.C. Hull. 2nd ed. Princeton, NJ: Princeton University Press.

———. 1975b. On psychic energy. In *The structure and dynamics of the psyche*. Vol. 8. 2nd ed. Bollingen Series XX, The Collected Works. Translated by R.F.C. Hull, Princeton, NJ: Princeton University Press.

———. 1975b-1. Spirit and life. In *The structure and dynamics of the psyche*. Vol. 8. 2nd ed. Bollingen Series XX, The Collected Works. Translated by R.F.C. Hull, Princeton, NJ: Princeton University Press.

———. 1975b-2. Basic postulates of analytical psychology. In *The structure and dynamics of the psyche*. Vol. 8. 2nd ed. Bollingen Series XX, The Collected Works. Translated by R.F.C. Hull, Princeton, NJ: Princeton University Press.

———. 1975b-3. Synchronicity: An acausal connecting principle. In *The structure and dynamics of the psyche*. Vol. 8. 2nd ed. Bollingen Series XX, The Collected Works. Translated by R.F.C. Hull, Princeton, NJ: Princeton University Press.

———. 1975b-4. On the nature of the psyche. In *The structure and dynamics of the psyche*. Vol. 8. 2nd ed. Bollingen Series XX, The Collected Works. Translated by R.F.C. Hull, Princeton, NJ: Princeton University Press.

————. 1975b-5. General aspects of dream psychology. In *The structure and dynamics of the psyche*. Vol. 8. 2nd ed. Bollingen Series XX, The Collected Works. Translated by R.F.C. Hull, Princeton NJ: Princeton University Press.

————. 1975c. Psychology and religion. In *Psychology and religion*. Vol. 11. 2nd ed. Bollingen Series XX, The Collected Works. Translated by R.F.C. Hull, Princeton, NJ: Princeton University Press.

————. 1975c-1. A psychological approach to the dogma of the trinity. In *Psychology and religion*. Vol. 11. 2nd ed. Bollingen Series XX, The Collected Works. Translated by R.F.C. Hull, Princeton, NJ: Princeton University Press.

————. 1975c-2. The psychology of Eastern meditation. In *Psychology and religion*. Vol. 11. 2nd ed. Bollingen Series XX, The Collected Works. Translated by R.F.C. Hull, Princeton, NJ: Princeton University Press.

————. 1975c-3. The holy men of India. In *Psychology and religion*. Vol. 11. 2nd ed. Bollingen Series XX, The Collected Works. Translated by R.F.C. Hull, Princeton, NJ: Princeton University Press.

————. 1975c-4. Foreword to Suzuki's Introduction to Zen Buddhism. In *Psychology and religion*. Vol. 11. 2nd ed. Bollingen Series XX, The Collected Works. Translated by R.F.C. Hull, Princeton, NJ: Princeton University Press.

————. 1975c-5. Psychological commentary on the Tibetan Book of the Dead. In *Psychology and religion*. Vol. 11. 2nd ed. Bollingen Series XX, The Collected Works. Translated by R.F.C. Hull, Princeton, NJ: Princeton University Press.

————. 1975c-6. Transformation symbol of the mass. In *Psychology and religion*. Vol. 11. 2nd ed. Bollingen Series XX, The Collected Works. Translated by R.F.C. Hull, Princeton, NJ: Princeton University Press.

————. 1975d. The mana personality. In *Two essays in analytical psychology*. Vol. 7. 2nd ed. Bollingen Series XX, The Collected Works. Translated by R.F.C. Hull, Princeton, NJ: Princeton University Press.

————. 1975d-2. The problem of the attitude type. In *Two essays in analytical psychology*. Vol. 7. 2nd ed. Bollingen Series XX, The Collected Works. Translated by R.F.C. Hull, Princeton, NJ: Princeton University Press.

———. 1975d-1. The relations between the ego and the unconscious. In *Two essays on analytical psychology*. Vol. 7. 2nd ed. Bollingen Series XX, The Collected Works. Translated by R.F.C. Hull. Princeton, NJ: Princeton University Press.

———. 1975d-3. The archetypes of the collective unconscious. In *Two essays on analytical psychology*. Vol. 7. 2nd ed. Bollingen Series XX, The Collected Works. Translated by R.F.C. Hull. Princeton, NJ: Princeton University Press.

———. 1975e. A study in the process of individuation: Appendix. In *The archetypes of the collective unconscious*. Vol. 9: I. 2nd ed. Bollingen Series XX, The Collected Works. Translated by R.F.C. Hull. Princeton, NJ: Princeton University Press.

———. 1975f. Instinct and the unconscious. In *The structure and dynamics of the psyche*. Vol. 8. 2nd ed. Bollingen Series XX, The Collected Works. Translated by R.F.C. Hull. Princeton, NJ: Princeton University Press.

———. 1975g. Answer to Job. In *Psychology and religion: East and West*. Vol. 11. The Collected Works. Translated by R.F.C. Hull. Princeton, NJ: Princeton University Press.

———. 1976a. Religion and psychology: A reply to Martin Buber. In *The symbolic life*. Vol. 18, The Collected Works. Translated by R.F.C. Hull. Princeton, NJ: Princeton University Press.

———. 1976b. The Tavistock lectures. In *The symbolic life*. Vol. 18, The Collected Works. Translated by R.F.C. Hull. Princeton, NJ: Princeton University Press.

———. 1976c. Religion and psychology: A letter to Père Lachat. In *The symbolic life*. Vol. 18, The Collected Works. Translated by R.F.C. Hull. Princeton, NJ: Princeton University Press.

———. 1976d. Jung and religious belief. In *The symbolic life*. Vol. 18, The Collected Works. Translated by R.F.C. Hull. Princeton, NJ: Princeton University Press.

———. 1976e. Psychology and national problems. In *The symbolic life*. Vol. 18, The Collected Works. Translated by R.F.C. Hull. Princeton, NJ: Princeton University Press.

————. 1976f. The symbolic life. In *The symbolic life*. Vol. 18, The Collected Works. Translated by R.F.C. Hull. Princeton, NJ: Princeton University Press.

————. 1977. *Psychology and alchemy*. Vol. 12. Bollingen Series XX, The Collected Works. Translated by R.F.C. Hull. Princeton, NJ: Princeton University Press.

————. 1983a. *The Zofingia lectures*. Supplementary vol. A. 2nd ed. Bollingen Series XX, The Collected Works. Translated by Jan Van Heurck. With an introduction by Marie-Louise von Franz. Princeton, NJ: Princeton University Press.

————. 1983. *Memories, dreams, reflections*. Recorded and edited by Aniela Jaffé. Translated from the German by Richard and Clara Winston. Rev. ed. New York: Vintage Books.

————. 1989. *Analytical psychology: Notes of the seminar given in 1925*. Edited by William McGuire. Bolligen Series XCIX. Princeton, NJ: Princeton University Press.

————. 2009. *The red book: Liber novus*. Edited and Introduced by Sonu Shamdasani. New York: W.W. Norton & Company.

Khanna, Parag. 2016. *Connectography: Mapping the future of global civilization*. New York: Random House.

Lammers, Ann Conrad and Cunningham, Adrian eds. 2008. *The Jung-White letters*. Consulting Editor, Murray Stein. New York: Routledge.

Lammers, Ann Conrad, ed. 2011. *The Jung-Kirsch letters*. Trasnslated by Ursula Egli and Ann Conrad Lammers. New York: Routledge.

Lindorff, David. 2009. *Pauli and Jung: The meeting of two great minds*. Quest Books. Wheaten, Ill: Theosophical Publishing House.

Magee, Glenn Alexander. 2008. *Hegel and the hermetic tradition*. Ithaca, New York: Cornell Paperbacks.

Maharshi, Ramana. 1985. *Be as you are: The teachings of Sri Ramana Maharshi*. Edited by David Godman. London: Penguin Books Ltd.

————. 1988. *The spiritual teaching of Ramana Maharshi*. Foreword by C.G. Jung. Compiled by Joe and Guivenere Miller. Boston: Shambhala Publications, Inc.

Maguire, Anne. 2006. Valedictory address for Marie-Louise von Franz at the burial service held in the Reformed Church, Kusnacht, Switzerland on February 26, 1998. In *The fountain of the love of wisdom: An homage to Marie-Louise von Franz*. Edited by Emmanuel Kennedy-Xypolitas. Wilmette, Illinois: Chiron Publications.

Anne Manne. *The Narcissism Epidemic.* YouTube. September 01, 2014.

McGuire, William and R. F. C. Hull, eds. 1980. *C.G. Jung speaking: Interviews and encounters*. Picador edition. London: Pan Books Ltd.

Monzo, Rafael. 2006. I had the privilege. In *The fountain of the love of wisdom: An homage to Marie-Louise von Franz*. Edited by Emmanuel Kennedy-Xypolitas. Wilmette, Illinois: Chiron Publications.

Mother, The (La Mère). 1971, December 22. *Auroville Gazette.*

———. 1978a. *Entretiens 1957–58*. Pondicherry: Éditions Sri Aurobindo Ashram.

———. 1978b. *Entretiens 1956*. 2ième Édition. Pondicherry: Éditions Sri Aurobindo Ashram.

———. 1978c. "Agenda de l'action supramentale sur terre." In *L'Agenda de Mère, 1961* [The Mother's agenda–1961]. Paris: Institut de Recherches Evolutives. Vol. 2: 280, 281.

———. 1979, 2003d, *Prayers and Meditations.* Vol. 1, Collected Works of the Mother. 2nd ed. Pondicherry: Sri Aurobindo Publications Department.

———. 1980. *L'Agenda de Mère:1966*. Vol. 7 (September 21) : 210.

———. 1981a. *L'Agenda de Mère:1968*. Vol. 9 (February 7) : 52–54 passim.

———. 1981b. *L'Agenda de Mère:1969*. Vol. X (December 31) : 44–51 passim, 524–536 passim.

———. 1997. *The Sunlit Path: Passages from conversations and writings of the Mother.* Pondicherry: Sri Aurobindo Ashram Publications Department.

———. 2001. *On thoughts and aphorisms*. Vol. 10, Collected Works of the Mother. 2nd ed. Pondicherry: Sri Aurobindo Publications Department.

———. 2003a. *Questions and answers 1950–1951*. Vol. 4, Collected Works of the Mother. 2nd ed. Pondicherry: Sri Aurobindo Publications Department.

———. 2003b. *Questions and answers 1953*. Vol. 5, Collected Works of the Mother. 2nd ed. Pondicherry: Sri Aurobindo Publications Department.

———. 2003c. *Questions and answers 1954*. Vol. 6, Collected Works of the Mother. 2nd ed. Pondicherry: Sri Aurobindo Ashram Publication Department.

———. 2004a. *Questions and answers 1955*. Vol. 7, Collected Works of the Mother. 2nd ed. Pondicherry: Sri Aurobindo Publications Department.

———. 2004b. *Questions and answers 1957–1958*. Vol. 9, Collected Works of the Mother. 2nd ed. Pondicherry: Sri Aurobindo Publications Department.

———. 2004c. *Being of gold: Our goal of self-perfection: A compilation from the Mother's writings*. Auroville: The Centre for Indian Studies.

———. 2004d. Collected Works of the Mother. *Words of the Mother—I*. Vol. 13, Collected Works of the Mother. 2nd ed. Originally published in 1980. Pondicherry: Sri Aurobindo Ashram Publication Department.

———. 2004e. *Words of the Mother—III*. Vol. 15, Collected Works of the Mother. 2nd ed. Originally published in 1980. Pondicherry: Sri Aurobindo Ashram Publication Department.

———. 2008. *Becoming One: The psychology of Integral Yoga: A compilation from the Mother's writings*. Pondicherry: Stichting De Zaaier: All India Press.

———. 2012. *The new being and a new society: A compilation of the Mother's words and archival material during the formative years of Auroville*. Auroville: SAHER

Monzo, Rafael. 2006. I had the privilege. In *The fountain of the love of wisdom: An homage to Marie-Louise von Franz*. Edited by Emmanuel Kennedy-Xypolitas. Wilmette, Illinois: Chiron Publications.

Murphy, Joseph. 1977. *Secrets of the I Ching*. West Nyack, NY: Parker Publishing Company, Inc.

Neusner, Rabbi Jacob. 1993. *A rabbi talks with Jesus: An intermillennial interfaith exchange*. New York: Doubleday.

Nagy, Marilyn. 1991. *Philosophic issues in the psychology of C.G. Jung*. Albany: State University of New York.

Norelli-Bachelet, Patrizia. 1985, October. *The VISHAAL Newsletter* 0, no.1: 5–10 passim, 5, 13, 14, 15, 31, 260, 299 passim.

———. 1986. *The VISHAAL Newsletter* 1, no. 5 (December).

———. 1987. *The VISHAAL Newsletter* 1, no. 6 (February).

Owens, Lance S. 2013. Foreword to *The search for roots: C.G. Jung and the tradition of gnosis,* by Alfred Ribi. 2nd printing. New York: Gnosis Archive Books.

Pandit, M. P. 1966. *Dictionary of Sri Aurobindo's yoga: Compiled from the writings of Sri Aurobindo.* Pondicherry: Dipti Publications.

Ratzinger, Joseph, Pope Benedict XVI 2007. *Jesus of Nazareth: From the baptism in the Jordan to the transfiguration.* Translated from the German by Adrian J. Walker. San Francisco: Ignatius Press.

Rib, Alfred. 2013. *The search for roots: C.G. Jung and the tradition of gnosis.* 2nd printing. New York: Gnosis Archive Books.

Romanyshyn, Robert D. 2013. *The Wounded Researcher: Research with Soul in Mind.* New Orleans, Louisiana: Spring Journal Inc.

Rosen, David, M. D. 1996. *The Tao of Jung: The way of integrity.* New York: Penguin Books USA, Inc.

Sabini, Meredith, ed. 2008. *The Earth has a soul: C.G. Jung on nature, technology & modern life.* Berkeley, Cal: North Atlantic Books.

Satprem 1982. *The mind of the cells: Or willed mutation of our species.* Translated from the French by Francine Mahak and Luc Venet. New York: Institute for Evolutionary Research.

Sen, Indra. 1986. *Integral psychology: The psychological system of Sri Aurobindo.* 1st ed. Pondicherry: Sri Aurobindo International Centre of Education.

Sengupta, Sulagna. 2013. *Jung in India.* New Orleans: Spring Journal, Inc.

Shakya, Jy Din. 1996. *Empty cloud: The teachings of Xu Yun: A remembrance of the great Chinese zen master.* As compiled from the notes and recollections of Jy Din Shakya and related to Ming Zhen Shakya and Upasaka Richard Cheung. A production of the Zen Buddhist Order of Hsu Yun. http://www.hsuyun.org.

Shamdasani, Sonu. 1998. *Cult fiction: C.G. Jung and the founding of analytical psychology*. New York: Routledge.

———. 2003. *Jung and the making of modern psychology: The dream of a science*. New York: Cambridge University Press.

———. 2009. Liber Novus: The Red Book of C.G. Jung in *The Red Book*. New York: W.W. Norton & Company.

Shedler, Jonathan. 2015, May. Where is the evidence for "evidence-based" therapies? *The Journal of Psychological Therapies in Primary Care*. Vol. 4.

Sheldrake, Rupert. 1995. *Morphic resonance and the presence of the past: The habits of nature*. Rochester, Vermont: Park Street Press.

Sarah Liuh, Shiyua. 2012. *Bridging West & East, C.G. Jung and Richard Wilhelm: A fateful relationship*. AJC Seminar #26. www.AshvilleJungCenter.org.

Siegel, Daniel J. 1999. *The developing mind: How relationships and the brain interact to shape who we are*. New York: The Guilford Press.

———. 2007. *The mindful brain: Reflections and attunement in the cultivation of well-being*. New York: W.W. Norton & Company, Inc.

———. 2011. *Mindsight: The new science of personal transformation*. New York: Bantam Books.

Sparks, J. Gary. 2010. *Valley of diamonds: Adventures in number and time with Marie-Louise von Franz*. Toronto: Inner City Books.

Spiegelman, J. Marvin and Arwind U. Vasavada. 1987. *Hinduism and Jungian psychology*. Phoenix, Arizona: Falcon Press.

Starbird, Margaret. 2005. *Mary Magdalene: Bride in exile*. Rochester, Vermont: Bear & Company.

Stein, Murray. 1998. *Jung's map of the soul: An introduction*. Peru, Illinois: Open Court.

———, presenter. *Jung and the religions of the East*. In Jung and the world religions. A Global Seminar. The Asheville center. March 28, 2015.

Stevens, Anthony. 1990. *On Jung*. New York: Routledge.

————. 2003. *Archetype revisited: An updated natural history of the self.* Toronto: Inner City Books.

Stevens, Anthony, and John Price 2000. *Evolutionary psychiatry: A new beginning.* 2nd ed. Philadelphia: Routledge: Taylor & Francis Inc.

Steyn, Mark. 2015, January 26. Free speech is the right to insult Islam, Steyn says. Toronto: *The National Post.*

Schweizer, Andreas. 2010. *The sungod's journey through the netherworld: Reading the ancient Egyptian Amduat.* Edited by David Lorton. Foreword by Erik Hornung. London: Cornell University Press.

Swimme, Brian, and Thomas Berry. 1992. *The universe story: From the primordial flaring forth to the Ecozoic era: A celebration of the unfolding of the cosmos.* New York: HarperCollins Publishers.

Tarnas, Richard. 2006. *Cosmos and psyche: Intimations of a new world view.* New York: Viking: The Penguin Group.

Thayer and Smith. The KJB New Testament Greek lexicon. BibleStudyTools. com

Tolkien, J. R. R. 1983. *The lord of the rings.* Boston: Houghton Mifflin Company.

————. 2004. *The Silmarillion.* Hammersmith, London: HarperCollins Publisher.

Twenge, Jean and Keith Campbell. 2010. *The narcissism epidemic: living in the age of entitlement.* New York: Atria.

von Franz, Marie-Louise. 1974. *Number and time: Reflections leading toward a unification of psychology and physics.* Translated by Andrea Dykes. Evanston: Northwestern University Press.

————. 1975. *C.G. Jung: His myth in our time.* Translated from the German by William H. Kennedy. New York: J. Putnam's Sons for the C.G. Jung Foundation for Analytical Psychology.

————. 1979. *Alchemical active imagination.* Revised Edition. Boston: Shambhala Publications Inc.

————. 1992a. Meaning and order. In *Psyche and matter.* Boston: Shambhalla Publications, Inc.

————. 1992b. Some reflections on synchronicity. In *Psyche and matter.* Boston: Shambhalla Publications, Inc.

————. 1992c. Time and synchronicity in analytical psychology. In *Psyche and matter.* Boston: Shambhalla Publications, Inc.

————. 1992d. *The golden ass of Apuleius: The liberation of the feminine in men.* Revised Edition. Boston: Shambhala Publications Inc.

————. (1997a*).* Individuation and social relationship. In *Archetypal dimensions of the psyche.* Boston: Shambhalla Publications, Inc.

————. 1997b. Jung's discovery of the self. In *Archetypal dimensions of the psyche.* Boston: Shambhalla Publications, Inc.

von Franz, Marie-Louise, with Claude Drey. 2004. Conversations on *Aion.* In *Lectures on Jung's "Aion."* Wilmette, Illinois: Chiron Publications.

Wertenschlagg-Birkhäuser, Eva. 2009. *Windows on eternity: The paintings of Peter Birkäuser: An interpretation based on depth psychology.* Einsiedeln, Switzerland: Daimon Verlag.

Wilhelm, Richard. 1962. *The secret of the golden flower: A Chinese book of life.* Translated and explained by Richard Wilhelm. Commentary by C.G. Jung. Appendix: memorial address on Richard Wilhelm by C.G. Jung.

Word-Origins.com 2011. *Err.*

INDEX

GLOSSARY OF TERMS AND DEFINITIONS

TERMS USED IN THE TEACHINGS OF
SRI AUROBINDO AND THE MOTHER

Ananda   Pure Bliss, Ecstasy, beyond joy and pleasure.

Asura   There are four Asuras, which were originally Beings of Light with great formative power. They became separated from the Divine Source and each Asura consequently became a perversion of *Sat Chit Ananda* and Truth (the Supermind). In place of *Sat* (Existence) one Asura became non-Existence (Death); in place of *Chit-Shakti* (Consciousness-Force) another became Ignorance; in place of *Ananda* (Bliss), a third became Suffering; and in place of Truth, there is the Asura of Falsehood. They are hostile beings that function according to mastery of the dark-side of the vital-mind. Two Asuras have converted back to the Divine, but not Falsehood and Death.

Atman   The *atman* is the Self or Spirit that remains above nature and is unaffected by the play of life. It is the true individual being, known as the *jivatman*, discussed below, as well as the cosmic Self that is the Self of all, the cosmic *atman*, and self-existence beyond both the individual and cosmic Self, the transcendent *atman*, the *Paramatma* the Supreme Divine Being.

Avatar   *Avatar* means descent of the Divine Consciousness and Being into the human world of being and dynamic action. The incarnation of the *Avatar* refers to the birth of the divine in the humanity, a descent and incarnation, where the human element is included. It involves complete conscious substitution of the Divine Person for the human person and expression. The two aspects of the incarnation are: Descent, where God, as the eternal *Avatar*, puts on human form and nature, and, then, the Ascent of the human into the Godhead. In this way, the *Avatar* serves the *Dharma*, meaning the moral, social and religious rule and conduct.

Chit   Pure Consciousness. The nature of *Chit* is *Shakti* (Power).

Higher Mind   The Higher Mind is the lower plane of spiritual consciousness that functions with day-like clarity while being constantly cognizant of the Self, unity of being and dynamic multiplicity. It is a delegate of the Overmind plane and mediates Truth to the human mind in an acceptable form, predominantly functioning with the power of higher Thought.

Ignorance
: Ignorance is the veil that separates Nature (Mind, Vital (Life) and the Body) from the Divine Source.

Illumined Mind
: The Illumined Mind is the higher plane of spiritual consciousness subsequent to the Higher Mind, no longer mainly functioning with Thought, but with spiritual illumination and light. Along with the down-pouring of Light from above, there is a descent of knowledge and peace, as well as the "enthousiasmos" of inner force and power.

Inconscient
: The Inconscient is absolute and an inverse copy of the supreme Superconscience, the final result of the Ignorance. It functions automatically, self-absorbed in its own abyss, an apparent infinite non-being. Yet, an ordered world is created from its self-absorbed trance and the oblivious automatic and apparently blind responses of the Inconscient. It is created by the infinite power of truth in manifest existence. Matter is an involved consciousness and force, and the Inconscient's first field of creation. The Inconscient's formations rise into waking consciousness or the subliminal self at the edge where the Subconscient meets the Inconscient.

Intellect
: The true intellect relates freely to ideas. It is a principle that reflects the Supermind, while being of a lesser status. The function of the intellect is to think, reason, and encourage perceiving and acting intelligently.

Intuitive Mind
: After the Illumined Mind, the next higher level of spiritual consciousness is the Intuitive Mind. It is a revelatory, visionary and inspired mind that functions according to higher Reason, with the authenticity and certitude of the light of truth and truth-discernment.

Jivatman
: The *jivatman* is the central being that presides over individual birth but is itself unborn and does not partake in the evolution. It is the individual Self and delegates a representative of itself in the psychic, the individual's inmost being. In addition, it puts forth a representation of itself on each level of being, a mental *purusha*, a vital (life) *purusha* and a physical *purusha*.

Mind of Light	The Mind of Light is a transitional state, a descent from Supermind beyond the Ignorance to an illumined humanity. Although knowledge for this new humanity is tied to the Ignorance, the new person is a seeker after light and open to the light. These new persons are capable of being truth-conscious, living in the truth and manifesting direct knowledge, while proceeding from knowledge to knowledge. Although there has been a descent from Supermind to Mind, the Mind of Light has maintained its connection with the supramental principle, and there is no error, Ignorance or Inconscience.
Mother, The	The Mother is the divine as Consciousness-Force. She gives birth to the *Ishwara,* the Cosmic Lord, and places herself beside him as the Cosmic *Shakti.*
Overmind	After the Intuitive Mind, the next highest spiritual plane, the highest plane in the Ignorance, is the Overmind, a direct delegate to the Ignorance from the Supermind. While the Supermind is integral Truth-consciousness, where all attributes e.g. Love, Power, Knowledge, are one, the Overmind is global consciousness full of divine attributes, where each attribute can exist on its own, while one attribute can disturb another, eg the expression of Peace can be deranged by ambition for Power. In addition, on the Overmind plane, each line of development in the manifestation needs to be worked through to its end as a separate truth.
Para Shakti/ Para Prakriti	The *Para Shakti* is the higher *Shakti* that works through the *Para Prakriti* as the supreme Consciousness-Force manifest in the multiplicity.
Physical Mind	The Physical Mind is concerned solely with the external world of physical objects and actions, for which it is dependent on the Sense-Mind. Its inferences and reasoning are based on data from the external world.
Prakriti	The working or executive force is *Prakriti,* the power behind which is *Shakti.*
Psychic Being	The psychic is a spark of the divine Fire involved in individual existence; while the psychic being is the developing soul-consciousness. It is the incarnated soul and emotional being found deep behind the heart that develops through evolution.

It turns naturally toward the divine, and brings discernment through feeling. When brought forward to consciousness, it has the effect of purifying and transforming the whole of one's nature.

Psychic Transformation	Psychic transformation emanates from within, from the influence and eventual domination of the psychic being on the mental, vital (life) and physical natures. The eventual effect is conversion of one's entire nature into an instrument of the soul.
Purusha	The *Purusha* is the conscious (witness) Soul that supports the workings of *Prakriti* (Nature). There is one *Purusha*, which has representatives on different planes of being, the mental *purusha*, the vital (life) *purusha* and the physical *purusha*. The psychic being is the *Caitya Purusha,* the inmost being that supports the other three *purushas* involved in the lower *Prakriti* (Nature).
Sat	Pure Existence, the One Existence, the Good.
Shakti	The *Shakti* is the self-conscious and effective power of the Lord as *Ishwara* or *Purusha*. She expresses herself in the workings of *Prakriti* (Nature), the executive force of Nature.
Spiritual Transformation	Spiritual transformation requires the Descent of a higher Light, Knowledge, Power, Force, Bliss and Purity from above into one's entire being and nature, the mental, vital (life), including its lower regions and the body, down to the darkness of the vital and physical Subconscient.
Subconscient	The Subconscient is a half-unconscious nether part of the being below body consciousness, generally without waking consciousness, where the light of awareness penetrates with difficulty. There is no thinking mind or feeling, organized response or control of will. It functions automatically and mechanically, constituted by obscure memories, repressed physical and vital reactions, and body-consciousness, including of the cells and nerves as well as the lower sense-mind. Memories and habitual movements come up in dreams and, when the light of consciousness is brought to bear and the old responses are trained to act more in truth, they eventually cease.
Subliminal	Behind the superficial waking consciousness, there is the Subliminal self, which refers to the inner mental, vital and physical which are all supported by the psychic. It is a luminous

and powerful self, the meeting place of the dynamic evolutionary consciousness emerging from below and the involution of the descending consciousness from above. It refers to the archetypes of the collective unconscious discovered and amplified by C.G. Jung.

Supermind

The Supermind is the connecting link between infinite *Sat Chit Ananda* and the multiplicity of the manifestation, and lower nature, consisting of the Mental, Vital (Life) and Physical Natures. The Supermind is the full Truth-consciousness or Real Idea inherent in all Existence and Cosmic Force, essential for order, relations and the intelligent unfolding of the manifestation. In itself, it is beyond the Ignorance.

Supramental Transformation

The supramental transformation is the third order of transformation grounded on the psychic and spiritual transformations. It requires the Ascent of being into the Supermind and the transforming descent of the Supermind consciousness into one's whole being and nature.

Vibhuti

The *Vibhuti* of the divine refers to manifestation in the human and the *Avatar* and the Divine Mother of a greater power of divine qualities and attributes, such as Knowledge, Strength, Energy and Love, through inner and/or outer achievement. The *Vibhuti* is the true hero who leads humanity towards fuller divine achievement.

Vital (Life) Mind

The Vital (Life) mind gives expression in thought or speech, etc. to all aspects of Life-nature, including, ambitions, desires, emotions, feelings, sensations, fears, greed, lust, attractions, repulsions, will, actions, passions, etc.

TERMS USED IN THE TEACHINGS OF C.G. JUNG

Alchemy

Although Gnosticism can be characterized as a spiritual discipline and path of knowledge, alchemy is a path of spiritual transformation which embraces the dynamic energy of the material world. As the word alchemy suggests, along with Babylonian metallurgy, an important source of Western alchemy is ancient Egypt, with its art of mummification and search for physical immortality. The primary source document of Western alchemy, probably written in Arabic between the 6th to 8th centuries C.E., is the *Tabula Smaragdina,* the Emerald Tablet, attributed to Hermes Trismegistus and, according to legend, found in a cave. Alchemy is derived from the Arabic words *Al Khemia,* which means the land of the black earth, an old name for Egypt.

Although in the West, over the past some 2000 years, Christianity has been the dominant religious and spiritual force, for the Christian alchemists, alchemy was practiced as a compensatory undercurrent. The laboratory practices of alchemy eventually evolved into chemistry and the physical sciences. The magical transformative aspect became depth psychology thanks to the discoveries of C.G. Jung. From the latter perspective, the alchemists were interested in extracting God from matter and the transformation of matter. Some alchemists understood the symbolic nature of the work, although, for the most part, they still did not realize they were projecting their own psyches into the chemical solutions and matter. Alchemical symbols include the psychological discrimination of opposites, the psychological movement to totality as understood by the Axiom of Maria and the movement from 3 to 4, and eventual unification of all opposites in the *mysterium conunctionis,* the *heiros gamos.*

Amplification   It is often helpful to work around the dream content with universal and archetypal images that come from humankind's collective heritage, for instance, from fairy tales, mythologies, religions, anthropology, alchemy, Gnosticism, other spiritual teachings, along with the historical meanings attributed to the images. This process can help the dreamer to widen understanding beyond the personal, and to enhance the dream's meaning with symbolic understanding.

Anima/Animus   The inner female image in a man is known as the anima, and the inner male image in a woman is the animus. They are dominant figures in the psyche; the anima that ideally relates the man to the archetypes of the collective unconscious and creative living, and the animus that ideally lights up the woman's archetypal unconscious and creative life. Individuals can become conscious of the anima and animus in dreams, visions and true fantasy, where they play the role described in the previous sentence.

Anima/animus images come in various guises representing different unconscious qualities and attributes, ranging from Eve to Helen of Troy, the Virgin Mary to Sophia-like anima images, and the equivalent animus figures such as Adam, the primal man, Paris, the perfect husband or lover, Christ, the divine man, and, finally, the Wise old man. Anima figures can also appear with shadow qualities as repressive mother, manipulative witch, seductive woman, and ambitious competitor. Likewise, animus figures can manifest as a brute, a tyrant for a father figure, the Devil and a black magician. Both anima and animus can act as a guide and *psychopompos* for individuals that potentially deepen and heighten relationship to the collective unconscious.

The anima represents the man's soul and inner attitude, the face turned toward the unconscious and creative living. It is the archetype of life itself. While Jung first refers to the animus as being the soul of woman, he later refers to it as her spirit and power of discernment. It is the archetype of the spirit and creativity. Both anima and animus are complementary to the persona, the outer attitude, while containing all the qualities lacking in consciousness, as can be surmised by the previous paragraph.

When the anima/animus is not in its proper place as mediator/rix to the unconscious, then the man identifies with and is, at times, possessed by the anima and the woman identifies with the animus and, occasionally becomes possessed by him. The factor of possession is painfully visible during heated arguments between men and women from all stations of life everywhere. When a man identifies with the anima, he acts in a garrulous, argumentative, moody, sentimental, or whining way, lacking typical masculine reason, steadfastness and purpose. When a woman is caught in the animus, she expresses collective opinions that are beside the point, while being opinionated, critical, argumentative, self-deprecating, and divorced from her deeper feeling and Eros nature.

Anthropos   The *Anthropos* is Greek for man, and refers to the Gnostic Original Man and wholeness, and according to Jung, corresponds to the Self. The *Anthropos* is traditionally depicted as splitting into male and female. According to Gnostic literature, it is the higher Adam and superordinate Self, of which Christ is the second Adam.

Archetype

Jung first used the term primordial image for fantasy images that have an archaic nature, meaning, when similar to a mythological motif. The primordial image is not personal but, primarily, is contained in the collective unconscious, from which it emerges when activated, giving a collective significance to the factors involved in the present context. The primordial image is the matrix for and source of the idea. Reason detaches the idea from the concrete reality of the primordial image and develops the idea into a concept.

The archetype-in-itself is irrepresentable and unknowable. As the archetype is perceived through the image, one typically refers to the archetypal image, which is affected by place, time and culture context, rather than the archetype-in-itself. The word type derives from blow or imprint, which assumes an imprinter. Any specific archetypal lens apprehends the world and provides a blueprint for action in a way characteristic to the archetype in question. The archetype is, accordingly, the instincts self-perception, while being subject to increasing development and differentiation. When activated, the subject perceives it as numinous. In fact, the archetype is psychoid, which means that it embraces and transcends both spirit and matter, which explains the non-dual experience of synchronicity.

Association

Personal associations of the dreamer to the dream content can help to understand the meaning of a dream.

Attitudes

There are two attitudes to consciousness, which reflect the orientation and readiness of the psyche to act and respond in either an introverted or extraverted way. In the case of the introvert, energy is withdrawn from the object toward the subject, while, in the case of the extravert, the subject's energy is directed toward the object. One typically adapts and functions mainly with either a differentiated introverted or extraverted attitude. Although the individuation process requires education of the inferior attitude, the dominant attitude typically does not change.

Axiom of Maria

The Axiom of Maria is a theme that runs throughout alchemy. It states: One becomes Two, Two comes Three, and out of the Third comes the One that is the Fourth.

Collective

Collective consciousness refers to general concepts and feelings

Consciousness	that are collectively current, for instance, ways of governing, practicing religion and administering justice and folk ways, along with the attending feelings. The collective dimension does not only include mental concepts but feelings.
Collective Shadow	The Shadow is fundamentally an archetypal phenomenon residing in the collective unconscious, and the dark side of the Self. The primal task of the individuation process is to come to terms with the paradoxical Self, which includes its dark side, the collective Shadow. This effectively means that, over and over again, the ego finds itself suspended between the light and dark sides of the Self, in Christian terms, between Christ and the Devil. The end result is increasing approximation of consciousness to the Self.
	From a psychological perspective, Jung regards both evil and good as aspects of God in their essential roots, and their conscious determination as principles of conscious human ethical judgment. They are both superordinate dimensions of the archetypal God-image, powerful beyond the human ego. Like all archetypes, the nature of good and evil cannot be known in themselves. Yet, Jung regards evil as a fact and not a privation of good or *privatio boni* as does Christianity. Given evil's power, daemonic and problematic aspects, Jung does not devalue evil, but encourages humans to not avoid it, and to deal with it as consciously as possible.
Collective Unconscious	The word collective refers to psychic contents that belong not just to the individual but to a people, a society or community and humankind in general. The Collective Unconscious consists of universal archetypes, including cultural archetypes and the archetype of the Self, and their counterpart, the instincts, linking psyche and the body. The archetypes are, in fact, psychoid and unite spirit with the physical world. The collective unconscious plays a compensatory role to consciousness, and, when activated, it brings to the individual and/or society supplementary images, feelings, concepts and other factors to adjust consciousness in order to bring it into balance.
Ego	The ego is a complex of ideas which are located the centre of the field of conscious awareness. The ego-complex is both a content of consciousness and the condition for consciousness.

It is differentiated from the Self, from which it emerges, and with which it keeps a connection in the form of the ego-Self axis. The role of the ego is to mediate between consciousness and the collective through the persona, as well as consciousness and, through the animus/anima, the unconscious, including the Self. The ego is charged with the task of working with and holding the tension of opposites until a resolution is found by the transcendent function.

Enantiodromia

Enantiodromia is a psychological law that was first introduced to the West by Heraclitus and, later, became an important ingredient in Jung's psychology. It means running in the contrary direction and refers to the fact that, eventually, everything turns into its opposite. It can affect both individuals in their beliefs and conduct of life, and the governing direction of society. One-sidedness can be compensated for by integrating creative messages from the unconscious that facilitate the impending change in consciousness.

Functions of Consciousness

In addition to the two attitudes, extraversion and introversion, there are four orienting functions of consciousness. Two functions, thinking and feeling, are rational, and two functions, sensation and intuition are non-rational. The favored function of consciousness is typically the one with which one identifies, as it generates the greatest adaptive success. The sensation function is what is, the intuition tells you about possibilities, the thinking function tells you what is and the feeling function evaluates what is. For any given individual, there is, typically, a superior function, a first and second auxiliary function and an inferior function. The superior function is the most differentiated function, the first auxiliary function is relatively differentiated, and the second auxiliary function less so, while the inferior function is relatively undifferentiated with part of it lying in the unconscious, not integrated to the ego, and functioning in an archaic and infantile fashion. Its inferior differentiation and unconsciousness relates it to the archetypes of the collective unconscious especially the archetype of the Self. One of the goals of the individuation process is to increasingly integrate all functions of consciousness, to consciousness, including, to the extent possible, the inferior function.

Gnosis	The word *gnosis* is of Greek origin and means Knowledge, for the Gnostics, this refers to self-knowledge as knowledge of the Self. It refers to knowledge of the heart and life processes, through revelation.
Gnosticism	Although Gnosticism originated prior to Christianity, it reached a creative crescendo during the first two centuries of the Christian era. Ideas and myths that had been around for centuries were consolidated into spiritual and philosophic Gnostic systems. Influential material for consolidation came from Iran (Mazdaism), Egypt, Greece (Philosophy), Babylonia (Astrology) and Jewish sources. For some teachings there is evidence of Buddhist and, possibly, Hindu, influence.

Gnostics tended to be individualists and there were, consequently, a variety of Gnostic systems with somewhat different orientations. For the most part, though, there was in common disdain for the material world and humans who did not share their views, along with contempt for the God of the Old Testament, spiritual elitism and belief of being above the moral law, which propagated inflation. In some Gnostic traditions, from Astrological influences, there was the development of an elaborate cosmology with different levels of being. From Buddhism and, possibly, Hinduism, there was recognition of the divine source the *Pleroma*, the Nothing that is the All. From Mazdaism, Gnostics tended to see the world as a moral battleground between the forces of good and evil and, from the Egyptian religion, the descent, ascent and liberation of the soul. They viewed the Old Testament creator God as an inferior Demiurge, who created an evil world, which is alien to the soul, with the cosmos governed by tyrant archons. The Gnostic Christ was an inner being of light that did not die on the cross. The main goal of most Gnostic systems was individual and cosmic redemption through individual knowledge, meaning knowledge of the Self, in contrast to mainline Christianity with its requirement for belief and faith, the elimination of sin and individual redemption. The Church Fathers considered the Gnostics to be heretics (holding opinions contrary to Church belief) and they were oppressed and, in some cases, exterminated.

The influence of Gnostic thought on Jung is evident early on with his Gnostic tract, *Seven Sermons to the Dead,* written as part of *The Red Book.* Then, late in life, in his book, *Aion,* in his discussion on and diagram of the Self, he uses a lot of amplificatory Gnostic material. Although the Gnostics were not self-conscious, Jung considered them to be psychologists who, in their own way, were concerned about the contents of the collective unconscious and who understood the psychological meaning of their myths. Jung found a historical link between Gnosticism and alchemy through Zosimos, which he felt substantiated his psychology of the unconscious.

Heiros gamos   The *heiros gamos* refers to the sacred marriage and mystical union.

Hermes   Hermes Trismegistus is sometimes referred to as one of the
Trismegistus   fathers, if not *the* father, of Western alchemy. In fact, he was a legendary figure who combined the qualities of the Greek god Hermes, the messenger of the gods, and the Egyptian, Thoth, god of magic and writing.

Holy Grail   During the Middle Ages in Europe there was fascination with the legend of the Holy Grail, which can still be considered a living tradition. The story is based on myth and fairy tale interwoven with the Christian legend of Joseph of Arimathea, who is reputed to have possessed a vessel that received the blood of Christ as he was taken down from the cross. The vessel is the Holy Grail, the principle of individuation, the goal symbolized by the spiritual quest of King Arthur and the Knights of the Round Table. The Grail legend finds sources in Persian stories, Islam and Celtic-Germanic pagan myth. There are also some associations with alchemy, Gnosticism, and the Knights Templars.

The Grail stories were a compensatory response to the psychological need of the time to elaborate the central theme of Christianity, the doctrine of redemption, as well as to creatively resolve complications of sexuality, the shadow and relationship with the collective unconscious. The stories emphasize knightly virtues and code of conduct, which included serving women. From the perspective of depth psychology, the quest for the Holy Grail contains much interesting symbolic and amplificatory material for understanding the individuation process today, as well as the necessary change in the culture's ruling consciousness. In fact, unsatisfactory endings of the legend in the most popular versions of the Grail tradition indicate that the psychological problems and the question of Christian redemption, were not resolved during the Middle Ages, but have remained until our time.

Individuation	Individuation refers to the formation and differentiation of individuals in their psychological uniqueness, although, as social animals, in relationship with the community.
Individuation Process	The individuation process refers to conscious development of the psychological individual as distinct from collective mentality. It requires conscious engagement with the unconscious, especially the collective (archetypal and instinctive) unconscious and the Self. It not only involves developing psychological distinction from the collective, but a more intense and broader relationship with the community.
Instinct	The archetype intrinsically interacts with the instinct to the point that they are two sides of the same coin. The specific archetype affects the spiritual dimension and the way one apprehends the world, while the instinctive side ideally acts dynamically, according to the archetypal image perceived. As indicated in the section describing the archetype, the archetype is psychoid, unifying both spirit and matter.
Persona	The persona is the adapted outer attitude and only concerned with relations to the outer object. It is a mask that serves a social purpose, although those who identify with the persona can be seen as personal but not individual. The persona is a utilitarian complex that is adapted for the sake of convenience or adaptation to a collective role, profession, social milieu or status. It is complementary to the anima/animus, the inner attitude. Inasmuch as there is a strong identification of the persona with the ideal, the persona is rigid and the personal shadow repressed. A feeling-supported persona is flexible and not repressive.
Lapis Philosphorum	Attaining the *lapis philosophorum*, the philosopher's stone, is an important goal of alchemy. It refers to the inner person that the alchemists sought to liberate. For the practicing Christian alchemist, it complemented the accepted version of Christ.

Lumen Nature   In alchemy the *lumen naturae* or the light of nature is the
source of temporal knowledge, one of two kinds of knowledge,
immortal and mortal. The eternal light finds its source in God
through the Holy Spirit, while the light of nature is found
in humans. It is the *quinta essentia* extracted from the four
elements, found in the heart and brought to consciousness by
the Holy Spirit. In nature there is a hidden light, a divine soul-
spark or *scintilla*. It is the *lumen naturae* that illuminates its
own darkness, in contemporary terms, the archetype [excluding
the archetype of the (descending) Holy Spirit] as the source
of enlightenment. Both sources of knowledge derive from the
unity of God.

Personal   The personal shadow refers to aspects of the psyche that could
Shadow   have become conscious but, for reasons of personal history,
have been repressed. It, consequently, resides in the personal
unconscious. Thus, the individuation process begins with
coming to terms with and assimilating to consciousness the
personal shadow, at least initial aspects. The personal shadow
is typically projected onto people of the same sex, usually close
friends of youth and siblings, brothers for men and sisters for
women. They involve qualities and attributes that one does not
wish to be or identify with, but which, when conscious, can be
modified according to context. They also often hold valuable new
life potential and energy. In the meantime, the undifferentiated
shadow is expressed through various psychopathologies and
affective explosions.

In the case of the introvert, the typical shadow projection is
directed toward extraverts, while the opposite is the case with
extraverts. In addition, the object of projection generally holds
a dominant function of consciousness that is inferior for the
individual doing the projecting. Often, one's choice of life-
partner reflects not only inferior conscious qualities carried
by the unconscious anima/animus, but also by aspects of the
unconscious personal shadow. Such shadow projections go
very deep, and represent attributes and qualities of the inferior
side of the psyche, that merge with the collective unconscious
and the archetypal Self.

Personal Unconscious	The contents of personal unconscious are mainly the personal shadow. Other psychic contents include (traumatic and other) memories and subliminal experiences that did not fully register in consciousness.

Psyche

The psyche is the world seen from within, where matter is the world seen externally. It is not *my* psyche, but *the* psyche, which is purposive living objective phenomena, living processes, in which humans are contained. The living processes including spiritual, take place in space-time as well as trans-personally and beyond space and time. The psyche-in-itself is an *ousia,* pure substance that transcends all dualities. The psyche per se is therefore "*unextended intensity.*"

The archetypes and attending emotions are the psyche's principal contents and the creative determinants of all psychic processes. They emerge into consciousness as archetypal images with feeling value, possessing both a spiritual and instinctual dimension. Given their personal historical nature, the complexes with their archetypal cores, are, consequently, included in the contents of the psyche.

Psyche and its contents are the only reality given to us *without a medium*. Thus, from the point of view of the psyche, what is generally considered illusory may be real. While the conscious mind serves as an instrument of adaptation and orientation, the unconscious psyche links to its spiritual and instinctive truth. Due to its psychoid nature, the archetype is an arranger of psychic forms inside and outside the psyche and, consequently, it is the dynamic source for experiences of synchronicity.

Jung differentiates between the psyche and psychoid processes. With psychic processes, there can be emancipation from instinctive functioning along with accessibility to consciousness and will, therefore potential for their modification. The psychoid functioning, in contrast, cannot be accessed to consciousness or will, as it is unknown and, as a direct phenomena unknowable. It has the compulsive character and drivenness of a drive.

Psychoid Unconscious

The psychoid unconscious is unknowable and not accessible to consciousness and will.

Rotundum   The nadir of the fourth level in descent of the Self as described by Jung in *Aion* is the alchemical *Rotundum*. It is at the base of the *Lapis* quaternio, which stands for the *prima materia* that contains something of the original chaos. The elements of the *Lapis* are not initially united but require alchemical procedures for the process.

The *Rotundum* is *increatum* (uncreated) and coeternal with God, the stone with a spirit. It is round and the fundamental building block of matter, but also consists of each of the four elements. It is subordinate and the vessel of transformation, the counterpart of the supraordinate *Anthropos,* the Original Man. Although the *Rotundum* is metal and has the heaviness of the earth, it has a secret relationship with the latter, meeting in the *uroborous* as the extreme union of opposites.

Scintilla   In alchemy, the scintilla is the divine soul-spark found in nature. As indicated in the section on *lumen naturae*, it is the hidden light of nature, the archetype.

Self   While the ego is the center and subject of consciousness, the Self is the subject of the whole psyche and represents its unity. It is not only the center of the psyche, but its circumference, incorporating both the conscious and unconscious. It is represented empirically by symbols of unity, including supraordinate personalities in the form of heroes, magicians, kings and queens, as well as totality symbols such as circle and square and other figures with united opposites. As a play of light and shadow, it not only includes light figures such as a hero, Christ or Buddha, but also the adversary, the dragon, the Devil and the Anti-Christ. From a psychological perspective, the archetypal Self represents totality and unity, while any dogmatic religious figure such as Christ or Buddha represents a symbol of the Self. Since it is both conscious and unconscious; given the latter, it is irrepresentable, and a *transcendental* concept.

Symbol   It is essential to distinguish the symbol from a sign. The sign stand for a known fact, like a company or product logo, which represents the product or company in question while the symbol represents a relatively unknown phenomenon, of which the symbol is the best possible formulation. The symbol is a living reality that is replete with meaning. The appeal of any given symbol depends on attitude of the observer towards the symbol in question, as well the spontaneous symbolic affect.

Inasmuch as the phenomenon expressed by the symbol is unconscious and widespread, it strikes a cord in everybody. For this to happen, on the one hand, it needs to be primal enough to appeal to everybody, yet, on the other hand, it requires the highest possible formulation. This explains the transformative power of certain living social symbols.

Likewise, through dreams, visions and true fantasy, individuals can access archetypal images that are highly symbolic, with individual transformative power. In this case, the traditional symbol, for instance, for some people today, the dogmatic Christian Cross, no longer fulfills the need of representing both the conscious, spiritual and rational, and the unconscious, primal and irrational. New symbol formation requires spiritual aspiration and springs from the dynamic primal level of the psychic depths.

Tabula Smaragdina

As indicated in the section on alchemy, the *Tabula Smaragdina*, the Emerald Tablet, is an important source document for alchemy, attributed to Hermes Trismegistus (Hermes, Thrice Great).

Transcendent Function

When there is a 'conflict of duties' and the ego is capable of fully participating in both sides of 'equal' opposites, there is a suspension of the conscious will. This damming up of libido results in its regression to the source of the conflict and an activation of the unconscious by way of the Transcendent Function. There is, as a result, the emergence of new content that answers the compensatory needs of both sides of the conflict.

ABOUT THE AUTHOR

DAVID T. JOHNSTON is a practicing psychologist in Victoria, BC, Canada. He resided and studied in Pondicherry (now Puducherry), India from 1970 to 1973, where he was introduced to the Integral Yoga of Sri Aurobindo and the Mother. He lived there during Sri Aurobindo's centenary in 1972. He subsequently studied at the C.G. Jung Institute in Zurich, Switzerland in 1975, the year of Jung's centenary. He has been an ardent student of Sri Aurobindo and the Mother, as well as Jung ever since. On several occasions, for extensive periods of time, he has visited Auroville, a township near Puducherry dedicated to the Mother's vision.

He received his Ph.D., phil. in Clinical Psychology at the Pacifica Graduate Institute in Carpinteria, California in 1996. He has written several studies about the Integral Yoga of Sri Aurobindo and the Mother in comparison to Jung's psychology of the individuation process, which he sharply differentiates from other approaches to psychology. Dr. Johnston is also an artist, where his art is a meditative means for him to enhance a living relationship between consciousness and the unconscious and to bring meaning to life and the individuation process.

CPSIA information can be obtained
at www.ICGtesting.com
Printed in the USA
FSOW03n2105190117
29851FS